PENITENCE AND SACRIFICE IN EARLY ISRAEL OUTSIDE THE LEVITICAL LAW

PENITENCE AND SACRIFICE IN EARLY ISRAEL OUTSIDE THE LEVITICAL LAW

AN EXAMINATION OF THE FELLOWSHIP THEORY OF EARLY ISRAELITE SACRIFICE

BY

R. J. THOMPSON

WITH A FOREWORD BY H. H. ROWLEY

LEIDEN
E. J. BRILL
1963

PRINTED IN THE NETHERLANDS

To my wife Shirley

co-worker

and

companion

CONTENTS

FOREWORD

It is a pleasure to welcome a new writer into the field of Old Testament studies, where there have been such exciting changes during the past generation. New discoveries have brought about the re-examination of views which had been regarded as established, and on many questions there is a greater fluidity of view than we should once have thought possible.

At the beginning of the present century the influence of Wellhausen on all critical scholars was immense, and while in many respects his views have had to be modified it is still considerable and likely to remain so. In the present study Dr. Thompson challenges Wellhausen's theories on the development and interpretation of sacrifice in ancient Israel. On many questions I too have been compelled to abandon Wellhausen's ideas on the religious history of the Israelite people. Yet I have retained a greater respect for Wellhausen than Dr. Thompson expresses, and have acknowledge with gratitude my debt to him. No man can attain all the truth, and the utmost any can hope to do is to make some contribution here and there to its full attainment.

My welcome to Dr. Thompson's study is precisely because I think he brings some contribution. At a number of points I am in agreement with him, and at many I have learned from him; at some I do not agree with him, as the reader will discover. But it is by the disagreements of scholars engaged on a common search for truth that we advance towards our goal.

For the fullness of his acquaintance with the literature relevant to every aspect of his study, and for the integrity with which he indicates views other than his own and the scholars who have held them, Dr. Thompson's work is to be most warmly commended. His diligence matches his independence. In not a few respects his views are in line with current trends: in some he stands aloof from them. This is all to the good. For it may well be that in a century from now views which are widely accepted today may be challenged from a new standpoint. When scholarship becomes static, it ceases to function. Happily it is far from static today, and while every man who offers to his colleagues of the fruits of his researches is welcomed to their ranks, none who is wise imagines that all he offers will survive their examination. It is my hope that Dr. Thompson will continue his researches, and will enrich us all by what he finds.

H. H. Rowley

PREFACE

Although the chorus of dissent to Wellhausen in Old Testament studies has grown in volume in the past decades, the alternative view desiderated by Rowley, which should deal not merely "piecemeal with this or that element of his view," but should be "worked out in as thorough a way in relation to all the facts and to the recorded history"[1] has not appeared. This will be no occasion of wonder to those, who like the writer, have attempted to come to terms with even one element of his view. Despite this, the larger work needs to be done for our generation and a beginning must be made somewhere.

The subject of sacrifice has been chosen for this beginning, not because it was the chief area of Wellhausen's interest, but because it is of greater importance to theology generally than the other areas. S. A. Cook has noted an early criticism of Robertson Smith's view of sacrifice, which was also that of Wellhausen, that it would "cut away the basis on which the whole doctrine of salvation rests,"[2] and asked the question whether this view may not have been unconsciously influenced by the author's Christology.[3] If an evolution really took place in Israelite sacrifice from the early fellowship meal to the idea of atonement by death only in the later time, it is not a far step to the assumption that the Pauline interpretation of the Lord's Supper as a memorial of the death of Christ was a later development of what at first had been a purely joyous, fellowship meal. This theological aspect cannot, in the nature of the case, be further discussed in the present work, but it may, in a sense, be said to be its justification, as it has been its inspiration.

My thanks are due to the librarians of some twenty libraries, to the scholars who have made available to me unpublished works,[4]

---

[1] H. H. Rowley. Review. " 'The Study of the Bible Today and Tomorrow,' Harold R. Willoughby (ed.)," *Theology Today* V (1948), p. 124.

[2] S. A. Cook (ed.), W. Robertson Smith, *Religion of the Semites*, London (^{3}1927), p. xxvii.

[3] *Ibid.*, p. 652.

[4] The important unpublished Habilitationsschrift, *Studien zur Geschichte des Opfers im alten Israel*, by R. Rendtorff only became available after this investigation was complete, and could only be noted in the Conclusion. (Announced for publication in 1963 by Neukirchener Verlag).

to the students and staff of the Rüschlikon Seminary, especially to Stud. Theo. W. Popkes, for linguistic and other help, to my wife for typing the manuscript, and to my professors—J. D. W. Watts of Rüschlikon and H. Wildberger and V. Maag of Zürich—particularly to Professor Maag, who although in disagreement at many points, has supervised this work, and brought his wide knowledge of religions in general and sacrifice in particular to bear upon it in advice and criticism. Professor Maag has asked that his disagreement be recorded.

EXPLANATORY NOTES

Transliteration

Hebrew short vowels are in ordinary script, *šewa* in raised letters, long vowels are overlined and long vowels written plene are indicated by a circumflex. The consonants follow the usual system, but *dageš* letters are not marked.

Bible References

The translation is chiefly that of the RSV. References are cited by the MT numbering, usually with the RSV numbering in brackets. Psalm references usually differ by one verse.

Publication Facts

These are not repeated in full in the footnotes after the first reference to a work, but may be found in the Bibliography. Titles of frequently quoted volumes are sometimes abbreviated in subsequent entries in the footnotes.

Abbreviations

See Appendix I.

INTRODUCTION

The Problem

With the current abandoning of much of Wellhausen's reconstruction of the religion of Israel, it is inevitable that the subject of Israelite sacrifice should come up again for discussion. A particular theory of the development of Israelite sacrifice was one of the five planks, on which Wellhausen built.[1] An evolution in Hebrew sacrifice, similar to that in the centralization of the place of worship, the growth of the festal calendar, the distinction of the priests and Levites and the increase in the endowments of the clergy was to be traced.[2] The association of sacrifice with a sense of sin was a late development.

> The ancient offerings were wholly of a joyous nature ... An underlying reference of sacrifice to sin, speaking generally, was entirely absent ... There was no such thought as that a definite guilt must and could be taken away by means of a prescribed offering ... Of this feature [reference to sin] the ancient sacrifices present few traces.[3]

It followed that sin offering, guilt offering and Day of Atonement had no existence before the exile, and the Priestly Code, which gave evidence of a more sombre view was to be dated late.

Many recent lines of enquiry suggest the need of a re-examination of this position. The form critical method has been able to go behind the laws of sacrifice in Leviticus to reconstruct their pre-history,[4] but can hardly go back further without a clearer understanding of just what elements in Hebrew sacrifice were early and what late.[5] The tradition historical method in its investi-

---

[1] J. Wellhausen, *Prolegomena to the History of Israel*, E. T. Edinburgh (1885).

[2] *Ibid.*, pp. 1-167.

[3] *Ibid.*, p. 81.

[4] See R. Rendtorff, *Die Gesetze in der Priesterschrift*, Göttingen (1954) and K. Koch, "Die Eigenart der priesterschriftlichen Sinaigesetzgebung," *ZThK* LV (1958), pp. 36-51; *Die Priesterschrift von Exodus 25 bis Leviticus 16*, Göttingen (1959).

[5] E.g. was the expiatory element an innovation or a revival? The words italicized (italics ours) in the following quotations should be noted. "It is no

gation of worship in ancient Israel has no difficulty in assuming rites of purgation in connection with the annual festivals, [1] and acts of penitence in amphictyonic worship.[2] One has only to compare a modern description of Israelite worship, such as that of Harrelson,[3] based on tradition historical methods with that of Wellhausen or Robertson Smith[4] to realize that modern scholars are living in another world.

To Wellhausen and Robertson Smith early Israelite worship centred in a joyous sacrificial meal, unshadowed by any sense of sin. Festal occasions and occasions of worship were identical. Robertson Smith wrote

> the identity of religious occasions and festal seasons may indeed be taken as the determining characteristic of the type of ancient religion generally; when men meet their god they feast and are glad together, and whenever they feast and are glad they desire that the god should be of the party . . .[5] The sacrificial meal . . .

---

accident that the stratum of Law that was added to the older narrative material of the Mosaic Age in the fifth century at the latest should, from *the abundance of old rituals*, have selected to a considerable extent just those that guarantee expiation, especially through the culmination of the festivals at the year's end in the great Day of Atonement." (J. Hempel, "The Literature of Israel," *Record and Revelation* (ed.) H. W. Robinson, Oxford (1938), p. 47). "The outstanding feature of the priestly code is this *revival of primitive customs and beliefs* . . . sacrifices are offered to appease an angry God . . ." (J. N. Schofield, *The Religious Background of the Bible*, London (1944), p. 176). "It is not likely that this [the priestly] code introduced any important innovations; it would rather systematize what had *for long been the practice* . . ." (G. Nagel, "Sacrifices," *A Companion to the Bible* (ed.) J.-J. von Allmen, E.T. New York (1958), p. 377b).

[1] See T. H. Gaster, *Thespis*, New York (1950), pp. 7ff. and the discussion of his view in Ch. VI below. N. H. Snaith, from his very different standpoint, writes: "There was from the first an element of penitence, as there must always be, among primitive peoples, and indeed cultured peoples also, in any festival which looks back into the year that has gone and forward on to the year that lies ahead. At times when the harvest had failed, or in the days when the Hebrews nationally met with increasing misfortune, the element of penitent concern would dominate" ("The Priesthood and the Temple," *A Companion to the Bible* (ed.) T. W. Manson, Edinburgh (1939), p. 440).

[2] See A. Weiser, "Das Deboralied," *ZAW* LXXI (1959), pp. 75ff.

[3] W. Harrelson, "Worship in Early Israel," *Biblical Research* III (1958), esp. pp. 8ff.

[4] W. R. Smith, *The Religion of the Semites*, London ([2]1894), pp. 254ff.

[5] *Ibid.*, p. 255. Cf. J. Wellhausen, *Prolegomena*: "a meal is prepared in honour of the Deity, of which man partakes as God's guest . . . (p. 62) A sacrifice was a meal, a fact showing how remote was the idea of antithesis between spiritual earnestness and secular joyousness . . . (p. 76)"

> may be regarded as common to all the so-called nature-religions of the civilized races of antiquity, religions which had a predominantly joyous character, and in which relations of man to the gods were not troubled by any habitual and oppressive sense of human guilt ...[1] In a religion of this kind there is no room for an abiding sense of sin and unworthiness, or for acts of worship that express the struggle after an unattained righteousness, the longing for uncertain forgiveness ... Men are satisfied with their gods, and they feel that the gods are satisfied with them.[2]

Behind Robertson Smith's description is his theory of an original totemism in which gods, men and sacrificial animals were all regarded as part and parcel of the same natural community. Religion is therefore not an appeasing of unknown gods who are feared, but a "loving reverence for known gods, who are knit to their worshippers by strong bonds of kinship."[3] The symbol of this kinship was the *zebaḥ* sacrifice, which provided a meal for the worshippers. By partaking of the flesh of the victim, in which in some sense the divinity resided, the worshipper came into a mystical union with the deity. With such a tie of kinship "there was no occasion and no place for a special class of atoning sacrifices."[4] Whenever the bond of kinship with the deity was broken or relaxed, it could be renewed by the "ceremony, in which the sacred life is again distributed to every member of the community."[5] From this point of view the sacramental rite was also the atoning rite and

> sacrificial communion includes within it the rudimentary conception of a piacular ceremony ... atonement being simply an act of communion designed to wipe out all memory of previous estrangement.[6]

"The atoning force of sacrifice is purely physical,"[7] and owes its "efficacy to a communication of divine life to the worshippers."[8]

---

[1] W. R. Smith, "Sacrifice," *EBrit* XXI (^{9}1886), p. 134.

[2] Smith, *Religion of the Semites*, p. 256.

[3] *Ibid.*, p. 54.

[4] *Ibid.*, p. 360.

[5] *Ibid.*, p. 320.

[6] *Loc. cit.*

[7] *Ibid.*, p. 400.

[8] *Ibid.*, p. 439. Atonement in this sense was quite old in Israel (pp. 217, 237-38, 397, 401), as were annual and other piacular rites (pp. 159, 405), but the latter were no more than survivals of ancient animal sacrifices of communion in the body and blood of a sacred animal and did not involve any sense of sin (pp. 405-406, 415).

It is to be "disassociated from the death of a victim and from every idea of penal satisfaction of the deity."[1]

Robertson Smith regarded the sin offering and burnt offering, and the ideas of sacrifice as a gift or a tribute, with which they are associated as much later developments, that arose out of the primary communion meal.[2] The burnt offering, with its implication of the divine dwelling place in heaven, was inconsistent with early Semitic beliefs in earth-dwelling deities,[3] and was not common early.[4] It is not to be associated with the idea of the etherealizing of food for the god, but arose out of piacular rites, like human sacrifice, which took place away from the altar.[5] The developed form of the altar, which could be used both for a ritual of blood and as a sacred hearth, was the result of the combining of two operations, which originally took place apart—the pouring out of the blood at a stone pillar, which had accompanied the old sacrificial meal, and the disposal, perhaps in a fire pit, of what was too sacred to be eaten.[6] The special piacular rites developed from the latter not the former. The blood did not wash away impurity but conveyed life.[7]

The rise of separate expiatory rites was traced by both Wellhausen and Robertson Smith to the time of the fall of the Hebrew kingdoms. The latter wrote:

> when a national religion is not left to slow decay, but shares the catastrophe of the nation itself, as was the case with the religions of the small western Asiatic states in the period of the Assyrian Conquest, the old joyous confidence in the gods gives way to a sombre sense of divine wrath, and the acts by which this wrath can be conjured become much more important . . .[8]

This change of outlook is thought to have taken place for Israel in the seventh century B.C.[9] Wellhausen mentions in particular the reign of Manasseh as the time, when "earnestness superseded the

[1] W. R. Smith, *Religion of the Semites*, p. 336.
[2] *Ibid.*, p. 351.
[3] Smith, "Sacrifice," *EBrit* XXI, p. 133. Cf. *Religion of the Semites*, p. 114.
[4] Smith, *Religion of the Semites*, p. 238.
[5] *Ibid.*, pp. 371ff.
[6] *Ibid.*, pp. 202, 377, 372.
[7] *Ibid.*, p. 427.
[8] Smith, "Sacrifice," p. 134.
[9] Smith, *Religion of the Semites*, p. 258, cf. p. 348.

old joyousness of the cultus" which "now had reference principally to sin and its atonement,"[1] and more remarkably thinks this rise into prominence of the cultus was "helped rather than hindered by the long reign of Manasseh, evil as is the reputation of that reign."[2] The new element in the cult had come to stay for

> even after the abolition of the horrid atrocities of Manasseh's time, the bloody earnestness remained behind with which the performance of divine service was gone about.[3]

The exile enforced the lesson: "the whole of the past is regarded as one enormous sin which is to be expiated in the exile,"[4] and the post-exilic period could not free itself from the "leaden pressure of sin and wrath,"[5] which became permanent in the consciousness of Israel[6] and dictated the forms of the Levitical cultus in the Priestly Code.[7]

In the following chapters this view of Wellhausen and Robertson Smith will be examined in the light of the Biblical materials, but some general considerations may be brought forward by way of introduction. First it needs to be said that Robertson Smith's view of the totemic origin of religion in general and of sacrifice in particular is not now considered valid.[8] Present day investigators have reacted against all such exclusive views and prefer to speak of the several roots of religion and sacrifice rather than of one.[9] The various

---

1 J. Wellhausen, *Prolegomena*, p. 486.
2 *Ibid.*, p. 421.
3 *Ibid.*, p. 421.
4 *Ibid.*, p. 279.
5 *Ibid.*, p. 112.
6 *Ibid.*, pp. 424-25.
7 *Ibid.*, p. 112.
8 It had a vogue for some time in the writings of F. B. Jevons (cf. *An Introduction to the History of Religion*, London ([3]1904)), and in the theories of Freud, applied in detail to sacrifice by R. Money-Kyrle, *The Meaning of Sacrifice*, London (1930), but was criticized by J. G. Frazer, *Totemism and Exogamy*, Vol. IV, London (1910), p. 231; A. L. Kroeber, "Totem and Taboo; an Ethnologic Psychoanalysis," *American Anthropoligist*, XXII (1920), pp. 48-55; W. Schmidt, "Ethnologische Bemerkungen zu theologischen Opfertheorien," *Jahrbuch des Missionshauses St. Gabriel*, I (1922), pp. 8, 12ff. and *The Origin and Growth of Religion*, E.T. London ([2]1935), pp. 103ff.
9 So, for the Old Testament, O. Schmitz (citing Stade), *Die Opferanschauung des späteren Judentums*, Tübingen, (1910), p. 35; C. R. North, "Sacrifice in the Old Testament," *ExpT* XLVII (1935-1936), p. 251; A. Lods, *The Prophets and the Rise of Judaism*, E. T. London (1937), pp. 293-96; E. Jacob, *The Theology of the Old Testament*, E. T. London (1958), pp. 268-69.

theories of sacrifice as "gift," "power," "communion," and "expiation" cross and recross each other in every cult.

The idea of gift in the gift theory (the oldest rival to Robertson Smith's view)[1] cannot be given a precise connotation. Van der Leeuw's definition of *dare* (to give) in the *do-ut-des* formula (I give that thou mayest give) as "to place oneself in relation to, and then to participate in, a second person, by means of an object, which is . . . a part of oneself"[2] would include Robertson Smith's communion theory. Such a law of participation in which power flows equally from receiver to giver, as from giver to receiver, in a cycle of giving also comes close to the "power-working" theories of sacrifice. Hubert and Mauss thought of sacrifice as a series of rites which concentrated mana in the victim and then discharged it for the benefit of gods and men.[3] For the gods the sacrifice would be a gift, but for men an atonement.[4] The negative side of the promoting of life and health is the removal of evil.[5] The blood, which was basically life-giving power, was at the same time an apotropaic, so that Bertholet could claim that the dynamistic theory of sacrifice could embrace each of the other three.[6]

---

[1] It was already represented in the epoch-making *Primitive Culture* of E. B. Tylor (Vol. II reprinted as *Religion in Primitive Culture*, New York (1958) pp. 461ff.).

[2] G. van der Leeuw, *Religion in Essence and Manifestation*, E. T. London (1938), p. 351; "Die *do-ut-des*-Formel in der Opfertheorie," *ARW* XX (1920-1921), pp. 241-53.

[3] H. Hubert and M. Mauss, "Essai sur la nature et la fonction du sacrifice," *L'Année Sociologique* II (1897-1898), pp. 29-138.

[4] On their theory there were thus two main types of sacrifice, which are summarized by E. E. Evans-Pritchard ("The Meaning of Sacrifice among the Nuer," *JRAI* LXXXIV (1954), p. 24) as follows: "In the first the sacred forces are transmitted through the victim to the sacrificer, who gains, often by partaking of its flesh, a sacred character he lacked before the sacrifice. These are sacrifices of sacralization. The other type of sacrifices is that of desacralization. In these the sacred forces are transmitted through the victim away from the sacrificer. They do not make sacred the profane but they make profane what is sacred. The sacrificer has in him religious forces which are harmful or dangerous to him and the rites get rid of them. This second type of sacrifice is therefore expiatory." Evans-Pritchard thinks this account too abstract and too much influenced by Vedic sacrifice and comments: "How fatal to compare Hebrew and Hindu sacrifices outside the contexts of these two religions, which are so entirely different" (p. 25).

[5] E. O. James, *The Origins of Sacrifice*, London (1933), p. 184. Cf. "Aspects of Sacrifice in the Old Testament," *ExpT* L (1938-1939), pp. 151-55 and W. R. Smith, *Religion of the Semites*, p. 427.

[6] A. Bertholet, "Zum Verständnis des alttestamentlichen Opfergedankens,"

In the same way communion and gift theories cannot be separated from expiation. An offering for fellowship already underlines a distance, and a gift may imply a debt, as one Brahmanic theory argued.[1] Köhler rightly pointed out that the purpose of the offering was quite a different subject from the meaning in itself,[2] and Berguer that the question to be asked was not so much "what is sacrifice" as "what impels man to sacrifice."[3] Berguer's answer that sacrifice was "a projection into the objective world of a psychological conflict" arising from the twin impulses to give the self to God and to withhold it, can be understood only on a doctrine of sin. The vast data of comparative religion cannot be canvassed here, but the viewpoint of the writer is well expressed by T. H. Robinson, when he suggests that universal sacrifice is the outcome of a universal sense of sin.[4] Man's failure to reach his ideals is not blamed on the object of worship, but on the worshipper himself. "Communion is hard to win, and when won seems only too easily lost." Ideal and failure bring the need of a third factor—atonement by sacrifice. This "explanation may be theological, but the fact is not... Sin is not... a theological... fabrication but a fact of experience."[5]

To establish this for Israel, however, involves a number of problems which must be briefly mentioned. There is first the question of the relation of the individual to the community. The nature of this relation will determine whether or not "sin" can be really spoken of.

JBL XLIX (1930), p. 232-33. Cf. also *Der Sinn des kultischen Opfers,* Berlin (1942), which through its dependence on Vedic parallels, is open to the same criticism as Hubert and Mauss' work.

[1] E. W. Hopkins, *Origin and Evolution of Religion,* New Haven (1923), pp. 163-66 citing Ait. Brah., 2, 3, 11 that in giving a sacrifice everyone "buys himself off." Hopkins remarks that such sacrifices have the form of gifts, but are not really gifts. Cf. the description of the aims of the gift sacrifice in the pre-exilic period given by A. R. S. Kennedy ("Sacrifice and Offering," *DB* (One Vol.) (1909), p. 812); "to secure and to retain favour," "to remove displeasure," and "to express gratitude for benefits." Perhaps only the last should be strictly classified as a gift.

[2] For example the same offering might serve as thanks, homage or atonement (L. Köhler, *Old Testament Theology* E. T. London (1957), p. 186).

[3] G. Berguer, "Les origines psychologiques du rite sacrificiel," *RThPh* N.S. XVII (1929), p. 10.

[4] T. H. Robinson, *A Short Comparative History of Religion,* London ([2]1951), pp. 13ff. [5] *Loc. cit.*

It is often asserted that the corporate consciousness of the people of Israel in ealier times makes it impossible to speak of a sense of personal sin. While the fact of corporate personality is certainly to be taken into account, it is not true even for races much less developed than Israel that a personal sense of sin was entirely absent.[1] It is not uncommon among primitives on critical occasions, such as when men are on the hunt or the warpath and when women draw near to childbirth, to find confession of sins, particularly those of a sexual nature.[2] Nor is it to be assumed that the individual sense of wrong-doing was later than the sense of national guilt. The reverse may have been the case in Israel, if Köberle is right in his claim that the consciousness of national guilt grew up independently of the sense of guilt through individual happenings.[3] It can scarcely now be argued with Stade that a sense of guilt was not yet possible, because duty had not yet been defined.[4] Israel from amphictyonic times was a people "under law."[5]

It is equally a mistake to think that communal sacrifice submerged the personal element, as Cheyne implies, when he says that the object of sacrifice "was not to produce peace of mind for the individual," but to maintain the consecrated character of the community unimpaired, because the individual who transgressed if unatoned for, "was a source of danger to the whole community."[6] This is hardly true for post-exilic Judaism, let alone for earlier times, if the sentiments of the Psalmists (cf. Ps. 32 : 1ff, 65 : 1ff.)

[1] Cf. the words of de Wette cited by F. Bennewitz, *Die Sünde im Alten Israel*, Leipzig (1907), p. 160: "Es sei die auszeichnende Eigentümlichkeit des hebräischen Volkes gewesen, dass in ihm von Anfang an wie in keinem Volke das Gewissen rege ist, und zwar das böse Gewissen, das Schuldgefühl, das Gefühl, dass ihm eine solche Aufgabe gestellt ist, die es nicht lösen kann noch will, das Gefühl des Zweispalts zwischen Erkenntnis und Willen."

[2] S. A. Cook, *The "Truth" of the Bible*, Cambridge (1938), pp. 119-20. The evidence from a hundred peoples of low culture collected by R. Pettazzoni in a series of works has been summarized by him in "Confession of Sins," *Essays on the History of Religions* (Numen Suppl. I), Leiden (1954), pp. 43-67.

[3] J. Köberle, *Sünde und Gnade im religiösen Leben des Volkes Israel*, München (1905), p. 48; cf. O. Procksch, *Theologie des Alten Testaments*, Gütersloh (1950), p. 553.

[4] B. Stade, *Biblische Theologie des Alten Testaments*, Vol. I, Tübingen (1905), pp. 196, 201.

[5] See below Ch. IV.

[6] T. K. Cheyne, *Jewish Religious Life After the Exile*, New York (1898), p. 74.

and sages like Ben Sirach (cf. Ch. 45) are any guide. The similar view of Robertson Smith,[1] and Wellhausen that Yahweh had little interest in the individual, and that "over him the wheel of destiny remorselessly rolled; his part was resignation and not hope,"[2] is contested by Knudson who claims that "there is no basis in the Old Testament for this line of distinction between the faith of the individual and that of the nation."[3]

The truth requiring to be emphasised is rather that sacrifice operated within the covenant and derived its efficacy from covenant grace.[4] This fact is perhaps not sufficiently recognized by Köhler, when he speaks of sacrifice as "man's expedient for his own redemption,"[5] and contrasts this way of "works" to divine "grace".

---

[1] "It was the community, and not the individual, that was sure of the permanent and unfailing help of its deity. It was a national not a personal providence that was taught by ancient religion." (pp. 263-64, cf. pp. 258-59) "In all discussion of the doctrine of substitution as applied to sacrifice, it must be remembered that private sacrifice is a younger thing than clan sacrifice, and that private piacula offered by an individual for his own sins are of comparatively modern institution" (p. 421) (W. R. Smith, *The Religion of the Semites*).

[2] J. Wellhausen, *Prolegomena*, p. 469.

[3] A. C. Knudson, *The Religious Teaching of the Old Testament*, New York (1918), p. 340. Cf. also Köberle, *op. cit.* pp. 322-25.

[4] "It is an institution provided by God for sins committed *within* the covenant. For some sins there was no atonement; sins done with a high hand cut man off from the covenant people" (A. B. Davidson, *The Theology of the Old Testament*, Edinburgh (1904), p. 310). "It was not supposed that any one conceivably a Gentile, might, by offering sacrifice, be admitted into that relationship. Sacrifice was intended rather to purge away uncleanness that would otherwise involve the breaking of a relationship already established" (C. R. North, op. cit., p. 252). If, however, Israel was from early times a covenant people, as is now generally recognized, the deductions drawn by Wellhausen, from the fact that it was only in later times that the divine wrath was regulated by covenant, are no longer valid. To him, the earlier times lacked this regulation, the divine wrath was unpredictable and incalculable—it was not "possible to enumerate beforehand those sins which kindled it and those which did not"—and sacrifice could not therefore be to avert it. In times of wrath not only was sacrifice not made, but the very name of Yahweh was not mentioned (Amos 6 : 10). (J. Wellhausen, *Prolegomena*, p. 81. Cf. also A. Lods, *The Prophets and the Rise of Judaism*, E. T. London (1937), p. 258 and O. Eissfeldt, "Opfer: II A. Im A.T." *RGG* IV (^{2}1930), col. 713).

[5] Köhler's section on the cult in his *Theology* bears this title (p. 181). He says the cult was no part of God's salvation, but only of man's self-help, and really has no place in the "theology of the Old Testament," because *Religionsgeschichte* can explain it all, except for a few usages, which distinguish themselves, not because they embody unique revelation, but only

Knudson was nearer the truth in his description of the offerings as "the fruit of grace, not its root,"[1] and Kautzsch, when he said that, since the sacrifices were commanded by God, divine grace was as much evident in the priest's revelation that God forgave through sacrifice, as in the prophet's that he forgave without it.[2]

The latter statement, however, is not without its difficulty,[3] especially in the form in which it is put by some scholars. Nagel agrees that there is an antithesis between the conception of expiation by sacrifice and forgiveness granted apart from sacrifice, but distinguishes between the sphere of law, which operates in the former case and the sphere of the interior life in the other. In the sphere of law the worshipper acts as a member of the community and must repair the damage done to the community by his sin. Sacrifices are efficacious only for this: "it is entirely a question of unwitting faults."[4] This may, however, be questioned.

This problem of advertence and inadvertence is equally important for the question of the sense of sin. If it could be established that sacrifice only involved matters of inadvertence, it would be pointless to talk about "sin" in any real sense of the word, but it is doubtful whether this can be maintained for the Priestly Code and quite improbable for the earlier period. Moral sins are expiated in some cases by the *'āšām* and *ḥaṭṭā't*—sins against the neighbour, misrepresentation, robbery and wrongful detention in Lev. 5 and Num. 5 : 5,[5] and sins of passion in Lev. 19 : 20-22.[6] That there was

because they are more antique (p. 181). The cult did not belong to the Old Testament revelation until the time of Ezekiel (p. 195).

[1] A. C. Knudson, *op. cit.*, p. 295. Th. C. Vriezen thinks Köhler's view refuted by the fact that the rite of expiation is preceded by a rite of consecration, in which God himself first consecrates the blood ("The Term *Hizza*: Lustration and Consecration," *OTS* VII (1950), p. 234 and the discussion of the cult as *Selbsterlösung* in his *An Outline of Old Testament Theology*, E. T. Oxford (1958), pp. 288ff.).

[2] E. Kautzsch, "The Religion of Israel," *DB* Extra Vol. Edinburgh (1904), p. 721.

[3] See Chs. VIII and IX below.

[4] G. Nagel, *op. cit.*, p. 379.

[5] See S. Herner, *Sühne und Vergebung in Israel*, Lund (1942), pp. 84-85.

[6] A. B. Davidson, *The Theology of the Old Testament*, pp. 315ff. *bišᵉgāgâ* may perhaps be defined as the occasions when a man is swept away by impulse, anger, passion, or overmastering temptation, and *bᵉyād rāmâ* as sins of deliberate apostasy like idolatry done in a spirit of rebellion against God. (W. Barclay, *The Letter to the Hebrews*, Philadelphia ([2]1957), pp. 43ff. Cf. H. H. Rowley, *The Meaning of Sacrifice*, Manchester (1950), pp. 96ff;

alongside this type of offence, others in which the evil to be cleansed was quasi-physical is apparent, but the relation between the two types cannot be solved simply by the categories of early and late. On this point, in the opinion of Hahn,[1] Robertson Smith supplied a corrective to Wellhausen by showing that the idea of ritual holiness was not confined to the post-exilic hierocracy, but went far back in Semitic life. Davidson thought the two conceptions ran right through the Old Testament. In the one Yahweh is the ruler, judge or governor, whose chief trait is righteousness, and to whom only moral offences are considered sin. In the other Yahweh, is thought of as a person dwelling in a house, whose chief trait is holiness, and to whom sin is uncleanness, which is not necessarily moral. The second conception he thought no less ancient than the first.[2]

These factors should be a warning against any theory of the development of a sense of sin in terms of a simple evolution.[3] The "sense of sin" in the late cult may easily be exaggerated—one wonders, for example, just how real it could be when the sacrifices for sin were offered only at a festival in Jerusalem perhaps six months later—and that in the early cult may be over-looked, as Bennett has noted: "it is often said that the special attention given to sin offerings in the Priestly Code is due to the deepened sense of sin in this period, but this is doubtful. In all times the idea that sacrifice atoned for sin was common."[4] It is not necessary to this

---

S. R. Driver, "Expiation and Atonement (Hebrew)," *ERE* V (1912), p. 658; E. Kautzsch, *op. cit.*, p. 721).

[1] H. F. Hahn, *The Old Testament in Modern Research*, Philadelphia (1954), pp. 50-51. The differences between Robertson Smith and Wellhausen on other points have perhaps been exaggerated by Hahn.

[2] A. B. Davidson, "The Word 'Atone' in Extra-Ritual Literature," *Exp.* 5th series, X (1899), pp. 92-93.

[3] So S. A. Cook in his notes to the 3rd edition of Robertson Smith's *Religion of the Semites* (1927) writes: "While it is tempting to contrast the happy type in Israel with the later gloom and undoubted timid notes of post-exilic Judaism, it can hardly be supposed that the Syro-Ephraimite Wars before the rise of Jeroboam II, or the earlier Philistine and other crises, did not cloud the more cheerful type of religion . . . The Semitic readiness to pass from one extreme to another . . . forbids simple theories of the development of religion" (p. 589). In this, however, Cook moves to a different position from that taken by Robertson Smith.

[4] Bennett says that what was new in the Priestly Code was the limitation of atoning value to special sacrifices, and of the efficacy of these sacrifices to sins that were not conscious or deliberate (W. H. Bennett, "Sin (Hebrew and Jewish)," *ERE* XI (1920), p. 558), but on this see above.

investigation to go more deeply into the theology of sin. The purpose of this work is not so much to show, that a fully developed consciousness of guilt accompanied early Israelite sacrifice, as that the fellowship theory of Wellhausen and Robertson Smith does not allow sufficiently for the element of solemnity in the early cult.[1]

Previous Contributions

Some account must now be given of the more important treatments of Hebrew sacrifice since Wellhausen. Around the turn of the century were published the major theologies, archeologies and dictionary articles of Smend, Nowack, Moore, Kautzsch, Stade and Benzinger,[2] which represented more or less closely the views of the Wellhausen school. Criticism of this point of view was expressed by Paterson, Orelli, Pohle, Lesêtre, Nötscher and Reeve.[3] Newer

---

[1] The term "solemnity" is chosen as a convenient one to include the several attitudes of awe, reverence and fear. The writer cannot follow Cook in his assertion that the presence of awe is not in contradiction to Robertson Smith's theory, because awe is "a recognition of greatness and a sense of a not unfriendly relation with the cosmos" (p. 519), and that this awe and confidence, and not fear, is the origin of religion. Nor does he agree that the alternative to Robertson Smith's view is "a gloomy type of religion" (pp. 588ff.), or such a theory as that of Westermarck that religion and sacrifice stem from fear (E. Westermarck, *The Origin and Development of the Moral Ideas*, London ([2]1917), Vol. II, pp. 612ff., Vol. I, p. 460). There is surely a middle position of reverence, which is neither wholly fearful, nor yet wholly confident but partakes of elements of both—"a religion of both fear and trust"—as Evans-Pritchard has so well described it (E. E. Evans-Pritchard, *Nuer Religion*, Oxford (1956), p. 316).

[2] R. Smend, *Lehrbuch der alttestamentlichen Religionsgeschichte*, Freiburg, i.B. (1893), pp. 25ff., 122-40, 319ff; W. Nowack, *Lehrbuch der hebräischen Archäologie*, Vol. II Freiburg, i.B. (1894), pp. 203-58; G. F. Moore, "Sacrifice," *EB* IV London (1903), cols. 4183-4233; E. Kautzsch, *op. cit.*; B. Stade, *op. cit.*, pp. 156-70; I. Benzinger, *Hebräische Archäologie*, Tübingen ([2]1907), pp. 362-86 and ([3]1927), pp. 358-73. The latter work and those of Smend and Kautzsch vary from Wellhausen at a number of points. Still more independent was E. König, *Geschichte der alttestamentlichen Religion*, Gütersloh (1912), pp. 138-40, 232-34, 500ff; *Theologie des Alten Testaments*, Stuttgart ([1] & [2] 1922), pp. 293ff.

[3] W. P. Paterson, "Sacrifice," *DB* IV (1902), pp. 329-49; C. Orelli, "Opferkultus des Alten Testaments," *PRE* XIV, Leipzig (1904), pp. 386-400 (E. T. (abbreviated) *The New Schaff-Herzog Encyclopedia of Religious Knowledge*, X New York (1911), pp. 163-66); J. Pohle, "Sacrifice," *CathEnc* XIII London (1912), pp. 309-21; H. Lesêtre, "Sacrifice," *Dictionnaire de la Bible* (ed.) F. Vigouroux, Paris ([2]1928), L, cols. 1311-37; F. Nötscher, *Biblische Altertumskunde*, Bonn (1940), pp. 320-32; J. J. Reeve, "Sacrifice," *ISBE* (ed.) J. Orr IV, Grand Rapids (reprint 1947), cols. 2638-51.

approaches to the subject find expression in the articles by James, Bertholet and Eissfeldt,[1] and in the works treated in detail below.

Most significant of the English contributions was the posthumous work of G. B. Gray, *Sacrifice in the Old Testament* (Oxford, 1925). This was a collection of studies on a number of topics related to sacrifice—the theory of sacrifice, the altar, the priesthood and the festivals—rather than a full-scale treatment of the Old Testament data. The first ninety-five pages, which dealt with sacrifice proper, consisted of a defence of the gift theory of sacrifice,[2] and a review of the evidence for the theory of propitiation. Gray's conclusion that "sacrifice was more often eucharistic than propitiatory" and "more often offered with feelings of joy and security than in fear or contrition"[3] supported the view of the Wellhausen school, but he laid a great deal more weight on the solemn element than Wellhausen and Robertson Smith,[4] and explicitly rejected the latter's view of mystical communion as invalid for Israel, whatever may have been the position in primitive times.[5]

On the Continent interest came to centre on one or other form of the "power-working" theories. Wundt had sought to show that behind the presentation of fruits and plants on the altar was the idea not of a gift to the deity, but of the magical re-creation of these materials by imitation.[6] In the later development the burning of

---

[1] E. O. James, "Sacrifice, (Introductory and Primitive)," *ERE* XI (1920), pp. 1-7; A. Bertholet, "Opfer: I. Religionsgeschichtlich," *RGG* IV (^{2}1930), cols. 704-11; O. Eissfeldt, "Opfer: II A. Im A.T." *Ibid.*, cols. 711-17.

[2] Gray appealed to such facts as the original meaning of the terms *minḥâ* and *qorbān*, the later commutation of some sacrifices to money and the prophetic criticism of sacrifice as a bribe to the deity (pp. 1-54).

[3] *Ibid.*, p. 95.

[4] In particular, he noted the allusive nature of the expiatory references in 1 Sam. 26 : 19 and 1 Sam. 3 : 14, as indicating the commonly understood theory of sacrifice, and thought that weight must also be given to the fact that the oft-told story of the founding of the major sanctuary in Jerusalem explained sacrifice as propitiatory (2 Sam. 24), (pp. 83ff). All the other *hieroi logoi* (Shechem, Beersheba, Bethel and probably Ophrah, Mizpah and Hebron), however, lacked this element (p. 90).

[5] *Ibid.*, pp. 1ff., 368ff. Cook's preference of Robertson Smith to Gray at this point again reads curiously, when he says that Gray's "more often eucharistic than propitiatory" overlooks "that early Israel undoubtedly suffered disasters enough to call for apotropaic and other rites." (*The Religion of the Semites*, (^{3}1927), p. 651). It is just this admission, which Robertson Smith does not make.

[6] W. Wundt, *Völkerpsychologie*, Leipzig II, 2 (1906), pp. 300-46, 446-50;

such "power-carriers" as the fat and the kidneys strengthened the god through strengthening the soul of the worshipper. Lagrange agreed with Robertson Smith that the eating of the sacrifice was central, but thought the rite one of deconsecration rather than of consecration. Just as the firstfruits were given to the deity to satisfy the tabu and make the remainder safe for food (cf. Lev. 19 : 23), so the dangerous blood was poured out in sacrifice to desacralize the rest for consumption.[1] Hubert and Mauss had thought the victim an intermediary to absorb the dangerous mana, and this was held by Bertholet to be a better explanation of the eating of the sin offering than Robertson Smith's. The eating in this case was a means of getting rid of what was dangerous to the community in a non-dangerous way.[2] The other rites of blood manipulation and burning released power.[3]

The idea of sacrifice as "the giving of life for the renewal of life," was represented by a series of scholars. Prominent among these was Dussaud, to whom the principle of sacrifice was the gaining of the life, which was set free by the pouring out of the sacrificial blood. Sacrifice released the power of the soul in the blood and part of this carried away sin and part brought covenant with God. The Wellhausen school was at fault in denying the early rise of the expiatory

II, 3 (1909), pp. 667-90; *Elemente der Völkerpsychologie*, Leipzig (1912), pp. 251ff., 427-38.

[1] M. J. Lagrange, *Études sur les religions sémitiques*, Paris (²1905), Ch. VII (esp. pp. 269-274).

[2] See the references cited in footnotes 3 and 6 on p. 6.

[3] Similar ideas were expressed by A. Loisy ("La notion du sacrifice dans l'antiquité israélite," *RHLR* N.S. I (1910), pp. 1-30); "Le sacrifice dégage une force qui s'impose, au moins dans une très large mesure, au dieu lui-même." (p. 18). On 2 Sam. 6 he wrote: "David . . . voulut transporter l'arche sur le mont Sion, il s'y risqua seulement en multipliant les sacrifices . .. Ce n'est pas là un service alimentaire. Le dieu en marche est une puissance redoutable dont les nombreux sacrifices accomplis sur sa route endiguent les débordements" (p. 19), and on Gen. 8 : 20: "L'odeur plait à la divinité, mais qui sans doute ont une raison plus profonde que celle de lui être agréable. Le sacrifice établit le rapport normal du monde avec Dieu, régularisant l'action de Dieu sur le monde et faisant refluer, pour ainsi dire, du monde vers Dieu la vie qui vient de lui." (pp. 20-21) See further his *Essai historique sur le sacrifice*, Paris (1920). The beginning of sacrifice in a magical fructifying of nature was also posited by G. Runze in his important articles "Die psychischen Motive der Opferbräuche in der Stufenfolge ihrer Entwicklung," *Zeitschrift für Religionspsychologie* II (1908-1909), pp. 81-89 and "Ursprung und Entwicklung der Opferbräuche," *Neue Weltanschauung*, I (1908), pp. 401-11, 453-57.

element.[1] In England, an Anglican school reaching back to Westcott had argued, in the interests of a priestly view of the Christian ministry[2] that the blood in sacrifice was the offering of life, rather than death, and this now found expression in Gayford's attempt "to justify the conception that sacrifice consists not merely in killing... but in the offering of a life that has passed through death."[3] The blood in the victim alone would be life unsurrendered, part of the blood would be part of the life surrendered, the whole life was needed and so the victim must die.[4] All the sacrifices had some element of expiation.[5]

Representing the same general standpoint, but seeking a wider basis in ethnology, was E. O. James. In his early works he looked chiefly to totemic communion ideas among the Central Australian aborigines,[6] but later writings drew on the cave evidence of France, where totemism found no support, and stressed rather the "blood as the vitalizing essence charged with life-giving power" as the fundamental conception of sacrifice.[7] Robertson Smith's view of an

---

[1] R. Dussaud, *Les origines cananéennes du sacrifice israélite*, Paris (1921), pp. 27ff, 3ff. Dussaud's views, as well as those of other scholars, who have treated specifically of the origin of Hebrew sacrifice, are discussed in the next chapter.

[2] Cf. W. Sanday (ed.) *Priesthood and Sacrifice*, London (1900).

[3] S. C. Gayford, *Sacrifice and Priesthood*, London (1924), p. 1.

[4] *Ibid.*, p. 116. Kennett added that no animal was of any use in sacrifice unless just slain that day, because it was not the dead body that mattered, but the transfer of the life ("Sacrifice," *The Church of Israel*, Cambridge (1933), p. 102). Similar views were expressed by F. C. N. Hicks, *The Fullness of Sacrifice*, London ([3]1946), but were denied by F. J. Taylor ("Blood," *A Theological Wordbook of the Bible* (ed.) A. Richardson, London (1950), p. 34. He writes: "the blood of a man after his death may have profound effects, not through the persistent activity of a life released, but because of the significance of the life taken"), and by L. Morris, *The Apostolic Preaching of the Cross*, Grand Rapids (1955), pp. 108-24 = *JTS* N.S. III (1952), pp. 216-27 (cf. the reply by L. Dewar, *JTS* N.S. IV (1953), pp. 204-208).

[5] "They all express the human desire for fellowship with God. We may perhaps go a step further and say that all of them, even the most confident and joyful, imply some sort of consciousness that the fellowship with God is not a continued, unbroken union but needs to be renewed (p. 33)."

[6] E. O. James, *Primitive Ritual and Belief*, London (1917), esp. pp. 122ff. "Sacrifice (Introductory and Primitive)," *ERE* XI (1920), pp. 1-7.

[7] E. O. James, *Sacrifice and Sacrament*, London (1927), pp. 1-11; *The Origins of Sacrifice*, London (1933); "Aspects of Sacrifice in the Old Testament," *ExpT* L (1938-1939), pp. 151-55; *History of Religions*, London (1956), pp. 13ff.

origin in totemism, or the communion meal is rejected. The blood offering for the increasing of life is older.[1] An analogy is to be seen in the rites of the killing of the divine king, and the human sacrifices which came to replace it.[2] Human sacrifice had originally the purpose of giving to the god the vitality of the life sacrificed and was not a substitution to save him from taking other lives.[3]

A synthetic account of Hebrew sacrifice, which drew on the three views of a gift to the deity, a means to communion and a liberating of life was put forward by Oesterley in 1937[4] and remains the last major work on the subject in English.[5] Chapters were devoted to primitive and Semitic sacrifice and then to Israelite sacrifice in the nomadic, agricultural, post-exilic and post-Biblical periods and to the attitude of the pre-exilic and post-exilic prophets and Jesus to sacrifice. The threefold scheme of classification into gift, communion and life-liberating elements is adhered to even for the nomadic period, where it is associated with a doubtful theory of moon-worship. Expiation, which has no separate category, receives some consideration under the other headings, but tends to be lost sight of, while more obscure elements are brought to the fore. It may be doubted whether the schematic treatment either as to type or to period is really satisfactory.[6]

A still more eclectic account was given by Wendel in his isolation of no less than nine motives for sacrifice.[7] The bulk of his book (pp. 32-206) is devoted to the discussion of instances of sacrifice culled from the historical books of the Old Testament in illustration of these nine themes—food for Yahweh, reconciliation of Yahweh,

---

[1] James, *Origins of Sacrifice*, pp. 42ff.

[2] *Ibid.*, pp. 73ff. J. G. Frazer, who had at first followed Robertson Smith, advanced the view that all sacrifice was to be traced to this root (*The Golden Bough* (one volume edition), New York, reprint (1948)).

[3] James, *Origins of Sacrifice*, p. 185. In this, like Runze (*op. cit.*) he perhaps leaned too heavily on the Mexican evidence.

[4] W. O. E. Oesterley, *Sacrifices in Ancient Israel*, London (1937).

[5] The book by R. K. Yerkes, *Sacrifice in Greek and Roman religions and early Judaism*, New York (1952), has much useful material, but is in some ways already dated (cf. the reviews by S. H. Hooke, *JTS* V (1954), pp. 240-42 and N. H. Snaith, *Theology* LVII (1954), pp. 188-89).

[6] Although six chapters are devoted to "the agricultural period," which was approximately from the entry to the land to the exile, the treatment is not historical and no clear picture of the historic movement emerges.

[7] A. Wendel, *Das Opfer in der altisraelitischen Religion*, Leipzig (1927).

fellowship with Yahweh, making present of Yahweh, destruction for Yahweh, gift to Yahweh, revitalizing of Yahweh, asceticism for Yahweh and service of Yahweh. The term "sacrifice" is given a wide connotation and includes such varied topics as anointing, circumcision, the ban, the *hierodouloi,* and tithes, firstlings and other gifts. Vestiges of animism and demonism are dealt with in an early chapter, and loom largely throughout the later sections. The various offering motives correspond to the many-sidedness of Yahweh—as war-god he received the ban, as wilderness demon the human first-born, as cattle-god the animals, and as lord of the land the fruits.[1] The solemn aspects of sacrifice are much more stressed than in the Wellhausen school,[2] and the element of expiation is seen to stand in no contradiction to that of rejoicing.[3]

In the works of Roman Catholic scholars the question of expiation and substitution has received special attention. The substitutionary theory was supported by Médebielle,[4] but the opposite view was taken by Metzinger in his series of articles in *Biblica,*[5] and by Moraldi in the most recent extensive investigation of Hebrew sacrifice.[6] Moraldi in Part I of his book makes a detailed study of the idea of expiation in Babylon-Assyria and among the Hittites, Canaanites and Egyptians. His conclusion is that expiation cannot be spoken of, because no real sense of sin was present. Part II comes to the Old Testament and after an introductory chapter on theories of sacrifice, expiation and human sacrifice, moves into a discussion of Lev. 4-5. Chapters describe in turn the *ḥaṭṭā't,* the *'āšām, kipper,* the blood and the *s^emîkâ* and the conclusion

---

[1] A. Wendel, *op. cit.*, p. 217.

[2] The view of Stade that Israelite sacrifices were normally joyous is rejected, along with that of Wundt that expiation was the main form (*ibid.*, p. 81).

[3] The joy of the communion meal might be the consequence of reconciliation (*ibid.*, pp. 105-106).

[4] A. Médebielle, *L'expiation dans l'Ancien et le Nouveau Testament,* Rome (1924), and "Expiation," *Dictionnaire de la Bible Suppl.*, III (1938), cols. 1-262 (esp. 48-81).

[5] A. Metzinger, "Die Substitutionstheorie und das alttestamentliche Opfer," *Bibl.* XXI (1940), pp. 159-87, 247-72, 353-77. Cf. also the discussion of Medebielle's book by J. Rivière, "Expiation et rédemption dans l'Ancien Testament," *Bulletin de littérature ecclésiastique,* XLVII (1946), pp. 3-22.

[6] L. Moraldi, *Espiazione sacrificale e riti espiatori nell'ambiente biblico e nell'Antico Testamento,* Rome (1956).

is reached that the Levitical ritual ignores penal substitution. It may be questioned, however, whether the method by which this conclusion is reached is really sound. The Levitical ritual is not fully handled. Lev. 1-3 and 6-7 are not discussed and the important evidence of the Day of Atonement is completely set aside. The history of Israelite sacrifice receives no separate attention and the question of the date of sources is left up in the air. The relevance of the discussion of Part I to that of Part II is thus nowhere demonstrated.

The idea of expiation has also been examined by Koch in an unpublished work.[1] Koch begins from the final form of P, and works back to the early materials. Expiation is not the atoning of God by man, but the cleansing of man by God. The subject of the verb *kipper* is either God, or the priest acting on God's behalf, not the sinful man. Lev. 17 : 11 is understood in a substitutionary sense.[2] The *s^emîkâ* signified a transfer of sin, and the fact that the victim was still spoken of as holy was not evidence to the contrary, when holiness was understood as "belonging to God."[3] Expiation, however, was in the blood-rite, rather than in the offering as a whole, and was not to be seen for example in the *'ōlâ*, either in P, or in earlier Old Testament references.[4] It involved ancient ideas of representation, which can only with caution be taken over into Christian soteriology.[5]

The Present Method

Many other works on sacrifice could be included in this brief review, but probably enough have been discussed to illustrate the main points that need attention and the methods that are required to meet them. Most of the scholars reviewed have conceded that

---

[1] K. Koch, *Die israelitische Sühneanschauung und ihre historischen Wandlungen*. Habilitationsschrift. (Typescript), Erlangen (1956).

[2] "Sühne durch Blut bedeutet also, dass an die Stelle des verwirkten Menschenlebens der Tod des Tieres auf dem Altar tritt" (p. 14). "Nach israelitischem Verständnis scheint der Tod des Tieres nicht durch die Schlachtung, sondern erst durch die Blutbespritzung und Blutausschüttung am Altar endgültig besiegelt und rechtmässig zu sein. Durch diesen Tod wird die Sünde ausgelöscht, die auf das Tier übertragen war" (p. 19).

[3] *Ibid.*, pp. 25, 29.

[4] *Ibid.*, pp. 8, 31, 75-77.

[5] *Ibid.*, pp. 95-96.

expiation had a larger place in early Israelite sacrifice than the Wellhausen school allowed, but none of them have devoted to it, a systematic and methodical investigation. Such an investigation must take up the sources seriatim in their order of date, and examine each reference to sacrifice. An *a priori* classification into a schematic framework must be avoided.[1] The Law Codes must be used only where their evidence can be shown to be contemporary,[2] and comparative materials only where they are relevant to Israel.[3] Individual and community aspects need to be distinguished and the results or accompaniments of sacrifice not confused with the cause and purpose.

With these principles in mind the following method will be adopted. A preliminary chapter will survey the comparative material, which may have influenced the beginnings of Israelite sacrifice. The chapters to follow will be devoted to the evidence of the Yahwist, the Elohist,[4] Joshua-Judges, Samuel, Kings, Psalms, the eighth century prophets, the seventh century prophets and

---

[1] Even the modern division "before the *Landnahme*," "the time of the amphictyony," "the formation of the state and after," favoured by R. Rendtorff, ("Der Kultus im Alten Israel," *JLH* II (1956), pp. 1-21) begs a number of questions (see next chapter) and thus shares the weakness of Oesterley's period divisions.

[2] While it may be agreed with M. Haran ("The uses of incense in the ancient Israelite ritual," *VT* X (1960), p. 122) that "the evidence of the non-Priestly sources is, for the most part, accidental and obscure and may even be misleading" his solution that "in all questions of Temple practice and ritual observance, we should usually begin by examining the authoritative evidence of the Priestly sources, and only then may we pass to the "external," non-Priestly sources for solving any difficulty raised by the latter" must be judged methodologically false. The Priestly Code is not good evidence for early Israel. It is left out of account in the present enquiry, not because old elements are not recognized, but because it is only possible to know what these are after their existence has been demonstrated by an independent historical enquiry. This is what is attempted here.

[3] The investigation therefore limits itself to Israelite sacrifice in the historic period, and passes no judgment on the validity of the views of Robertson Smith and other scholars, for earlier times, or other peoples.

[4] A study of the history of criticism has convinced the writer of the necessity for the continued use of these sigla (J, E, D, P) in discussion with the Wellhausen school. This study of the history also suggests that modifications in the view of the religious history carry with them consequences for source criticism, which have not yet sufficiently been drawn. (Cf. the writer's *The Rise and Decline of the Grafian Hypothesis*, Th. M. Thesis, Typescript, Rüschlikon (1959), pp. 63, 132. On the question of method see Th. C. Vriezen, *An Outline of Old Testament Theology*, p. 39).

Deuteronomy.[1] Each reference to sacrifice will be examined as to terms used, source (whether secondary or primary), background (whether Israelite or non-Israelite), scope (whether individual or communal), occasion (whether special or regular) and mood (whether a sense of sin or solemnity is present).

---

[1] With Wendel a date about 600 B.C. would seem to be as late as one need go in discussing "early Israelite sacrifice."

CHAPTER ONE

BEGINNINGS

Where is the discussion of the religion of Israel to begin? S. H. Hooke spoke for many of his generation, when he said in 1954, that whereas twenty years earlier he would have regarded the eighth century prophets as the true founders of Israel's religion, he had come to see in the tradition of the double call and choice of Israel in Abraham and Moses an authentic tradition.[1]

The view that the *prophets* were the founders of Israel's religion was persuasively propounded in the first flush of the critical movement by Kuenen, who began his "Religion of Israel" with the eighth century B.C.[2] The same emphasis on the prophets as founders was present in Wellhausen's work, although ostensibly he took back to Moses the beginnings of both the history,[3] and the religion.[4] The view of the *Mosaic* origin of Israel's religion, went along with that of nomadic antecedents, Marti, for example, dividing his history of Israelite religion into four periods—the nomad religion of polydaemonism, largely indifferent to sacrifice, which characterized the early period, the peasant religion of Canaanitism, which was responsible for the sacrificial cultus, the religion of the prophets, which introduced monotheism, and legal religion, which produced

---

[1] S. H. Hooke, "Myth and Ritual Reconsidered," *The Siege Perilous*, London (1956), pp. 182-83. Cf. also Hooke, "Myth and Ritual: Past and Present," *Myth, Ritual, and Kingship*, Oxford (1958), p. 19.

[2] A. Kuenen, *The Religion of Israel*, E.T. 3 vols London (1874-1875). Kuenen claimed to be following "not the course of the history itself, but the path which we must take in order to learn to know it." (I, p. 30) He recognized, of course, that there was a religion of Israel before the prophets and devoted a later chapter (I, Ch. V) to it, but he had little confidence in pre-prophetic sources (I, pp. 17ff, 108ff), or in the quality of the pre-prophetic religion (I, pp. 270ff).

[3] Wellhausen wrote ("Israel," *EBrit* XIII, p. 397 reprinted in *Prolegomena*, p. 432): "In point of fact the history of Israel must be held to have begun then . . ."

[4] "We can begin the history of the religion only with the history of the people, that is with Moses at the earliest" (Wellhausen, "Israelitisch-jüdische Religion," *Die Kultur der Gegenwart*, (ed.) Paul Hinneberg, Div. I Vol. IV, Part I, Berlin ([2]1909), p. 7).

the law after the exile.[1] *Patriarchal* religion found a defender in König,[2] but only with the work of Alt[3] can the focus of interest be said to have shifted back to this time.

The present chapter will be devoted to a review of these and other theories of the beginnings of Israel's religion, which have particular bearing on the origin of Hebrew sacrifice.

The Nomadic Origin

Israel's nomad origin became axiomatic for a long line of writers on Israelite religion, and to some extent determined the view of Israelite sacrifice. Vegetable offerings, appropriate only in an agricultural people, could not have been offered in the Mosaic period.[4] The *minḥâ*, as a gift or tribute, was equally inappropriate in a free Bedouin people, among whom all were equal and no man acknowledged as master.[5] The *ʿōlâ*, or whole burnt offering, was unknown to the pre-Islamic Arabs and could not therefore have been offered in Israel till a late period. The *ʾāšām* and *ḥaṭṭāʾt*, as altar sacrifices, were equally unknown. The sacrificial practice of Arabic heathendom was appealed to as the definitive description of early Israelite sacrifice by both Wellhausen and Robertson Smith.[6] The *zebaḥ* or sacrificial meal was the typical sacrifice.

---

[1] K. Marti, *The Religion of the Old Testament*, E. T. London (1907).

[2] Two works of König a generation apart may be compared. In 1884 for him *Die Hauptprobleme der altisraelitischen Religionsgeschichte*, Leipzig (1884) were the questions whether the religion of Israel had begun with the prophets or with Moses, while in 1921 "The Burning Problem of the Hour in Old Testament Religious History," (*Exp* 8th series XXI (1921), pp. 81-106) was whether it had begun with Moses or the patriarchs. See his *Geschichte der alttestamentlichen Religion*, Gütersloh (1912), pp. 1-147, and his Genesis commentary *Die Genesis*, Gütersloh ([2] & [3] 1918).

[3] A. Alt, "Der Gott der Väter," Stuttgart (1929) reprinted in *Kleine Schriften zur Geschichte des Volkes Israel*, Vol. I, München (1953), pp. 1-78.

[4] Cf. W. R. Smith, *Religion of the Semites*, pp. 244ff.

[5] *Ibid.*, pp. 458ff.

[6] J. Wellhausen, *Reste arabischen Heidentumes*, Berlin (1887), p. 110-24; W. R. Smith, *The Religion of the Semites*. Robertson Smith argued that Arabia, where nomadic life had remained unchanged from generation to generation, was a better starting point for the study of primitive Semitic religion than Babylonia where "society and religion alike were based on a fusion of two races, and so were not primitive but complex . . .," and where "the official system of Babylonian and Assyrian religion, as it is known to us from priestly texts and public inscriptions, bears clear marks of being something more than a popular traditional faith; it has been artificially moulded by priestcraft and statecraft . . ." (pp. 13, 14).

Various elements in this view were challenged from time to time. In 1899 Curtiss went to Syria firmly persuaded of Robertson Smith's view of the sacrificial meal as the earliest form of Semitic sacrifice, but investigations over seven years among present day Arabs convinced him that still more fundamental was the vicarious principle. The sacrificial meal was frequent but not essential. The central feature was "the bursting forth of the blood" and its interpretation in a substitutionary sense of "blood for blood."[1] Other investigators noted the much fuller sacrificial vocabulary in the South Arabian (Sabean and Minean) inscriptions and felt that this should be placed alongside the Arabian evidence adduced by Robertson Smith and Wellhausen.[2] Lods also argued for a more elaborate nomad ritual and believed that the pre-Yahwist Israelites practised a form of *kālîl* or whole offering, the prototype of the burnt offering, in addition to the communion meal.[3]

---

[1] S. I. Curtiss, *Primitive Semitic Religion Today*, Chicago (1902) and in more detail in a series of articles in the *Exp*—"Discoveries of a Vicarious Element in Primitive Semitic Sacrifice," 6th series, VI (1902), pp. 128-34, "The Semitic Sacrifice of Reconciliation," VI (1902), pp. 454-62, "Some Religious Usages of the Dhîâb and Ruala Arabs and their Old Testament Parallels," IX (1904), pp. 275-85, "The Origin of Sacrifice among the Semites as deduced from Facts gathered among Syrians and Arabs," X (1904), pp. 461-72, "Survivals of Ancient Semitic Religion in Syrian Centres," XI (1905), pp. 415-431.

[2] So F. Hommel, *The Ancient Hebrew Tradition*, E.T. London (1897), who sought to prove from the parallels that P could not be a late document (cf. pp. 271ff), and J. A. Montgomery, *Arabia and the Bible*, Philadelphia (1934) who noted that the use of *ḥaṭṭā't* for sexual irregularities offending sacred places and seasons paralleled the Hebrew sin and trespass offerings of Lev. 4 and 15 and indicated a sensitiveness towards sexual offences unique in the old Semitic world (pp. 157-58). I. Benzinger, *Hebräische Archäologie*, Tübingen (³1927) compared the early Old Testament use of *ḥaṭṭā't* for a money fine, which Wellhausen had recognized, but was more impressed by the presence of fire offerings among the Mineans and in Israel: "Dagegen ist das minäische Opfer ein Feueropfer gewesen, wenn anders die Deutung von *mabschal* 'Heiligtum' der Inschriften = Ort wo das Opfer gekocht oder gebraten wird, richtig ist." (pp. 371, 67) The argument from *ḥaṭṭā't* is also discounted by G. B. Gray, *Sacrifice in the Old Testament*, pp. 63ff. The relevant inscriptions are collected *ibid.*, p. 406.

[3] Lods wrote: "Probably, like the ancient Arabs and Moslem pilgrims of today, they would practise a sort of *kālîl*, or 'whole gift'—a prototype of the burnt offering—in which the victim's flesh was given over to the wild beasts of the sacred place. It is very probable that, like the present-day Bedouin and a good many 'primitives,' they also slaughtered animals with the intention of getting rid of a sickness or a fault. They were certainly familiar with the covenant sacrifice (Exod. xxiv. 4b, 6-8), and with the use

Sporadic voices were also raised against the assumption that the Israelites had been nomads at all. Sayce claimed that Pharaoh could not have enslaved true Bedouins, who would have flitted in a night.[1] Hommel noted that in the time in Egypt, on the testimony of Deut. 11 : 10, Israel had engaged in agricultural as well as pastoral pursuits "You sowed your seed and watered it with your foot."[2] E. Robertson said "The Hebrews were never an Arab tribe, and their wanderings for a short period in the desert could not turn them into one."[3] Albright remarked that the Israelites were never at home in the desert, and unlike the Transjordanian nomads, who have never settled in the Transjordan despite their centuries of residence,[4] Israel settled quickly to sedentary life.[5]

Eerdmans and others drew attention to the local colour of the Genesis traditions as inconsistent with nomadic conditions. Abraham had flour (Gen. 18 : 6), Isaac sows grain and drinks wine[6] (Gen. 26 : 12, 27 : 25), Jacob had lentils and mandrakes (Gen. 25 : 34, 30 : 14), Joseph dreams of sheaves of grain (Gen. 37 : 7) and receives gifts of fruit (Gen. 43 : 11). The true Bedouin lives without bread and with little water, but the patriarchs must dig wells (Gen.

---

of the victim's blood as a protection against . . .evil spirits. The various types of ritual slaughter, the theory of which was to be provided by the priestly legists of the Exilic period . . . existed already . . ., at least in germ, among the Hebrews of nomadic times." ("The Religion of Israel I. Origins," *Record and Revelation*, pp. 190-91. Also in "Eléments anciens et éléments modernes dans le rituel du sacrifice israélite," *RHPhR* (1928), pp. 399-411 (esp. pp. 406ff); "Israelitische Opfervorstellungen und—bräuche," *ThR* N.F. III (1931), pp. 347-66; *Israel from its Beginnings to the Middle of the Eighth Century*, E.T. London (1932), p. 279).

[1] A. H. Sayce, in preface to V.Z. Rule, *Old Testament Institutions*, London (1910).

[2] Hommel, *op. cit.*, p. 229.

[3] E. Robertson, *The Old Testament Problem*, Manchester (1950), p. 66. So also now Y. Kaufmann, *The Religion of Israel*, E. T. Chicago (1960), pp. 205, 218, 221, 339.

[4] G. A. Smith found the Beni Mesaid pitching their summer camp, where a Greek inscription of A.D. 214 indicated that the *phulē Mozaiedēmōn* had also encamped (vide S. A. Cook, "Semites," *Cambridge Ancient History*, Vol. I, Cambridge (1923), p. 190).

[5] W. F. Albright, *Archaeology of Palestine*, Middlesex (Penguin) (^{3}1956), p. 119; *Archaeology and the Religion of Israel*, Baltimore (^{3}1953), p. 102.

[6] The latter is perhaps more striking than the former. Corn can be grown by a nomad in a stay of a few months, but vines require years of residence.

26 : 18) and seek corn in Egypt (Gen. 42 : 2).[1] The animals of the patriarchs were not only those of nomads—camels and small head of sheep and goats, but included the larger bovines—cows, oxen and asses. De Vaux noted the interesting fact that Jacob in Haran (Gen. 28-29) has only small stock, but when he reaches Esau (Gen. 32-33) has large cattle also. In this is typified the approach of the pastoralist to more fertile land. The patriarchs in Palestine were no longer nomads, nor yet peasants but semi-nomads.[2] The upshot of the discussion has been the recognition of an intermediate category half-way between the Bedu nomad and the fellahin settled peasant.[3] The scholars listed above recognized that Israel had some nomadic background,[4] but preferred to speak of the Israelites as semi-nomads.[5]

Along with this change of opinion about Israelite nomadism has gone a corresponding modification in the view of Arabian religion itself. The confidence with which Robertson Smith drew upon

---

[1] B. D. Eerdmans, "Have the Hebrews been nomads," *Exp* 7th series, VI (1908), pp. 118-31. See also the reply by G. A. Smith, *ibid.*, pp. 254-72 and the rejoinder by Eerdmans *ibid.*, pp. 345-58.

[2] R. de Vaux, "Les patriarches hébreux et les découvertes modernes," *RB* LVI (1949), pp. 11ff. De Vaux points out that camel breeding is possible with less than 10 cm. rainfall a year, sheep and goat breeding with 10 to 25 cm. while cattle breeding requires considerably more. His map (p. 13) indicates that the western and northern zones of Canaan had a rainfall in excess of 50 cm., the central and eastern zone in excess of 25 cm. and the south and further east 10 cm. or over. See also his *Les institutions de l'Ancien Testament* Vol. I, Paris (1958), pp. 15-17.

[3] For the various stages of nomadism see S. Nyström, *Beduinentum und Jahwismus*, Lund (1946), pp. 5-6, 71-72.

[4] De Vaux (*Institutions* I, p. 30) cites the survival of nomadism in such expressions as "to your tents, O Israel," death as cutting a cord (Job 4 : 21 etc.), the nomadic ideal of the prophets, and like E. Dhorme, *L'évolution religieuse d'Israël*, Vol. I, Bruxelles (1937), writes the first volume of his *Institutions* in the framework of nomadic life. Lods, *Israel*, p. 190 listed such terms as *nasa*ᶜ "to pull up tent-pegs" for "setting out," *derek* "way" for "conduct" and *naweh* "pasturage" for "abode" as evidence of nomadic origins. For a full list of such survivals in Israelite food, clothing, shelter, organization and religion see J. W. Flight, "The Nomadic Idea and Ideal in the Old Testament," *JBL* XLII (1923), pp. 158-226.

[5] So W. F. Albright, *Archaeology and the Religion of Israel*, p. 97, who distinguishes camel nomads, who live in the desert miles from water and subsist on a diet of camel milk and flesh and use camel skin and hair for their tents and equipment, from ass nomads, who must keep close to water and whose animals supply little milk or hair and cannot be eaten.

Arabian sources for pure Semitic religion is no longer shared by investigators.

According to Guillaume all Arabian religion had been Sumerianized except in the most inaccessible places. The sanctuaries of pre-Islamic times that are known to us were one and all from settled areas around oases.[1] Primitive Semitic nomadism was an abstract concept that corresponds to nothing in reality. Arabian religion was the result of attrition—the shedding of all complications of ritual and pantheon.[2] Arabia may well have been an example, for which other parallels existed, of the nomad being a displaced settler, rather than the fellahin a settled nomad. In some areas the hunter first turned agriculturalist and only later moved out into the desert.[3] Communal animal sacrifices thus took their rise in the cattle breeding of the civilized fringes of Arabia, as might have been deduced from the fact that only domestic animals and not such creatures as deer and hares, as would have been expected on Robertson Smith's animal kinship theory, were sacrificed.[4]

It was a short step from this position to the conclusion that the antecedents of Semitic religion were to be sought in Babylonia rather than Arabia,[5] and this step was taken by the adherents of the Pan-Babylonian school.

The Mesopotamian Origin

Mesopotamian antecedents of Israelite sacrifice found spokesmen in two different schools, which have flourished since Wellhausen—the Pan-Babylonian school around the turn of the century, and the Myth and Ritual school of the present generation.

In 1906, Winckler made his celebrated attack on the evolutionary scheme of Marti.[6] Marti's nomad and peasant stages in Israel's religion were imaginary. The religion of the Bible was as little "Bauernreligion" as Luther's or Zwingli's.[7] Wellhausen's cult-less

---

[1] A. Guillaume, *Prophecy and Divination*, London (1938), pp. 61ff.

[2] *Ibid.*, pp. 73-74.

[3] *Ibid.*, pp. 71-72. Guillaume remarked that the Cain and Abel story reflected this order of the nomad as the child of the agriculturalist (*loc. cit.*).

[4] *Ibid.*, p. 73.

[5] D.M.L. Urie, "Sacrifice Among the West-Semites," *PEQ* LXXXI (1949), pp. 80-81.

[6] H. Winckler, *Religionsgeschichtler und geschichtlicher Orient*, Leipzig (1906).

[7] *Ibid.*, p. 21.

wilderness period was a fiction: "Es hat nie und nirgends eine Religion ohne Kult und ohne Opfer gegeben, ebensowenig wie einen Staat ohne Gesetze, Regierung und 'Opfer,' d.h. Leistungen (Steuern)."[1] In similar strain A. Jeremias stressed the early origin of the propitiatory element in Israel's religion on the analogy of what he believed was true of Babylonian sacrifice. Of the offering of Isaac he wrote: "The thought that at the altar the sacrifice of an animal takes the place of a human being, is at the root of the sin-offering throughout the whole of the antique world,"[2] and of the Passover: "The striking of the doorposts with blood presupposes in the religion of the Patriarchs an acquaintance with a sin offering of which our sources of Israelite primitive histories say nothing."[3] J. Jeremias shared the view that Babylonian sacrifice had the purpose of influencing the deity in favour of the sacrificer. The gods rejoice over it, but "predominant... over this joyous note... is a feature which is common to all Semitic religions—the element of propitiation."[4] M. Jastrow also saw evidence for the sombre side of Babylonian religion in the frequent references to the sense of guilt, and the unfavourable days in the calendar, which outnumbered the favourable.[5]

Later investigation has cast doubt, both on this description of the nature of Babylonian religion and of the extent of Israel's indebtedness to it. Galling, writing of the oldest period, emphasised that the offerings were regarded as food for the gods, rather than as expiatory: "the old Babylonian brought his offering with a joyful heart... A band of confidence linked the offerer and the deity."[6] Dhorme, while acknowledging the alimentary aspect thought expiation and substitution more dominant,[7] but Moraldi replied that: "in the ritual are lacking those notes, moral and religious,

---

[1] *Ibid.*, p. 32.

[2] A. Jeremias, *The Old Testament in the Light of the Ancient East*, E.T. Vol. II ([2]1911), London, p. 49.

[3] *Ibid.*, pp. 103-4.

[4] J. Jeremias, "Ritual (Assyrio-Babylonian Ritual)," *EB* IV, London (1903), col. 4120. He agreed with Wellhausen, however, that in Israel the joyous sacramental meal was the typical sacrifice (cols. 4120, 4124ff).

[5] M. Jastrow, "Religion of Babylonia and Assyria," *DB* Extra Vol. p. 581a.

[6] K. Galling, *Der Altar in den Kulturen des alten Orients*, Berlin (1925), p. 38.

[7] E. Dhorme, "Le sacrifice akkadien," *RHR* CVII-CVIII (1933), pp. 107-25. See also *L'évolution religieuse*, Vol. I, pp. 215ff.

which are necessary and characteristic of expiation."[1] These different verdicts are in part due to the complexity of the material, the long period involved,[2] the disagreement as to what is to be classed as sacrifice,[3] and the uncertainty as to the use of the various altars and cult installations.[4]

Israel's indebtedness to Babylonian ritual was stressed by Haupt[5] who after citing many parallels concluded that although:

> the comparative study of the ante-islamic religions of the Arabs undoubtedly throws much light on certain forms of ancient Israelite worship... if we want to trace the origin of the later Jewish ceremonial of the Priestly Code, we must look for it in the cuneiform ritual texts of the Assyro-Babylonians

and to a lesser by Barton,[6] who thought he found a parallel to the Israelite *'āšām* in the offering of doves referred to in Eannatum's Stele of the Vultures. The great difference between Babylonian and Israelite ritual must, however, be noted. Most striking is the complete omission of any blood rite analogous to that of the Old Testament, and the pervading atmosphere of magic, which determines the character of so much of Babylonian sacrifice, but scarcely figures at all in the Old Testament. Guillaume has well remarked that the Akkadians, while vastly superior to the Hebrews in material

---

1 L. Moraldi, *op. cit.*, p. 32.

2 The evidence for propitiation seems to be more marked in the new Babylonian period.

3 Are the rites for the healing of sickness and the expulsion of demons to be included, or only altar offerings?

4 Galling, *op. cit.*, p. 27 disputes W. H. Ward's identification ("Altars and Sacrifices in the Primitive Art of Babylon," in S. I. Curtiss, *Primitive Semitic Religion Today*, pp. 266-77) of the leaf-shaped designs rising above the vase altars as flames, but his own treatment needs supplementing by the evidence of burnt offering altars at Mari (A. Parrot, "Autels et installations cultuelles a Mari," *Congress Volume Copenhagen* 1953 (*VTSuppl* I), Leiden (1953), pp. 112-19, and elsewhere (E. D. van Buren, "Places of Sacrifice," *Iraq* XIV (1952), pp. 76-92). Perhaps L. Rost has drawn the line too close when he limits the occurrence of burnt offerings to the Western Semites in the area bordered by the Taurus in the north, the Mediterranean in the west and the desert in the east and south ("Erwägungen zum israelitischen Brandopfer," *Von Ugarit nach Qumran* (Eissfeldt Festschrift), Berlin (1958), p. 179). Cf. J. de Groot, *Die Altäre des Salomonischen Tempelhofes*, Berlin (1924), pp. 39-40, 67.

5 P. Haupt, "Babylonian Elements in the Levitic Ritual," *JBL* XIX (1900), p. 61.

6 G. A. Barton, "A Comparison of Some Features of Hebrew and Babylonian Ritual," *JBL* XLVI (1927), pp. 79-89.

resources, were a stupid people religiously. They had all the materials for a doctrine of a transcendent God, but came instead under demons.[1]

The theory of Babylonian influence in the Pan-Babylonian school had been associated with an astral myth theory, which had never won much acceptance. It came into new favour, however, with the much more acceptable divine kingship theory of the Myth and Ritual school. If a common ritual pattern was indeed to be discerned in Israel along with the other nations of the ancient Near East, it was to be expected that Israelite sacrifice would also have much in common with the sacrifice of her Mesopotamian neighbours. Hooke, therefore, claimed that Hebrew sacrifice began in a substitution for the death of the king, in a placation and removal of guilt, rather than in communion, as Robertson Smith had thought. Unconnected with this was the idea of the god of the land needing a daily meal, which gave rise to the gift aspect of the *minḥâ*.[2] These two lines—substitution, placation and purification (*ʿōlâ, kālîl, ʾāšām, ḥaṭṭāʾt*) from the ritual of the death of the god, and the gift aspect (*minḥâ*) from the idea of the god's ownership were common to both Israel and Mesopotamia.[3] Particularly striking was the Babylonian *puhu* ceremony in which a kid was sacrificed in the desert as a substitute for a sick man. Hooke found similar ideas of substitution to be a present at many points in the Old Testament.[4]

The Myth and Ritual theories received a powerful stimulus through the publication of the materials from Ras Shamra (1929ff). Here was material that was nearer to Israel both in place and time. Snaith felt that Hooke was on stronger ground in his use of this material, than of the Babylonian. The direct influence of Babylon on Judah dated only from Nebuchadnezzar and of Assyria only a little earlier, but Canaanite influence had been constant. Jewish

---

[1] A. Guillaume, *op. cit.*, pp. 18, 57.

[2] S. H. Hooke, *The Origins of Early Semitic Ritual*, London (1938), pp. 64-65.

[3] Hooke, *Babylonian and Assyrian Religion*, London (1953), p. 45.

[4] Hooke, "The Theory and Practice of Substitution," *VT* II (1952), pp. 1-17. An origin for sacrifice in a substitution for the dying divine king is common also to the Scandinavian school, who are not separately treated in this chapter. Cf. Engnell's explanation of the rite in the Baal Hunting text (75. 1 : 26-33) "an expiatory sacrifice, where the god-king, substituted by the bull, brings about the atonement by his 'vicarious suffering' " (*Studies in Divine Kingship in the Ancient Near East*, Uppsala (1943), p. 127).

religion had never been astral as Babylonian had been.[1] For these and other reasons Canaanite antecedents came to be seen as a more likely background for Israelite religion.

The Canaanite Origin

Theories of a Canaanite origin of Israelite sacrifice have also passed through two stages—the first in which the evidence from Phoenician sacrifice at Marseilles and Carthage was drawn on, and the second after the Ugaritic materials became available.

In 1914 Dussaud argued that Wellhausen's late dating of Lev. 1-7 and the expiatory element in Israelite sacrifice was disproved by the Carthaginian sacrificial tariffs. He thought Eerdmans' attempt to take it back to Moses was no happier. It came from the temple of Solomon and was borrowed from the Canaanites, whose sacrifices as revealed in the Carthage lists were clearly the same as those of Israel.[2] It was true that the terms did not closely coincide (except for the general words *zebaḥ* and *minḥâ*) but the disposal of the sacrifices—whether to priests alone (*kālîl*), or to both priests and worshippers (*ṣewʿat*) or to neither (*šelem kālîl*)—permitted the identification of the Phoenician *kālîl* with the Hebrew sin and guilt offerings, the *ṣewʿat* with the *zebaḥ šᵉlāmîm* and the *šelem kālîl* with the *ʿōlâ*.[3]

These conjectures were, however, open to objection at a number of points. The two surviving tariffs—that from Marseilles and that from Carthage—did not precisely agree on the usage of the terms. It was not certain that the *kālîl* was not shared by the worshippers, or that the *ṣewʿat* was the shared sacrificial meal, or that the *šelem kālîl* was a complete holocaust. Langdon thought the *šelem kālîl* a vow offering from the root *šlm* to "requite" or "to pay," but the Hebrew vow offering provided a meal for the worshipper.[4] The *ṣewʿat* was thought to be related to an Ethiopic root "to call together, to invoke," or "to call upon,"[5] but this could be variously

[1] N. H. Snaith. *The Jewish New Year Festival*, London (1947), pp. 207-209.

[2] R. Dussaud, *Le sacrifice en Israël et chez les Phéniciens*, Paris (1914), p. 7. Dussaud's later volume, *Les origines cananéennes du sacrifice israélite*, Paris (1921) incorporated this earlier work, along with much additional material.

[3] R. Dussaud, *Le sacrifice en Israël* . . ., pp. 50-51.

[4] S. Langdon, "The History and Significance of Carthaginian Sacrifice," *JBL* XXIII (1904), p. 85.

[5] *Ibid.*, p. 87.

interpreted as a sacrificial meal (Langdon), a prayer offering (Kent)[1] or even as *'āšām* and *ḥaṭṭā't* (Ginsberg).[2] Urie rightly concluded that etymology was no guide to usage and the disposal of the victim no guide to the purpose of the rite.[3] Dussaud had not produced any convincing proof of the early existence of the expiatory sin or trespass offerings, and his general assumption of a Canaanite origin for Israelite sacrifice was no difficulty to the Wellhausen school, which took this for granted.[4] His position was incompatible, however, with Lods' theory of a nomadic origin and evoked some discussion.[5]

The Phoenician materials thus far used in the discussion were of comparatively late origin,[6] but this situation was greatly changed by the discoveries at Ras Shamra in 1929. Here was a large corpus of Canaanite materials from before the time of Moses with numerous references to sacrifice and with evidence of a fully developed cult. It is not surprising that the discovery of the presence of sacrificial terms dated late by Wellhausen, led to the claim that the new materials overthrew his position. Dussaud quickly identified the *mtn tm* with the "perfect offering" of the Old Testament, the *dbḥ bšt* with the *ḥaṭṭā't* sin offering, the *šlm* with the communion offering, the *šrp* with the holocaust[7] and found confirmation for his earlier rejection of the Graf-Wellhausen view and his assumption of a Canaanite origin for Israelite sacrifice, except in the one point that the borrowing had taken place, not at the conquest, but in the

---

[1] C. F. Kent, *Israel's Laws and Legal Precedents*, London (1907), pp. 297-9.

[2] H. L. Ginsberg, "A Punic Note," *AJSL* XLVII (1930-1931), pp. 52-53. See now F. Rosenthal *ANET* (²1955), pp. 502, 503 "substitute offering."

[3] D.M.L. Urie, *op. cit.*, p. 69.

[4] J. Wellhausen, "Israel," *EBrit* XIII, p. 409 wrote: "The cultus, as to place, time, matter, and form belonged almost entirely to the inheritance which Israel had received from Canaan . . . (Footnote—The description of the cultus by the prophet Hosea shows this very clearly) . . . It was the channel through which paganism could and did ever anew gain admittance into the worship of Jehovah." So also W. R. Smith, *The Prophets of Israel*, London (²1895), p. 38; K. Marti, *Religion of the Old Testament*, Ch. 2.

[5] For Lods see the literature cited on p. 24 and for Dussaud's replies *RHR* C (1930), pp. 125-28, CIII-CIV (1931), pp. 205-11.

[6] Carthage was not founded before 850 B.C. and the tariffs probably date from between the sixth and third centuries B.C. (Langdon, *op. cit.*, p. 81); G. A. Cooke, *North Semitic Inscriptions*, Oxford (1903), pp. 112-24.

[7] R. Dussaud, "Le sanctuaire et les dieux phéniciens de Ras Shamra," *RHR* CV-CVI (1932), pp. 285-86.

time of the patriarchs.[1] Other scholars who expected much from the Ugaritic materials were Jack,[2] Hooke,[3] Hyatt,[4] and Gaster.[5] In particular the *'āšām* was thought to be referred to in the *'aṭm* (*'ašm*) in UH 27 and 45.

Greater restraint was exercised by de Vaux,[6] Snaith,[7] and Urie,[8] who pointed out that the fragmentary nature of the texts prevented any conclusion as to the nature of *'aṭm* from being drawn, and that it could not be inferred from Ugarit that there was an *'āšām* sacrifice among the ancient Hebrews. It was useful, however, to have this evidence of the developed nature of the Canaanite cultus at the time of the entry of the Israelites and the attestation of the existence of the whole burnt offering and incense.[9] More recently J. Gray has reviewed the whole evidence afresh in relation to Wellhausen's position, and has concluded that although it was chronologically possible, that Israel had such a cult as that at Ras Shamra in the time of Moses, it was socially improbable in view of her desert

---

1 Dussaud, *Les découvertes de Ras Shamra et l'Ancien Testament*, Paris (1937), pp. 110-113.

2 J. W. Jack, *The Ras Shamra Tablets: Their Bearing on the Old Testament*, Edinburgh (1935), pp. 29-31.

3 S. H. Hooke, "The Early Background of Hebrew Religion," *A Companion to the Bible* (ed.) T. W. Manson, Edinburgh (1939). He wrote: "The (Ras Shamra) names of the various types of offering present surprising parallels with the Levitical nomenclature in the Old Testament, proving that many of the technical terms which Old Testament criticism has hitherto regarded as the product of the post-exilic period belong in fact to the early background of Hebrew religion" (p. 283).

4 J. P. Hyatt, "The Ras Shamra Discoveries and the Interpretation of the Old Testament," *JBR* X (1942), p. 72. Hyatt wrote: "It is very probable that some of the elements in the Hebrew ritualistic system, which do not appear until exilic or post-exilic times, so far as the literature now indicates, were actually of very early origin."

5 T. H. Gaster, "The Service of the Sanctuary: A Study in Hebrew Survivals," *Mélanges Syriens* (Dussaud Festschrift), Vol. II, Paris (1939), pp. 577-82.

6 R. de Vaux, "Les textes de Ras Shamra et l'Ancien Testament," *RB* XLVI (1937), p. 549. De Vaux thought the parallels further away than those with the Marseilles tariff.

7 N. H. Snaith, "The Religion of Israel—Worship," *Record and Revelation*, p. 268.

8 D. M. L. Urie, *op. cit.*, p. 72.

9 W. Baumgartner, "Ras Schamra und das Alte Testament," *ThR* N.F. XIII (1941) wrote, p. 169: "*šrp* und die mehrfache Erwähnung von *'išt* "Feuer" in Zusammenhang mit einem Opfer zeigen, dass das Brandopfer schon in vorisraelitischer Zeit bekannt war. Ebenso ist das Vorkommen des Räucheropfers für die Frage nach seinem Alter in Israel . . . von Belang."

environment.[1] Baumgartner thought the borrowing theories of Dussaud, Hooke and Gaster unlikely for the same reason. Ugarit was sedentary and agricultural, while Israel was a desert people, and a section of Israel at least had a tribal organization in marked difference from the type of society at Ugarit.[2] Attention came more and more to centre on this group—the patriarchs.

The Patriarchal Origin

The book of Genesis described divine appearances to the patriarchs at various sanctuaries and the revelation of different El Names—El Bethel (Gen. 35: 7), El Elohe Israel (Gen. 33 : 20), El Olam (Gen. 21 : 33), El Roi (Gen. 16 : 13). These El deities were formerly thought to be local numina half-way between a spirit and a god.[3] The Ras Shamra materials, however, revealed a supreme God, El, who was creator, king and father of gods and men, and head of the pantheon. The present text of Genesis identifies Yahweh with El, but this seems to be the result of a syncretism of Yahweh and El which took place later in the history.

As is well-known the three major Pentateuchal sources appear to speak with a different voice on this matter. The Yahwist source regards the history as one and uses Yahweh as the divine name from the beginning. To him primeval, patriarchal and Mosaic religion are all on a level, and the revelation to the last-named is no more than an episode in the unfolding of the whole. Not once but twice this view of the history was challenged—first by the Elohist and second by the Priestly writer. The Elohist saw the history in two great parts—the Yahweh religion of Moses and the Elohim religion of the patriarchs. Between the two he built a bridge in Exod. 3 : 15 by his identification of the Yahweh of Moses with Elohim, the God of the fathers, the God of Abraham, the God of Isaac and the God of Jacob. The Priestly writer is even more persuaded of the primacy of Mosaic revelation. Yahweh was not

---

[1] J. Gray, "Cultic Affinities between Israel and Ras Shamra," *ZAW* LXII (1949-1950), pp. 207-20; *The Legacy of Canaan*, Leiden (1957), pp. 140-47 (esp. p. 143).

[2] Baumgartner, "Ugaritische Probleme und ihre Tragweite für das Alte Testament," *ThZ* III (1947), pp. 91ff.

[3] W. O. E. Oesterley and T. H. Robinson, *Hebrew Religion*, London (^{2}1937), pp. 52ff.

known to the fathers, but El Shaddai was their God (Exod. 6 : 3).[1]

If the Yahwist's position of patriarchal Yahweh worship must be set aside, and the Priestly writer's El Shaddai theory also, can more credence be given to the Elohist's interpretation? This question was subjected to careful examination by Alt, who came to the conclusion that E's formula "the God of Abraham, the God of Isaac and the God of Jacob" also covered a syncretism. Behind this was a time, when three separate deities were referred to—the God of Abraham, the Fear (*Paḥad*) of Isaac and the Mighty One (*'Ābîr*) of Jacob.[2] This earlier stage is reflected not only in the separate use of these titles (Gen. 31 : 53b; Is. 1 : 24; Gen. 49 : 24), but in the different stages in the textual tradition in a verse like Gen. 31 : 53a "the God of Abraham and the God of Nahor be judge," where the Hebrew read a plural verb, the LXX a singular and the Samaritan a singular verb and an additional singular subject "the God of Abraham" expressly identifying the two subjects.[3] Behind the patriarchal narratives localizing El at various sanctuaries was a faith independent of particular places (*Ortsgebundenheit*), a faith in a wanderer's God who went forth with a particular people on their wanderings, a God of families or clans. The cult founders in the clans concerned were Abraham, Isaac and Jacob. Parallels for such "gods of the fathers" (*theoi patrōoi*) were found by Alt in the much later use of the Nabatean and Palmyrene nomad tribes.[4]

It will be readily agreed that this attempt to take seriously the patriarchal traditions and to find a place for them in the history has been a great step forward, but not all will be persuaded by Alt's arguments. Foundational for the discussion will be the question as to whether the worship of the patriarchs was of one God or of several. Meek has said that "no modern scholar of any standing

---

[1] Support for this view is sought by Hooke, (*In the Beginning* (*ClarB*) VI, Oxford (1947), p. 137) in the absence of names compounded with Yahweh in the book of Genesis. He writes: "Hence we see that the Jahvist, in spite of his own beliefs that the name of Jahveh was known to the patriarchs, has borne witness to the fact that this was not actually the case by recording in his narrative no names compounded with Jahveh."

[2] Alt suggested that Abraham's God may have been known as "the Shield" (Gen. 15 : 1) (A. Alt, *op. cit.*, p. 67), and Albright that *Paḥad* might be rendered "kinsman" (*From the Stone Age to Christianity*, Baltimore (²1946), p. 189).

[3] Reading *ʾelōhê ʾabrāhām* for *ʾelōhê ʾabîhem* of MT, which the Greek omits.

[4] A. Alt, *op. cit.*, pp. 68-77.

today believes that the Hebrews of the Patriarchal Period were anything but polytheistic,"[1] but the tradition speaks only of "the God of the Fathers," not "the Gods of the Fathers."[2] Alt wrote before the Ugaritic El was known, and in Eissfeldt's opinion allowed too little for the universal scope of a high God.[3] Gemser thought of only one Fathers'-God in different appearance forms. The God of Abraham is the God of his son and grandson also (Gen. 31 : 5, 42a, 53a, 32 : 10, cf. 48 : 15), while the God of the father of Jacob is not distinguished from El (Gen. 46 : 3).[4]

Evidence for the perpetuity of the individual Fathers'-God names is also meagre. Jacob founded no cult of the *'Ābîr*, but was rather associated with Bethel.[5] The *Paḥad* of Isaac is of doubtful meaning,[6] while no name for the Fathers'-God of Abraham survives.

It is not denied that polytheism lay in the background of the fathers'-religion as indeed the Biblical tradition acknowledges (Gen. 35 : 2; Josh. 24 : 14) but this was "beyond the river" and is possibly to be connected with the families of Terah, Nahor and Laban rather than Abraham, Isaac and Jacob. Hooke's statement that "according to the tradition preserved in Joshua 24, the ancestors of the Hebrews after their entry into Canaan both continued to worship the gods of Mesopotamia and also adopted

---

[1] T. J. Meek, "Monotheism and the Religion of Israel," *JBL* LXI (1942), p. 21.

[2] R. Brinker, *The Influence of Sanctuaries in Early Israel*, Manchester (1946), p. 26.

[3] So O. Eissfeldt, "El and Yahweh," *JSS* I (1956), p. 34. M. H. Pope, however, thinks (*El in the Ugaritic Texts*, Leiden (1955), pp. 85ff.) that Eissfeldt makes too much of the monarchical position of El.

[4] B. Gemser, "God in Genesis," *OTS* XII (1958), pp. 20-21.

[5] H. G. May, "The Patriarchal Idea of God," *JBL* LX (1941), p. 126. This point is of importance in view of Alt's remark in "Zum Gott der Väter," *PJB* XXXVI (1940), pp. 100-103. Commenting on Lewy's claim to have found comparative material in the old Assyrian "Assur and the God of thy father, shall be witness" (J. Lewy, "Les textes paléo-assyriens et l'Ancien Testament," *RHR* CX (1934), pp. 29-65 esp. pp. 50ff), Alt remarked that only if the existence of a special god and a *continuing cult* could be established —an impossible undertaking in view of the fact that each man had his own god—could the cases be regarded as parallel (p. 103).

[6] May, "The God of my Father—A Study of Patriarchal Religion," *JBR* IX (1941), p. 158, thought it a late word and claimed that all three "father-god" terms occurred only in late passages.

the cult of the local gods of Canaan"[1] overlooks the disjunctive between the two parts of vs. 15 "*whether* the gods your fathers served in the region beyond the River, *or* the gods of the Amorites in whose land you dwell." It is nowhere said that Abraham, Isaac and Jacob were worshippers of "other gods."

This point should, perhaps, not be stressed, in view of the willingness of Alt and his successors to speak of the fathers'-religion as monolatrous, for although in the total view a monolatry limited to a clan is a virtual polytheism, a real connection between the fathers'-gods, at least as far as type is concerned, is acknowledged. This type of tribe or clan religion had been well illustrated from the ethnological background and conclusions drawn for Hebrew sacrifice by Maag.[2]

Arguing from the frequency of the "shepherd" metaphor for the God of Israel (Gen. 49 : 24, 48 : 14, 15, cf. Ps. 23 : 1, 80 : 1) Maag located these Hebrew ancestors in the shepherd culture of the steppes. Here the deity, as a kindly Providence, led and protected his clan members, as the shepherd led and cared for his sheep. Here too, where the life of man and animal were intimately bound up together, the typical Hebrew *zebaḥ* sacrifice had its origin.[3] It corresponded to the hunting ritual of the primitive hunting culture where the old hunters, afraid of the revenge of the "lord" of the animals which they killed ("the bush spirit"), practised various rites of appeasement.[4] Chief among these was the proper treatment of the blood. This survived in the shepherd culture in the ritual slaughter in which the blood was poured out on the ground.[5] After this a communion meal with the deity followed and the god, by his presence and participation, took over the responsibility for the

---

[1] S. H. Hooke (*ClarB*) VI, pp. 135-36.

[2] V. Maag, "Der Hirte Israels," *Schweizerische Theologische Umschau* XXVII (1958), pp. 2-28. Cf. also Maag "Malkût Jhwh," *Congress Volume Oxford 1959* (*VTSuppl* VII), Leiden (1960), pp. 129-53, esp. 131-42.

[3] V. Maag, "Erwägungen zur deuteronomischen Kultzentralisation," *VT* VI (1956), pp. 10-18, esp. pp. 14-16.

[4] A. E. Jensen, "Über das Töten als kulturgeschichtliche Erscheinung," *Paideuma* IV (1950), pp. 23-38; H. Baumann, "Nyama, die Rachemacht," *ibid.*, pp. 191-230.

[5] For a description of the evolution of sacrifice from the hunting to the shepherd culture in Asia, and its further development in Greek sacrifice see K. Meuli, "Griechische Opferbräuche," *Phyllobolia für Peter von der Mühll*, Basel (1946), pp. 185-288, esp. pp. 223ff.

slaughter. As the divine shepherd he protected and granted security for his people at the sacrificial meal. In this sense God is the shield between the worshipper and danger, and sacrifice a freeing from anxiety.[1] The fathers'-god is a brother-god (*'Aḥiel*), whose sacrifice is the communion *zebaḥ*, not the *minḥâ-ʿōlâ*.[2] This communion meal with the deity remained the background of Israelite sacrifice until the Deuteronomic Reform, when the quite different *minḥâ-ʿōlâ* arising from the plant culture side displaced it.[3]

The discussion of this theory, together with that of Robertson Smith, to which it has some parallels, will be the task of the sequel and only a few comments in the form of questions can be made now. One must ask first concerning the relevance of the ethnological material.

With Frobenius, Jensen and Naumann, the theory takes its cue from African religion, but a completely different account of sacrifice among one African people is given by Evans-Pritchard. The second half of Evans-Pritchard's work on Nuer religion[4] is devoted to Nuer sacrifice, and draws conclusions for sacrifice as a whole, which must be taken into account by all investigators.

The Nuer are a cattle-herding tribe of the Sudan, with marked similarities to the Hebrews of the Old Testament,[5] yet for whom sacrifice on Evans-Pritchard's account is closely related to the confession of sin and to ideas of substitution. The chief sacrificial animal is the ox, which is slain in expiation of the fault of its owner, on the principle of a life for a life.[6] There is no fear of the shedding

---

[1] Maag, "Der Hirte Israels," p. 27 compares the stress on lay communion in both kinds at the Reformation as an assurance of deliverance from Purgatory and Hell-fire.

[2] ". . . der Jahwist, der seine Väter doch opfern lässt, erzählt nie, dass sie eine *ʿōlâ* dargebracht hätten" (V. Maag, "Der Hirte Israels," p. 5). Cf. also Jensen *op. cit.*, p. 27 for the opinion that sacrifice was not a gift to the godhead in the old planter culture.

[3] Maag, "Erwägungen zur deuteronomischen Kultzentralisation," *VT* VI (1956), pp. 10-18.

[4] E. E. Evans-Pritchard, *Nuer Religion*, Oxford (1956).

[5] *Ibid.*, p. vii, referring also to C. G. Seligmann, *Pagan Tribes of the Nilotic Sudan*, London (1932) and in *JRAI* (1913), pp. 593-705; Ray Huffmann, *Nuer Customs and Folk-Lore* (1931).

[6] "To sum up the meaning of Nuer piacular sacrifice in a single word or idea I would say that it is a substitution—a life for a life" (Evans-Pritchard, "The Meaning of Sacrifice," *JRAI* LXXXIV (1954), p. 29).

of the blood,[1] no eating with a friendly deity,[2] and no rites for rain and the fertility of the soil.[3] Holocausts, in which the flesh of the victim is not eaten, but is left lying intact in the bush to avert a disaster from the whole people, are not unknown.[4] Yet the Nuer also are a "primitive people," despite these refinements, which stand in contradiction to current ethnological theories.[5]

It is not claimed that this interpretation of sacrifice is of universal validity, or that it provides a better background for Hebrew sacrifice than that given by Maag, but it does raise the question of whether the description of the shepherd's god as virtually a clan member, and invariably favourable to his clan does not leave out of account the more solemn element, which connects sacrifice to sin.[6] If fear of vengeance, consequent upon the shedding of blood lies behind sacrifice in the hunting culture, confidence in the deity can hardly be posited for the shepherd culture, without further proof.[7] Is the Yahwist really silent concerning the *ʿōlâ* in the patriar-

---

[1] *Nuer Religion,* p. 215.

[2] Evans-Pritchard agrees with G. Gusdorf (*L'expérience humaine du sacrifice,* Paris (1948)) that sacrifice is against the gods, rather than for the gods. It is because of the presence of spiritual influence in a bad sense in trouble or sickness that the sacrifice is offered to separate God and men not to unite them. The final purpose is, however, union—union on the material plane is dissolved, to bring about union on the moral plane—but this is achieved by the initial rites of expiation, which are the sacrifice proper, and not by the meal which follows ("Meaning of Sacrifice," pp. 23-24).

[3] *Nuer Religion,* p. 199.

[4] *Ibid.,* p. 219.

[5] *Ibid.,* p. 311.

[6] Whatever one may think of the stratified "culture circles" of Wilhelm Schmidt, the evidence for a sense of sin and sacrifices of expiation collected by him—even for the shepherd-culture—("Ethnologische Bemerkungen," pp. 48ff) must be given some weight. Cf. A. Vorbilcher, *Das Opfer,* Wien (1956).

[7] Maag recognizes that there was a fear of spirits and dangerous powers, but these were appeased by ritual, not worshipped ("Der Hirte Israels," pp. 18-20). Such a malignant being met Jacob at Jabbok, but the God of Israel stood by him to fight the demon. (The name Israel means "God striving for," not "striving against God"). Only later was the demon identified with Yahweh (pp. 20-21). But on this method all the evidence for a contrary view may be removed and investigation becomes subjective. Just how subjective investigation may become is illustrated by the following description of life in the Arabian steppes, given by an Old Testament scholar of another day, to support his view of the nomadic deity as destructive and the agricultualist's as beneficent (C. F. Burney, "Israelite Religion in Early Times," *JTS* IX (1908), p. 324): "To the nomad, and more especially to

chal period? Vriezen viewed the evidence differently when he wrote:

> The Yahwist presupposes in the times of Abraham a cult at an altar, but this is apparently especially for *ʿōlâ*-offerings as sacrifices in honour of Yahweh.[1]

Finally one may ask whether the suggested development in terms of parallel *zebaḥ* practice from the patriarchal side and *minḥâ ʿōlâ* from the Canaanite side down to the Josianic Reform is not too simple. Other elements belonging to neither of these categories entered in. In particular the distinctive Yahweh faith of Moses and Sinai with its solemn overtones must have left some mark on the cultus.[2] This subject must therefore also receive attention.

The Mosaic Origin

One of the remarkable changes of emphasis in the Old Testament discussion of this generation is the loss of stature of Moses, who figured so centrally in Old Testament religion a generation ago. The positive gains for patriarchal and amphictyonic religion have been largely at the expense of Moses. The Exodus and Sinai covenant-making have been ousted from the centre of the stage by the *Landnahme* and the Shechem covenant-making. Some groups of the later Israel may have been in Egypt and at Sinai, but the

---

the nomad of the barren Arabian steppe, life is to a great extent a struggle against the antagonistic forces of nature. He is exposed to the rigours of climatic change. By day the sun strikes upon him and scorches him, while at night he is a victim to the frost. The thunderstorm inspires him with well-founded terror, since without a harbour he may perish by the lightning. He pitches his tent, and the sandstorm lays it low, or a sudden torrent from the mountain sweeps it away . . . The agriculturist dwelling in a kinder land, views nature as beneficent power." He is of course leading up to a description of Sinai religion, but when one hears of the nomad as both fearless and fearful, and the agriculturist as both fearful and fearless (cf. R. Anderson's remark ("The Role of the Desert in Israelite Thought," *JBR* XXVII (1959), p. 42) that the nomad does not have to appease the gods for harvests and rain as the agriculturist does) one wonders whether the criteria for discrimination are really available. Is not that just the problem? Archeology cannot uncover the tracks of nomads, which remained but for an hour and then were lost for ever in the shifting sands.

[1] Th. C. Vriezen, *An Outline of Old Testament Theology*, p. 26. The point turns on the narrative of Gen. 22. Cf. the footnote of Maag, "Der Hirte," p. 26 and the discussion of the passage below (Ch. III).

[2] Maag treats briefly of this element on p. 23 ("Hirte") but hopes to return to it in a separate publication.

silence of the old credos to a Sinai covenant (von Rad),[1] and the impossibility of speaking of "Israel" before the constitution of the nation of Israel in Canaan (Noth)[2] make it unlikely that the majority of the people shared in these events. The writer is strongly of the opinion that this position, so contrary to the major Biblical tradition cannot possibly endure,[3] but for the meantime it has the effect of rendering discussion of the various hypotheses of the origin of Mosaic religion of less moment than was formerly the case.

The older theory of Egyptian influence, which once had some vogue, is now only an antiquarian curiosity, but is included for completeness. Hengstenberg and some conservatives argued for the Mosaicity of the cult on the ground that Egypt already had similar sacrifices and institutions,[4] but more usually the differences rather than the similarities of the two cults have been stressed.[5] Kyle remarked the absence of the sacrificial meal, burnt offerings, expiatory rites, substitution and the *s^emîkâ*.[6] How the offerings were disposed of—if by the worshippers or by the priests—is unknown, but the pictorial representations showed the altars heaped too high for burning and revealed no trace of ashes. There were possibly some exceptions as, for example when Egyptian shipmen on a foreign shore conveyed their offerings by burning to gods at home,[7] or when animals were slaughtered to get pieces of meat to lay as food on the altar,[8] or when in later time enemies of the gods in symbolic representation were both killed and burnt,[9] but basically

[1] G. von Rad, *Das formgeschichtliche Problem des Hexateuch*, now reprinted in *Gesammelte Studien*, München (1958), pp. 9-86.

[2] M. Noth, *The History of Israel*, E. T. London (1958), p. 5.

[3] Cf. C. A. Keller, "Von Stand und Aufgabe der Moseforschung," *ThZ* XIII (1957), pp. 430-41.

[4] An argument which was an embarrassment to his English editor. See the introduction to the English Translation of Hengstenberg's *Egypt and the Books of Moses*, Edinburgh (1845).

[5] So already John Spencer in his theory of Israelite sacrifice as a contempt of heathen gods. "The Jews sacrifice a ram in contempt of Amon and the ox, which the Egyptians call Apis." (*De Legibus Hebraeorum ritualibus* (1686) cited W. H. Green, *The Hebrew Feasts*, New York (1886), p. 56). Is this "the abomination of the Egyptians" in Exod. 8 : 26?

[6] M. G. Kyle, *Moses and the Monuments*, Oberlin (1919), pp. 240-69.

[7] A. Erman, *Die ägyptische Religion*, Berlin (²1909), p. 59.

[8] This was no *zebaḥ* with the blood to the god in the Semitic sense (K. Galling, *Der Altar*, p. 14).

[9] H. Junker, "Die Schlacht — und Brandopfer im Tempelkult der Spätzeit," *ZÄS* XLVIII (1911), pp. 69-77.

Egyptian sacrifice was the laying of a table of food for the gods.[1]

As with Babylonia, however, a long history and a conglomerate of cults provides many varieties of ritual from the Osiris rites for fertility in nature,[2] to the myth which described the origin of sacrifice to destruction averted by a vicarious human sacrifice.[3] The omission of the rites characteristic of Israel makes it fruitless to continue the enquiry further. The Egyptians unlike the other groups dealt with in this chapter were probably not Semites,[4] despite the arguments of Barton,[5] and had no great influence on Israelite sacrifice.

More popular has been the theory, held by perhaps the majority of Old Testament scholars, of the Kenite origin of Mosaic Yahwism. If indeed Yahweh was not known to the patriarchs, but first revealed to Moses at the Holy Mount as Exod. 3 and 6 seem to indicate, what more probable than that Yahwism was indigenous there. The mountain is already called "the mount of God" before Moses' arrival there (Exod. 3 : 1), and is holy ground (Exod. 3 : 5). The priest from this region, Jethro, who becomes Moses' father-in-law, rejoices in the triumphs of Yahweh (Exod. 18 : 10-11) and superintends the offerings of sacrifice from which Israel partakes (Exod. 18:12). Yahweh is hereafter associated with Sinai, or the south as if this is his seat (Judg. 5 : 3-5;[6] Deut. 33 : 2ff). The tribes of this area continue in friendly relation to Israel and join the tribe of Judah under David (1 Sam. 30 : 26ff). From their number come such Yahweh zealots as Jael and Jonadab and the Rechabites

[1] Galling, *op. cit.*, p. 14. For the view that burnt offerings were not un-Egyptian, with details of recent literature see A. H. Gardiner and T. E. Peet, *The Inscriptions of Sinai*, Pt. II, London (1955), p. 46.

[2] A. Moret, "Du sacrifice en Egypte," *RHR* LVII (1908), pp. 81-101. The sacrifice of the god preceded sacrifice to the god, and eating the sacrificed god also had a place. Cf. also E. O. James, *Myth and Ritual in the Ancient Near East*, London (1958), Ch. 2 and H. W. Fairman, "The Kingship Rituals of Egypt," *Myth, Ritual, and Kingship* (ed.) S. H. Hooke, pp. 74-104. Fairman concludes that: "In Egypt sacrifice bore no implication of atonement, but enshrined a double concept, on the one hand the destruction of the enemy, e.g. by the burning of the slaughtered offering, and on the other hand the absorption of certain desirable qualities and powers by eating the sacrifice" (p. 91).

[3] Cited by E. Naville, *Old Egyptian Faith*, London (1909), pp. 298 ff.

[4] W. O. E. Oesterley and T. H. Robinson, *Hebrew Religion*, p. 13.

[5] G. A. Barton, *Hamitic and Semitic Origins*, Oxford (1934), Ch. 1.

[6] "*zeh sînay*" is rendered by many as "possessor" or "owner" of Sinai (cf. the Ugaritic *d*) but RSV still prefers the demonstrative "Yon Sinai."

(Judg. 4 : 17; 2 Kings 10 : 15ff; 1 Chron. 2 : 5). In the Judahistic south also, the Yahwistic source, which knows no time when Yahweh was not worshipped, is written.[1]

Not all these considerations are of equal weight. It cannot be proved from Exod. 3 : 1ff. that Sinai before the story was "the mount of Yahweh,"[2] or from Exod. 18 : 1ff. that Jethro was officiating as priest of Yahweh.[3] The latter passage might equally be read as the conversion of Jethro to Yahwism (see the discussion below in Ch. III). Moses equally with the patriarchs speaks of "the God of my father" (Exod. 18 : 4, cf. Exod. 15 : 2) and it is this "God of thy father" who appears to him on the mount (Exod. 3 : 6). Hyatt has, therefore, concluded that Yahweh was the god of one of the ancestors of Moses—possibly not of his father, but of his mother, who in the P tradition bears a name compounded with Yahweh—Jochebed. Israel therefore followed Moses, because Yahweh was already known to be the god of Moses' clan.[4] Buber also sees a true "Fathers'-God" in Yahweh, who came to Egypt with Jacob, went from Egypt to Midian with Moses, wandered with his people and like the God of the patriarchs approached men for covenant.[5]

On the other side it is objected that this does not allow for the great differences between the kindly God of the fathers and the jealous and violent Sinai deity Yahweh. These differences have perhaps been exaggerated,[6] but some difference may, however, be granted. The present case is not that the Yahweh of Moses was

---

[1] For these and other arguments see G. A. Barton, *A Sketch of Semitic Origins*, New York, (1902), pp. 275-78 and H. H. Rowley, *From Joseph to Joshua*, London (1950), pp. 149ff.

[2] The phrase may be anachronistic for what, through the present events, became the later designation. The text reads "mount of Elohim" not "Yahweh."

[3] Jethro also has an El name—Reuel.

[4] J. P. Hyatt, "Yahweh as "The God of My Father,"" *VT* V (1955), pp. 130-36.

[5] M. Buber, *Moses*, Oxford (1946), pp. 39ff. He writes: "The two likenesses will be found to differ in a special manner; namely, just as a clan god in non-historical situations might be expected to differ from a national god in an historical situation" (p. 43).

[6] B. Gemser, "God in Genesis," *OTS* XII (1958), pp. 17-18 thinks that Böhl's contrast between the God of Genesis and the God of Exodus ("Das Zeitalter Abrahams," *Opera Minora*, Groningen (1953), pp. 26ff.) too lightly goes over "less idyllic episodes like the terrifying nightly appearance of Yahweh to Abram Ch. xv, the terrible punishment administered to sinners

known to the patriarchs, but only that a borrowing from the Kenites is not the only or most probable explanation of the origin of Yahwism. Moses may well be calling Israel back to an older faith, while at the same time being the recipient of new revelations. The point has ceased to be of central significance, now that Old Testament studies no longer speak of "Israel" in Egypt or at Sinai.

On the modern view not all the tribes were involved in the events associated with Moses. The strongest case can be made for the Joseph tribes as the Egyptian tribes. The tradition of "Joseph in Egypt" is attested not only by the double record of his sale in Gen. 37,[1] but by the assertions of the prophets Amos and Hosea that Ephraim had been brought from Egypt, and the assumption of the Song of Deborah that the tribes gathered for the battle knew of the Holy Mount.[2] Whether the Leah and concubine tribes were also in Egypt is more debateable. Asher is named in the early inscriptions of Seti I and Raamses II as the name of a people, already resident in what was to be their later tribal territory. Simeon and Levi are apparently tribes in central Canaan in Gen. 34. Judah is a people apart at the time of the *Landnahme*, and is thought to have entered the land in a northward movement from the wilderness (Num. 21 : 1-3) rather than a southward move from Gilgal (Judg. 1 : 1ff).[3] Yet according to the tradition it was of Levite parents that Moses and Aaron were born in Egypt, and Egyptian names that the sons of the latter, Hophni and Phinehas bore.[4] Meek and Albright,[5] are therefore of the opinion that the Leah tribes were also in Egypt, but possibly at a different time. Time cannot be taken to explore these possibilities further,[6] particularly as the discussion has moved to another level with the view of Noth that the tribes came into being as tribes, and Israel as a people only in the land of Canaan, when diverse elements from many sides first came together as one.[7]

---

in Sodom and Gomorrah Ch. xix, the dark background of the severe testing of Abraham's faith in Ch. xxii etc."

[1] W. J. Phythian-Adams, *The Fullness of Israel*, London (1938), pp. 37-38, 104ff.

[2] H. H. Rowley, *From Joseph to Joshua*, p. 142.

[3] C. F. Burney, *Israel's Settlement in Canaan*, London (1918).

[4] T. J. Meek, *Hebrew Origins*, New York ([2]1950), pp. 31ff. Cf. G. von Rad, *Theologie des Alten Testaments*, Vol. I, München (1957), p. 22.

[5] W. F. Albright, *BASOR* LVIII (1935), pp. 10-18.

[6] The full discussion of Rowley, *From Joseph to Joshua* may be consulted.

[7] M. Noth, *The History of Israel*, pp. 5ff., 53ff.

The Composite Origin

Basic to the theory of Noth is the assumption that at the *Landtag* at Shechem in Joshua 24 groups of disparate origin banded themselves together to form the people of Israel.[1] At least three major groups are thought to have been present—a group which had not been in Egypt and were not worshippers of Yahweh, but of the gods of the fathers, the gods of Mesopotamia (Josh. 24 : 15b), a group more fully identified with Canaanite culture and religion, who were worshippers of the Canaanite deities (vs. 15c) and the group, who had been in Egypt and had entered under Joshua (vs. 15d).[2] The third group are called upon to renew their allegiance to Yahweh, and the other two groups to become Yahweh worshippers for the first time. Israelite faith was thus a syncretism of all the elements which have been examined in this chapter. The older theories were wrong only in so far as they sought to take all back to one root, when the final Israel that emerged was rooted in them all—the Yahwism of Moses, the El religion of Canaan, the father-gods of the patriarchs and the nomad and sedentary backgrounds.

A long process of growing together preceded and followed this synthesis. Patriarchal religion was already a syncretism of the old Father-God faith, which may be thought of as having come from the north-east[3] with the local cults of Canaan at such places as Bethel. Yahweh religion had also had a complicated history involving groups in Midian, Egypt and Kadesh and an early synthesis with patriarchal religion in the Transjordan.[4] The process of fusion was not complete with the formation of the amphictyony, but rather reached its height with the monarchy, when vast numbers of Canaanites were incorporated into Israel.[5] Israel's sacrificial cultus was largely taken over from the Canaanite side and was resisted by

---

[1] Noth, *Das System der zwölf Stämme Israels*, Stuttgart (1930).

[2] Cf. W. Harrelson, *op. cit.*, p. 7.

[3] So the old cultic confession of Deut. 26 : 5 "a wandering Aramean was my father."

[4] Just how complicated the explanation must be to account for all the facts may be seen in Maag's reconstruction ("Der Hirte," pp. 23-24) where the elements of leading, and "going with" in the Sinai god (cf. Buber's remark mentioned on p. 42) are derived from an earlier father-god tradition.

[5] S. A. Cook summarizing R. H. Kennett, *Church of Israel* says that Saul and David ruled over a people for the most part Canaanite rather than

the prophets in consequence.[1] One naturally thinks of the northern kingdom as the area of greatest Canaanite influence, but many find it stronger in the luxurious dynastic court and Phoenicianized royal temple in Jerusalem, rather than in the prophet-inspired rulers of the north.

This new reconstruction, so different from the traditional view based on the present form of the Biblical materials, fails to convince at a number of points. There is a difference between a recognition of the Canaanizing of the Yahweh cult in times of apostasy to which the Books of Judges, Kings and the prophets bear witness and the assumption that the religion of Israel in its high points as, for example, in the Book of Psalms and the piety of the "good" kings was a thinly veneered Yahwized Canaanitism. The distinction between aberration and norm is not entirely the work of the Deuteronomic historians. Behind the modern view lies the theory of a peaceful *Landnahme*, in which new settlers and old lived side by side in harmony, rather than of a "holy war" against the Canaanites and a conquest.[2] This theory which reduces much of Deuteronomy and the Deuteronomic Work of History to insubstantial dreams, had its origin in the pre-archeological period.[3] It is having difficulty in maintaining itself today against the archeological denials.[4]

Israelite (p. xxxvii) and Lods ascribes the difference between the army of David (1,300,000) and that of Deborah (40,000) to the accession of Canaanites (*Israel*, p. 333).

[1] Barton thinks 2 Kings 17 : 25ff. an illustration of what might have happened. At first the new settlers worshipped their own gods, as the Mosaic group may be expected to have worshipped Yahweh, but then when disaster overtook them, they busied themselves to learn the law of the god of the land (*Sketch of Semitic Origins*, p. 147). For a maximal view of the Canaanite impact see E. Leslie, *Old Testament Religion in the Light of its Canaanite Background*, New York (1936). Cf. also J. Pedersen "Canaanite and Israelite Cultus," *Acta Orientalia* XVIII (1940), pp. 1-14.

[2] It is recognized, of course, that the amphictyony was anti-Canaanite (cf. Judg. 5), but this does not go far enough. A. C. Welch pointed out (*Prophet and Priest in Old Israel*, London (1936), pp. 12ff) that much of the misunderstanding of the Israelite cult in the Wellhausen school was due to the failure to realize that the Israelite entry had been a conquest. Cf. Y. Kaufmann, *The Biblical Account of the Conquest of Canaan*, Jerusalem (1953), p. 90; *The Religion of Israel*, pp. 245-61.

[3] It is represented in Stade's, *Geschichte des Volkes Israel*, Vol. I, Berlin (1887), pp. 133, 141.

[4] The debate between Albright and Noth now extends to a whole series of articles (see most recently M. Noth, "Der Beitrag der Archäologie zur

Wright has remarked one curious effect of the theory:

> [Noth's] perspective makes it necessary to assume that the Period of the Judges was Israel's great creative period, though Biblical tradition remembered it differently as precisely the time when the new nation failed to "get off the ground" in its flight through time and space.[1]

By eliminating the dimension of depth in which the tradition has placed Joshua, Moses and the patriarchs[2] it removes the causes which brought the people of Israel to a unifying faith—the revelation to Moses and the call of Abraham.[3]

The criticisms offered at this point are against details of the construction, rather than against the theory of composite origin as a whole. That Israelite religion received accretions in the course of its history, and was thus in a sense composite, is not denied. The writer thinks of these elements, not so much as like the various spokes going to make up the wheel on a flat temporal plane, as tributaries flowing into the stream of a faith continuing from generation to generation. Once this is granted, the contributions of Alt and Noth can be welcomed for the light they throw on particular periods. Their strength lies in what they affirm about the patriarchal religion on the one hand and amphictyonic religion on the other. Their weakness is the denial of a connecting link in the work of Moses. Inability to follow them there explains the independence of treatment in the present work. The fact, that the many different views surveyed in this chapter have been possible in a little over a generation, is a warning against adopting the framework of any one of them. It may well be that the Biblical material will fall into the pattern of one of them, but for the first it must be allowed to speak for itself. This, is of course the advantage of the composite

---

Geschichte Israels," *Congress Volume Oxford 1959* (*VTSuppl* VII), pp. 262-82), and with the publication of John Bright's *A History of Israel*, Philadelphia (1959), is not likely to die down.

[1] G. E. Wright, "Old Testament Scholarship in Prospect," *JBR* XXVIII (1960), p. 184. Wright sees no future for the first hundred pages of Noth's history.

[2] The family sequence of Abraham, Isaac and Jacob as father, son and grandson is thought by Alt (*Der Gott der Väter*, p. 56) a late attempt to bring the disparate father-god cults into relation with one another.

[3] Cf. G. E. Mendenhall, *Law and Covenant in Israel and the Ancient Near East*, Pittsburgh (1955), p. 5.

theory over its predecessors. Its very eclecticism offers a broader base for working, than was possible with the more narrowly conceived theories of the earlier schools, and thus permits a relatively free enquiry. In this, attention will be given to the views of the various schools, where applicable, but adherence withheld from any one of them.

CHAPTER TWO

THE YAHWIST

Introduction

In assembling the Pentateuchal material under the captions of "Yahwist" and "Elohist", the standpoint of Wellhausen is adopted, so that the case can be argued from his premises, and the material passed quickly in review. The issue raised by Gunkel, as to whether these writers were authors or collectors—"masters or servants of their material"[1] cannot be gone into. Skinner[2] and Simpson[3] have followed Gunkel in speaking of the diversity, rather than the unity of the material, while Luther[4] and Fleming James[5] have been impressed rather by the Yahwist as a "personality" with a distinctive point of view. Both opinions are represented in von Rad, who on the one hand has filled out the personality and theology of the Yahwist in a new way,[6] and on the other has shown that these characteristics are to be looked for, not so much in the individual narratives, but in the links made between them and in the framework of the composition as a whole.[7]

Corresponding to these different approaches have been widely different assessments of the attitude of the Yahwist to sacrifice.[8] Some scholars, noting the occurrence of sacrifice at such integral points in the narrative as the expulsion from Paradise, the cessation of the flood, the covenant with Abraham and the deliverance from Egypt, along with the many references to the patriarchs building altars, have come to a positive verdict on the Yahwist's relation to

---

[1] H. Gunkel, *Genesis* (*HK*) ([5]1922), p. lxxxv.

[2] J. Skinner, *Genesis* (*ICC*) ([2]1930), pp. xxi, xlviff.

[3] C. A. Simpson, *The Early Traditions of Israel*, Oxford (1948); and *IB* I (1952), pp. 185-200, 439-57.

[4] B. Luther, "Die Persönlichkeit des Jahwisten," in E. Meyer, *Die Israeliten und ihre Nachbarstämme*, Halle (1906), pp. 105-73.

[5] Fleming James, *Personalities of the Old Testament*, New York (1939), pp. 196-209.

[6] G. von Rad, *Das formgeschichtliche Problem des Hexateuch*, *GS*, pp. 58ff.

[7] Von Rad, *Das erste Buch Mose* (*ATD*) ([5]1958), p. 28.

[8] Cf. what was written above on the *ʿōlâ* in the Yahwist (See pp. 37, 39).

the cult.[1] Others have retorted that no sacrifices are recorded as having been offered on the patriarchal altars, and have argued that the Yahwist shared the prophets' rejection of sacrifice, and was not responsible for the passages in the Primeval History and elsewhere of a different point of view.[2] In what follows the position is adopted that, while the form of the stories may be that of the older material and details should not be pressed for the Yahwist's own theology, the presence of these stories at all in his narrative is an indication of his interest in them and general agreement with their view-point. It would extend the enquiry beyond all limits to go into each story for its own history, and it is not necessary for the summary purpose of the present work.

The Sacrifices of Cain and Abel (Gen. 4 : 1-16)

The discussions of Gunkel and Mowinckel[3] may be consulted for the earlier history of the chapter,[4] but study here must be limited to the present form of the story, which is apparently that in which it was known throughout the greater part of the historic Israelite period.

It is assumed by the author—the Yahwist or another—that it was a perfectly natural thing, that the two workmen—the brothers Cain and Abel[5]—should bring an offering "at the end of days"

---

[1] F. Tuch thought Levitical interests indicated by the mention of "fat" in Gen. 4 : 4 and "clean" and "unclean" in Gen. 7 : 2ff. (*Genesis*, Halle (^{2}1871), pp. lii-liii.)

[2] Luther, *op. cit.*, pp. 138-40; R. H. Pfeiffer, *Introduction to the Old Testament*, New York (^{2}1948), p. 173; I. Lewy, *The Growth of the Pentateuch*, New York (1955), pp. 197-201. These authors achieve their result by the division of the J source—Luther by the omission of the Primeval History, Pfeiffer by a late source S2, which added the sacrificial references to J and S (p. 161), and Lewy by a priestly annotator, JP, who supplemented the early anti-sacrificial JN (p. 152). In contrast, Eissfeldt's "J2" is a "lay source" furthest from P and the cult, and J retains the sacrificial references (*Hexateuch-Synopse*, Leipzig (1922).)

[3] H. Gunkel, *Genesis* (*HK*), pp. 40-55; S. Mowinckel, *The Two Sources of the Predeuteronomic Primeval History* (*JE*) *in Gen.* 1-11, Oslo (1937), pp. 25-43.

[4] A lengthy and complicated pre-history seems suggested by the bewildering complexity of the figure of Cain, who appears as the first city-builder (vs. 17), the ancestor of a fierce Bedouin race (vss. 18-24) and also of a despised vagrant group (vss. 12-16), a *fellahin* offering the agriculturalist's *minḥâ* (vss. 2-3), and the child of the first human pair (vs. 1).

[5] Mowinckel (*op. cit.*, pp. 22ff.) thinks this an example of the "hostile brothers" motif, and notes the connection, which also appears in the Romulus-

(vs. 3).[1] The use of the normal sacrificial verb *hēbîʾ* and the reference to "the fat" (vs. 4), makes it plain that a sacrifice is being described, but whether an altar or a burnt offering is to be understood is left uncertain. What is important is, that the sacrifice is a *minḥâ*, not a *zebaḥ*, and no sacrificial meal follows.[2] The *minḥâ*, which simply means a "present" or "tribute" in 34 of its 212 uses,[3] is confined to cereal offerings in its 97 occurrences in P, but apparently had a wider use for both animal and vegetable sacrifices outside of P,[4] and is so used here.[5] It seems to have been linked to the *ʿōlâ* rather than to the *zebaḥ*, but whether Köhler is to be followed in his suggestion that the two terms were originally one *ham-minḥâ hā-ʿōlâ* "the present that ascends (in the fire)"[6] is not so clear.

The interest of this investigation centres in the motives for the bringing of the offerings, rather than the reasons for their rejection or acceptance, debated though the latter are.[7] That the offering

---

Remus story, to the building of a city. Ehrenzweig's suggestion ("Kain und Lamech," *ZAW* XXXV (1915), pp. 1-11) that foundation sacrifices for this city are being described (cf. the reference to a "door" in vs. 7) seems far-fetched, as is also the "myth and ritual" interpretation of Brock-Utne ("Die religions-historischen Voraussetzungen der Kain-Abel-Geschichte," *ZAW* LIV (1936), pp. 202-39) and S. H. Hooke (*The Siege Perilous*, pp. 66-73 and (*ClarB*) VI, pp. 38-42), which sees in the murder of Abel "in the field" (LXX vs. 8) a sacrifice for fertility and in the punishment and protection of Cain, the ritual flight of the cult officiant.

[1] If Snaith is to be followed in his rendering "at the end of the year," (*The Jewish New Year Festival*, pp. 12-13) and his identification of this with an annual autumn rite, the normality of the sacrifice would be further attested, but the meaning may simply be as in RSV "in the course of time."

[2] It may well be that in one of the twists of the story, by which finally the figures of pastoralist and agriculturalist were reversed, the pastoralist's *zebaḥ* was replaced by the agriculturalist's *minḥâ*, but this cannot be proved.

[3] E.g. Judg. 3 : 15; 1 Kings 4 : 21.

[4] Of animal sacrifices clearly in 1 Sam. 2 : 12-17.

[5] Snaith's suggestion that *minḥâ* slipped in inadvertently in vs. 4b and that here, and in the rest of the Old Testament, was a cereal offering ("Sacrifices in the Old Testament," *VT* VII (1957), pp. 314-16) can hardly be followed.

[6] L. Köhler, *Old Testament Theology*, p. 184.

[7] Among the theories, three are worthy of mention. The LXX with its rendering of *dielēs* probably read *lntḥ*, as in Lev. 1 : 12, for *lptḥ*, and sought an explanation in some fault in the ritual: "if thou didst rightly offer, but didst not rightly divide, thou didst sin." *Ntḥ*, however, is only applicable to animal sacrifice, which Cain's was not. The traditional view, that the passage teaches that animal sacrifice is better than vegetable, overlooks the point that cereal offerings were also acceptable (1 Sam. 1 : 24, 10 : 3, 21 : 6), and not only as an accompaniment of animal sacrifice, but as a substitute

was a gift offering, does not rule out a possible propitiatory sense, as noted in the Introduction. It is this sense, which *minḥâ* has in 1 Sam. 3 : 10-14 and 1 Sam. 26 : 19.[1] The same may be true of the firstlings and firstfruits, which were probably at first offered for a more serious reason than thanksgiving.[2] The sacrifices are not spoken of, however, as expiating sin,[3] and so while possibly nearer to the solemn theory, than to the fellowship meal theory of Wellhausen and Robertson Smith, cannot be used for evidence either way.

The Sacrifice of Noah (Gen. 8 : 20-22)

Three of the four chief accounts of the deluge—the Sumerian, Akkadian and Yahwist—relate how the hero—Ziusudra, Utnapishtim or Noah—offered a sacrifice when the waters abated. The Yahwist, like the Akkadian version, places the scene of the sacrifice on the dry land, where in the Sumerian account it is apparently still on ship-board.[4] In common with the

---

for it (Lev. 5 : 11-13). The third suggestion, that something in the mind of the offerers was determinative, might be borne out by the order "Cain and his offering," "Abel and his offering," and the words "if thou doest well," but this latter phrase can scarcely be taken as a prophetic preference of conduct to animal sacrifice, as Vriezen proposes (*An Outline of Old Testament Theology* p. 44). On the textual problem in vs. 7 see G. E. Closen "Der Dämon Sünde," *Bibl.* XVI (1935), pp. 431-42.

[1] Cf. S. R. Driver: "it does not express the neutral idea of gift, but denotes a complimentary present, or a present made to secure or retain goodwill" ("Offer, Offering, Oblation," *DB* III (1900), p. 587).

[2] Produce and offspring were probably thought of as sacred to the deity until "deconsecrated" by the offering to him of a first portion (Lev. 19 : 23-25). They must at first have been accompanied by a feeling of solemnity in the presence of the tabu (cf. J. A. MacCulloch, "Firstfruits (Introductory and Primitive)," *ERE* VI (1913), p. 41).

[3] F. Delitzsch wrote: "Der Mensch wie er nach dem Falle ist kann weder sich selbst noch irgend etwas Gotte darbringen als eine Gabe die ihm gefiele; er bedarf vor allem der Sühne seiner todeswürdigen Sünde, und dieser Sühne dient das mittelst Schlachtung des Thieres gewonnnene Blut" and added "warum nicht auch in Abels Bewusstsein—der Gedanke der Sühne?" (*Genesis*, Leipzig (^{4}1872), p. 165), but this presupposes a connection to the Fall story which was probably not present to the original teller of the stories, nor to the Yahwist, for whom the connections of the story are rather forward to the increase of sin among mankind, than backward to Paradise.

[4] Lines 209-11 (*ANET*, p. 44) place Ziusudra's adoration of Utu the sun-god, on board the ship, but the lines following 211 are destroyed and there is no record of the coming out of the ark. L. W. King (*Legends of Babylon and Egypt*, London (1918)), thinks this the original form of the story: "Ziusudu

latter, however, he has Noah, like Ziusudra offer animal sacrifices.[1]

The offering might seem to be one of simple thanksgiving for deliverance, but this does not suit the Mesopotamian versions, where the anger of the gods had brought the calamity. Even there, however, the polytheistic nature of the accounts makes it difficult to determine, whether the intention of the offerer is to thank his patron Ea, through whose intervention he has been preserved, or to propitiate the other gods, and in particular Enlil, who is angry at his escape. The order of events supports the propitiation of the gods in general, for it is not until after the majority of the gods have "smelled the sacrifice" and have been appeased, that the strife of Enlil and Ea breaks out, and the particular anger of the former is revealed.

The Biblical account subsumes the various elements under a monotheistic belief. If stress is given to the mercy of Yahweh toward Noah, in securing his preservation, his offering will be seen as a thank-offering,[2] but if the wrath of God at human sin is stressed a propitiatory intention will have to be acknowledged.[3] The fact that Noah is described as a "righteous man" (Gen. 6 : 9, 7 : 1) does not rule out the possibility of a propitiatory sacrifice, for any confidence arising therefrom must have been shaken by the terrors of the judgment he had witnessed.

Again it must be noted that no fellowship meal is involved in the sacrifice. It is the *ʿōlâ*, which ascended entirely in smoke to God.

---

regards himself as saved when he sees the sun shining" (p. 83) not when he landed. All other accounts, including Berossus, place the sacrifice on dry land (see A. Heidel, *The Gilgamesh Epic and Old Testament Parallels*, Chicago ([2]1949), p. 255).

[1] Noah offers of "every clean animal and of every clean bird" (Gen. 8 : 20). Ziusudra "kills an ox, slaughters a sheep," (*ANET*), "kills an ox, offers an abundant sacrifice of sheep" (A. Heidel, *op. cit.*, p. 104). The Akkadian account does not list the animal victims but reads "offered a sacrifice . . . poured a libation . . . heaped cane, cedar and myrtle" (Lines 155-58, *ANET*, p. 95; Heidel, p. 87).

[2] So S. R. Driver, *Genesis* (*WC*) ([15]1948), p. 94; A. C. Welch, *The Religion of Israel under the Kingdom*, Edinburgh (1912), p. 246; W. B. Stevenson, "The Hebrew ʿOlah and Zebach Sacrifices," *Bertholet Festschrift* (1950), p. 489; W. Zimmerli, *1. Mose* 1-11, (Proph) II, Zürich (1943), pp. 67-69; R. Rendtorff, "Opfer," *EKL* II, Göttingen (1958), col. 1693.

[3] So J. Skinner, (*ICC*), p. 157; H. Gunkel (*HK*), p. 65; O. Procksch, *Genesis* (*KAT*) ([2] & [3]1924), p. 69; E. Lewis, "Propitiation," *Harper's Bible Dictionary* (eds.) M. S. and J. L. Miller, New York (1952), p. 585.

In the earlier time this offering seems to have been limited to occasions of some solemnity (cf. Gen. 22; 1 Sam. 7: 9; 2 Kings 3 : 27; Job 1 : 5; 2 Sam. 24 : 25)[1] and this would support a propitiatory significance for the present passage. Vs. 21 confirms this by speaking of Yahweh smelling the pleasant odour (*rēaḥ nîḥōaḥ*), and being moved to grant the assuring promise of vs 22. The *rēaḥ nîḥōaḥ* is best understood in a propitiatory sense in earlier passages, although Gray doubts whether this was still the case in the time of P.[2] Procksch speaks of a new religion of atonement established after the flood in which one animal of seven was to be for offering,[3] and von Rad of the provision for a new humanity's expiation:

> Diese neue Einstellung zum Menschen ist nun doch tatsächlich zusammengeordnet mit dem Zeichen des Opfers als einem menschlichen Bekenntnis zur Versöhnungsbedürftigkeit.[4]

The Sacrifices of the Patriarchs

The negative conclusions drawn by some scholars from the lack of explicit descriptions of patriarchal sacrifice have been shown above to be without foundation. On the contrary there is scarcely any important centre of patriarchal habitation that was not marked by an altar. In addition there are references to patriarchal covenants and hospitality, which may have involved sacrifice.

The Patriarchal Altars

In three of the four centres with which Abraham is associated an altar is built—Shechem (12 : 6-7), Bethel (12 : 8, 13 : 4) and Hebron (13 : 18). At Beersheba it is Isaac, who builds the altar (26 : 25), while Abraham's part is limited to the planting of a tree

---

[1] "It always contained an element of solemnity and awe, if not also of actual apprehension of evil to be averted by the offering. It was used on occasions of special gravity e.g. the deliverance of the Flood" (A. T. Chapman and A. W. Streane, *Leviticus and Numbers* (*CamB*) (1914), p. li).

[2] Gray finds it surprising that this term, used more than 30 times in P, is not used where it ought to be on the propitiatory theory—with the sin offering and guilt offering—but is used where it ought not to be—with cereal, *zebaḥ* and *ʿōlâ* offerings (*Sacrifice in the Old Testament*, pp. 77-81).

[3] O. Procksch, (*KAT*), p. 71. This may have been the intention from the beginning, if the animals that went into the ark were not seven pairs, but a total of seven (*śibʿâ śibʿâ* "by sevens" (Gen. 7 : 2))—three pairs and an extra male for sacrifice.

[4] G. von Rad (*ATD*), p. 100.

(21 : 33). It may be assumed that animal sacrifice was offered on these altars,[1] "since the altar had no use or significance except as a means of sacrifice,"[2] but nothing is known of the motives prompting these sacrifices, nor of the sacrifices themselves. Those after the arrival in Canaan, and the promise of seed (12 : 7, 26 : 25) might have expressed thanksgiving,[3] and that after the wife-denying episode (13 : 4) penitence for sin. However, if the stories are aetiological in character, and seek to legitimate the later worship of these sanctuaries by taking back its beginning to a theophany to Abraham, the fact that similar aetiologies trace the first worship of Shechem and Bethel to Jacob (33 : 20, 28 : 18) makes it uncertain if these contexts can be taken seriously.[4] The type of sacrifice offered is not stated, and the assumption of Maag that they were not *ʿōlôt*, can no more be proved than that of Vriezen, that they were.[5]

The Patriarchal Covenants

These are described in Gen. 15 : 9-18 (Abraham and Yahweh), Gen. 21 : 28-30 (Abraham and Abimelech), Gen. 26 : 26-33 (Isaac and Abimelech) and Gen. 31 : 44-53 (Jacob and Laban). No common pattern unites these covenants with each other, nor with that of Exod. 24 : 3-11 (effected by the throwing of blood on each party), and those of Josh. 9 : 14 (eating bread) and Num. 18 : 19 (sharing salt). Gen. 15 has no common meal, but a rite of dividing a number of sacrificial victims into two halves.[6] In Gen. 21 : 27 Abraham gives Abimelech sheep and oxen in the E version, but in the J version sets aside seven lambs as a witness—an act which

[1] Cf. J. Bright, *A History of Israel*, p. 92: "The cult of the patriarchs is depicted as exceedingly simple, as one would expect it to be. At its centre was animal sacrifice, as among all the Semites."

[2] J. Skinner (*ICC*), p. lii.

[3] S. Nyström, *op. cit.*, pp. 103-4.

[4] E.g. 13 : 4 is usually regarded as a redactional bridge linking Chs. 12 and 13 (Skinner (*ICC*), p. 243; Holzinger, *Genesis* (*KHC*) (1898), p. 140). More confidence is usually placed in the connection of Abraham with Hebron, as of Isaac with Beersheba and Jacob with central and east Palestine.

[5] See p. 39 above.

[6] Jer. 34 : 18-19 implies that the parties passed between the halves. This is omitted in the LXX, but Heinisch is hardly to be followed in his assumption (*Genesis* (*HS*) (1930), p. 231) that this element comes into Jeremiah from Genesis, in view of the fact that in Genesis the human partner Abraham sleeps (vs. 12), and what passes between is a "smoking fire pot and a flaming torch" (vs. 17).

even Abimelech does not understand. No meal or sacrifice is mentioned. In 26 : 30 and 31 : 46, where sacrificial terminology is again not used, feasts are made, and an eating together takes place before the covenant is consummated. In the last three cases a dispute has preceded the treaty, so that the thought of reconciliation between the human participants cannot be far away. The presupposition of the covenant meal was not undisturbed fellowship, but the ending of a dispute.[1]

The peculiar ritual of the Gen. 15 covenant has been much discussed. Older writers denied that any sacrifice was to be seen here, as no altar was mentioned. It is significant, however, that all the victims required by the Levitical Law were offered—heifer, goat, ram, pigeon and dove—and no others than these—e.g. neither camel nor ass. Three year old animals are favoured as in 1 Sam. 1 : 24. The Levitical requirement that the birds should not be divided (Lev. 1 : 17) is observed.

Among the various explanations of the meaning of the rite, perhaps three theories, which might be called the imprecatory, the sacramental and the purificatory, may be distinguished. In Jer. 34 : 18ff. it seems plain from the punishment pronounced on the violators of the covenant (that they should be made like the calf that was cut in two) that the cutting in two had been a symbolic *self-imprecation*: "may this be done to me, if I do not keep the covenant."[2] That this was an integral part of ancient treaty-making seems attested by such inscriptions, as that from Sujin, of the treaty between *KTK* and Arpad.[3] Robertson Smith, however, felt that this did not explain so characteristic a feature as the passing between the two parts, and proposed a more *sacramental* interpretation. The two parties had joined in eating and when it ceased to be eaten, stood between the pieces, as a symbol that they were

[1] So S. I. Curtiss, "The Semitic Sacrifice of Reconciliation," *Exp* 6th series, VI (1902), pp. 454-62 with illustrations of the Jacob and Laban covenant from the practices of modern Semites.

[2] So H. Schultz, *Old Testament Theology*, Vol. II, E. T. Edinburgh (²1909), p. 4: "it is simply a form of oath, like the symbolical sending out of dismembered bodies of animals sacrificed, by which the curse of a like destruction was called down upon the heads of laggards."

[3] *ANET* (²1955), pp. 503-504. F. Rosenthal renders "(as) this calf is slaughtered . . .thus Matti ʿel shall be slaughtered." Cf. A. Dupont-Sommer, *Les inscriptions araméennes de Sfiré* (Stèles I & II), Paris (1958), pp. 21, 57-58.

"taken with the mystical life of the victim."[1] This explanation still commends itself to Henninger,[2] but one may wonder whether the *purificatory* aspect mentioned both by him and Robertson Smith is not better grounded, seeing that an eating of the victims cannot be proved. In a remarkable Hittite text translated by Masson,[3] when the Hittite army has been defeated, sacrificial victims are cut in two, and the halves placed over against each other to form a "street" through which the troops march. Accompanying rites of passing between fires and sprinkling with water, confirm that the purpose is purificatory, and perhaps propitiatory, to avert the wrath of the gods.[4] In Gen. 15 the meaning might also be that of purification for covenant.[5] There is certainly nothing of joyous communion in the passage, but rather solemn awe as Abraham meets Yahweh (vs. 12, vs. 17).[6]

The Patriarchal Hospitality

Apart from meals in connection with the treaties, to which reference has already been made, the Yahwist gives only one other incident of patriarchal hospitality—Abraham's meal for his three visitors in Gen. 18 : 1-8. Here a fellowship meal is certainly in view, but mention of any religious rite is lacking. Abraham is not aware at the time of the meal that his guests are deity, does not eat with them, nor, as far as is recorded, perform the slaughter at an altar.[7]

[1] W. R. Smith, *The Religion of the Semites*, p. 481. Holzinger (*KHC*), pp. 150-51 also thought of an original meal, omitted as inappropriate to Yahweh, who now acts alone while Abraham sleeps.

[2] J. Henninger, "Was bedeutet die rituelle Teilung eines Tieres in zwei Hälften," *Bibl.* XXXIV (1953), pp. 344-53.

[3] O. Masson, "A propos d'un rituel hittite," *RHR* CXXXVII (1950), pp. 5-25. Also in O. R. Gurney, *The Hittites* (Penguin), London (1952), p. 151 and E. Nielsen, *Shechem*, Copenhagen (1955), pp. 115-16.

[4] So Nielsen, *ibid.*, p. 116. Masson says that in none of the texts describing this rite is there the idea of a pact in Robertson Smith's sense, but only of purification and expiation (pp. 18, 25).

[5] Nielsen suggests that by passing between the halves the partners had all their impurity absorbed by the corpse.

[6] Cf. the theory of L. A. Snijders ("Genesis XV. The Covenant with Abram," *OTS* XII (1958), p. 276) that the sleep of Abraham was a kind of "death" and that the covenant was made in death.

[7] So D. Schötz, *Schuld — und Sündopfer im Alten Testament*, Breslau (1930), p. 72, who thinks the slaughter was not a sacrifice. Similarly J. Pedersen, *Israel* III-IV, E.T. London (1940), p. 339. One would expect the head of the house rather than a servant to offer sacrifice, but this cannot be pressed.

Vital links of the Robertson Smith-Wellhausen chain are therefore missing, and the passage, which comes nearer to their view than the others thus far handled, has actually been used by their critics to deny that "all slaughter was sacrifice."[1]

The Sacrifices of Moses

The commissioning of Moses included the command to call Israel to a sacrifice in the wilderness. The sacrificial terminology in the requests to Pharoah for permission to leave Egypt, and in the replies of Pharoah must be noted.

The requests to Pharoah are —

Exod. 3 : 18 " 'The Lord, the God of the Hebrews, has met (*qārâ*) with us; and now, we pray you, let us go a three days' journey into the wilderness, that we may sacrifice (*zābaḥ*) to the Lord our God.' "

5 : 3 adds "lest he fall upon us with pestilence or with the sword."

7 : 16 "let my people go that they may serve (*'ābad*) me in the wilderness." So also 4 : 23, 7 : 26 (8 : 1), 8 : 16 (8 : 20), 9 : 1, 9 : 13, 10 : 3.

"Meeting" with Yahweh is a solemn matter, and failure to sacrifice to Him may result in pestilence, or sword.[2] The sacrifice in such a context, although described by the word *zābaḥ*, must have been much more than a fellowship meal.[3] The third verb *'ābad*, which normally means "serve", in cultic passages is to be understood in the sense of the Vulgate's "*sacrificere.*"[4]

---

[1] A number of similar passages will be noted at later points, but finally it will be the decision on Deut. 12 that determines the interpretation of all such passages.

[2] Cf. H. Gressmann, *Die Anfänge Israels* (*SAT*) ([2]1922), p. 44: "Jahve sei ihnen "begegnet" (IV Mose 23, 3f.), ein deutliches Zeichen seines Zorns, denn er wolle ein Opfer haben und müsse wieder versöhnt werden."

[3] The word *zābaḥ*, which makes its first appearance in the Yahwist here, occurs 133 times as a verb, and 162 times as a noun for the slaughtering of an animal. In the majority of cases the killing is for sacrifice, as the use of the word *mizbēaḥ* for altar also confirms.

[4] Cf. C. Lindhagen, *The Servant Motif in the Old Testament*, Uppsala (1950), pp. 93-94 and R. B. Y. Scott, "The Service of God," in *A Stubborn Faith* (ed.), E. C. Hobbs, Dallas (1956), pp. 133-34. Scott compares the Egyptian cult attendant, who like a slave, awoke, washed and clothed the god. Jehu's intention to "serve Baal much" (2 Kings 10 : 18) and the Psalmists call to "serve the Lord with singing" (Ps. 100 : 2) illustrate the use of the verb.

The replies of Pharoah are —

Exod. 8 : 4 (8 : 8) "I will let the people go to sacrifice (*zābaḥ*) to the Lord."

8 : 21 (8 : 25) adds "within the land."

8 : 24 (8 : 28) adds "not very far away. Make entreaty for me."

10 : 24 adds "only let your flocks and herds remain behind."

From the answers of Moses it is apparent that Hebrew sacrifice, if conducted in the land, would be an abomination to the Egyptians (8 : 22 (8 : 26)), that it would comprise *zᵉbāḥîm* and *ʿōlôt* of animal victims from the flocks and herds (10 : 25-26), and that the precise details of the ritual were unknown (10 : 26, 8 : 23 (8 : 27)). It may probably be concluded that Hebrew sacrifice was different from that of the Egyptians,[1] and had been in suspension during the time in Egypt.[2] Pharoah's request "make entreaty for me" (8 : 24 (8 : 28)), might indicate the understanding of sacrifice in a propitiatory sense,[3] but more probably the collocation of entreaty and sacrifice is accidental, in view of the different order, in which the two items appear in 8 : 4 (8 : 8).

The Sacrifice of the Passover (Exod. 12 : 21-28)

Despite the dictum of Wellhausen that "the exodus is not the occasion of the festival, but the festival ... the occasion of the exodus,"[4] it is not clear that the Passover was the sacrifice to which Israel was called in the wilderness.[5] It may, however, have contained elements of an older ritual,[6] but whether this was from the old

---

[1] The "abomination of the Egyptians" is usually taken to be the repugnance with which the Egyptians would have viewed the Hebrew sacrifice of animals held sacred in their various temples. A similar Egyptian antipathy to Jewish worship at a later time may be reflected in their destruction of the Elephantine temple (see Papyrus No. 30, lines 8 and 23 in A. Cowley, *Aramaic Papyri of the Fifth Century B.C.*, Oxford (1923). pp. 112-14).

[2] This was not, however, because Yahweh's rule did not extend to Egypt. See G. Beer *Exodus (HAT)*, Tübingen (1939), p. 52.

[3] E. Power, "Exodus," (*CatholicC*) (1953), p. 212.

[4] J. Wellhausen, *Prolegomena*, p. 88.

[5] A. C. Welch, *Prophet and Priest in Old Israel*, p. 39 says: "The two are entirely distinct. For the same sources which record the demand agree in stating that Passover was celebrated on Egyptian soil and on the night of the Exodus". A sacrifice after three days' journey was also inconsistent with the command for an immediate killing of the Passover.

[6] The J passage begins abruptly with the command "kill the passover," but no definition of *pesaḥ* is given.

nomadic exchange of pastures,[1] or the annual sacrifice of firstlings,[2] or from sedentary New Year rites of purgation[3] can no longer be ascertained.

On any view a hard core of old apotropaic rites must be acknowledged. These include the smearing of the blood to ward off evil,[4] the use of hyssop and bitter herbs for the same purpose,[5] and the prohibition of leaven, the breaking of the bones of the victim and the going out of doors before the morning.[6] These elements, which are not all in J, are shared by both the blood ritual and the sacrificial meal, and lend no support to the suggestion that an early fellowship meal, without any apotropaic purpose once existed.[7]

In the Yahwist passage it is the blood rite, rather than the meal, which is being described. The sacrificial blood has a protective purpose, whether one thinks the story is "intended to correct a popular conception of Yahweh, or to counteract a popular recognition of other divine powers than Yahweh,"[8] and thinks of the word *pesaḥ* as a passing into the house, of Yahweh, as guest and protector,[9] or a protective covering by one stationary upon or

---

[1] This theory, elaborated by L. Rost in "Weidewechsel und altisraelitischer Festkalender," *ZDPV* LVI (1943), pp. 205-16 and in part also represented in G. Dalman (*Arbeit und Sitte in Palästina,* Gütersloh Vol. I, pp. 40, 169, Vol. VI, pp. 204-07) and A. Brock — Utne ("Eine religionsgeschichtliche Studie zu dem ursprünglichen Passahopfer," *ARW* XXXI (1934), pp. 272-78), well accounts for the staff, shoes and girded loins, but in the opinion of J. Henninger ("Les fêtes de printemps chez les Arabes et leurs implications historiques," *Revista do Museu Paulista,* N. S. IV (1950), p. 421) does not make enough of the first-born element.

[2] N. H. Snaith, however, doubts the connection to first-born and firstlings (*The Jewish New Year Festival,* p. 17).

[3] S. H. Hooke, *The Origin of Early Semitic Ritual,* p. 48; I. Engnell, "Paesaḥ—Maṣṣōt and the Problem of 'Patternism,'" *Orientalia Suecana,* Vol. I, Uppsala (1952), esp. pp. 45-48 and in part N. H. Snaith, *op. cit.,* p. 20.

[4] Cf. W. Brandt, "Zur Bestreichung mit Blut," *ZAW* XXXIII (1913), pp. 80-81.

[5] Cf. G. Beer, "Die Bitterkräuter beim Paschafest," *ZAW* XXXI (1911), pp. 152-53.

[6] Cf. A. Bertholet, *A History of Hebrew Civilization,* E.T. London (1926), pp. 348-49, and Snaith, *op. cit.,* pp. 21ff.

[7] It can hardly be argued with G. Beer, *Pesachim,* Giessen (1912), p. 17 that the door rite, implying a house cult, must be younger than the meal, which could belong to an open-air cult.

[8] G. B. Gray, *Sacrifice in the Old Testament,* p. 364 cited by E. O. James, *The Ancient Gods,* London (1960), p. 149.

[9] H. C. Trumbull, *The Threshold Covenant,* Edinburgh (1896), pp. 209ff.

at,[1] rather than of the passing over of the house by the destroyer. To quote Gray's criticism of Robertson Smith's theory "the blood is not, as Smith suggests, a tonic but a disinfectant."[2]

The Yahwistic Code (Exod. 34 : 14-26, also 13 : 11-13)

The various attempts that have been made to reduce the fourteen items of this code to ten, are of no great importance to this discussion.[3] The code takes for granted the bringing of sacrifice and makes several provisions for it. In vss. 19-20 (paralleled by 13 : 11-13) the command for the bringing of firstlings, and for the redemption of the first-born is given. Similarly the firstling of the unclean ass is to be redeemed, because it cannot be sacrificed. If it is not redeemed it must be killed, by the breaking of the neck.[4]

Vs. 25 prohibiting the offering of the blood of the sacrifice with leaven, and leaving the Feast of the Passover till the morning presents some difficulties. Nowhere else is the "blood of the *zebaḥ*" used as a direct object of the verb *šāḥat*. The second half of the verse is overfull with its *zebaḥ* of the *ḥāg* of the *pesaḥ*. It is tempting to see *pesaḥ* as an addition by some one to whom the only sacrifice that could not remain until the next day was the Passover.[5] May finds it a palpable insertion, and argues that had it been genuine, it should have come in after vs. 18.[6] On the other hand the addition might be of *ḥāg* rather than of *pesaḥ*, as this is unparalleled for the Passover.[7] Beer accepts the Passover reference, and thinks that

[1] T. Glasson, "The 'Passover,' a Misnomer: The Meaning of the Verb *Pasach*," *JTS* N.S. X (1959), pp. 79-84. Glasson thinks the other meaning of "to be lame, to limp," throws no light on Exodus 12 and Is. 31 : 5 (p. 79).

[2] Gray, *op. cit.*, p. 359. Cf. also pp. 368ff, and S. A. Cook's attempted refutation of these strictures in *Religion of the Semites* ([3]1927), pp. 651ff.

[3] Probably the simplest is that which includes the three separate feast laws in vs. 18 and vs. 22, under the one comprehensive law of vs. 23. This has the advantage of removing the disorder and restoring the parallel to the Exod. 23 code.

[4] This would add some support to the view that ordinary slaughter was sacrifice.

[5] B. D. Eerdmans, "The Book of the Covenant and the Decalogue," *Exp* 7th series VIII (1909), p. 225.

[6] H. G. May, "The Relation of Passover to the Festival of Unleavened Cakes," *JBL* LV (1936), pp. 65-66. May claims, that the Passover is not referred to in any pre-Deuteronomic source, and regards Exod. 12 : 21-28 as of the same date as 12 : 1-20.

[7] MT reads "the Feast of the Passover" in Ezek. 45 : 21, and uses *ḥāg* in references which might be to the Passover in Ps. 118 : 27 (text corrupt);

Passover belonged to the south, where the present code originated, while the Feast of Unleavened Bread, which is the only one mentioned in the Book of the Covenant, belonged to the north.[1]

The rule of vs. 26b against seething a kid in the mother's milk is probably directed against a Baal fertility rite like that referred to in the Ugaritic Text 52 : 14.[2] A similar command, occurring earlier in vs. 15, forbids sacrificing to the gods of the inhabitants of the land, and accepting invitations to eat of their sacrifices. The phraseology in the context is Deuteronomic, but the command itself need not be, as J preserves at least one story of such a sin (Num. 25 : 1-5).

The Sacrifices of Baal-Peor (Num. 25 : 1-5)

The repetitions in the narrative suggest parallel J and E versions of this short incident. In one, the god of Moab is worshipped, in the other, the Baal of Peor. The punishment of vs. 4 is repeated in a different form in vs. 5. Gray assigns vss. 1a, 3a and 5 to E, and 1b, 2, 3b and 4 to J.[3] The sacrificial reference comes in J. The Israelites are invited to the sacrifices (*zᵉbāḥîm*) of the gods of Moab. They ate and bowed down to these gods. This non-Israelite worship centred in a sacrificial meal.

More important for the thought of Israel is the following punishment, which appeases Yahweh's wrath.[4] The passage is remarkably parallel to the P passage, which follows, where Yahweh's wrath is appeased by Phinehas' action or by the death of the wrongdoers, and the verb *kipper* is actually used (vs. 13). There seems little distinction to be drawn between P's idea of expiation and that of the earlier source.[5]

Is. 30 : 29 and Exod. 12 : 14 (P). It cannot certainly be said that *ḥāg* is impossible for Passover, in view of the fact that references to the Passover are rare in early documents, and in later documents are always associated with *maṣṣôt* which is the *ḥāg* proper.

[1] G. Beer, *Pesachim*, p. 23ff.; (*HAT*), p. 163.

[2] See *UH*, p. 144, *UL*, p. 59.

[3] G. B. Gray, *Numbers* (*ICC*) (1903), p. 381. W. Rudolph, *Der "Elohist" von Exodus bis Josua*, Berlin (1938), pp. 128ff. sees no need for analysis.

[4] What the punishment is, is obscure. The verb *hôqâʿ* referring to the punishment of the evildoers can hardly have as its object the "chiefs of the children of Israel." Something seems to have fallen out, or else the text should be emended from *roʾšê* to *hā-rᵉšāʿîm*.

[5] Jewish tradition made much of the heroism of Phinehas and ascribed the atonement to his "sacrifice" in risking his life. See Ps. 106 : 28-31.

Conclusion

Twenty references to sacrifice in the Yahwist have now been reviewed. The Wellhausen-Robertson Smith theory is borne out in only one case—and that a non-Israelite sacrifice—(Num. 25 : 2). In about half the other references the purpose of the sacrifice cannot be ascertained and some of these, which involved meals, might possibly support the fellowship theory. Against this, however, are the significant number of cases—and these include the most important sacrificial narratives—where more solemn ideas are present.[1]

This is what one would expect from a writer with so profound an understanding of sin as the Yahwist. Mowinckel rightly says that the early chapters of Genesis show that "the sinfulness of man is a fact which must be taken into account in real life" and enable the readers to see "why the later temple rites of expiation are necessary."[2] This does not prove, of course, that sacrifices for the expiation of sin were offered in the time of the Yahwist,[3] but the above investigation makes it probable that they were, or at least that the fellowship theory is a too simple explanation of early Israelite sacrifice.

[1] In some cases the sacrifices were expiatory, and in others propitiatory. L. B. Cross claimed that there was no evidence that the early offerings were made as a result of any consciousness of sin, but saw them rather as propitiatory or placatory, to bias the deity on the side of the worshipper in view of possible future calamity, or to turn away His wrath ("Sacrifice in the Old Testament," *The Atonement in History and Life* (ed.) L. W. Grensted, London (1929), pp. 53-54). Welch, however, doubted that there was propitiatory sacrifice in J or E, and saw them as reacting against the presence of this element in the Books of Samuel (*The Religion of Israel under the Kingdom*, pp. 16-22, 246).

[2] S. Mowinckel, *The Two Sources of the Predeuteronomic Primeval History (JE) in Gen. 1-11*, p. 48.

[3] Wellhausen acknowledged the sense of sin in the Yahwist, when he spoke of him as "rattling the chains" of bondage (*Prolegomena*, pp. 314, 301), but did not allow that this had any bearing on sacrifice.

Reference	Incident	Terms Used		or Secondary	or Foreign	or Individual	or Regular
A. WHERE A SENSE OF SIN OR SOLEMNITY IS PRESENT							
Gen. 8 : 20-22	Sacrifice of Noah	*ʿōlōt*	*ʿālâ*	Primary	Universal	?Family	Special
15 : 8-12	Covenant with Abraham		*bātar*	Primary	Israelite	Individual	Special
Exod. 3 : 18, 5 : 3,	Request to Pharoah		*zābaḥ*	Primary	Israelite	National	?Festival
7 : 16			*ʿābad*				
8 : 4(8), 8 : 21(25)	Replies of Pharoah		*zābaḥ*	Primary	Israelite	National	?Festival
8 : 24(28)							
10 : 24-26		*zebāḥîm ʿolôt*	*ʿāśâ*				
12 : 21-28	Sacrifice of the Passover	*pesaḥ*	*šāḥaṭ*	Primary	Israelite	National	Annual
Num. 25 : 1-5	Punishment at Baal Peor						
B. WHERE A SENSE OF SIN OR SOLEMNITY NOT PRESENT							
Num. 25 : 1-5	Sacrifices of Baal Peor	*zebāḥîm*	*ʾākal*	Primary	Non-Isra.	?National	?
C. DOUBTFUL OR UNCLASSIFIABLE PASSAGES							
Gen. 4 : 1-16	Sacrifices of Cain and Abel	*minḥâ*	*hēbīʾ*	Primary	Universal	Individual	?Regular
	Patriarchal Altars						
12 : 6-7	Shechem	*mizbēaḥ*					
12 : 8, 13 : 4	Bethel	*mizbēaḥ*					
13 : 18	Hebron	*mizbēaḥ*					
21 : 33, 26 : 25	Beersheba	*mizbēaḥ*					
	Patriarchal Covenants						
21 : 27-30	Abraham and Abimelech						
26 : 26-33	Isaac and Abimelech		*ʾākal*				
31 : 44-53	Jacob and Laban		*ʾākal*				
	Patriarchal Hospitality						
18 : 1-8	Abraham and the Three Men		*ʿāśâ ʾākal*				
	Yahwistic Code						
Exod. 34 : 15	Not to other gods	*zebāḥîm zābaḥ*	*ʾākal*				
34 : 19-20	Firstlings and First-born						
13 : 11-16							
34 : 25a	Not with Leaven	*zebaḥ*	*šāḥaṭ*				
34 : 25b	Not left over	*zebaḥ pesaḥ*	*ḥāg*				
34 : 26b	Kid in Mother's Milk		*bāšal*				

CHAPTER THREE

THE ELOHIST

INTRODUCTION

The question of the existence of the Elohist, as raised by Volz and Rudolph,[1] and that of the nature of his work as independent author,[2] or supplementer[3] must be left on one side. The sacrificial narratives to be treated in this chapter, in most cases have no parallel in the Yahwist, but this fact alone scarcely warrants any conclusions as to the "priestly" or "prophetic" nature of the compiler.[4] Pfeiffer thought of the Elohist as a priest, in whom could be discerned the germs of the interests that were to produce the Priestly Code,[5] while the majority of scholars have come to the opposite conclusion and have placed him among the prophets.[6] A narrative like Gen. 22, which is both E's masterpiece as literature, and his fullest treatment of sacrifice, combines both obedience and sacrifice.[7] Procksch remarked that the Elohist connected the two great events of the past, the exodus and the covenant to sacrifice (Exod. 12 : 21-23, 34 : 7 (cf. 11b).[8] While he has not been followed in the analysis, which gives the former passage to E, it remains true that sacrifice occupies an important place in this source.

---

[1] P. Volz and W. Rudolph, *Der Elohist als Erzähler: ein Irrweg der Pentateuchkritik* ? Giessen (1933); W. Rudolph, *Der "Elohist" von Exodus bis Josua.*

[2] O. Procksch, *Das nordhebräische Sagenbuch*, Leipzig (1906).

[3] Cf. M. Noth, *Überlieferungsgeschichte des Pentateuch*, Stuttgart (1948).

[4] The opposing of "prophet" to "priest" in this sense is now seen to have been an error of the Wellhausen school.

[5] R. H. Pfeiffer, *Introduction*, pp. 173-76. He cites E's references to libations of oil (Gen. 28 : 18, 35 : 14), tithes (Gen. 28 : 22), the avoidance of eating the ischial nerve (Gen. 32 : 32) and to the priestly functions of Moses appearing in Exod. 19 : 14ff, 24 : 6-8, 33 : 5ff.

[6] Older writers ascribed to E the words of Samuel "to obey is better than sacrifice," and cited the presence of the Ephraimite Joshua instead of a Levite in the tabernacle. The latter to E is a place of consultation, not a tent of meeting. E gives the name of prophet to Abraham (Gen. 20 : 7), Miriam (Exod. 15 : 20) and the Lord's people (Num. 11 : 25-29).

[7] Human sacrifice is not required, but animal sacrifice is.

[8] O. Procksch, *Das nordhebräische Sagenbuch*, p. 185.

Abraham's Sacrifice of Isaac (Gen. 22 : 1-14)

Basic to the interpretation of this story is the question of whether it is aetiological in character, and if so whether the aetiology is of a particular sanctuary or of a way of sacrifice. The present form of the story is that of the testing of a righteous man,[1] but this may have been laid over a cult saga. In vs. 14 the words after "he called the name" do not read like a place name (*Yahwê Yireʾê*), and Gunkel proposed,[2] that Jᵉruʾel, on the analogy of Penuel, would be a more convincing reading in an E narrative than Moriah.[3] Jᵉruʾel, however, is not even known to have been a sanctuary,[4] and a more prominent place seems required. Procksch and others have therefore argued for Shechem, in the sanctuary of which E is thought to have had a special interest,[5] but this does not seem in any way superior to the Chronicler's theory that it was Jerusalem (2 Chron. 3 : 1).[6]

If this story was indeed told of so important a sanctuary as Jerusalem, its significance goes beyond that of a purely local usage and approaches to an aetiology of sacrifice. It is then not merely the record of the passing of human sacrifice in a particular sanctuary, but rather in Israel as a whole.[7] Its full sacrificial voca-

---

[1] H. Gunkel (*HK*), p. 240.

[2] *Ibid.*, p. 241.

[3] The form Moriah based on a combination of *Yahweh* and *rāʾâ*, and the interpretation "*Yahwê Yireʾê*" could hardly be original in an E narrative. The latter is also superfluous in view of the further interpretation in vs. 14b.

[4] It is a place in the wilderness of Tekoa in 2 Chron. 20 : 16 and 20. Gunkel thought the distance from Beersheba would be about right, and such factors as the carrying of the wood and the fire, and the unlikelihood of being able to purchase a victim on the spot would agree with some such unpopulated waste, but less so the fact that Moriah was a mountain.

[5] Among the arguments advanced for Shechem have been the possibility of a confusion with Moreh (Gen. 12 : 6), the Samaritan tradition that it was Gerizim, the Syriac reading "land of the Amorites" and Wellhausen's suggested emendation to "sons of Hamor" (*Composition des Hexateuchs*, Berlin (²1889), p. 21). See O. Procksch (*KAT*), pp. 314ff.

[6] Against Jerusalem it is objected, however, that the identification is late and very likely of priestly origin, that the expression "land of Moriah" is inaccurate and the description "one of the mountains" too vague and that the later temple mount was in the hands of the Jebusites at the time.

[7] Cf. Procksch, *Theologie des Alten Testaments*, p. 53. While it is true that "the story contains no word in repudiation of human sacrifice" (Skinner (*ICC*), p. 332) it does not follow that "it rather implies the Jahveh might desire such a sacrifice" (Hooke (*ClarB*), p. 89). The astounding thing was not that Abraham's God should ask for human sacrifice, but that he should

bulary[1] suggests a developed cult, while the question of Isaac witnesses to the fact that Abraham was accustomed to sacrifice, that the customary sacrifice was likely to be an *ʿōlâ* and that for this a lamb (*śe*) was the appropriate victim.[2] The motive of the sacrifice was certainly a solemn one,[3] and Procksch's use of the incident as an illustration of Abraham's religion as an *"islâm,"* a total surrender to God, carried out in the fear of God (vs. 12),[4] seems better than Gray's attempt to make it illustrate "the completest harmony that existed between God and Abraham."[5]

The Sacrifices of Jacob

Although E has Jacob explicitly sacrificing in 31 : 54 and 46 : 1, he also shares J's practice of referring to patriarchal sacrifice obliquely under the terminology of the building of an altar, or the erection of a *maṣṣēbâ*. Jacob receives theophanies at Bethel (28 : 18, cf. 35 : 7), Mahanaim (32 : 2), Peniel (32 : 30) and Shechem (33 : 20, cf. 35 : 1), but only at the first and last is said to have erected an altar,[6] and only at Galeed-Mizpah, where no theophany is related, offers sacrifice (*zebaḥ*) (31 : 54).

Jacob at Bethel (Gen. 28 : 18, 31 : 13, 35 : 7)

This passage, although of great interest as a cult aetiology,[7] is

---

interpose to prevent it (J. H. Hertz, *Genesis*; *The Pentateuch and Haftorahs*, London (1929), p. 182). Further on the question of child sacrifice see below.

[1] E.g. *ʿōlâ, ʿāqad, šāḥat, ʿārak, śe, ʾaîl.*

[2] On the other side Maag's argument ("Der Hirte Israels," p. 26, A. 13) should be noted: "Man wird Gn. 22, 6ff. im Rahmen dieser Beobachtungen übergehen müssen; denn hier handelt es sich um ein Problem, das sich erst bei der Übernahme des Moria-Heiligtums durch die Vätergottverehrer ergeben hat. Erstgeborenenopfer hängt religionsgeschichtlich eindeutig mit landsässigem Bauerntum zusammen."

[3] Isaac was more than first-born child and highest natural gift. He was child of promise (G. von Rad (*ATD*), p. 209) and centre of the purpose of God.

[4] O. Procksch, *Theologie*, p. 54 (cited by B. Gemser, "God in Genesis," *OTS* XII (1958), p. 18). Procksch thinks that as a result of this incident Abraham came to a milder view of God, but that was later ((*KAT*), p. 319, *Das nordhebräische Sagenbuch*, pp. 342-43). He sees the offering as expiatory (*Theologie*, pp. 560, 656).

[5] G. B. Gray, *Sacrifice in the Old Testament*, p. 92.

[6] In 28 : 18 it is a *maṣṣēbâ* Jacob sets up, and this is probably also the case in 33 : 20, where the use of the verb *nāṣab* strongly suggests that *maṣṣēbâ* should be read for *mizbēaḥ*. At Bethel, however, in 35 : 7 an altar is built.

[7] G. von Rad (*ATD*), p. 250 finds the aetiology more prominent here than in Ch. 22, where it has been subordinated to an event in Abraham's life. In

less so for Israelite sacrifice, as the ritual in use at Bethel does not seem to have been followed elsewhere. The oil (*šemen*) which is poured (28 : 18 *yāṣaq*) or smeared (31 : 13 *māšaḥ*) and the drink-offering (*nesek*), which was poured out (*nāsak*) (35 : 14)[1] on the *maṣṣēbâ*, were in a sense sacrificial, but do not throw light on the altar sacrifices, with which this investigation is concerned.[2]

In the "return to Bethel" passage, however, in 35 : 7, an altar is built, as commanded in 35 : 1, and sacrifices apparently offered. From the context of "the putting away of the foreign gods" (vss. 2-4), these would appear to have been of penitence. If Alt is right in seeing in this passage the *hieros logos* of a pilgrimage from Shechem to Bethel,[3] the element of penitence seems to have been to the fore in this worship.

Jacob and Laban (Gen. 31 : 43-55)

This passage in E gives the full account of the covenant between Jacob and Laban of which the J fragments were discussed above. Vs. 45 describes Jacob's setting up of a *maṣṣēbâ*, but as the verb *rûm* is used and the references which follow are not to worship, but to territorial boundaries, it is probable that the pillar was a boundary stone.

A minor difficulty is presented by the "brethren" of vs. 54, whom Jacob calls to the sacrificial meal. Presumably it is a covenant meal, that is being described, yet Laban is not said to partake, but the "brethren" of Jacob. If the passage stood alone, it would be

---

particular the giving of tithes (cf. Amos 4 : 4), and the practice of anointing the Bethel *maṣṣēbâ* with oil are explained. For the pre-history of the Bethel sanctuary see V. Maag, "Zum Hieros Logos von Beth-El," *Asiatische Studien* (*Zeitschrift der Schweizerischen Gesellschaft für Asienkunde*) V (1951), pp. 122-33.

[1] The suggestion that vs. 14 should be read after vs. 8, as a continuation of the obsequies of Rebekah's nurse, Deborah, although favoured by Gunkel (*HK*), p. 379, and Skinner (*ICC*), pp. 424ff. proceeds from the perhaps unnecessary assumption that neither J nor P would have spoken of a *maṣṣēbâ*.

[2] The oil was probably thought of as an anointing with an unguent (W. R. Smith, *The Religion of the Semites*, pp. 232ff, 383ff), rather than as a drink-offering poured out like blood or wine. However, on the use of the verb *yāṣaq* instead of *māšaḥ* in 28 : 18 see C. R. North, "The Religious Aspects of Hebrew Kingship," *ZAW* L (1932), p. 15.

[3] A. Alt, "Die Wallfahrt von Sichem nach Bethel," now in *KS* I, pp. 79-88. When Ch. 34 is removed as a separate source, 35 : 1ff. follows directly on the reference to Shechem in 33 : 20.

more natural to see Jacob's sacrifice, as one of thanksgiving at the satisfactory settlement that had been reached. In such a sacrifice (*zebaḥ*) a meal for his retinue would naturally be included. Laban is still present on the morning of the morrow, however, (32 : 1 (31 : 55)) and it is probable that it was the covenant meal with him that was described in vs. 54, as in vs. 46 (J), and that the difficulty occurred in the combination of the two sources.[1]

Some scholars speak of the parties spending the night together in the holy place (sanctuary), but this may be building too much on the words "they tarried all night in the mount." The eating together may be the sign of restored friendship and trust, or in itself the end of the feud.

Jacob at Beersheba (Gen. 46 : 1)

Zebāḥîm now occurs in the plural for the sacrifices Jacob offered in Beersheba, before going down to Egypt to see the long lost Joseph. Source analysis is necessary to determine, whether the passage goes with what precedes, or with what follows. Holzinger thinks that it has nothing to do with the following theophany, but concludes the preceding narrative. Jacob offers a thankoffering for the preservation of Joseph.[2] This is unlikely and has not been generally followed.

Alternatively the sacrifice may be seen as a thank offering for the accomplishment of the first stage of the journey from Hebron to Beersheba. It is not clear, however, that the scene in Ch. 45 is Hebron, although Jacob was there, when last noticed in Ch. 37 : 14 (J). A journey to Egypt from Hebron would hardly go via Beersheba especially with the wheeled waggons Pharoah had sent, and in fact it is only from Beersheba forwards that the waggons are mentioned

---

[1] H. Gunkel (*HK*), pp. 345-46, 351 thinks that the subject of vs. 54 was really Laban, who alone in the narrative has brethren (vs. 23), but that his name was replaced by that of Jacob to avoid the scandal of having this Israelite sanctuary erected by foreigners (p. 350).

[2] H. Holzinger (*KHC*), p. 248. So also O. Procksch, *Das nordhebräische Sagenbuch*, p. 54: "Man hat an ein Dankopfer zu denken und darum 46. lb noch zu c. 45 zu ziehen." He omits "and came to Beersheba" as redactional. W. Zimmerli, *Geschichte und Tradition von Beerseba im Alten Testament*, Göttingen (1932), p. 13 begins the E section with vs. 2, and says that to have E relate the offering is to destroy the surprising element in E. He thinks the offering stood in J and regards the passage as the *hieros logos* of a pilgrimage to Beersheba to offer to the "Fear" of Isaac.

as the means of transport (vs. 5). It is probable then, that E's tradition placed Jacob's home in Beersheba,[1] and that it was in Beersheba that the journey began.

There seems no good reason to deny then that the reassuring vision preceded Jacob's departure for Egypt, and was in fact the answer to a request made in his sacrifice. Viewed in this light, the sacrifice had been an expression of Jacob's fears and uncertainties. His fears were not so much of Joseph's displeasure at his brethren (Gen. 50 : 15), as of possible divine displeasure if he should leave the Land of Promise. This course had been forbidden to Isaac in this very town of Beersheba in 26 : 2. Weighty consequences might follow from such a step (as in fact they did) and only the assurance of the divine will could persuade him to go forward. Solemn motives must, therefore, be seen as actuating his sacrifice.[2]

Sacrifices in the Wilderness

Although E has no account of the Passover, nor of the request to leave Egypt to offer a sacrifice, he describes a number of sacrifices offered in the wilderness, chiefly in the vicinity of Sinai. The first of these with its reference to a named altar, but not to any sacrifice offered on it is reminiscent of the patriarchal materials examined above.

The Altar at Rephidim (Exod. 17 : 15-16)

The victory over Amalek is celebrated by the erection of a named altar, but as is so often the case with such altars, the meaning of the name is uncertain.[3] Although the purpose of the altar seems to

---

[1] Zimmerli thinks that for E all the patriarchs live in Beersheba (*ibid.*, pp. 13-26).

[2] L. Rost ("Die Gottesverehrung der Patriarchen," *Congress Volume Oxford* 1959 (*VTSuppl.* VII), p. 354) thinks of a rite of "atonement" in preparation for the shepherd's half-yearly exchange of pastures: "Hier könnte ein alter Brauch von Kleinviehnomaden im Hintergrund stehen, wie er ähnlich auch in den Böcken für Jahwe und Azazel im Ritual vom Versöhnungstag erhalten geblieben ist: Vor dem herbstlichen Auszug der Herden in das Weidegebiet ruft man den Segen der Gottheit an. Dann handelt es sich hier um eine der üblichen Historisierungen eines viel älteren Brauchs."

[3] Vs. 15 reads "Yahweh is my banner" (*Yahwê nissî*), but vs. 16 has the difficult reading "a hand upon the *kēsyāh*." The latter could be simply emended to read "throne of Yah" (*kissê Yāh*), and understood as the ark (K. Möhlenbrink, "Josua im Pentateuch," *ZAW* LIX (1942-1943), pp. 16-24),

have been commemorative, a *mizbēaḥ* must have been also for sacrifices, and these may be assumed to have been of thanksgiving for the victory over Amalek. Whether *ʿōlâ* or *zebaḥ* were offered is not known.

Jethro's Sacrifice (Exod. 18 : 12)

Neither the conversion of Israel to the God of Jethro, as on the Kenite hypothesis,[1] nor the conversion of Jethro to the faith of Israel, is required by the wording of the chapter.[2] Nor is it clear that Israel is seeking covenant with Jethro,[3] rather than Jethro with Israel.[4] While the sacrifice could be explained as a simple thanksgiving meal, it is probable that covenant ideas were also present, and that these would partake to some extent of the solemn nature of those described in Exod. 24 : 1-11. *ʿōlôt*[5] and *zᵉbāḥîm*

---

but this introduces the ark into a narrative from which it is missing (R. Rendtorff, "Der Kultus . . .," *op. cit.*, p. 13) and requires the emendation of vs. 15 to "Yahweh is my throne," (*Yahwê kisʾî*) to bring it into line. It is simpler, and more in keeping with the narrative to read "banner" in both verses (M. Noth, *Das zweite Buch Mose* (*ATD*) (1959), p. 115), and to connect this to the "staff" of Moses, which has acted as an ensign. Sacrifices to this standard in the Assyrian sense (H. Gressmann (*SAT* 1, 2), p. 101) need not, however, be understood. The aetiology is rather of the holy war with Amalek, than of a Rephidim or Kadesh sanctuary, or the cult objects or usage there.

[1] See above pp. 41ff.

[2] C. Brekelmans has pointed out ("Exodus XVIII and the Origins of Yahwism in Israel," *OTS* X (1954), p. 216) that statements similar to Jethro's "Now I know that Yahweh is greater than all gods" (vs. 11) occur in 2 Kings 5 : 15, where a conversion is described, and in 1 Kings 17 : 24, where no more than a confirmation of something already acknowledged before is required.

[3] Much less that Israel was being inaugurated into a cult not previously practised.

[4] In favour of the former might be Jethro's superintendence at the sacrifices, and the fact that these were held at the sacred mountain of Midian, where he was priest, but Brekelmans, notes that it is Jethro, who comes to Moses, not Moses to Jethro, and compares the kings in Genesis, who seeing the prosperity of the patriarchs, seek covenant with them (pp. 217ff). Jethro was no more a convert to Israel's God, than Abimelech had been, when he said "we see plainly that the Lord is with you," (Gen. 26 : 28), nor does Israel become a convert to Jethro's God by partaking of his sacrificial meal, any more than Isaac became a convert to Abimelech's by accepting his hospitality (Gen. 26 : 30). Possibly the one seeking alliance had to offer the sacred meal (p. 221).

[5] So LXX probably rightly understanding the MT *ʿōlâ* as a collective.

are offered,[1] and Aaron and the elders of Israel eat bread (*ʾākal leḥem*) with Jethro.[2]

The Making of the Covenant (Exod. 24 : 3-8)

The E account of the covenant in vss. 3-8 describes the erection of an altar and twelve *maṣṣēbôt* (or stones) (vs. 4),[3] the offering of *ʿōlôt* and *zᵉbāḥîm šᵉlāmîm* by the young men (vs. 5), and the throwing of half the blood on the altar and half on the people (vss. 6-8).[4] The meal which follows in vs. 11 is probably not from the same source,[5] and cannot be certainly identified as a covenant meal, nor made integral to the present ritual.[6] It is improbable, therefore, that Robertson Smith's explanation of this ritual as a sharing in mystical life is the correct one.[7] The blood rite is more naturally understood with Davidson as "piacular, atoning for and consecrating the people on their entering upon their new relation to J",[8] or with Morris as purificatory "to signify the entry into a new state marked by cleansing from defilement and consecration to a holy purpose."[9]

---

[1] The use of the verb "took" (*lāqaḥ*), when followed by *lʾēlōhîm* is peculiar, and is emended by BH, with Syriac, Targum and Vulgate to "offered" (*qārab*).

[2] Why Moses is omitted is a matter of conjecture. Possibly he was already in covenant with Jethro, or the text is in disorder.

[3] MT reads "*maṣṣēbâ*" (sing.), and LXX and Samaritan "stones."

[4] One wonders if in an earlier version, the blood was not thrown on the *maṣṣēbôt* as representing the people. In the present version these play no role.

[5] The usual analysis gives vss. 1-2, 9-11 to a second source. Many scholars think this was J (cf. G. von Rad, *Das formgeschichtliche Problem . . ., GS*, p. 24), but others see in Exod. 34 the J account (cf. M. Noth (*ATD*), p. 161), and see here an unknown source (B. Baentsch, "Exodus . . ." (*HK*) (1903), p. 213). Alternatively, it might be vss. 3-8, that are from the unknown source and vs. 11b from E (M. Noth, p. 159).

[6] While not going so far as G. Beer (*HAT*), p. 126 in deleting "ate" and reading "drank" as "worshipped," one hesitates to assume with E. Meyer, *Die Israeliten*, p. 558 and L. Köhler, *Lexicon*, p. 152 a derivation of *bᵉrît* from *bārâ* "to eat." Cf. now the full discussion of E. Nielsen, *Shechem*, pp. 110-18 and what was written above on Gen. 15.

[7] See on Gen. 15. There is nothing to show that the division of the blood, the division of the animal into two parts and eating of a share of the flesh all stem from the same idea.

[8] A. B. Davidson, "Covenant," *DB* I (1898), p. 512.

[9] L. Morris, *The Apostolic Preaching of the Cross*, p. 71. The objection from the double application of the blood, that a consecrating of the divine partner was as unnecessary, as the propitiating of the human partner was unintelligible, cannot be pressed in view of the wide use of blood in the laws for the

With this would agree the use of *'ōlôt* and *šelāmîm*.[1] The common assumption that the latter were purely fellowship offerings is not borne out by the early references, in which they are associated with new ventures,[2] and occasions of solemnity in battle and disaster,[3] nor by the Ugaritic usage, where a propitiatory sense seems to predominate.[4]

The Sin in the Wilderness (Exod. 32 : 1-6)

It is unimportant for this investigation to determine if the golden calf motif is original to the present context, or a later addition.[5] The tradition of a great sin in the wilderness seems amply attested by such passages as Hos. 9 : 10 and Num. 25 : 1-5, and whether this took place in Moab (Num. 25) or Midian (Exod. 32), and whether or not it involved Baal worship,[6] it seems to have centred in such an orgiastic festival as that described in vs. 6.[7]

'Ōlôt and *šelāmîm* are offered and eating and drinking and "playing" follows. This included shouting and singing (vss. 17-18). The essentially joyous, and probably licentious nature of the occasion

---

purification of both persons and things. *Hizzâ* would, however, be more usual for this use than the *zāraq* of the present passage.

[1] The juxtaposition of *zebāḥîm* and *šelāmîm*, without the subordination of the former to the latter, as in later passages, occurs also in 1 Sam. 11 : 15 and Josh. 22 : 27, and perhaps indicates that they were once separate sacrifices.

[2] Exod. 32 : 6; 1 Sam. 11 : 15; 2 Sam. 6 : 17; 1 Kings 8 : 63.

[3] 1 Sam. 13 : 9; Judg. 20 : 26; 2 Sam. 24 : 25.

[4] So D. M. L. Urie, *op. cit.*, pp. 75-77. The references are examined below (Conclusion).

[5] It has long been held to be a criticism of Jeroboam's calf worship projected back into the wilderness period. The plural forms in vs. 8 "these be your gods, which brought you out of Egypt" are thought to point to Jeroboam's two images, rather than Aaron's one. For the bull figure, however, it is not necessary to come down to the time of Jeroboam, as it is known from Ugarit as the symbol of Baal, and is thought by Eissfeldt ("Lade und Stierbild," *ZAW* LVIII (1940-1941), pp. 190ff., esp. p. 203) to have been the symbol of a pre-amphictyonic Israelite group.

[6] Baal worship was not impossible in view of the presence of a name like Baal-Zephon in Egypt (Exod. 14 : 2). Cf. J. Gray, *The Legacy of Canaan*, p. 71.

[7] The analysis of R. H. Pfeiffer ("Images of Yahweh," *JBL* XLV (1926), p. 216), which makes the calf references in vss. 1b-5a, 7-8, 20-24, (30-34), 35 post-Jeroboamic, nevertheless allows vss. 1a, 5b, 6, (9-14), 15-19, 25-29 to an old source describing an orgiastic festival. Cf. now S. Lehming, "Versuch zu Ex. xxxii," *VT* X (1960), pp. 16-50.

is apparent, but what is not clear is that this was typical Israelite worship, rather than a foreign innovation.

The Intercession of Moses (Exod. 32 : 30-34)

These verses although containing no reference to a sacrifice have come into the discussion, through their employment by some recent scholars, as descriptive of the role of a covenant-mediator, who had regularly to intercede for the people, and if need be offer his life as expiation for them.[1] Without pronouncing on the existence of such an office, the interpretation of Moses' words as expressing the desire to die "for" the people, rather than simply "with" them, as favoured by some exegetes,[2] is in keeping with the suffering prophet role, which is so prominent in the later Old Testament. No object of the verb *kipper* is expressed in vs. 30, but it is not impossible that a propitiation of God is in view, unusual as this usage is.

Balaam and Balak (Num. 22 : 40-23 : 30)

The analysis of the whole Balaam pericope need not be gone into, as the sacrificial references occur only in the section 22 : 40-23 : 17, which is usually assigned to E.[3] They comprise the *zebaḥ* of 22 : 40, with which Balaam is greeted, and the *ʿōlôt* of 23 : 1-6 and 23 : 13-17, which precede the E oracles. The latter are a part of a supplicatory ritual, while the former is naturally understood as a sacrificial feast of welcome. Von Gall, however, notes the strangeness of the words "and sent to Balaam" in vs. 40, and explains them of the entrails of the sacrificial animals sent to him for hepatoscopy.[4]

[1] H. J. Kraus, *Gottesdienst in Israel*, München (1954), pp. 60-61.

[2] E.g. F. Hesse, *Die Fürbitte im Alten Testament*, Hamburg (Mikrodruck) (1951), p. 33 argues that Moses in vs. 32a prays first for forgiveness, without the offer of his life, and only in the event of his request being denied, is it his wish not to survive his people, but to die with them (vs. 32b). (So also J. J. Stamm, *Das Leiden des Unschuldigen in Babylon und Israel*, Zürich (1946), p. 71 and *Erlösen und Vergeben im Alten Testament*, Bern (1940), p. 60). The alternative view favoured above sees the offering of Moses' life in vs. 32b, rather than the prayer of vs. 32a, as the means of making the atonement mentioned in vs. 30 (so L. Morris, *op. cit.*, p. 144).

[3] The sacrificial section in 23 : 27-30 can hardly be introductory to Ch. 24, and by its repetition of the initial instructions of 23 : 1-6, which are no longer necessary in 23 : 13-17, shows itself as secondary.

[4] A. F. von Gall, *Zusammensetzung und Herkunft der Bileam-Perikope*, Giessen (1900), pp. 10-11.

On this view 22 : 40 becomes the first of the supplicatory rituals.[1] It is doubtful, however, if the passage is to be interpreted in this divinatory sense, for although divination might seem to be present in the number seven in the ritual,[2] and in some other obscure terms in the text,[3] a supplicatory ritual would hardly begin so casually, in view of the concern on the morrow for an auspicious site. It is not even certain that the verb *zābaḥ* is cultic in this case.[4]

The *ʿōlôt* of the next day, however, are solemn sacrifices to favourably dispose the deity. They were offered in each case by Balak, the Moabite king,[5] but the initiative lay with Balaam the Aramean, who prescribed the ritual. It is not clear that such sacrifices were thought of as un-Israelite,[6] or that the narratives need be dated late.[7]

The Elohistic Code (Exod. 20 : 23-23 : 19)

The Book of the Covenant deals for the most part with civil and humanitarian matters, with the exception of four sections which are so parallel to the Yahwistic Code of Exod. 34 that they must be an alternative version of the same original viz. 20 : 23-26, 22 : 20, 22 : 28-30 and 23 : 12-19. The majority of scholars have argued that the J version is the earlier,[8] but the strong defence of the priority

[1] Von Gall differs from most scholars in assigning the sacrificial references of 23 : 1, 2a, 3b and 4 to J, and 23 : 3a, 5 and 22 : 40 to E, as parallel rituals.

[2] Seven altars also figure in Babylonian incantation rituals, and were possibly associated with the seven evil spirits.

[3] *Šepî* in 23 : 3 might describe some kind of enchantment, and *śᵉdê ṣōpîm* in 23 : 14 a watching for bird-omens, but the reference to omens in 24 : 1 cannot be called in as evidence, as this is a J passage.

[4] So W. Rudolph, *Der "Elohist . . .,"* pp. 111-12; "Das "Opfer" in v. 40 hat nichts mit dem von 23 lf. zu tun; es handelt sich hier gar nicht in erster Linie um einen kultischen Akt, sondern um eine Bewirtung Bileams . . . (*zābaḥ* heisst hier "schlachten" nicht "opfern")."

[5] The singular verb in 23 : 2 and the pronoun "thy" in 23 : 3 show that Balaam should be deleted from vs. 2.

[6] 23 : 23 is probably not intended to distinguish Israelite ritual from that of Balaam, and should be read with RSV "no divination against Israel," rather than "no divination in Israel."

[7] The stereotyped form describing the offering ritual suggests a long history in the oral tradition, before it was written down. Perhaps 23 : 30 is due to this popular usage.

[8] E.g. J. Morgenstern, "The Oldest Document in the Hexateuch," *HUCA* IV (1927), pp. 1-138; G. R. Berry, "The Ritual Decalogue," *JBL* XLIV (1925) pp. 39-43; L. Waterman, "Pre-Israelite Laws in the Book of the Covenant," *AJSL* XXXVIII (1921-1922), pp. 36-54.

of the E version by other scholars[1] suggests that there is little to choose between the two in age.

In the altar law of Exod. 20 : 24-26 the reference to sacrifice is subordinated to the rule for the construction of the altar. It is implied that *ʿōlôt* and *šᵉlāmîm* of sheep and oxen will be sacrificed (*zābaḥ*)[2] in "all places" where God records His name. In 22 : 19(20) sacrificing (*zābaḥ*) to any god save to Yahweh is forbidden under threat of the *ḥērem*.[3] The prohibition of leaven, left over sacrifice and seething a kid in the mother's milk (23 : 18-19) have been discussed in connection with Ch. 34 and offer little of further interest, except that it is the "fat of my feast (*ḥāg*,)" rather than "the sacrifice of the Feast of the Passover" that is not to be left over until the morning.

The law of the first-born, however, in 22 : 28 (29) is different in form from that in 34 : 19, and in this difference presents one of the most discussed problems of Old Testament sacrifice. Are the words "the first-born of your sons you shall give to me" to be read as a command to child sacrifice? The presence of this command in the document that had related the story of Abraham's sacrifice of Isaac,[4] together with the implication of Ez. 20 : 25-26 that Yahweh had given commands that were not good[5] have led to the suggestion that child sacrifice must have been enjoined in the first codes.[6]

---

[1] E.g. R. H. Pfeiffer, "The Oldest Decalogue," *JBL* XLIII (1924), pp. 294-310; "The Transmission of the Book of the Covenant," *HTR* XXIV (1931), pp. 99-109.

[2] It is doubtful if anything is to be made of the fact, that the verb *zābaḥ* embraces both the *ʿōlôt* and the *šᵉlāmîm* (as e.g. that the burning of the *ʿōlâ* on the altar was not yet secure, as W. R. Smith, *Religion of the Semites*, p. 378 or that like the Phoenician *kālîl* it might have been eaten, as G. A. Cooke, *North Semitic Inscriptions*, p. 117). The omission of the appropriate verb in a list of sacrifices is paralleled in 2 Kings 16, where in vs. 13 the drink offering has its own verb (*nāsak*), while in vs. 15 it comes under the first verb (*qāṭar*).

[3] Many scholars emend *yoḥᵃrom* to *ʾᵃḥērîm* on the grounds that the application of the *ḥērem* against an individual was unlikely in an early document. This, however, leaves the sentence incomplete.

[4] But Isaac, while Abraham's first-born, is not a child in the narrative, and his consent to the transaction makes his sacrifice quite different from child sacrifice.

[5] The context in Ezekiel is of child sacrifice, but see the discussion of the passage below.

[6] O. Eissfeldt, *Molk als Opferbegriff im Punischen und Hebräischen und das Ende des Gottes Moloch*, Halle (1935) thinks sacrifices to Moloch were not to a separate god, but were in "votive offering" to Yahweh, and occurred in

Against such an interpretation, however, must be placed a number of considerations. The instances of human sacrifice in the Old Testament, those of Jephthah, Hiel, Mesha and Ahaz, are clearly regarded as exceptional and called forth by grave circumstances.[1] No support can be found in such instances for a universal sacrifice of first-born. A greater or lesser degree of non-Israelite influence is present in most cases. They stand at most on the outer edge of Yahwism, and can hardly be cited for the practice of Yahwism, when such prohibitions as Lev. 18 : 21, 20 : 2-5 and Deut. 12 : 31, 18 : 10 stand in the Codes. While these prohibitions no doubt have in view the later Moloch worship, which became rife in the last days of the kingdom, the tradition of the redemption of the first-born is already in the Yahwist Codes, and there is no good reason for interpreting the "giving to" Yahweh of Exod. 22 : 28(29) in any other way.[2]

Conclusion

The Elohist mentions sacrifice about the same number of times as the Yahwist. A significant number of cases still come into the first category of "occasions marked by a sense of sin or solemnity." Only two—and both possibly non-Israelite sacrifices—come into the second category lacking these elements. The necessity of purification before the approach to Yahweh is stressed in an incident like that of Gen. 35 : 2,[3] while in Exod. 24 : 5 this purification is expressly achieved by sacrifice.

Yahwism down to the Deuteronomic Reform. The rendering of Moloch as "votive offering" does not, however, suit such passages as Lev. 20 : 5 and 1 Kings 11 : 7, where the name of a god seems required (So E. Dhorme, *L'évolution religieuse* . . . Vol. I, pp. 213-14; E. Jacob, *Theology of the Old Testament,* p. 60).

[1] The point made by A. S. Kapelrud, "King and Fertility," *Interpretationes ad Vetus Testamentum pertinentes Sigmundo Mowinckel,* Oslo (1955), pp. 118ff. that these sacrifices were from the families of kings and leaders and possibly connected with fertility rites should not be missed (see below on 2 Sam. 21 : 1-14).

[2] On this Wellhausen may be quoted with approval "The offering of the human first-born was certainly no regular or commanded exaction in ancient times; there are no traces of so enormous a blood tax . . ." *Prolegomena,* p. 89.

[3] Such an incident could not have been exceptional. The Yahwist also stresses that the people must be clean to stand before Yahweh (Exod. 19 : 22; Num. 11 : 18). Köhler thinks the question of Abimelech to David at Nob (1 Sam. 21 : 5) must have been typical (*Hebrew Man,* E. T. London (1956), p. 88). Wellhausen (*Prolegomena,* p. 71) and Robertson Smith (*Reli-*

That the Elohist has a sense of sin, few will be disposed to deny,[1] but that this need not be a post-prophetic development, has not perhaps been sufficiently recognized.[2] The discovery that the "prophetic" concern for the widow and the orphan was a Ugaritic commonplace[3] greatly modifies the picture of pre-prophetic religion drawn by Wellhausen.

---

gion of the Semites, p. 434) agree that there was a sanctifying before sacrifice, but the latter warns against understanding this as sorrow for sin (see below in Ch. VI).

[1] He is thought to have consciously corrected the Yahwist in the direction of a higher moral standard in the narrative of Abraham's wife-denial and expulsion of Hagar, and in that of Jacob's deceiving of Esau and Laban.

[2] Among older scholars, who recognized an ethic before the prophets, R. Dobbie ("Deuteronomy and the Prophetic Attitude to Sacrifice," *SJT XII* (1959), p. 71) lists H. G. Mitchell, *The Ethics of the Old Testament*, Chicago (1912), pp. 19ff. and J. M. P. Smith, *The Moral Life of the Hebrews*, Chicago (1923), pp 1-70, and among recent discussions N. Porteous, "The Basis of the Ethical Teaching of the Prophets," *Studies in Old Testament Prophecy* (ed.) H. H. Rowley, Edinburgh (1950), pp. 154-56.

[3] E. Hammershaimb, "On the Ethics of the Old Testament Prophets," *Congress Volume Oxford* 1959 (*VTSuppl* VII), pp. 75-101.

REFERENCES TO SACRIFICE IN THE ELOHIST

Reference	Incident	Terms Used		Primary or Secondary	Israelite or Foreign	National or Individual	Special or Regular
A. Where a sense of sin or solemnity is present							
Gen. 22 : 1-14	Abraham's Sacrifice of Isaac	*ʿōlâ*	*ʿālâ*	Primary	Israelite	Individual	Special
35 : 7	Jacob at Bethel	*mizbēaḥ*		Primary	Israelite	Individual	Special
46 : 1	Jacob at Beersheba	*zᵉbāḥîm*	*zābaḥ*	Primary	Israelite	Individual	Special
Exod. 24 : 3-8	Making of the Covenant	*ʿōlôt* *šᵉlāmîm zᵉbāḥîm*	*ʿālâ* *zābaḥ*	Primary	Israelite	National	Special
32 : 30-34	Intercession of Moses		*kipper*	?Primary			
Num. 23 : 1-6	Balak's Sacrifice	*ʿōlâ*	*ʿālâ*	Primary	?Non-Isra.	Individual	Special
23 : 13-17				Primary	?Non-Isra.	Individual	Special
23 : 27-30				Secondary			
B. Where a sense of sin or solemnity not present							
Exod. 32 : 1-6	Sin in the Wilderness	*ʿōlôt* *šᵉlāmîm*	*ʿālâ* *nāgaŝ* *ʾākal* *zābaḥ*	?Primary	?Non-Isra.	National	Special
Num. 22 : 40	Balak's Feast		*zābaḥ*	Primary	?Non-Isra.	Social	Special
C. Doubtful or unclassifiable passages							
Gen. 28 : 18	Jacob at Bethel	*maṣṣēbâ šemen*	*yāṣaq*				
31 : 13			*māšah*				
35 : 14	Jacob at Bethel	*maṣṣēbâ nesek* *maṣṣēbâ šemen*	*nāsak* *yāṣaq*				
33 : 20	Jacob at Shechem	*maṣṣēbâ*					
31 : 43-55	Jacob and Laban	*zebaḥ* *zābaḥ*	*ʾākal*	Primary	?Israelite	?Covenant	Special
Exod. 17 : 15-16	Altar at Rephidim	*mizbēaḥ*		Primary	Israelite	National	Special
18 : 12	Jethro's Sacrifice	*zᵉbāḥîm ʿōlâ ʾākal*	*lāqaḥ*	Primary	?Midianite	National	Special
	Elohistic Code						
20 : 24-26	Altar of Earth	*šᵉlāmîm ʿōlâ*	*zābaḥ*	Primary	Israelite	Individual	Regular
22 : 19	Not to other gods		*zābaḥ*				
22 : 28(29)	Firstlings & First-born		*nātan*				
23 : 18a	Not with leaven	*zebaḥ*	*zābaḥ*				
23 : 18b	Not left over	*ḥāg*					
23 : 19	Kid in Mother's milk		*bāšal*				

CHAPTER FOUR

JOSHUA AND JUDGES

Joshua

The traditions of the *Landnahme* in the Book of Joshua are more difficult to work with than those of any other part of the Deuteronomic Work of History. It is well known that the cultic tradition of this book and that of Chronicles were the first casualties to the attack of the higher critical school.[1] Passages that would have given support to traditional views of a cultus, instituted by Moses were ascribed to the inventive partisanship of P. This explanation may still be resorted to for 13 : 14, 20 : 1-6, but it is doubtful whether the traditions of cultic celebrations of such sanctuaries as those of Gilgal, Shechem and Shiloh can be so easily disposed of. The tradition history school has done much to restore the balance at this point.

The Passover at Gilgal (Josh. 5 : 10-12)

The grounds on which this passage was assigned to P were numerous,[2] but in the opinion of recent investigators do not rule out the possibility that behind the present form of the narrative is to be discerned the *hieros logos* of the sanctuary at Gilgal.[3] This

[1] See the author's work, *op. cit.*, p. 8ff.

[2] When the two aetiologies of the name Gilgal in 4 : 20-5 : 8 were removed, the passage followed immediately on P in 4 : 19 and gave a typical P dating of the 10th and the 14th of the first month for the Passover. The P rule of Exod. 12 : 48, that only the circumcised could partake of the Passover, was taken care of by the fiction of 5 : 2-8. The link between Passover and Unleavened Bread, which is not earlier than D, already occurs in 5 : 11. The words "the parched corn" and "on the morrow" were thought to be derived from the sheaf offering of the 16th Nisan in Lev. 23 : 9-14, and the continuance of the manna till this date, was in contradiction to E's view (Exod. 16 : 35) that the manna had ceased at the border of Canaan i.e. before crossing the Jordan. P stylistic traits were found in such terms as "the selfsame day" (vs. 11).

[3] The words "on the morrow" were not read by the LXX, and an original core, which was not in contradiction to Exod. 16 : 35, or dependent on Exod. 12 : 48 and Lev. 23 : 9-14, might once have existed. That Passover and Unleavened Bread were connected before Deuteronomy, is suggested by

great rallying-place of the tribes under Samuel and David[1] was the scene of the many "returns" of Joshua (10 : 6, 10 : 43, 14 : 6), and must have become an Israelite sanctuary at this time.[2] Möhlenbrink thought that it had been the cultic centre for the three tribes of Benjamin, Reuben and Gad,[3] but Kraus argued from the motif of the "twelve stones" that no less than the twelve tribe amphictyony had met at Gilgal.[4] He saw in the difficult geographical note of Deut. 11 : 29 connecting Gilgal to Shechem a suggestion that the old ceremonies of Shechem had been transferred to Gilgal.[5] He believed he could construct from the sources a description of a Gilgal *Maṣṣôt* festival centring in an ark procession and a ritual re-enactment of the crossing of the Red Sea.[6]

Various elements of Kraus' theory have been challenged,[7] but

---

the old law of Exod. 34 : 25 forbidding the bringing of leaven near the blood of the Passover (cf. J. Pedersen, *Israel*, E.T. III-IV, London (1940), p. 385). One tradition at least reflects an important celebration of Passover early in Israel's possession of the land (2 Kings 23 : 22).

1 It was the place of Saul's accession to the kingship in 1 Sam. 10 : 8 and 11 : 15, and of David's renewal of his kingdom in 2 Sam. 19 : 15. See K. Galling, "Bethel und Gilgal," *ZDPV* LVI (1943), pp. 140-55, and J. Muilenburg, "The Site of Ancient Gilgal," *BASOR* CXL (1955), pp. 11-27.

2 The view of Y. Kaufmann, *The Biblical Account of the Conquest of Palestine*, p. 67 that Gilgal's significance was not cultic, but purely military, as a base camp, does not explain its prominence as a sanctuary in the time of Samuel and the later period (2 Kings 2 : 1, 4 : 38; Amos 4 : 4; Hos. 4 : 15, 9 : 15, 12 : 11.)

3 K. Möhlenbrink, "Die Landnahmesagen des Buches Josua," *ZAW* LVI (1938), pp. 238-67.

4 H. J. Kraus, "Gilgal," *VT* I (1951), pp. 181-99.

5 *Ibid.*, p. 194. E. Sellin, *Gilgal*, Leipzig (1917) thought of a Gilgal near Shechem, but the location of Gilgal near the Jordan is well attested (2 Kings 2 : 1; 2 Sam. 19 : 15; Judg. 3 : 19).

6 Kraus' arguments for the existence of this combined Passover-*Maṣṣôt* feast in the time of the amphictyony were further elaborated in "Zur Geschichte des Passah-Massot-Festes im Alten Testament," *EvTh* XVIII (1958), esp. pp. 54-58, and p. 65.

7 M. Noth doubts the repetition of the Red Sea wonder, but acknowledges the connection to the ark (*Das Buch Josua* (*HAT*) (²1953), p. 33). C. A. Keller, "Über einige alttestamentliche Heiligtumslegenden II," *ZAW* LXVIII (1956), p. 91 thinks, however, that the tradition elements, which contain the ark, do not belong to the oldest tradition strata. R. Rendtorff, "Der Kultus," *op. cit.*, pp. 10-11 remarked that although the transfer of the amphictyonic centre from Shechem to Gilgal stood in tension with Alt's theory of the transfer from Shechem to Bethel (see above), it was an unproved postulate that the amphictyony always needed to meet in the same place. E. Kutsch ("Erwägungen zur Geschichte der Passafeier und des Massotfestes," *ZThK*

the basic assumption of the antiquity of the three main elements—the circumcision (5 : 2-9), the Passover (5 : 10-12) and the appearance (5 : 13-15) seems sound.[1] The suggestion of the narrative, that a preparation for the Passover by circumcision was required, is significant for the solemn view.

The Curse on Jericho (Josh. 6 : 26)

What were the misfortunes of Hiel? Kuenen assumed that the two sons of Hiel were "sacrificed ... " to avert the wrath of the deity whose possession he violated,[2] but Dillmann thought this "an unprovable assumption."[3] Foundation sacrifices might explain the reference,[4] but so also might sickness or some other untoward circumstance. It is not therefore certain that the passage should be classed as a sacrifice, but if so it would come under the heading of propitiation.[5]

The Covenant at Shechem (Josh. 8 : 30-35, Josh. 24; Deut. 11 : 26-32, Deut. 27)

The latter two of these passages stand to the former two in the

N.F. LV (1958), pp. 20off) objected that Passover and *Maṣṣôt* were not combined until the exile, and restated the argument from the calendrical framework, that the passage was from P. See further on Deut. 16 below.

[1] Cf. J. Bright, *Joshua* (*IB*) II (1953), pp. 573ff.

[2] A. Kuenen, *An Historico-Critical Inquiry into the Origin and Composition of the Hexateuch*, E.T. London (²1886), p. 240.

[3] A. Dillmann, *Die Bücher Numeri, Deuteronomium und Josua* (*KEH*) (²1886), p. 466.

[4] So T. K. Cheyne, "Hiel," *EB* II (1901), col. 2063.

[5] Opinions differ on the relation of this curse on the rebuilder of Jericho, to the record of the misfortunes that befell Hiel, when he rebuilt that city in 1 Kings 16 : 34. Noth thinks its presence in an appendix here implies that it was not known to the collector of the aetiological traditions, but came in only with Dtr. The formulation of the Book of Kings is therefore the earlier ((*HAT*), p. 41; "Bethel und Ai," *PJB* XXXI (1935), pp. 27ff.). Steuernagel thought, however, that the curse was very old, and like the oracle of Ch. 10 : 12, possibly came from the Book of the Upright. He said that the misfortunes of Hiel would have raised no interest had the ancient curse not been remembered, and concluded "es ist daher falsch, wenn man meint, unser Spruch sei auf Grund jenes Ereignisses formuliert," (*HK*), p. 231. It is possible, of course, that the curse belonged originally to some unnamed city, as the name of Jericho is missing in the LXX and seems to spoil the metre. It is certainly difficult to reconcile it with the continuous occupation of Jericho, which seems to be implied in Judg. 3 : 13 and 2 Sam. 10 : 5. A. Dillmann (*KEH*), p. 467 thought an unwalled hamlet grew up again on the site and that this was fortified by Hiel, but Steuernagel doubted if the verb *yāsad* could be used for the fortifying of the city.

relation of command to fulfilment. There are good grounds for assuming that both pairs were once more closely related than at present, and that Deut. 27 is to be connected to Deut. 11 : 31-32,[1] and Josh. 8 : 30-35 read as part of Josh. 24.[2] A satisfactory reconstruction has been worked out by Simpson who gives the sequence of the command as Deut. 27 : 2, 11 : 29b-30, 27 : 5-8 and the fulfilment as Josh. 24 : 1-18, 25, 8 : 30-34.

What was the origin of these sources? It is almost universally recognized that they were not free constructions of the Deuteronomist.[3] The use of *šelāmîm* rather than *zebāḥîm* for sacrifice (Deut. 27 : 7; Josh. 8 : 31) is unparalleled in the Deuteronomist, while the injunction to raise an altar on Mt. Ebal seems inconsistent with the demand for centralization.[4] The injunctions for the altar (Deut. 27 : 5-6) are closely related to those of the Book of the Covenant (Exod. 20 : 24-25) and suggested to older critics the presence of an E core in these verses.[5] Gressmann thought that the earliest reference was to a *maṣṣēbâ* (as in E), rather than an altar

---

[1] The removal of the Deuteronomic Code (Chs. 12-26) from its present position, and the omission of the bridge words in 11 : 31-32 and 27 : 1 would bring together the two Deuteronomy passages so that the second (27 : 2ff.) would closely follow the first (11 : 26-30).

[2] Josh. 8 : 30-35 should be removed from its present unsuitable position. 9 : 3 connects to 8 : 29, and both the MT order of 8 : 30-35 after 8 : 29, and the LXX order of it after 9 : 2, breaks this connection. A later place in the book is necessary, if the book's own account, that the central highlands did not fall into the hands of Ephraim until Ch. 17, is to be accepted. Only after this had taken place could the festival of the text have been celebrated on Mt. Ebal. Cf. E. Meyer, *op. cit.*, pp. 542-61; C. A. Simpson, *The Early Traditions of Israel*, pp. 644 and 646-7.

[3] E. Auerbach, "Die grosse Überarbeitung der biblischen Bücher," *Congress Volume Copenhagen* 1953 (*VTSuppl.* I) (1953), p. 3 is almost alone in his view that Josh. 24 is a "typical Deuteronomic construction of exilic origin."

[4] It might be argued from the fact that the Deuteronomist made no effort to bring the material of his history of the earlier time into line with this demand, that he did not expect centralization before the temple was built. It is more probable, however, that while allowing older materials to stand, he would not himself in a narrative of his own composition, have encouraged another altar.

[5] So Dillmann (*KEH*), Holzinger (*KHC*), Steuernagel (*HK*) and especially Sellin, *Gilgal*, pp. 22, 28, 50-52; S. Mowinckel, *Segen und Fluch in Israels Kult und Psalmdichtung* (*Psalmenstudien* V), Kristiana (1924), pp. 97-107. M. Noth, however, *Das System*, pp. 140ff. strongly argued against an E core and saw only the hand of D. Cf. now the very full discussion of E. Nielsen, *Shechem*, pp. 37-141, esp. p. 61.

on the ground that "*maṣṣēbôt* are older than altars,"[1] but Meyer took the altar and sacrifice to be the original part of the story.[2] The sacrifices mentioned are *ʿōlôt* (verb *ʿālâ*) and *šelāmîm* (verb *zābaḥ*).[3] Meyer's emphasis on the centrality of the covenant meal[4] has been referred to in connection with Exod. 24 : 5-8, but again it must be noted that no meal is specifically mentioned here. The references to "eating" and "rejoicing before Yahweh" in Deut. 27 : 7 are typical for Deuteronomy and are probably to be regarded, with Simpson,[5] as Deuteronomic additions.

If the sacrifice is rightly in place in Josh. 24, purification for covenant would again have to be seen as in Exod. 24. The motif of repentance and putting away of sin is in the foreground (vss. 19-24).[6]

The Covenant with Gibeon (Josh. 9)

It is not necessary to go into the problem of this chapter, as there is no reference to sacrifice in connection with this covenant.

The Inheritance of the Levites (Josh. 13 : 14; 20 : 3-6)

These passages are clearly secondary—in the former case to D and the latter to P. Neither are read by the LXX. The "offerings made by fire" (*ʾiššê*) in 13 : 14 are not read in the parallel in vs. 33,[7]

---

[1] H. Gressmann (*SAT*) I, 2, (^{2}1922), pp. 160-61.

[2] E. Meyer, *op. cit.*, p. 555. So also Holzinger (*KHC*), p. 99 suggested "Vermutlich ist v. 22-24 Ersatz für ursprüngliche Schilderung eines Bundesschlusses mit Opfer; ein Fragment eines solchen Berichts begegnet 8.30ff." Vss. 22-24, however, need not be a later substitution in view of the presence of this motif in Gen. 35 : 2.

[3] LXX *Thysian sōtēriou* apparently read *wa-yizbeḥû* as a substantive. Nielsen, *op. cit.*, p. 61 thinks the Shechem covenant involved only *šelāmîm*, but his grounds for omitting the *ʿōlôt* are not convincing, in view of his admission that they appear in four covenant traditions. Meyer, *loc. cit.* thought the adjective *šelēmôt*, in connection with the stones of the altar, and the verb *nûp*, forbidding the wielding of an iron tool, to go back in some way to the *šelem* offering and its "waving" (*nûp*).

[4] There is no ground for his view that the Israelites were taking over the regular Canaanite meal festival of Baal Berith.

[5] C. A. Simpson, *op. cit.*, pp. 316-17.

[6] W. Harrelson, *op. cit.*, p. 8 speaks of the "utmost seriousness" of the occasion, and thinks this element of ritual cleansing, along with the covenant renewal sacrifice, which followed it, an integral part of old Israelite worship.

[7] LXX reads vs. 14 with the exception of *ʾiššê*, but does not read vs. 33.

but come in apparently from Deut. 18 : 1.[1] The insertion in vs. 14 is impossible grammatically in view of the pronoun indicating that "the Lord God of Israel" alone is the Levites' inheritance. The original form is found therefore in vs. 33, and vs. 14 is superfluous.

Similarly the LXX does not read the reference to the manslayer's pardon at the death of the high priest (20 : 3-6). This comes in from Num. 35 and Deut. 19, although as a summary of the longer sections there, rather than a verbal citation. The fact that what are alternatives in Num. 35 "until the death of the high priest" and "until he stand before the congregation for judgment," are combined into one in vs. 6 proves that it is Josh. 20 which is the borrower.[2] The significance of the high priest's death as atoning belongs therefore to the discussion of Num. 35.

The Altar of the Eastern Tribes (Josh. 22 : 9-34)

This section has long been regarded as purely from P,[3] and "absolutely unhistorical."[4] It was a *midrash* to enforce the point of centralization, or some other post-exilic question, such as that of the loyalty to Yahweh of either the Transjordanian community,[5] or of the community in exile, who perhaps had built a symbolic altar. It was even suggested that it might have been a vindication of the growth of the synagogue.[6]

To the tradition history investigators, however, the story must go back to some altar or sanctuary, which was not acceptable to the Yahweh amphictyony at Shiloh. Can this altar be identified? The name *ʿēd* (witness) occurs more than once in connection with

---

1 The need of the Levites for sustenance was more a matter of concern consequent upon centralization than earlier, and the same is in part true of the cities of refuge in the next reference.

2 In Num. 35 the manslayer, if he had been adjudged innocent, remains in the city of refuge "until the death of the high priest" but if guilty is handed over to the avenger of blood for punishment. In either case he must stand before the congregation.

3 So J. Wellhausen, *Composition*, p. 135. P characteristics were seen in the designation of Israel as an *ʿēdâ* under the rule of *neśîʾîm*, in the leadership assigned to Phinehas rather than Joshua, in the mention of the tabernacle (*miškān*) which nowhere else appears in Joshua, and in the emphasis on centralization, which goes beyond Deuteronomy in taking the law of one altar back to the beginning.

4 This was Kuenen's phrase, *Hexateuch*, p. 107.

5 But was this under Jerusalem jurisdiction?

6 Cf. A. Menes, "Tempel und Synagoge," *ZAW* L (1932), pp. 270ff.

stones erected as memorials or boundary limits (Gen. 31 : 48; Josh. 24 : 27), but in the present chapter it has probably been substituted for a place name in vs. 34. Möhlenbrink believed this place was Gilgal,[1] and saw in the story a cult polemic saga of Shiloh against her rival Gilgal.[2] He claims that the sanctuary must have been in West Jordan, if it was to serve its purpose of binding eastern and western tribes together. While this would seem to be supported by "in the land of Canaan" in vs. 10, vs. 11 speaks of the altar as "facing the land of Canaan," and this together with *'el 'ēber*, would naturally suggest the east side. With this would go the reference to an "unclean land" in vs. 19. If the altar was originally on the east side, and vs. 10 was inserted to transfer it to the west, as Simpson suggests,[3] Gilgal can hardly have been the original reading.[4]

It is unlikely that a solution to this problem will ever be found, or that an analysis of the narrative could succeed in disentangling the early core. There is no way of knowing e.g. if the sacrificial references, which are repeated again and again, are evidence for an earlier time, or only for the time of P. Some points of interest arise. *'ōlâ* and *zebaḥ* in vs. 26 and vs. 28 are unexceptional, as are the *zibḥê šelāmîm* in vs. 23. But what is to be made of the distinction between *zebāḥēnû* and *šelāmēnû* separated by a *waw* conjunction in vs. 27.[5] Is *minḥâ* in vs. 23 and 29 to be read in P's sense of the cereal offering accompanying the other sacrifices, or is it an independent offering as in the earlier time?[6] What is to be made of an "altar not for sacrifices?" Did such purely memorial altars exist and could the altars of Exod. 17 : 15 and the patriarchal narratives have been such altars? Is vs. 17 with its reference to the guilt of Israel at Peor which had hardly yet been cleansed,[7] despite the

[1] LXX^B for *Gelîlôt* of vs. 10 is *Gilgal*, which is also an alternative to *Gelîlôt* in 15 : 7 and 18 : 17.

[2] K. Möhlenbrink, "Die Landnahmesagen," *op. cit.*, pp. 246-50.

[3] The name would then be dropped at the time of the transfer (Simpson, *op. cit.*, p. 399).

[4] The alternative explanation, that, it is vs. 11 which is added is favoured by Noth (*HAT*), p. 134.

[5] For the possibility of a distinction between *zebaḥ* and *šelem* see the Conclusion.

[6] Or is it to be read at all? Steuernagel (*HK*), p. 295 thinks that the LXX omits *minḥâ* and renders *zbḥ* twice in vs. 29, but this is uncertain. *Minḥâ* may, however, have been omitted in the LXX of vs. 23.

[7] The verb is *ṭāhar* not *kipper*.

plague that had been in the congregation evidence only for the post-exilic sense of sin (Holzinger), or for that of an earlier time?

Judges

The references to sacrifice in the Book of Judges played an important part in Wellhausen's treatment, but here as elsewhere his work was vitiated by the assumption that "the nearer history is to its origin the more profane it is."[1] He made much of the primitive elements revealed in the stories of Gideon, Manoah and Jephthah, but disallowed entirely such sacrifices of national penitence as those of 2 : 1-5, 20 : 26 and 21 : 4. The religio-pragmatic framework of the first of these was deuteronomic and late, while the "all Israel" motif of the others was a Priestly figment and even later—not earlier than the post-exilic theocracy.

More recent work, particularly that of Noth, has rendered both these judgments unlikely. An amphictyonic organization of the twelve tribes of Israel may be discerned in the period of the Judges, and to this organization the greater part of Chs. 20-21 belong.[2] In addition, investigations of the historical books have shown that much material, which was formerly assigned to a Deuteronomic redactor of the sixth or fifth century (as e.g. the cyclic scheme of idolatry, oppression, penitence and divine grace), must have belonged to the eighth century or earlier.[3] The early cult must, therefore have included such elements as the confession of national guilt in the turning away after foreign gods.[4] These considerations

---

1 J. Wellhausen, *Prolegomena*, p. 245.

2 M. Noth, *Das System*, pp. 162-70. It should be added, however, that Noth thought sacrifice to have played no great part in the amphictyony. He says that "religious observances apparently were not regarded as of prime importance in Israel," and that compared with such documents as those of Ugarit "the Old Testament shows surprisingly little interest in purely devotional events and problems" (*History of Israel*, p. 99). His argument that sacrifice has no place in Josh. 24 has been considered above. Evidence for sacrificial worship on the occasions of the meeting of the amphictyony is just as good as that for the recitation of the law, and even were it not, that fact would not tell us very much about the daily devotional life of the people.

3 O. Eissfeldt, *Geschichtsschreibung im Alten Testament*, Berlin (1948), p. 43.

4 A. Weiser, "Das Deboralied," *ZAW* LXXI (1959), p. 75 finds evidence for this in Judges 5 : 6-8 "they chose new gods, then was war in the gates." *Lāḥem* for *milḥāmâ* (war) is admittedly difficult and many emendations have

must have their bearing on the estimate of early Israelite sacrifice.

The Sacrifice at Bochim (Judg. 2 : 1-5)

The usual analysis of these verses gives the angelic movement of vs. 1a and the sacrifice of vs. 5b to an early source,[1] but deletes the mention of the people's repentance following the angelic rebuke as Deuteronomic. It is true that Deuteronomic phraseology is to be discerned in vss. 1b-3, but this is not so clear in vs. 4, which speaks of the people's weeping. If vs. 4b is allowed to stand, Bochim can be accepted as original in vs. 1 and vs. 5, and the aetiological explanation of this name becomes the point of the narrative.[2]

This seems preferable to the view that the intention of the narrative was to authenticate Bethel as the successor of Gilgal as the central sanctuary. There is no mss evidence for the deletion of Bochim. The LXX reading of "Bochim, Bethel and the house of Israel" seems to be an attempt to identify Bochim with the Bacuth of Gen. 35 : 8.[3] It is obviously conflate and cannot be held to be superior to the shorter reading of the MT text, which is confirmed by vs. 5. The site of this "Bochim" was probably as unknown to the LXX translators as it to us, but some old tradition of penitence must have been associated with the name. That sacrifice should be central in this tradition is significant.[4]

---

been proposed. The "choosing" of gods, however, is spoken of in 10 : 14, and "new gods" in Deut. 32 : 17. Weiser believes the Song of Deborah was a liturgy of the Yahweh cult before the monarchy. To him therefore, the theme of apostasy and penitence belongs to the earliest history of the Book of Judges.

[1] Many writers think the passage a continuation of the J account of Ch. 1, but C. A. Simpson, *op. cit.*, p. 327 and J. A. Bewer, "Critical Notes on Old Testament Passages," *Old Testament and Semitic Studies* (in Memory of W. R. Harper) Vol. II, Chicago (1908), pp. 211-14 favour E.

[2] So Gressmann (*SAT*), p. 144 and Hertzberg (*ATD*) (1953), p. 155.

[3] Other possibilities are *b*ᵉ*kā*ʾ*îm* (2 Sam. 5 : 23) and *bākā*ʾ (Ps. 84 : 7). LXX reads *klauthmōn* for both. Gressmann (*SAT*), p. 144 wonders if there is not some connection with the Valley of Achor, which was in the same general locality (Josh. 7 : 24). Bewer, who rejects the rendering of Bethel on the grounds that there was no evidence for Bethel as the central shrine, favours an emendation to *šekem*, and regards the passage as parallel to Josh. 24 (p. 213).

[4] The words "they sacrificed there" (*zābaḥ*), vs. 5, are not those used by J and E to record the first act of worship at a newly authorized sanctuary. Other aetiologies of cultic places follow the theophany with the words "he built an altar there to the Lord"—presumably the altar still stood in the time of the writer.

The Sacrifices of Gideon (Judg. 6 : 11-32)

It is evident that a number of accounts of the early worship at Ophrah are here combined. Leaving aside the account of the making of an ephod in Ch. 8 : 24-27, and the threshing-floor incident in 6 : 36-40, there still remains in 6 : 11-32 the following four elements —the call of Gideon (vss. 11-17), the entertainment of a stranger (vss. 18-21), the building of the altar *"Yahwê Šālôm"* (vss. 22-24) and the building of the Yahweh altar in place of the Baal altar on the hill-top (vss. 25-32). The problem of the chapter is whether all, or any of these elements originally belonged together. The first section can be shown to share with several Old Testament passages the form of a prophetic call.[1] The second section is also not without parallels, which may indicate a stereotyped description of hospitality.[2] Similarly vss. 22-24, if they had stood alone, would have been but one of many accounts of an altar building after a theophany, and the same is true of vss. 25-32.

Vss. 25-32 are usually regarded as an independent account of the transition from Baal worship to Yahweh worship, at the central sanctuary of the family of Joash.[3] Kittel found in the earlier sections also, an account of a transition in sacrificial ritual from food offerings laid out on a rock to an earth spirit, to a fire offering conveying the food in spiritualized form to a god, now conceived of as in heaven.[4] It is a question, however, whether Gideon intended an offering from the first, or a meal for a stranger.[5] It is unsafe

[1] E. Kutsch, "Gideons Berufung und Altarbau Jdc 6, 11-24," *ThLZ* LXXXI (1956), cols. 75-84 finds the four steps of vss. 14-17—the call, the objection, the over-ruling of the objection and the sign—also present in the calls of Moses (Exod. 3 : 10-12), Jeremiah (Jer. 1 : 5-10) and Saul (1 Sam. 10 : 1-7, 9 : 21).

[2] Cf. esp. Gen. 18 : 3-8.

[3] With this is combined the aetiology of the name Jerubbaal.

[4] R. Kittel, *Studien zur hebräischen Archäologie und Religionsgeschichte*, Leipzig (1908), pp. 98ff. and also in (*HSAT*) I (^{3}1909), p. 352.

[5] The word *minḥâ* is vs. 18 is a little strange for a meal, but is not necessarily an offering. The unleavened cakes of vs. 19 would be appropriate in an offering, but also in a meal prepared in haste. The provision was large for a meal, but so was that of Abraham in Gen. 18. The pouring out of the soup on the rock in vs. 20 sounds like a sacrifice, but this was not done by Gideon on his own initiative. Vs. 17b, in which Gideon already recognizes the supernatural quality of his visitor, does not go well with the suggestion of a meal, but is probably too early in its present place in the story, as it is only in vs. 21 that Gideon is aware of the identity of his visitor. On the other hand nothing is made of the slaughter of the kid (the verb is *ʿāśâ*), or any blood

therefore to assume a necessary connection between the meal and the sacrifice.

It is equally uncertain, whether the sacrifice is to be connected to the forgiveness of sin. An altar bearing the name "peace" possibly speaks of a reassurance of divine favour received through sacrifice, but it must be admitted that in the present obscure state of the narrative, thanksgiving might be the motive. In the second narrative, where a burnt offering of a bullock is offered,[1] together with the wood of the Baal asherah as fuel, a dedication offering for the new altar (vss. 25ff.) may be in view. Although this second account is later than the former, both are relatively early.[2]

The Shechemite Vintage Festival (Judg. 9 : 27)

The men of Shechem, who engaged in this wine feast, are Canaanites. Having gathered the grapes from their vineyards, they eat and drink and hold festival *'āśâ hillûlîm* in the house of their god. The word *hillûlîm* is used elsewhere only in Lev. 19 : 24, where it describes the fruit of a tree offered in its fourth year as *qōdeš hillûlîm* to the Lord. It would seem in this instance to be connected to the festival of firstfruits. There is probably also a connection to *hillēl* "to praise." The thanksgiving for the grape harvest degenerates into noisy hilarity and drunkenness, as the later Hebrew Feast of Tabernacles was inclined also to do. A festal meal is described here.

The Vow of Jephthah (Judg. 11 : 29-40)

A hero saga of Jephthah is here brought into connection with the aetiology of a women's festival in Gilead. The Gileadite hero

ritual. Moore (*ICC*) (1895), p. 183 and others, who were not convinced of a sacrificial intention, suggest that *minḥâ* and vss. 17b and 20, are additions to the story. Kutsch argues for the unity of vss. 11b-18, but must treat the story of the call as quite distinct from that of the altar building. His suggestion that the original nucleus was vss. 11a, 19-24, later supplemented by vss. 11b-18, is also not without its difficulties.

[1] There are some difficulties here also. Why the "second bull" (vs. 25)? And why "seven years old?" The latter words, which have no proper grammatical connection with the former, may in some way reflect the seven years of the Midianite bondage, but the former are unintelligible.

[2] C. F. Whitley ("The Sources of the Gideon Stories," *VT* VII (1957), pp. 157-64) sees no reason to make the theme of the destruction of the Baal altar late. He thinks vss. 25-32 link to vss. 7-10, where Israel's afflictions are attributed to her associations with the gods of the Amorites. He believes this to be an E theme rather than D (p. 160).

Jephthah, in a desperate situation comparable to that of Mesha, king of Moab, in 2 Kings 3 : 27, made a vow to sacrifice to Yahweh the first "comer out who comes out of the doors of my house to meet me." It was obviously a human rather than an animal sacrifice he intended, for although animals might be housed within, and even come out of the same door, by no stretch of imagination could they be said to be coming to "meet" him.[1] One might think he must have already had in view his daughter—who more likely than she to come to meet him?—but this was not the thought of the story-teller, who records the father's grief and prostration in vs. 35. This grief of the father and the annual mourning of the women are intelligible only on the view that the sacrifice of the girl was consummated. Dedication to religious life like that of Samuel (1 Sam. 1 : 11), or to unmarried seclusion, totally fail to explain the tragic pathos of the narrative.

Was human sacrifice then encouraged in Israel? This would be too far-reaching a conclusion to draw from the story. While it is true that Jephthah comes forward as a Yahweh enthusiast, it can hardly be pretended that a robber captain, of half Canaanite origin, who was *persona non grata* with his own tribe, represented the normal faith of Israel. It is misleading to say that his action is not condemned by the narrator. It is the latter's high art to leave the story to teach its own truth, untouched by moralizing. The lesson of this father's folly was unforgettable and unforgotten in Israel.[2]

The Sacrifice of Manoah (Judg. 13 : 15-23)

This story has both parallels with,[3] and differences from that of

---

[1] Not even a dog does this in the East. Kimchi's suggestion (cited Moore (*ICC*), p. 300) of alternatives to be understood in vs. 31 "(if unfit for sacrifice) will be the Lord's" and "(if suitable) I will offer it up as a burnt offering" makes nonsense of the suffix on the Hebrew verb *weha ʿalîtihû*.

[2] The later festival of the women (vs. 40) may have been linked to the "weeping for Tammuz," but, if so, the virgin's death has replaced that of the god. S. A. Cook, "The Theophanies of Gideon and Manoah," *JTS* XXVIII (1927), pp. 368-83 arguing from the name *Iphtah-el* (cf. Josh. 19 : 14, 27), which he rendered "El opens the womb," suggested the annual sacrifice of a virgin for fertility. Manoah's barren wife was benefited by such a rite in Zorʿah. The tradition of the disappearance of the "angel" in fire may reflect a burnt offering.

[3] In both an angel appears and a kid is prepared as a meal. The kid is placed on a rock and this by fire becomes an altar. Even the *minḥâ* reappears

Gideon in Ch. 6. Gideon had been permitted to prepare the meal before it was turned into a burnt offering, but Manoah is refused this permission and bidden offer a burnt offering.[1] When he does so, there is no suggestion of a miraculous flame coming out of the rock to consume it as in the former incident. In the second incident there is also the exchange of dialogue in which Manoah seeks to know the name of his visitor and receives the answer—possibly evasive—"wonderful."[2] Moore thinks that there is no need to find a change of source in the use of altar instead of rock in vs. 20, as the *ʿōlâ* would in any case convert the rock into an altar. A flat rock with cup-marks discovered by Hanauer at Zorʿah in 1885 has been suggested[3] as the altar of the text, but it is doubtful that Gressmann is right in seeing the narrative as an aetiology of this Zorʿah altar (pp. 240ff).The sacrifice of Manoah is one of reverence, but hardly of expiation, although its acceptance is interpreted as proving that Yahweh is peacefully disposed towards the worshippers (vs. 23).

The Sacrifice of the Philistines (Judg. 16 : 23)

In this case there is rejoicing "*śimḥâ*" (the first occurrence of this word, the verbal form of which, is to be so popular in Deuteronomy) as the *zebaḥ* is sacrificed[4] as a thanksgiving to Dagon for victory over

---

here, but is generally judged out of place alongside of *ʿōlâ*, as it was only in much later times that the *ʿōlâ* required the cereal accompaniment. These parallels probably belong to the "form" of this type of narrative.

[1] It is not certain that this more spiritualized trait is later. Moore remarks, that while there seemed to be a development from Gen. 18, where the divine visitors partake of the meal, to Judg. 6, where the meal is transmuted into a sacrifice, and Judg. 13, where the very idea of a meal is rejected (cf. C. F. Burney, *The Book of Judges*, London (1918), p. 348), this gives no guide to relative dating because in any case it was thought that Yahweh had been more intimate with man in early times (*op. cit.*, p. 320).

[2] It has been suggested by E. J. Young, *The Study of Old Testament Theology Today*, London (1958), pp. 97, 108 from this passage and Is. 9 : 6 that this was a divine name. The difficult words of vs. 19 are perhaps to be rendered with the LXX "who works wonders" (Moore (*ICC*)). The following words "and Manoah and his wife looked on" are best omitted.

[3] K. Galling (*Der Altar*), p. 64 thinks wrongly so. The Zorʿah altar is stepped, while that of the text was a primitive flat rock.

[4] Some have thought the verb *zābaḥ* inappropriate for the worship of a grain god Dagon. Philo Byblius attests the character of Dagon as a grain god (derived from *dāgān*) but Moore thinks that it is not until Rashi and Kimchi—possibly in explanation of 1 Sam. 5 : 4—that the legend of the fish form and the derivation from *dāg* arises (Moore, *op. cit.*, pp. 359ff.). If this is so, it is scarcely possible to see in the fish god the food god of a

the national enemy Samson.[1] Moore rightly warns against the assumption that the worship of Dagon always had a joyous and festive character.[2]

The Sacrifices of the Benjamite War (Judg. 20 : 26, 21 : 4)

The worth of these two chapters, Judg. 20 and 21, as a historical source, has been hotly contested since Wellhausen's emphatic rejection.[3] The negative attitude of the older critics has gradually given way to a more positive estimate,[4] but this does not carry with it the justification of the present form of the narrative, or of the references to sacrifice. The section 20 : 20-28 is probably the most suspect part of the chapter. The repetitiousness of the battle, extending into three days, and the large numbers of the slain—22,000 the first day and 18,000 the second day—are in contradiction to the more realistic figure "about 30 men" which shows through the narrative in vs. 31. The extension of "the weeping of Israel before the Lord" (vs. 23) into "weeping, fasting and offering burnt offerings and peace offerings" (vs. 26), is in contradiction to the late development of penitence and fasting in Israel. The justifi-

---

maritime people replacing the grain food god of the Canaanites (J. N. Schofield, *Religious Background of the Bible*, p. 82).

[1] The objection that this could not have been a victory festival (Kittel (*HSAT*), Hertzberg (*ATD*)) because of the time that had elapsed in which Samson's hair had grown, is not weighty.

[2] Moore (*ICC*), p. 358.

[3] Wellhausen regarded the exaggerated numbers and the picture of Israel as an *ʿēdâ* with the twelve tribes acting together under *neśîʾîm* as "priestly" in the worst sense. (*Composition*, pp. 232-38, *Prolegomena*, pp. 236-37).

[4] Gressmann (*SAT*), p. 262 thought that "the shame of Gibeah" at least stood in the tradition in the time of Hosea. He argued that it was better to refer Hosea 9 : 9 "they have deeply corrupted themselves as in the days of Gibeah" to this incident than to an extreme anti-monarchic judgment on the accession of Saul, who after all had been not crowned in Gibeah. Bewer ("The Composition of Judges, Chaps. 20, 21," *AJSL* XXX (1913-1914), pp. 149-65) raised a protest against theories of compilation, and argued for one basic document, worked over with only minor additions such as the large numbers and *šibṭê Yiśrāēl* or *benê Yiśrāēl*. Noth (*Das System* . . . Excursus IV, pp. 162-70 and on the *nāśî* Excursus III, pp. 151-62) showed that this latter element "the tribes of Israel" was the earliest, rather than the latest part of the chapters and belonged, along with the *neśîʾîm*, to the tribal amphictyony of the times of the judges. Eissfeldt ("Der geschichtliche Hintergrund der Erzählung von Gibeas Schandtat (Richter 19-21)", *Festschrift Georg Beer*, Stuttgart (1935), pp. 19-40) in his summing up of the discussion, emphasised the basic agreement of the chapters with the history as it can be reconstructed.

cation of these sacrifices at a place other than the central sanctuary, by the device of bringing, not only the ark, but an Aaronic high priest, to the shrine of Bethel, is in contradiction to all we know of the religion of Israel in the days of the judges, and betrays the hand of P.

Most of these objections have been met in one way or another by the writers mentioned above. Bewer thought the action limited to two days, rather than three, and deleted vs. 23, and the words "the second day," where they occurred. This would leave vs. 26 as the original narrative. Noth preferred the alternative that vs. 23 was an earlier form of vss. 26, 27a and 28, although itself not original.[1] He saw no reason to deny, however, that the ark had been at Bethel, and with this opinion Eissfeldt concurred.[2]

Whether the sacrificial reference is to be accepted, will perhaps turn on the question of the fasting and the meaning of *šelem*. Smend's view, based on 1 Sam. 31 : 13; 2 Sam. 1 : 12, 2 Sam. 12 : 16 that in the older time fasting was confined to mourning rites, and that such passages as Judg. 20 : 26 and 1 Sam. 7 : 6, which associated fasting with penitence were late, proceeded from the assumption that the early cult was uniformly joyful.[3] This assumption is the point at issue in the present discussion, and may not be taken for granted. Fasting as a means of supplication is resorted to by David on behalf of his sick child (2 Sam. 12 : 16), and was not impossible in the cult (cf. the Nazirite vows), and on the battlefield (cf. 1 Sam. 14 and the institution of the holy war). A similar answer must be given to the objection, that *šelem* had only a joyful sense in the earlier time, in view of the uncertainty of its original meaning.[4]

---

[1] M. Noth, *Das System*, p. 167.

[2] O. Eissfeldt, *op. cit.*, p. 38. M. Noth, *History of Israel*, p. 94 thought the verse evidence for the change of the amphictyonic central shrine from Shechem to Bethel, which had been hinted at in Gen. 35 : 2ff. W. F. Albright, *Archaeology and the Religion of Israel*, pp. 104, 108 who thinks that the high priesthood functioned in the time of the judges, accepted the reference to Phinehas also. (Also in "Excavations and Results at Tell-el-Fûl," pp. 47-48 cited by J. M. Myers, *Judges* (*IB*) II (1953), p. 819).

[3] R. Smend, *Lehrbuch der alttestamentlichen Religionsgeschichte*, p. 125. In later times a seer might also fast to get a revelation (Exod. 34 : 28; Deut. 9 : 9, 18; Dan. 9 : 3).

[4] The argument of S. Herner, that the use of this term for a fast, instead of a joyful meal, is a clear sign of P (*Die Opfermahle nach dem Priesterkodex*, Lund (1911), pp. 37-38, 40 and *Sühne und Vergebung in Israel*, p. 91) overlooks the probable more solemn early use. See on Exod. 24 : 5.

It would seem then that, if the arguments from "all Israel" and "Bethel" validate vs. 26a, no objection can be made to vs. 26b. The commentators are quite unanimous on the propitiatory purpose of the sacrifice here.[1]

A second sacrificial reference in somewhat similar terms in 21 : 4 is usually judged a doublet of the above, in view of the fact that the Israelites are again described as building an altar at Bethel, where this had already been done in 20 : 26. The occasion in Ch. 20 is, of course, different, but the relation of the two narratives is complicated. Possibly only the words regarding the altar are late, or vss. 4-5 should be read after vs. 7 with Gressmann. It is not possible to go into this further, but the passage, if not a doublet of 20 : 26, would be a verse of a similar kind and to be classified along with it.

Conclusion

Some seventeen instances of possible sacrifice in thirteen passages in Joshua and Judges have now been examined. Two have been deleted as very late additions (Josh. 13 : 14, 20 : 3-6). Two others are not definitely sacrifices (Josh. 6 : 26, Josh. 9), and one further case is of doubtful date (Josh. 22 : 9-34). In only two cases— both of them non-Israelite—does the fellowship theory find clear support (Judg. 9 : 27, 16 : 23). Parts of the passages concerning Gideon and Manoah might seem to belong in this category, but in both cases the evidence is uncertain. The solemn view is found then in the largest number of cases—five different passages. One of these, however, is a human sacrifice (Judg. 11 : 29-40).

These results depend in part on a new estimate of the age of the sources, and it must be asked if the attempt made here to push back the references to a sense of sin and sacrifice for sin into earlier times is legitimate. It is obviously necessary to distinguish between the theology of the Deuteronomic framework and the theology of the old sagas. An attempt to do this for Judges has been made by

---

[1] W. O. E. Oesterley, *The AbingdonC* (1929), p. 375 speaks of "an accumulation of propitiatory acts," Moore (*ICC*), p. 433 of "the most strenuous efforts to propitiate Yahweh." So also Burney, *Judges*, p. 477, Myers (*IB*), p. 818. W. B. Stevenson ("Hebrew ʿOlah and Zebach Sacrifices," p. 493) can hardly be followed in his description of the sacrifices here as "the return to normal life" after a day of mourning and fasting.

Jenni.[1] The newness of his approach is indicated in the opening sentences, where he remarks that the only commentary with a section on the theology of the Book of Judges is that of Burney, and then only four pages out of six hundred and sixty-two are devoted to this theme. Even the least theological of the old sagas (the story of Judges 9) is not free of theology, as the closing verses clearly show. It is interesting to find that under both of the headings, which Jenni employs to describe amphictyonic theology—"Jahwe, der Schutzherr Israels" and "Israel, die auf das Recht Jahwes verpflichtete Gemeinschaft"—the themes of the present discussion emerge. The sin of Baal worship is an offence against Yahweh as the only Lord (Judg. 6 : 25-32 — p. 269). Yahweh is a God who punishes sin (Judg. 16 : 28-31 — p. 271). Israel must serve only Yahweh and observe the law of the covenant of Yahweh (p. 271), and of its own inner life as a community (272). Offences against either law are judged and punished (Judg. 19-21). This concept of Israel under the judges as a people "under law" would have been incredible to Wellhausen, and in the writer's opinion, justifies the present attempt to modify his interpretation of early Israelite sacrifice.

---

[1] E. Jenni, "Vom Zeugnis des Richterbuches," *ThZ* XII (1956), pp. 257-74.

REFERENCES TO SACRIFICE IN JOSHUA AND JUDGES

Reference	Incident	Terms Used		Primary or Secondary	Israelite or Foreign	National or Individual	Special or Regular
A. WHERE A SENSE OF SIN OR SOLEMNITY IS PRESENT							
Josh. 5 : 10-12	Passover at Gilgal	*pesaḥ*	*ʿāśâ*	?Primary	Israelite	National	?Regular
Josh. 8 : 30-35, 24 : 1ff	Covenant at Shechem	*ʿōlôt* *šᵉlāmîm*	*ʿālâ* *zābaḥ*	?Primary	Israelite	National	?Regular
Deut. 11 : 26-32, 27 : 1ff							
Judg. 2 : 1-5	Sacrifice at Bochim		*zābaḥ*	?Primary	Israelite	National	?Regular
Judg. 11 : 29-40	Vow of Jephthah	*ʿôlâ*	*ʿālâ*	Primary	Israelite	Individual	Special
Judg. 20 : 26, 21 : 4	Sacrifices of the Benjamite War	*ʿōlôt* *šᵉlāmîm*	*ʿālâ*	?Primary	Israelite	National	?Regular
B. WHERE A SENSE OF SIN OR SOLEMNITY IS NOT PRESENT							
Judg. 9 : 27	Shechemite Vintage Festival	*hillûlîm*		Primary	Non-Isra.	Local	Regular
Judg. 16 : 23	Sacrifices of the Philistines	*zebaḥ*	*zābaḥ*	Primary	Non-Isra.	National	?Regular
C. DOUBTFUL OR UNCLASSIFIABLE PASSAGES							
Josh. 6 : 26	Curse on Jericho			?Primary	Israelite	Individual	Special
Josh. 9	Covenant with Gibeon						
Josh. 13 : 14	Inheritance of the Levites	*ʾiššê*		Secondary			
20 : 3-6	Death of the High Priest			Secondary			
Josh. 22 : 9-34	Altar of the Eastern Tribes	*ʿôlâ minḥâ* *zibḥê šᵉlāmîm* *ʿōlâ zebaḥ* *ʿōlôt zᵉbāḥîm šᵉlāmîm* *ʿōlâ minḥâ zebaḥ*	*ʿālâ* *ʿāśâ*	?Primary	Israelite	Tribal	Regular
Judg. 6 : 11-32	Sacrifices of Gideon	*minḥâ ʿôlâ*	*ʿālâ*	Primary	Israelite	Individual	Regular
Judg. 13 : 15-23	Sacrifice of Manoah	*minḥâ ʿōlâ*	*ʿālâ*	Primary	Israelite	Individual	Regular

CHAPTER FIVE

SAMUEL

The importance of these books for the history of Old Testament ritual was fully recognized by Wellhausen.[1] The formal pattern, which the Deuteronomic editor had imposed on his material in Judges and Kings, is almost completely missing here, and such unadorned narratives as those of 1 Sam. 9 and 2 Sam. 21 are valuable evidence, both for the popular sacrifice, which was little more than a festal meal, that Wellhausen chiefly stressed, and for the propitiatory element, which he thought less important. Not all the materials are of the same date. In addition to the old materials of "The Court History of David" (2 Sam. 9-20), and the History of the Ark (1 Sam. 4-6; 2 Sam. 6),[2] there are probably to be discerned biographies of Saul, Samuel and David, which are of varying ages.

From the Biography of Samuel (1 Sam. 1-3)

Elkanah at Shiloh (1 Sam. 1, 2 : 19)

The sacrifices of Elkanah in 1 : 3, 1 : 21, 1 : 24 and 2 : 19 are apparently at yearly intervals.[3] What was the occasion of the sacrifice? One naturally thinks of the provision of the oldest Codes for three visits to the sanctuary in the year (Exod. 23 : 14, 34 : 23). One of these feasts—that of Ingathering—was to be celebrated at either *bᵉṣēt haš-šānâ* (Exod. 23 : 16) or *teqûpat haš-šānâ* (Exod. 24 : 22). This latter phrase is possibly to be read in 1 : 20 as the time of the birth of Samuel,[4] and of the following sacrifice.[5] This

[1] Cf. Index to *Prolegomena*. See also A. T. Chapman, *Introduction to the Pentateuch*, Cambridge (1911), pp. 192-95 for a discussion of 1 Sam. 1-7 as witness to an early Israelite ritual different from that of P.

[2] Cf. L. Rost, *Die Überlieferung von der Thronnachfolge Davids*, Stuttgart (1926).

[3] The phrase *mîyyāmîm yāmîmâ* (vs. 3) although literally reading "from time to time," is defined by vs. 7 as *šānâ bᵉšānâ*, and is employed for an annual occasion in Exod. 13 : 10. *Zebaḥ hay-yāmîm* in vs. 21 is to be interpreted in the same sense.

[4] It is read by eight MSS and requires only the slightest change in the MT *tᵉqûpōt*.

[5] See BH. The LXX by the addition of the words *tas dekatas* in vs. 21 thought of the bringing of tithes, but this is only an interpretative addition.

might support the identification of the occasion with the end of the year Feast of Ingathering, which is thought to be the only one well attested in the early period.[1] It is possible, however, that the pilgrimage of the story was not one of the three feasts at all, as these were more likely to have been observed by Elkanah at his local sanctuary at "Ramah."[2] Some scholars have argued from the mention of "his" vow in vs. 21, rather than Hannah's, which is the only vow so far in the story, that "Elkanah's visit was a private family festival held in fulfilment of a vow."[3]

The sacrifices are consummated in a family meal at which portions are distributed to the two wives and the children. It is possible that a dining hall similar to the *liškâ* of 9 : 22 was attached to the Shiloh shrine for this purpose, but it is not certain that *bališkâ* should be read with BH for MT *bešilô* (in Shiloh) in vs. 9[4]. Eli is accustomed to such meals being times of drunkenness and excess (vss. 13ff.), and this fact alone suggests the joyful nature of the occasion.

After the birth and weaning of the child, an even more elaborate provision is made for a festal meal at Shiloh (vs. 24). Possibly others beside the family are to be guests. A bull of three years—the most valuable age,[5] flour in large measure and wine are provided. The slaying of the bull is described by *šāḥaṭ* (vs. 25), but no sacrificial terminology, or other description of what follows, appears, except for the final words that "they worshipped the Lord."

The Sacrificial Dues at Shiloh (1 Sam. 2 : 12-17)

The details of priestly ritual for a festal meal, which had been missing in Ch. 1, are now supplied. The sons of Eli are charged with the hasty and forcible appropriation of portions of the sacrifice.

---

[1] But are such local celebrations as Judg. 9 : 27, 11 : 40, 21 : 19 really examples of the celebration of this feast?

[2] Or Shiloh, as a national amphictyonic centre, might have been the scene of one of the feasts, while the others were celebrated at local sanctuaries.

[3] So, G. B. Caird, *Samuel* (*IB*) II (1953), p. 877. Alternatively "his vow" might have been interpolated as Smith, *Samuel* (*ICC*) (1899), p. 12 supposes.

[4] The proposed emendation is perhaps supported by the LXX's introduction of a *katalyma* in vs. 18, but not by the LXX of vs. 9. Wellhausen's suggestion (*Der Text der Bücher Samuel*, Göttingen (1871), p. 38 and *Prolegomena*, p. 68) of *bešēlâ* "boiled flesh" is also unlikely.

[5] So LXX.

In the first case, described in vss. 13-14, the priest's servant inserted a fork into the pot, and secured for the priest whatever the fork would bring up. This was consistent, neither with the laws, which assigned specific portions to the priests,[1] nor with the supposedly earlier practice alleged by Wellhausen,[2] by which the decision as to the priests' portion was left to the freewill of the worshipper.[3] In the second case (vss. 15-16) the sacrifice was not permitted to come as far as the pot, on the ground that the priest wanted to have it roasted and not boiled. The sin was not so much the roasting of the meat,[4] as the fact that the priestly allocation

---

[1] "The shoulder, the two cheeks and the stomach," (Deut. 18 : 3), "The right leg and breast" (Lev. 7 : 28-36).

[2] J. Wellhausen, *Prolegomena*, p. 153. But now see G. E. Wright, *Biblical Archaeology*, Philadelphia (1957), p. 115 for a description of the sacrificial bones found in the Lachish Canaanite temple (destroyed c. 1220 B.C.), and apparently representing the priestly dues, all which were identifiable being the upper part of the right foreleg. This coincides, not with the practice of the passages cited by Wright from Leviticus (Lev. 3, 7 : 32 right hindleg—*šôq*), but with that of Deut. 18 : 3 (right fore-leg—*zᵉrōaʿ*) as Wright notes in connection with the latter verse (*IB*, II (1953), p. 445). It cannot be assumed that this Canaanite practice prevailed at Shiloh, or that Shiloh was still a Canaanite shrine as Nielsen, following Nyberg, supposes ("Some Reflections on the History of the Ark," *Congress Volume Oxford* 1959 (*VTSuppl.* VII), p. 64).

[3] The rendering favoured by many commentators, which combines vss. 13 and 12b to read "they knew not the Lord, nor what was due to the priest from the people" renders *mišpāṭ* by "due." It is supported by the LXX and by Deut. 18 : 3, but requires the addition of *ʾet* before *mišpāṭ*, if this is to be a second object parallel to *ʾet Yahwê*, and also of the reading of *mēʾēt* for *ʾet* before *hāʿām*. On these objections, however, see the discussion of S. R. Driver, *Notes on the Hebrew Text of the Books of Samuel*, Oxford (²1913), p. 29.

[4] Not enough is known of the method of preparing the sacrificial meal to assert with Wellhausen (*Prolegomena*, p. 68), that sacrifices were only boiled (*bāšal*) in the early time, and that P introduced the refinement of roasting (*ṣālâ*). Cf. K. Galling, *Der Altar*, p. 72: "Dass das Fleisch roh verbrannt wird, ist nicht—wie Wellhausen anzunehmen scheint—eine Verfeinerung des Priesterkodex, sondern . . . alter (nomadischer) Brauch gewesen;" A. Wendel, *Das Opfer*, p. 50: ". . . die Frage nach der Priorität von Braten oder Kochen . . . Die Wahrscheinlichkeit ist vorläufig auf der Seite des Bratens, denn der Nomade hat nicht immer Wasser zur Hand zum Kochen;" so also G. Beer, *Pesachim*, p. 15. W. R. Smith, however, writes: ("A Journey in the Hejâz," *Lectures and Essays*, London (1912), pp. 526-27) "Boiled meat is the rule, but two other methods of cooking are known in the desert. One is to cut the meat in slices and broil them on hot stones, the other to improvise an oven by digging a hole . . . I have seen it argued that boiling is the most ancient form of Semitic cookery, but the other methods which I have mentioned

was demanded before the fat had been burned as God's share. This was an offence against the fundamental principle of "the first" for God. Nothing was to intervene between the presentation of the offering and the burning of the fat. Vs. 17 concludes that these offences led to "the men" (*hāʾᵃnāšîm*) despising the offering (*minḥâ*) of Yahweh, but it is not clear if this is to be understood with the LXX as referring to the priests,[1] or to the effect on would-be worshippers, who were discouraged from coming to the Shiloh shrine.

The Sin of Eli's House (1 Sam. 2 : 27-36, 3 : 10-14)

The first of these passages is almost universally regarded as a *vaticinium ex eventu* describing the fortunes of Eli's house in the various phases of its history—the extermination at Nob, the replacement by Zadok, the outlawing of the country Levites under Josiah —down to 621 B.C. It is not improbable, however, that a core at least of the passage should be accepted as older, in view of the reference back to a word against Eli's house in 3 : 12. Late characteristics are chiefly apparent in vss. 32-33 and 35-36, but some of the remainder might be the original core.[2] The identification of the sin of Eli's sons with their offences against the sacrifices (vs. 29) is expressed in vigorous language and is reminiscent of 2 : 12-17. *Minḥâ* for offering has already occurred in 2 : 17 and *zebaḥ* in 2 : 13. *Qᵉṭōret* for incense, and *ʾiššê* "fire offerings" (vs. 28) are not otherwise attested early. The verb *qṭr* BH may, therefore, refer to the burning of the fat as in 2 : 16.[3]

The second prophecy of doom on Eli's house in 3 : 10-14 may be later, but 3 : 14 at least, with its reference to *minḥâ* as well as *zebaḥ* as expiatory offerings, is not likely to be too late. If in this special

---

seem at least equally primitive." He agrees that boiling was more common among the Hebrews from an early date, and this seems true of the Canaanite practice at Lachish, where the bones showed no trace of burning. (So Wright, *Biblical Archaeology, loc. cit.*).

[1] LXX omits *hāʾᵃnāšîm* and refers the verb *niʾᵃṣû* to *han-nᵉʿārîm* as subject.

[2] C. Steuernagel, "Die Weissagung über die Eliden," *Alttestamentliche Studien Rudolf Kittel*, Leipzig (1913), pp. 204-21 argues for an original core consisting of vss. 27-31a, 33aᵃb, 34 (p. 220). From the sacrificial verses he seems to delete only "fire offerings" (vs. 28) and "which I commanded" (vs. 29) as from D or P (p. 209). His date in the eighth century seems too late.

[3] But see below, Ch. VI.

case the iniquity of Eli's house, will not be expiated[1] by *zebaḥ* or *minḥâ* for ever, it must follow that the normal purpose of sacrifice was the expiation of sin.[2] The coexistence of this solemn view of sacrifice, alongside the more festal aspect of the other Shiloh traditions, must not be forgotten.

From the History of the Ark (1 Sam. 6 : 3-9, 14-15)

The ʾĀšām of the Philistines (1 Sam. 6 : 3-9)

The plague which broke out among the Philistines concurrent with their possession of the ark has led them to return the ark to Israel, and along with it as an expiatory offering (*ʾāšām*), symbolic representations of their affliction made from gold.[3] It is not clear whether these were a money compensation, or like the brazen serpent in the wilderness, a means to healing actuated by the principle of homeopathic magic that like produces like. Schötz finds evidence for an early form of the guilt offering of the Levitical Code, and like it expressing penitence for an act of sacrilege.[4] Wellhausen's theory, that there was no guilt offering proper, but only a money compensation until Ezekiel, seems to reverse the

---

1 The Hithpael *yitkappēr* is unparalleled and should perhaps be emended to the form which occurs elsewhere *yekuppar*.

2 The exegesis of A. B. Davidson ("The Word "Atone" in the Extra-Ritual Literature," *op. cit.*, p. 96), which makes the sacrifice and offering refer to the sin, rather than the means of atonement ("the iniquity of Eli's house (in regard) to sacrifice and offering,") is rightly rejected by J. Herrmann (*Die Idee der Sühne im Alten Testament*, Leipzig (1905), pp. 52-53). The preposition *b* after *kipper*, except in a few cases of local use (e.g. Lev. 6 : 23(30), 16 : 17), is instrumental, expressing the means by which the atonement is made (Gen. 32 : 21; Lev. 5 : 16, 7 : 7; Num. 5 : 8; 2 Sam. 21 : 3; Is. 27 : 9; Prov. 16 : 6).

3 The number and nature of these is confused. According to vs. 4 there are to be five golden tumours and five golden mice, while in vss. 17-18 the number of golden tumours is still five, but that of the mice apparently much larger. The question arises concerning the bringing in of the mice at all. They are not referred to in Ch. 5. LXX prepares for Ch. 6 by introducing them in 5 : 6 and by reading in 6 : 1 "and their land swarmed with mice," and removes the difficulty of the numbers by confining vs. 4 to the tumours and by leaving the number of the mice in both vss. 5 and 18 unspecified. The alternative of removing all the references to the mice and deleting vss. 17-18 as a gloss is favoured by Smith (*ICC*), pp. 41, 47. The association of plague with mice, however, is frequent in antiquity and is thought to be the reason why the reverse of Sennacherib in 2 Kings 19 : 35 is reported in Herodotus II, 141 to be due to mice in the "quivers."

4 D. Schötz, *Schuld- und Sündopfer im Alten Testament*, pp. 35ff.

natural evolution from animal sacrifice to a money substitute, which is seen, for example in the redemption of the first-born.[1] The Ugaritic references to *ʾāšām* have been claimed to support the view, both of an offering, and of a monetary compensation, but the references are too meagre to decide the point.[2] In the present passage an expiation is in view, but no blood sacrifice is involved.

The Return of the Ark to Bethshemesh (1 Sam. 6 : 14-15)

The men of Bethshemesh are in the harvest field when they see the ark returning. "They rejoiced to see it" (vs. 13), and proceeded to offer on a great stone the wood of the cart and the cows, which had drawn it. Vs. 15 makes the stone merely a depository for the ark and the box containing the golden figures, and implies that a separate altar was used for the *ʿōlôt* and *zᵉbāḥîm*. The secondary nature of the verse is apparent, not only from this repetition of the sacrifices already offered in vs. 14, but also in the obvious attempt to meet Levitical requirements, both as to the altar, and to the transport of the ark by Levites. The purpose of the sacrifices was apparently thanksgiving, but other motives may have been present.[3]

From the Biography of Samuel

Samuel at Mizpah (1 Sam. 7)

Wellhausen's judgment that this chapter was post-Deuteronomic and "can not [have] a word of truth in it," and that Samuel as "a

---

[1] So B. Stade, *Biblische Theologie des Alten Testaments*, Vol. I, pp. 165-66.

[2] See above, p. 32.

[3] N. H. Tur-Sinai, "The Ark of God at Beit Shemesh (1 Sam. VI) and Peres Uzza (2 Sam. VI; 1 Chron. XIII)," *VT* I (1951), pp. 275-86 has drawn attention to the doublet of this incident in vss. 18bff. and has argued for the rendering *ʾAbhel* instead of stone (*ʾeben*) in vs. 14 as in vs. 18. He finds an aetiology of this place name in the following account of the "mourning" of the people over the disaster of Bethshemesh. A further doublet is to be found in the story of Uzzah in 2 Sam. 6. The connections, however, between *ʾAbhel* and *gōren* in Gen. 50 : 11, and between *nākâ* and *gōren nākôn* in 2 Sam. 6 : 6 and *gōren ʾᵃrawnâ* in 2 Sam. 24 : 18, and between *ʾāḥaz* of Uzzah in 2 Sam. 6 and *ʾāḥaz* of Joab at the *ʾeben gādôl* of Gibeon (2 Sam. 20 : 8-9) and his following pursuit to *ʾĀbēlâ*, which would link all these references to the same aetiology, are tenuous. A. Bentzen in "The Cultic Use of the Story of the Ark," *JBL* LXVII (1948), pp. 37-53 sought to extend the liturgical explanation of the entry of the ark, to include also this earlier story of its loss and return. Its experiences in the Philistine country were those of the god in the underworld, while its happy return was the rising of the god.

saint of the first degree (Jer. 15 : 1)" had to be made "to take his place at the head of the whole,"[1] overlooks the fact that the reputation of Samuel as an intercessor to which Jeremiah refers, could only have come from the incident of the text.[2] Kittel argued for a date at least before Jeremiah.[3] Budde found predominant E influence and assigned the chapter to his E2 source prior to 650 B.C.[4] The chief difficulty of going back earlier is the contradiction between the picture of Samuel as a deliverer from the Philistines, and the low state of Israel beneath Philistine subjection in the time of Saul and David. This tradition of a deliverance under Samuel is, however, inextricably interwoven with his reputation as an intercessor, and it seems therefore necessary to allow that on at least one occasion in his long life he was responsible for such an act of deliverance as Ch. 7 relates. It is suggested, therefore, that only the formalized "rest" notice of vss. 13-14, which reflects the Deuteronomic framework of the lives of the judges need be questioned. Alternatively the story might stop with vs. 9, or even be limited to the central core in vss. 5 and 6.

Do the various elements of the story agree with this suggestion of an older core? The assembling of Israel at Mizpah as an amphictyony (vs. 5) seems adequately attested in the sources (Judg. 20 : 1; 1 Sam. 10 : 17). The water pouring rite of vs. 6 is nowhere described in the Levitical law, and seems more likely to have belonged to an earlier time, than to that of P. It can scarcely be identified with the rain-making ceremonies of the Feast of Tabernacles in late Judaism,[5] which seem only reflected in the Old Testament in Zech. 14 : 17. The water drawing of Isaiah 12 : 3, and the water pouring of Lam. 2 : 19 seem to be metaphorical. It is not certain that an offering is being described in the present passage.[6]

---

[1] J. Wellhausen, *Prolegomena*, p. 249.

[2] Or that of Ch. 12 : 18, on which Wellhausen is equally harsh. The same tradition is also reflected in Ps. 99.

[3] R. Kittel, *A History of the Hebrews*, Vol. II, E.T. London (1896), p. 25.

[4] K. Budde, *Samuel* (*SBOT*) (1894). So also O. Eissfeldt, *Einleitung in das Alte Testament* ([2]1956), Tübingen, p. 326.

[5] Cf. D. Feuchtwang, "Das Wasseropfer und die damit verbundenen Zeremonien," *MGWJ* LIV, N.F. 18 (1910), pp. 535-52, 713-29, LV, N.F. 19 (1911), pp. 43-63.

[6] J. A. Kelso, "The Water Libation in the Old Testament," *Exp* 8th series XXIV (1922), pp. 226-40 thought that "before the Lord" supported a water libation, but S. R. Driver, *Text of Samuel*, p. 64, argued that *nāsak*

As a picture of penitence, however, following the call to "put away the foreign gods" in vs. 3 the symbolic water pouring might be appropriate.[1] This "putting away of foreign gods" has been noted above, in connection with Gen. 35 : 2; Josh. 24 : 23 and Judg. 5 : 8, as possibly a part of an ancient ritual. The reply of the people "we have sinned (*ḥāṭānû*)" also has early attestation in E passages (Num. 14 : 40, 21 : 7 and ? Judg. 10 : 10, 15). Possibly an early rite of national fasting and penitence is to be discerned in the present passage.[2]

It cannot of course be certainly affirmed that the sacrifices related in vss. 9 and 10 belonged to such a service, rather than to the preparation for the battle which follows, but it is possible.[3] A "sucking lamb" *ṭᵉlê ḥālāb* as a victim is nowhere else specifically mentioned, and is not necessarily to be identified with P's lamb of the first year (P's word is uniformly *kebeś*). *ʿôlâ kālîl* is also unusual,[4] but is not impossible in view of *šelem kālîl* in the Carthaginian sacrifices of the Marseilles list.[5] The purpose of the sacrifice here is undoubtedly expiatory.[6]

---

should have been used instead of *šāpak* if this had been the case. However, in 2 Sam. 23 : 16 where both *lᵉYahwê* and *nāsak* are used it is still not certain that David was making an offering.

[1] Cf. the call to "pour out your hearts before the Lord" (Lam. 2 : 19; Ps. 62 : 9). In other verses it is the "complaint" that is poured out (Ps. 102 : 1, 142 : 3; 1 Sam. 1 : 15; Job 3 : 24), while in still others it is the strength of of life poured out in sufferings (Ps. 22 : 15; Is. 53 : 12).

[2] Cf. R. Rendtorff, "Opfer," *EKL* II, col. 1693. M. Buber ("Die Erzählung von Sauls Königswahl," *VT* VI (1956), p. 118) writes: "die Riten haben einen frühen Charakter, die Wasserlibation kennen wir von Ägypten her als Wiederbelebungsriten, auch das Fasten ist ein alter Trauerbrauch (vgl. 2 Sam. i 12; iii 25), und das kollektive Sündenbekenntnis brauchte nicht späterer Herkunft zu sein als das individuelle (vgl. 2 Samuel xii 13)."

[3] A. R. S. Kennedy, *Samuel* (*CB*) (1905), p. 70.

[4] It is not necessary, however, to delete *kālîl* with Schulz, *Die Bücher Samuel*, Münster (1919) or *ʿôlâ* with Caspari (*KAT*) (1926). LXX reads *kālîl* as *syn panti tō laō* presupposing *bᵉkol hāʿām*.

[5] In some references in the Phoenician texts the *kll* seems to belie its name. The Marseilles *kll* apparently goes wholly to the god and the priests, while that at Carthage might be shared by the worshippers. D. M. L. Urie, ("Sacrifice Among the West-Semites," *PEQ* LXXXI (1949), pp. 70-71). In the Old Testament *kālîl* occurs five times for sacrifice—twice as a prohibition of eating the *minḥâ* (Lev. 6 : 15-16 (= 22-23)) and in the other cases either in connection with the *ʿōlâ* or as a substitute for it. (Ps. 51 : 21; Deut. 13 : 17, Deut. 33 : 10).

[6] A further reference to be noted is Samuel's building of an altar in 7 : 17.

From the Biography of Saul

The Anointing of Saul (1 Sam. 9 : 11-24)

No problems of date are raised by this old narrative, which begins the biography of Saul. The passage is rightly regarded as one of the most important in the Old Testament for the early festal meal. Other such references are usually of family occasions, but here "thirty men" are the invited guests.[1] One can only conjecture, who they were or what the occasion was. It is usually supposed that they were the influential citizens of the place,[2] but no clue to the nature of the occasion is given. Was it sacrificial at all? The only sacrificial term used is *zebaḥ*[3] and the question has been asked above whether a secular meaning is not possible.

In favour of a secular meaning is the fact that the *zebaḥ* is not further defined as *l^eYahwê* as in 1 : 3, questions are not asked as to cultic purity as in 1 Sam. 21 : 1-6, a cook not a priest supervises (vs. 23), Samuel is not necessary to kill the sacrifice, but only to bless it, and the implication of the narrative is that eating rather than worship was the main point of the *zebaḥ* (vs. 13).

It is possible, of course, that there had been a sacrifice, but that this had taken place earlier, when Samuel made the arrangement for the reservation of a certain portion of the victim (vs. 23).[4] The present passage describes only the meal made from the sacrificial flesh and can scarcely be used as evidence for the sacrifice itself.[5]

---

[1] LXX has seventy men.

[2] Some recent scholars see in them the representatives of the amphictyony and hold that Saul was their appointee. See H. Wildberger, "Samuel und die Entstehung des israelitischen Königtums," *ThZ* XIII (1957), p. 465.

[3] Unless *rûm* in vs. 24 is to be translated "heave."

[4] There is a difficulty in the text of the MT between vs. 13 and vs. 24. According to the former verse, the guests will not eat until Samuel has blessed the sacrifice, but in vs. 24 the words "whatever was left over is set before you" and "it was kept for you to the appointed time" imply that the meal has already been in progress. The suggestion that *haš'^eēr* be read for *šāmûr* is forced, as is that of *rē'šît* for a possible *š^e'ērît*. In the next clause, however, "with the guests" is a plausible emendation of *hā'ām qārā'tî*. That the *šôq*, the most prized portion, which in P is the prerogative of the priests (Lev. 7 : 32), should go to Saul as the honoured guest is not surprising. More difficult is the meaning of *w^ehe'ālehâ*, which has been variously explained as the preposition *'al* with the suffix as in the Levitical Code (Exod. 29 : 22), or "the fat tail" *hā'alyâ* (Wellhausen), or *hakilyâ* (Klostermann, *SZ*), or "upper portion" (RSV).

[5] Cf. Prov. 7 : 14, where the hospitality offered by the harlot from the

Offerings for Bethel (1 Sam. 10 : 3)

In continuation of the above narrative of Saul's anointing it is related how several signs were to be given to Saul. The second of these was that he should meet, by the oak of Tabor,[1] three men "going up to God at Bethel." Their gifts of kids, loaves and wine are similar to those in 1 Sam. 1 : 24 and suggest a sacrificial meal. If the offerings were firstfruits as in the LXX,[2] the giving up of two of the loaves to a traveller before their being presented would be strange. Perhaps this constituted the sign.

From the Biography of Samuel or Saul

The four sections which follow are complicated by the two accounts of Saul's accession and the two accounts of his rejection. 10 : 8 and 13 : 8-15 belong together and possibly 11 : 12-15 and 15 : 2-23.

Saul at Gilgal (1 Sam. 10 : 8)

10 : 8 is clearly out of place in its present position on any view of the composition of the book. It is inconsistent with the preceding verse which leaves the initiative to Saul to "do whatever your hand finds to do." This prepares the way for the exploit of Jabesh-Gilead (Ch. 11), while vs. 8 prepares for 13 : 8-15 and should be in closer connection with it. It owes its present position to an attempt to bring together into a chronological scheme the very different materials of Chs. 10-15. This is not to say that it has no place in the narrative. It is necessary to the understanding of 13 : 8-15.

The Renewal of the Kingdom (1 Sam. 11 : 12-15)

The suggestion of a renewal of the kingdom in vss. 12-14 is probably a further editorial device to harmonize the accession of Saul, after the Jabesh-Gilead episode,[3] with the other account of his

sacrificial flesh, has little to do with the sacrifice, which had taken place earlier.

[1] Perhaps the oak which marked Deborah's burial place (Gen. 35 : 8).

[2] LXX reads *aparchas* for MT *leḥem* in vs. 4, probably understanding *kikrôt* in vs. 3 as *bikrôt*, although its reading of *aggeia* in vs. 3 presupposes *kᵉlûbê*.

[3] Reference should perhaps have been made to the "fiery torch" of a divided animal sent into all Israel by Saul in 1 Sam. 11 : 7. G. van der Leeuw, *Religion in Essence and Manifestation*, p. 357 thinks it to have been a sacrifice to effect the unity of the tribe, but this is unlikely.

accession that has already been described. Vs. 15 is plainly the account of Saul's accession as it lay in the old source of Ch. 11. Peace offerings (*zᵉbāḥîm šᵉlāmîm*) are sacrificed before the Lord and a great rejoicing follows. The two absolute nouns in Hebrew are in an awkward apposition, instead of the usual construct relation, and this may reflect a time when the *zebaḥ* and *šelem* were separate sacrifices (cf. on Exod. 24 : 5 and Josh. 22 : 27).[1] These offerings may have been sacrifices of dedication for the new kingdom, but if so no hint to this effect is given.

The First Rejection of Saul (1 Sam. 13 : 8-15)

Of the two accounts of the rejection of Saul this one from its connection with the Philistine war, its less theological tone and its milder reproof is usually judged the older.[2] Smith referred it to his Saul source and assigned Ch. 15 to the later Samuel source.[3] Budde thought it an addition made to the old J source before 650 B.C.[4] He questioned the representation of war beginning with sacrifice as inadequately attested for Israel.[5] The context in Ch. 13, however, when taken with 10 : 8 suggests that the sacrifices were to have been offered in any case, but that the threat of a Philistine attack precipitated Saul into action before the arrival of Samuel.

10 : 8 had spoken of *ʿōlôt* and *zibḥê šᵉlāmîm*, and in 13 : 9a Saul asks for *hā-ʿōlâ* and *haš-šᵉlāmîm*, but only the *ʿōlâ* had been offered, before Samuel came.[6] The propitiatory purpose, not only of this

---

[1] LXX separates *šᵉlāmîm* from *zᵉbāḥîm* by *kai* (waw).

[2] Some recent investigators have expressed the contrary opinion e.g. H. Wildberger, *op. cit.*, p. 460.

[3] H. P. Smith (*ICC*), pp. xxi, 94.

[4] He argued that a relatively high age was indicated by the fact that it was not because the king did not have the right to offer sacrifices that Saul was condemned, but because of his disobedience to a particular command (*KHC*), p. 87. Gressmann, however, took the opposite view and found this a late trait (*Die älteste Geschichtsschreibung und Prophetie Israels* (*SAT*) ([2]1921), p. 52).

[5] He pointed out that Judg. 6 : 19 was an undesigned sacrifice, Judg. 6 : 26 the dedication of a new altar, Judg. 20 : 26 followed two disastrous days of fighting and 1 Sam. 7 : 9 was to be related to the preceding religious assembly, rather than to the ensuing battle (p. 87). On the other side the phrase "to consecrate war" *qiddēš milḥāmâ* (Jer. 6 : 4; Job 4 : 9 (3 : 9); Mic. 3 : 5; Jer. 22 : 7) implies some kind of religious ceremonies.

[6] So A. Klostermann (*SZ*), p. 42. This is better than Caspari's deletion of *šelem*, as an addition to turn it into a joyful occasion (*KAT*), p. 156.

offering, but of sacrifice in general, is indicated by the use of the verb *ḥālâ* "to entreat the favour of the Lord" in vs. 12.[1]

From the Biography of Saul

Saul at Michmash (1 Sam. 14 : 32-35)

The old Saul source is resumed in this incident. The army, famished by Saul's restriction, fall upon the spoil and eat it *ʿal had-dām*. Just what the offence is, is not clear from the Hebrew.

(a) "*Eating the blood*" does not seem a possible translation.[2] The phrase occurs elsewhere only on Lev. 19 : 26 and Ezek. 33 : 25, but in the former the LXX reads "eating upon the mountains," and in the latter this should probably be read also, in view of Ezekiel's frequent condemnation of this sin (e.g. Ezek. 18 : 6 etc.). Robertson Smith argued that the change should be made the other way, and all these passages understood in the sense of his mystical communion theory of an eating of the blood,[3] but this is rightly rejected for Ezekiel by Cooke.[4]

(b) "*Eating with the blood*" i.e. "containing the blood," "with the blood improperly drained off" is favoured by some scholars, who think the concern was with *kosher* killing.[5] That the preposition *ʿal* can have the meaning of "in addition to," "together with" is plain from the many examples collected by BDB on p. 755. In many of these cases substantives are conjoined, and the local use of the preposition in its basic sense of proximity is not far away. Num. 9 : 11 and Exod. 12 : 6 "with unleavened bread," "with bitter herbs" are, however, parallel to the present passage.

(c) "*Eating upon the blood.*" Is the local use possible here? Pedersen thought so, when he interpreted the offence as the failure

---

[1] BDB gives the meaning of *ḥālâ* as "mollify, appease, entreat the favour of . . ., to induce . . . to show favour in place of wrath," p. 318.

[2] The Hebrew for this should be *ʾākal had-dām*, as in the many prohibitions in the laws (Lev. 7 : 26, 17 : 12; Deut. 12 : 23 etc.).

[3] W. R. Smith, *The Religion of the Semites*, pp. 342-43.

[4] G. A. Cooke, *Ezekiel* (*ICC*) (1936), p. 198. The recent commentaries on Ezekiel by Eichrodt (*ATD*) (1959) and Zimmerli (*BK*) (1959) differ on this point, Eichrodt favouring "samt dem Blut," (p. 144) and Zimmerli "auf den Bergen" (pp. 404-405).

[5] LXX (*syn tō haimati*) and the other versions understood the phrase in this sense, but one would expect the preposition *b* not *ʿal* for "with" (cf. Gen. 9 : 4). *ʿal* can, however, have the sense of "containing the blood."

to keep blood and food apart: "the sin of the people consists in letting the blood run out on to the ground, where they will eat their meal."[1] The killing on the stone provided by Saul, was not to make the slaughter into a sacrifice, but to remove the blood from the body of the animal, so that it could be consumed elsewhere. There was no evidence that the stone was holy, or that all slaughter had to be sacrifice. This was in opposition to the view of Wellhausen and Robertson Smith, who interpreting the stone as an altar, deduced that the offence had been the failure to first offer the blood to God. This also is possible from the Hebrew.

(d) *"Eating concerning the blood"* i.e. "in the matter of," "with regard to." The possibility of this vague use indicates that the linguistic aspect cannot be final, and that the context both of the passage, and of the Old Testament in general must be taken into account. From the nearer context Pedersen's view would be perfectly possible, seeing that the altar building (vs. 35) seems to be separated from the provision of the stone (vs. 33), but most scholars feel that the Wellhausen-Robertson Smith view is more consistent with the Old Testament evidence as a whole, and permits of a more satisfactory explanation of Deut. 12. In the present passage, however, it is not the only possibility.

The Redemption of Jonathan (1 Sam. 14 : 45)

No sacrifice is mentioned, but the verb *pādâ* implies that a substitute took the place of Jonathan. Since Ewald, it has been supposed by many that a human sacrifice—perhaps of a prisoner of war— was the redemption price.[2] It is improbable, however, that such would have been passed over in silence, and an animal sacrifice or even money was acceptable as a ransom in such early laws as Exod. 13 : 15, 34 : 20.[3] The operation of a substitutionary principle here hardly warrants any conclusion as to the nature of Hebrew sacrifice.

From the Biography of Samuel

Saul's Second Rejection (1 Sam. 15 : 1-23)

The dating of the chapter and the determination of its relation

[1] J. Pedersen, *Israel* (III-IV), p. 339.

[2] So Budde (*KHC*) arguing from the seriousness of the occasion, Gressmann (*SAT*) and others.

[3] So Kittel (*HSAT*), Driver (*Text . . .*), p. 119 and others.

to Ch. 13 : 8-15 is not easily settled. Smith argued that the scene of the action would have been Mizpah, which in his late Samuel source, is the centre of Samuel's public activity, had not the writer already had 13 : 8-15 before him, compelling the change to Gilgal. He assigns the story therefore to the later source.[1] The oracle on sacrifice in vs. 22 is to him "a summary of later Jewish theology" of the time of Ps. 50.[2] Budde argued, however, that there was no need to come down later than Amos and Hosea for the sentiments of this verse.[3] It is now known that such sentiments were expressed in Egypt a thousand years before.[4] A late date might seem to be favoured by the Deuteronomic flavour of the institution of the ban, but it can no longer be argued that the idea of the "holy war" was late in Israel. A later element might be the condemnation of teraphim and divination (vs. 23), but the obscurity of the Hebrew is against this.

The sacrificial reference occurs first in Saul's excuse for not carrying out the ban "the people spared the best of the sheep and oxen to sacrifice (*zābaḥ*) to Yahweh" (vss. 15, 21). Such a sacrifice would possibly have been in thanksgiving for victory, and would have been shared in by man.[5] Samuel's reply makes it plain that

---

[1] Smith (*ICC*), p. xxi. The LXX addition of "behold he has offered burnt offerings to the Lord of the first of the booty which he brought out of Amalek" to vs. 12 is also probably an attempt to link the two rejection stories. Budde was inclined to accept this addition as original but A. Weiser "1 Sam. 15," *ZAW* LIV (1936), p. 8 fn. points out that according to vs. 30 Saul is not at the sanctuary during the conversation. The sacrifices are not offered until vss. 30-31.

[2] Smith (*ICC*), p. 137.

[3] Budde (*KHC*), pp. 111, 107. In *SBOT* he had accepted an early date for the whole narrative.

[4] Gressmann (*SAT*), p. 60. W. A. L. Elmslie also favours an early date for the oracle (*How Came Our Faith,* Cambridge (1948), p. 231). R. Press ("Der Prophet Samuel," *ZAW* LVI (1938), pp. 221-23) goes further than most in making Samuel an earlier Hosea in his rejection of the Canaanizing of the cult—particularly the sacrificial meal. He sees in Samuel's condemnation of Eli's sons and Saul "prophetic" resistance to the increasing sacrificial meals coming in under Canaanite influence (p. 222). The present narrative is interpreted in the sense that obedience to the ban is better than the sacrificial meal Saul had planned (p. 211). Press objects to Kittel's view of a "priestly" Samuel and treats the altar building of Ch. 7 and the blessing of the sacrifice of Ch. 9 as legendary (p. 223). These passages have been differently estimated above.

[5] Some commentators have seen in the condemnation of witchcraft in vs. 23 a hint that Saul had retained the sacrifices for some magical purpose, but this is unlikely. On this difficult verse the larger works must be consulted.

the ban, by which all is devoted to God must take precedence over sacrifice.[1] God delights in obedience more than sacrifice, burnt offerings, and the fat of rams.

The Anointing of David (1 Sam. 16 : 1-13)

Budde and Kittel include this story in their Midrash source, which consists of the latest material in the Book of Samuel.[2] The elements of the story would then owe their origin to an attempt to give to David an anointing like that of Saul. Samuel comes to Bethlehem as once he went to "Ramah." A sacrificial meal in the family of Jesse, borrowed from the reference in 20 : 6, to a sacrifice in the house of Jesse in Bethlehem,[3] is extended to include the chief men of the place as in 1 Sam. 9. In their presence David is anointed. That the whole thing was a fiction is clear from the history, where Saul does not even know David, and his brothers treat him with scant respect. This would be incomprehensible if he had already been designated by Samuel as the future king.

On the other side, it must be said that the picture of David given by Noth,[4] as one who had had his eye on the throne from the beginning, and moved toward it with unswerving purpose and considerable strategy, almost requires an anointing as the initial impetus. An earlier form of the story might have lacked those traits which suggest an imitation of 1 Sam. 9. The elders of the village do not appear after vs. 5.[5] Nothing more is said of a sacrificial meal.[6] A heifer *ʿeglâ* would be unusual for this, but would possibly be more suitable for a consecration rite.[7] Caird suggests that each son was

---

[1] It is probably best therefore to see in the killing of Agag in vs. 33 the fulfilment of the ban, rather than a human sacrifice, so R. de Vaux, *Samuel* (*JerusB*) (1953), p. 78.

[2] Budde (*SBOT*) thought it was added after 400 B.C., Kittel (*HSAT*) thought of it as beginning the David series, but Smith (*ICC*) assigned it to his Samuel source.

[3] So Budde (*KHC*), p. 114.

[4] M. Noth, *The History of Israel*, pp. 179ff.

[5] This was a difficulty for the LXX translators who therefore read *ûśᵉmaḥtem ʾittî hay-yôm* for *bāʾtem ʾittî baz-zābaḥ*.

[6] A hint is perhaps contained in vs. 11 but only if *nāsōb* be read as *nēšēb*. LXX^{BA} reads *kataklithōmen*. W. O. E. Oesterley (*Sacrifices*, p. 73) thinks the MT *sbb* should be followed and renders "go around" in the sense of "march about the altar" (cf. also Smith (*ICC*), p. 146).

[7] Cf. Gen. 15 : 9; Deut. 21 : 3.

sanctified separately by the sacrifice (cf. Job. 1 : 5).[1] The act of anointing might then have been secret between Samuel and David. In this case the sacrifice would have been one of consecration.

From the Biography of David

David's Family Sacrifice (1 Sam. 20 : 5-6, 24-29)

As an excuse for his absence from Saul's table at the special meal occasion of the new moon, David pleads the pretext of a *zebaḥ hay-yāmîm* for *kol-ham-mišpāḥâ* at Bethlehem. The phrase *zebaḥ hay-yāmîm* is used in 1 : 21 of Elkanah's sacrifice, which was shown above to have been a yearly one. The *mišpāḥâ* in Bethlehem might have been the clan, "the father's house," rather than the family, and would involve a larger group than Elkanah's sacrifice.[2] A further difference is that Elkanah's sacrifice took place at a sanctuary distant from his home, while that of the family of Jesse was celebrated at home. It is difficult to identify such a family celebration with any of the feasts of the law. Luther argued that such a feast of "brethren" at a new moon could only be the Passover,[3] but the fact that Saul's celebration continued on to the morrow and to the third day would not agree with this.[4] Snaith thought of the annual harvest feast,[5] but again there is little ground for this identification. All that can be said is that some festal meal was contemplated.[6]

---

[1] G. B. Caird (*IB*), pp. 967-68.

[2] With this would agree the LXX rendering of *ʾaḥay* BH for *ʾāḥî* in vs. 29.

[3] B. Luther, "Davids Passahopfer," in E. Meyer, *op. cit.*, pp. 170-73.

[4] Luther thought Saul's *lḥm*, which he took to be flesh, as with the Arabs, evidence of a feast, but it is possible that it was David's custom to dine every day at the king's table—apparently only the four men sat down together. The requirement of cultic purity might support a festal interpretation. It is interesting to note that uncleanness would be only until the evening, so that David might be expected to put in an appearance the next day.

[5] N. H. Snaith, *The Jewish New Year Festival*, pp. 44-45. The fact that it was a new moon, rather than a full moon, would argue against it (cf. B. D. Eerdmans, *The Religion of Israel*, Leiden (1947), p. 99) but see Snaith (*op. cit.*, p. 98) for the suggestion that *ḥōdeš* was the New-Month Day, not the New-Moon Day.

[6] At this point the omission of the narrative of 1 Sam. 21 : 1-6 should perhaps be remarked on. The incident of David's eating the shew-bread at the sanctuary of Nob, and the requirement that he should be culticly clean is of interest to this discussion, although not listed as a sacrifice.

David's Reply to Saul (1 Sam. 26 : 19)

This verse, which has often been quoted in its latter portion for the religious beliefs of the early Hebrews, clearly understands the offering (*minḥâ*) to be efficacious in removing the anger of Yahweh. The propitiatory purpose is apparent in the words "let him smell (*rîaḥ*) a *minḥâ*."

The Removal of the Ark (2 Sam. 6 : 12-19)

The possibility of this narrative being a doublet of 1 Sam. 6 is mentioned above to be rejected. Its liturgical significance has also been stressed by a series of scholars,[1] but such considerations must be left on one side at present. The passage describes three sacrifices. The *zebaḥ* of vs. 13 after the first six paces of the journey, the *ʿōlôt* of vs. 17,[2] and the *hā-ʿôlâ* and the *haš-šelāmîm* of vs. 18.

The offering of vs. 13 is apparently one of thanksgiving for the safe commencement of the journey. The element of fear of the wrath of Yahweh is not completely absent,[3] but vs. 12 seems to indicate, that it was only when the prosperity of Obed Edom's house has convinced David that the anger of Yahweh was now appeased, that he concluded it was safe to move the ark. The burnt offerings of vs. 17 might well be of consecration of the new dwelling of the ark. From the peace offerings *šelāmîm* which follow, portions are apparently distributed to the assembled people.[4] The music and dancing of David indicate that the occasion was one of joy, but this was not inconsistent with more solemn thoughts.[5]

---

[1] J. R. Porter, "2 Sam. VI and Ps CXXXII," *JTS*, N.S. 5 (1954), pp. 161-73 discusses the view of Mowinckel, Bentzen and Kraus, and makes a further contribution of his own.

[2] *Šelāmîm* at the end of vs. 17 seems to be in the wrong place, and perhaps came in by assimilation from vs. 18. 1 Chron. 16 : 1 reads *ʿōlôt* and *šelāmîm* in both verses, but *šelāmîm* in vs. 17 is before *lipnê Yahwê*.

[3] Cf. the Chronicler's remark "God helped the Levites" (1 Chron. 15 : 26), and the citation from A. Loisy on p. 14 above.

[4] This is not quite certain. The loaves of bread and raisin cakes could accompany the distribution of the sacrificial meat but it is not known if *ʾešpār* represents the latter. J. R. Porter, *op. cit.* pp. 168-69 thinks this the distribution of food that took place at coronation rites and cites the evidence of the Ramesseum Papyrus. He compares Ps. 132 : 15.

[5] L. Rost, *Thronnachfolge*, p. 47 writes: (on the whole ark narrative) "Jahve erscheint als der übermächtige, zwar nicht willkürlich handelnde, meist Unheil, aber auch Heil bringende Gott; dementsprechend ist die Frömmigkeit von Furcht, aber auch von freudiger Verehrung bestimmt."

The Sacrifice of Absalom (2 Sam. 15 : 7-12)

This is the only reference to sacrifice in the Court History Document.[1] It is usually assumed that Absalom, like Adonijah in 2 Kings 1, celebrated his proclamation as king by a coronation feast to which his supporters had been invited. The meal would have been a large one, involving about two hundred men. However, nothing is said of a meal in this case,[2] and the *zᵉbāḥîm* of vs. 12 may be only the vowed offering referred to in vs. 8.[3] Such an offering in fulfilment of a vow would be a thank offering, while sacrifices at a coronation might be dedicatory.

The Execution of the Sons of Saul (2 Sam. 21 : 1-14)

There is little doubt that this story should come earlier in the narrative, and in particular, before the question of 9 : 1 was asked "Is there anyone left of the sons of Saul?" Probably the original setting was immediately before 9 : 1, and in connection with it. The verses preceding its present position (20 : 23-26) are a doublet of the verses preceding 9 : 1 (8 : 15-18). The Court History (Ch. 9-20) has been inserted before this narrative instead of after it.[4]

It is not known which of Saul's crimes is referred to in vs. 1. Some identify Gibeon with Nob, where Saul massacred the entire priestly family. 2 Sam. 4 : 3 refers to Beerothites having fled to Gittaim on some unspecified occasion. This may have been the result of Saul's attack, for Beeroth was one of the four cities of Gibeon in Josh. 9 : 17. Malamat suggests that the disaffection of these cities was as big a security risk to Saul, as it had been to the Canaanites, who attacked them in Josh. 10.[5] He points out that it was not merely that Saul had killed the Gibeonites, that was his

---

[1] Unless a sacrificial reference be found in 2 Sam. 15 : 24, where the verbs *way-yaṣṣiqû* and *wayyaʿal* might mean "poured a libation and offered" (Hertzberg). This is impossible, however, with *ʾet-ᵃrôn* as the object of the first verb and not very probable in the context. BH suggests *wayyaṣṣēg* for the first verb and *ʿal* for the second. LXX has *anebē*.

[2] Unless *qᵉruʾîm* in vs. 11 can only mean "guests," which is doubtful.

[3] The verb in vs. 8 is *ʿābad* as in Exod. 4 : 23.

[4] Cf. A. S. Kapelrud, "King and Fertility," *op. cit.*, p. 113 (citing Mowinckel). There is no need to suppose, however, that D had omitted the narrative because it told of a human sacrifice.

[5] A. Malamat, "Doctrines of Causality in Hittite and Biblical Historiography: A Parallel," *VT* V (1955), pp. 1-12.

offence, for he had killed others also, but that he had killed them in defiance of the treaty made by Joshua.

The savage Gibeonite demand for compensation in the form of human hostages (money would not do) illustrates the strength of the law of blood-revenge.[1] There is more than the *lex talionis* however, in the incident. It is a three year famine that brings to light the unexpiated guilt of Saul.[2] The anger of Yahweh as well as the lawful demands of the Gibeonites must be appeased (*kipper*) vs. 3. The victims are therefore "hanged on the mountain before the Lord" (vs. 8).[3] The result is that the Lord is "entreated for the land."[4]

It was only to be expected that this narrative, in which royal deaths are brought into relation to famine and fertility, should have been interpreted in terms of the divine king myth. Kapelrud has worked out this interpretation in detail.[5] Stressing the time reference "from the beginning of harvest until the rain fell" (vs. 10), he argued that the death of the royal victims was a powerful fertility rite recommended to David by the non-Yahweh-worshipping priests of Gibeon, whose shrine David patronized, just as he did that of El Elyon in Zion. This is not the place to offer a criticism of the divine kingship theory, but it may be said that it is hardly necessary as an explanation in the present chapter, when the details are sufficiently illustrated by ideas better attested in Israel.

---

[1] And many would add "the political sagacity of David" in getting rid of his political rivals by conniving with the oracle. This is as maybe. At least justification is sought for the blood purge of the royal predecessor's survivors, which otherwise was regarded as quite normal in the ancient world.

[2] Malamat compares the remarkable parallel in a Hittite source. Murshili the Hittite king (1340-1310 B.C.) prays for the end of a twenty year long plague which had begun in the time of his father Shuppiluliuma. The cause is revealed to him as a breach of a treaty by his father. Murshili tries to appease the gods by humbling himself and bringing offerings.

[3] The meaning of the verb *hôqaʿ* is uncertain, as is noted above on Num. 25 : 4. From the Qal used in Gen. 32 : 36 of putting a bone out of joint Köhler suggests "expose (with legs a. arms broken)" (*Lexicon*, p. 398). In both passages exposing beneath the heat of the sun is prominent.

[4] The verb translated "entreated" *ʿātar* is in Arabic "to slaughter for sacrifice." The weakened sense "to make entreaty for" clearly shows the connection of propitiation and sacrifice.

[5] A. S. Kapelrud, *op. cit.*, pp. 113-22. Also *ZAW* LXVII (1955), pp. 198-205.

David's Water Libation (2 Sam 23 : 16)

Many writers speak of this as an offering, and this might be thought to be clear enough when the phrase *way-yassēk l^eYahwê* is used (cf. on 1 Sam. 7 : 6). If an offering is thought of, however, it was not of water *per se,* but rather as a symbol of blood (vs. 17), and so is illustrative of blood libations rather than water libations.

David and Araunah (2 Sam. 24 : 15-25)

As the *hieros logos* of the Jerusalem sanctuary, this passage is of great importance. The sacrificial practice here may be that which became normative in Jerusalem. The context is of sin and penitence and expiation, but the crucial question of whether the latter was achieved by sacrifice, or preceded the sacrifice, is unfortunately not clear. Smend arguing against sacrificial expiation, claimed that this was an example of a bad case, where the cultus had ceased to operate and could only be resumed after the assurance that God was already expiated.[1] Welch on the other hand believed that Jerusalem might well have been the sanctuary which maintained the expiatory tradition, and traced it back to this propitiatory sacrifice on the floor of Araunah.[2]

Those who maintain the non-expiatory view have difficulty with vs. 17. Without this verse the narrative would run smoothly from vs. 16, where Yahweh stays his hand, to vs. 18, where David offers a sacrifice of thanksgiving. Vs. 17 however, brings in a prayer of David and his confession of penitence, which taken in conjunction with vs. 18, would support the expiatory view of the sacrifices. Those who argue that vs. 17 does not follow on vs. 16 seem in the right in view of vs. 17a. Three possible courses are open—1. to omit the verse as an interpolation (Nowack)[3]—2. to read it before vs. 16 (Budde)[4]—3. to assign it to a second source.

Neither the first nor second views are satisfactory. There are no textual grounds for either supposition. The third view would allow one tradition, in which Yahweh stopped the plague at the gates of Jerusalem, and David offered a sacrifice of thanksgiving, and another in which deliverance was obtained after David's inter-

[1] R. Smend, *op. cit.*, p. 126.
[2] A. C. Welch, *Post-Exilic Judaism,* Edinburgh (1935), pp. 294ff.
[3] W. Nowack (*HK*) (1902), p. 261.
[4] K. Budde (*KHC*), p. 330.

cession and sacrifice.[1] David is then able to say to Araunah in vs. 21 that he buys the threshing-floor "in order to build an altar to the Lord, that the plague may be averted from the people." It must be concluded that the view, which omits the expiatory meaning, is unsatisfactory, if only for the reason that the last verse of the narrative—and of the book—sums up that, after the sacrifice, Yahweh was entreated for the land (the same phrase as in 21 : 14). The sacrificial words are *'ōlôt* (vs. 22, vs. 24, vs. 25), and *šᵉlāmîm* (vs. 25).

Conclusion

This chapter has examined approximately twenty-five instances of sacrifice in twenty-one passages. In eleven passages it has not been possible to decide into which of the two main categories they fall. Seven passages reflecting the more solemn view have been assigned to category A. One of these is a special case, which perhaps should be set on one side (1 Sam. 6 : 3-9), and two others might justifiably be questioned as somewhat late (Ch. 7, Ch. 13 : 8-15). The human sacrifice of 2 Sam. 21 is possibly also not good evidence, but three clear cases which may be taken as indicative of the regular Israelite view remain (1 Sam. 3 : 14, 1 Sam. 26 : 19; 2 Sam. 24 : 15-25).

This is a more impressive list than the few cases that can be assigned to category B as reflecting a purely joyous view. Although Ch. 1, 2 : 12-17 and Ch. 9 have been included under this second heading, not enough is known about the motives of the sacrifice in these passages to prove that they really belong here.

From the category C—the doubtful or unclassifiable cases—1 Sam. 16 : 1-13, 1 Sam. 20 : 5-6, 24-29; 2 Sam. 15 : 7-12 could possibly go into category B as sacrificial meals. Four other cases—those dealing with the removal of the ark (1 Sam. 6; 2 Sam. 6) and Saul at Gilgal (1 Sam. 11 : 12-15, 1 Sam. 15) might go into either category as both rejoicing and solemnity are in the contexts. Two cases which are not clearly sacrifice (1 Sam. 14 : 45; 2 Sam. 23 : 16), a reference to sacrificial materials (1 Sam. 10 : 3), and the problem passage (1 Sam. 14 : 32-35) make up the list of eleven in category C.

The conclusion must therefore be that the more solemn view of

[1] R. de Vaux, (*JerusB*), p. 237. See J. J. Stamm, *Erlösen und Vergeben im Alten Testament*, pp. 106-107 for a possible analysis.

sacrifice is not only present in the sources, but is even better attested than the opposite view of Wellhausen and Robertson Smith, and again it must be asked if this is credible in the light of general considerations. Wellhausen's comment on this period was that "the ancient Israelites did not build a church first of all; what they built first was a house to live in,"[1] and that therefore all theologically tinted narratives were suspect. This judgment is not even probable for the early evolution of man—altars and sacrifice are at least as old as human dwellings—and is certainly not true of a people of revelation. There is no untheological writing in the Books of Samuel, least of all in "the Court History of David," which is shot through and through by a moral and theological purpose.[2] A. George has collected an impressive list of "faults against Yahweh" in the Books of Samuel,[3] and one is impressed by the constant shadow of cultic prohibitions (1 Sam. 20 : 26, 21 : 4 etc.) and the awe of Yahweh's transcendent personality (1 Sam. 6 : 19; 2 Sam. 6 : 7, 2 Sam. 24). With such a background a solemn view of sacrifice is consistent, but the light-hearted joyousness of the fellowship theory impossible.

---

[1] J. Wellhausen, *Prolegomena*, p. 255.

[2] So M. Smith, "The So-Called 'Biography of David,' " *HTR* XLIV (1951), pp. 167-69, who describes it as a moral tract illustrating the punishment of sin, and the reward of penitence and humility. To him these motives are late. G. Gusdorf, *op. cit.*, pp. 129, 138, 157-58 has chosen the story of 2 Sam. 12 to illustrate how the sinner may find peace of mind through sacrifice. When David accepts the death of his child as a sacrifice for his sins, he regains moral integrity.

[3] A. George, "Fautes contre Yahweh dans les livres de Samuel," *RB* LIII (1946), pp. 161-84. His larger work *Le péché dans les livres de Samuel*, Lyon (1944) was unfortunately not available to the writer.

REFERENCES TO SACRIFICE IN SAMUEL

Reference	Incident	Terms Used		Primary or Secondary	Israelite or Foreign	National or Individual	Special or Regular
A. Where a sense of sin or solemnity is present							
1. S. 3 : 10-14	Sin of Eli's House	*zebaḥ minḥâ*	*kipper*	?Primary	Israelite	Individual	Regular
1. S. 6 : 3-9	ʾĀšām of the Philistines	*ʾāšām*		Primary	Non-Isra.	National	Special
1. S. 7	Samuel at Mizpah	*ʿôlâ kālîl*	*ʿālâ*	?Secondary	Israelite	National	Special
1. S. 13 : 8-15	First Rejection of Saul	*ʿōlâ š*^{e}*lāmîm*	*ʿālâ*	?Primary	Israelite	National	Special
1. S. 26 : 19	David's Reply to Saul	*minḥâ*		Primary	Israelite	Individual	Regular
2. S. 21 : 1-14	Execution of Sons of Saul		*kipper*	Primary	?Israelite	National	Special
2. S. 24 : 15-25	David and Araunah	*ʿōlôt š*^{e}*lāmîm*	*ʿālâ*	Primary	Israelite	National	Special
B. Where a sense of sin or solemnity is not present							
1. S. 1	Elkanah at Shiloh	*zebaḥ*	*zābaḥ ʾākal*	Primary	Israelite	Family	Regular
1. S. 2 : 12-17	Sacrificial Dues at Shiloh	*minḥâ zebaḥ*	*zābaḥ*	Primary	Israelite	Individual	Regular
1. S. 9 : 11-24	Anointing of Saul	*zebaḥ*	*ʾākal*	Primary	Israelite	Local	Regular
C. Doubtful or unclassifiable passages							
1. S. 2 : 27-36	Sin of Eli's House	*minḥâ zebaḥ q*^{e}*ṭôret ʾiššê*	*ʿālâ qṭr*	?Secondary	Israelite	Priestly	Regular
1. S. 6 : 14-15	Return of the Ark	*ʿōlâ zebaḥ*	*zābaḥ ʿālâ*	Primary	Israelite	Local	Special
1. S. 10 : 3	Offerings for Bethel			Primary	Israelite	Individual	Regular
1. S. 11 : 12-15	Renewal of the Kingdom	*z*^{e}*bāḥîm š*^{e}*lāmîm*	*zābaḥ*	?Primary	Israelite	National	Special
1. S. 14 : 32-35	Saul at Michmash		*ʾākal*	Primary	Israelite	National	Regular
1. S. 14 : 45	Redemption of Jonathan		*pādâ*	Primary	Israelite	National	Special
1. S. 15	Second Rejection of Saul	*ʿōlôt z*^{e}*bāḥîm*	*zābaḥ*	?Secondary	Israelite	National	Regular
1. S. 16 : 1-13	Anointing of David	*zebaḥ*	*zābaḥ*	?Secondary	Israelite	Local	Regular
1. S. 20 : 5-6, 24, 29	David's Family Sacrifice	*zebaḥ*		Primary	Israelite	Family	Regular
2. S. 6 : 12-19	Removal of the Ark	*ʿōlôt š*^{e}*lāmîm*	*ʿālâ zābaḥ*	Primary	Israelite	National	Special
2. S. 15 : 7-12	Sacrifice of Absalom	*z*^{e}*bāḥîm*	*zābaḥ*	Primary	Israelite	Individual	Regular
2. S. 23 : 16	David's Water Libation		*nāsaq*	Primary	Israelite	Individual	Special

CHAPTER SIX

KINGS

Introduction

The next period of Israelite history was marked by significant changes which must have had their effect on sacrifice. First among these was the building of the temple, and closely associated with it, the establishment of the monarchy on dynastic lines. Much attention has been given these subjects in recent years, so that it is no longer possible to dismiss the temple, as some were formerly inclined to do, as an insignificant and unpopular royal shrine with little place in the lives of the people. Noth has asked whether the fundamental significance which Jerusalem came to assume[1] was due to her connection with the Davidids or to the presence of the ark, and concludes that it was the latter, as much as the former which hallowed Jerusalem as the Holy Mount for Israel.[2] The ark as the central shrine of the Israelite amphictyony, had no less significance on Mt. Zion and must have hallowed the temple also for every Israelite.[3] The temple was a royal chapel it is true,[4] but it was also very much more.[5]

The second chief factor with a bearing on the subject of sacrifice is the question of sacral kingship. To what extent was the king

---

[1] He remarks on the startling difference in the short four hundred years between the Pentateuch sources with their complete omission of Jerusalem and the sentiment of such a psalm as Ps. 137 "if I forget thee O Jerusalem" (M. Noth, "Jerusalem und die israelitische Tradition," *GS*, München (1957), pp. 173-74).

[2] He claims that Jerusalem is central in prophetic visions of the future, not because of her connection to the future of the House of David—in the 'Messianic' prophecies the Jerusalem reference is largely lacking—but in her own right as the place of Yahweh's enthronement over the ark, pp. 176-84.

[3] The strength of this feeling over the whole period is attested by such an early song as Exod. 15 on the one hand with its *Landnahme* culminating on the Holy Mount (so H. Schmid, "Jahwe und die Kulttradition von Jerusalem," *ZAW* LXVII (1955), pp. 168-97), and by such a record as Jer. 41 : 5 describing pilgrimages from Ephraim to Jerusalem in 586 B.C. on the other.

[4] So W. F. Albright, *Archaeology and the Religion of Israel*, p. 139.

[5] Cf. C. R. North, "The Religious Aspects of Hebrew Kingship," *ZAW* L (1932), p. 20.

of Israel a sacral figure reproducing in Jerusalem the ritual pattern common to the rest of the ancient Near East? This question is of utmost importance to the discussion of penitence and sacrifice. The ritual pattern as reconstructed by Gaster[1] consisted of a *kenosis* (mortification and purgation) and a *plerosis* (invigoration and jubilation). In his description of the second half of this ritual, Gaster quotes with approval Robertson Smith's view that the communion meal was so much a part of the festivals that they were called feasts, and joy was so much the essence of them that Amos could practically identify the two, when he said "I will turn your *ḥaggîm* (E.V. feasts) into mourning."[2] He is not satisfied, however, with Robertson Smith's explanation of fasting as nothing more than a preparation before eating holy flesh.[3] Israel fasted also at other times and this fasting must express penitence and purgation of national sin.[4]

The atonement for this national sin was achieved by the king in the Mesopotamian cult.[5] The ritual humbling of the king is thought to but thinly disguise the older practice of the death of the king, or a king substitute for the sins of his people. Many scholars have pointed out that traces of this role of the king are to be found in the Israelite high priest, who inherited the functions of the king in the downfall of the monarchy in the exile. His death apparently atones for the manslayer in Num. 35. His garments symbolized his bearing Israel on his shoulders (Exod. 28 : 29-30). He entered the Holy of Holies at risk to himself ("lest he die" Exod. 28 : 34-35).[6]

[1] T. H. Gaster, *Thespis*, pp. 6ff.

[2] *Ibid.*, pp. 27, 29-30.

[3] *Ibid.*, p. 9. Robertson Smith wrote (*Religion of the Semites*, p. 434), "The usage of religious fasting is commonly taken as a sign of sorrow, the worshippers being so distressed at the alienation of their god that they cannot eat; but there are very strong reasons for believing that, in the strict Oriental form in which total abstinence from meat and drink is prescribed, fasting is nothing more than a preparation for the sacramental eating of holy flesh. Some savage nations not only fast, but use strong purges before venturing to eat holy meat . . ."

[4] Gaster's illustration (pp. 44ff) from the Book of Joel shows the close connection of fasting (Ch. 1 : 14-17) and the sense of sin (1 : 18-20)—cf. also 2 : 15-18, but this is of course late. In *Festivals of the Jewish Year*, New York (1952), (repr. 1955), pp. 182-86 he argues, however, that the Day of Atonement is early not late.

[5] S. Mowinckel, *He That Cometh*, E.T. (1956), pp. 38ff.

[6] J. Morgenstern, "A Chapter in the History of the High Priesthood," *AJSL* LV (1938), pp. 1-25 thought this danger reflected in the tradition of

Some have thought that the bells on his garment were intended to reassure the worshippers by their ringing, that all was well with him, while he was out of sight.[1]

Various hints of this sacral role of the king have been found in the Book of Kings e.g. the king's power to heal (2 Kings 5 : 6), the king's responsibility for fertility (1 Kings 18), the king as mediator of the covenant (2 Kings 23 : 3ff)[2] and the king as sacrificing (1 Kings 8 : 5, 63ff., 9 : 25, 12 : 32ff, 16 : 32; 2 Kings 10 : 24, 16 : 12ff). For the king as a divine person, as favoured by some advocates of this theory, recourse must be made to the evidence of the "royal psalms" in the Book of Psalms.[3] If these "messianic" psalms belong to the reigning king, rather than to a coming saviour, some support for the semi-divine role of the king might be forthcoming. After a thorough canvassing of this position, present day discussion tends to veer away from the ascription of divinity to Israel's kings,[4]

---

the death of several chief priests while officiating, and the provision of a substitute high priest to step in in the case of accident. He thought the high priest's task was to rekindle the sacred fire from the rays of the sun.

[1] The alternative explanation regards the bells as a survival of the belief in demons of the threshold requiring to be expelled.

[2] See, G. Widengren, "King and Covenant," *JSS* II (1957), pp. 1-32.

[3] The situation would be different if one could accept Morgenstern's ingenious reconstruction (in his *Amos Studies*, pp. 127-79 = *HUCA* XII-XIII (1937-1938), pp. 1-53) of the sacral function of Solomon, Jeroboam, Jeroboam II and Uzziah. Morgenstern noted the likeness between Uzziah's sin and its punishment in 2 Chron. 26 : 16-21 and Jeroboam's in 1 Kings 12-13, between Amos' encounter with a king called Jeroboam and prophecy of the destruction of the Bethel altar in Amos 7-9 and the unknown prophet's in 1 Kings 13, and between Jeroboam's temple dedication and Solomon's. All these stories reflect the king's annual offering at peril to himself in the New Year's Day rite on which the fertility for the forthcoming year depended. Now see also Morgenstern, "The King-God," *VT* X (1960), pp. 138-97, esp. pp. 191ff.

[4] Frankfort showed that the Babylonian king occupied a much lower place than the divine kings of Egypt (*Kingship and the Gods*, Chicago (1948), esp. pp. 297ff.), and Gray that this was still further reduced among the Canaanites, and in Israel ("Canaanite Kingship in Theory and Practice," *VT* II (1952), pp. 193-220). In Egypt the king as divine visits the queen to beget an heir. In Babylon the goddess is divine, and only if the king is called to her couch is he in some sense divine. He was the servant of the goddess. The ceremony, in which he gave his regalia to the high priest, was unthinkable in Egypt (E. O. James, *The Nature and Function of Priesthood*, London (1955), pp. 130-31, 282). In Egypt the king was an incarnate god and in Babylon a deified man (S. Mowinckel, *He That Cometh*, p. 55). In Babylon the king is prayed for, not to (*ibid.*, p. 48), and the same is true in Ugarit, where Engnell's rendering of Keret 128, col. iv, 28 "sacrifice to your lord

and to speak rather of sacral than of divine kingship.[1]

The evidence of the Book of Kings supports this contention. Ten out of the eighteen sacrifices recorded are offered by the kings themselves. In some cases it is not clear that the king sacrificed personally, rather than through his priesthood, but in five cases this seems plain,[2] and for the other cases may perhaps be assumed.[3] The king's general responsibility for and superintendence of the cult is clear, but the case for his mediatory role in the sense of carrying and atoning for the people's sins cannot be said to be proven. It is possible, however, that the Deuteronomic editor has played down the sacral king element as inconsistent with later ideas of the cult.

The problem of separating earlier sources from the Deuteronomic framework must be met in each case. Most of the sacrificial references belong in the earlier sources—whether the acts of Solomon, the lives of the prophets, or the annals of the kings. In a few cases

---

krt" is to be rejected, in favour of "your lord *krt* hath a sacrifice" (Gray, *op. cit.*, p. 202). Gray's further argument drawn from the Ugaritic data tends to support the view of Alt ("Die Staatenbildung der Israeliten in Palästina," now in *KS* II, pp. 1ff), that by the time of the entry of Israel into Canaan, Canaanite kingship had been much attenuated, and could scarcely have had a great influence on the Israelite monarchy.

[1] So already C. R. North, "The Religious Aspects of Hebrew Kingship," *op. cit.*, p. 37 ("he represented the people to God rather than God to the people"). This is approximately the position, with some variations, of A. Johnson in "Hebrew Conceptions of Kingship," *Myth, Ritual, and Kingship* (ed.) S. H. Hooke, pp. 204-35; "Divine Kingship in the Old Testament," *ExpT* LXII (1950-1951), pp. 36-42; "Old Testament Exegesis Imaginative and Unimaginative," *ibid.*, LXVIII (1956-1957), pp. 178-79 (replying to W. S. McCullough, "Israel's Kings, Sacral and Otherwise," *ibid.*, pp. 144-48), and above all in *Sacral Kingship in Ancient Israel*, Cardiff (1955). Johnson rejects the reading of "O God" in Ps. 45 : 6 as an address to the king (*ibid.*, p. 27). To V. Maag, however, the distinction drawn by these scholars between sacral and divine kingship is a false one. The question is not whether the king was more or less divine, but whether he was seen in the framework of "cosmostatic" myth and magic. Maag argues that this is shown to be the case in Israel (within limits), not only by the royal psalms, but also by the later Messianism, and the fact that the anti-christ is an appearance form of chaos ("Malkût Jhwh," *op. cit.*, pp. 144ff). For the extreme opposite of this view see Kaufmann's presentation of Israel's religion as rejecting all myth and magic, and with it divine kingship (*The Religion of Israel*, pp. 1-149, 266). The divinity of the king, which was possible in polytheism was quite inconceivable in Israel.

[2] 1 Kings 3 : 15, 13 : 1; 2 Kings 10 : 24, 16 : 12-13 (3 : 27).

[3] 1 Kings 3 : 4, 8 : 64, 9 : 25, 10 : 5 (1 : 9).

interpolation may have to be reckoned with. The Deuteronomic framework has also a stereotyped phrase to describe the ritual of apostatizing kings "sacrificing and censing" (1 Kings 3 : 3 (cf. 3 : 2), 11 : 8, 22 : 44(43); 2 Kings 12 : 4(3), 14 : 4, 15 : 4, 15 : 35, 16 : 4 (cf. 18 : 4 also 2 Kings 17 : 32, 35, 36)). The RSV rendering "sacrificed and burned incense" is rejected by Snaith[1] who claims that *qṭr* did not mean incense until post-exilic times. Montgomery, however, is prepared to accept a much earlier origin of incense in Israel,[2] and suggests that sacrificing and censing represent the round of worship.

Adonijah's Accession (1 Kings 1)

Adonijah gathers his supporters at a sacrificial banquet, at which he is proclaimed king. This takes place "by the Serpent's Stone (*'eben haz-zōḥelet*) which is beside En-rogel," (vs. 9). It is not certain that this was an ancient Jerusalem sanctuary with the stone a *maṣṣēbâ* connected to a serpent cult,[3] or whether the well had particular significance in coronation rites.[4] Even the place of sacrifice in the coronation ritual is not securely attested. The only full accounts of coronations—those of Solomon (1 Kings 1 : 33-40) and Joash (2 Kings 11 : 12-14) do not mention it,[5] and the case of Absalom has been seen above to be doubtful. On the present occasion Adonijah sacrifices (*zbḥ*) sheep, oxen and fatlings (vs. 9) in abundance (vss. 19, 25), and invites all the king's sons and royal officials of Judah to eating and drinking (vs. 25) and feasting (vs. 41). If religious rites marked the occasion, they have been passed over by the narrator.

---

[1] N. H. Snaith, "Kings," *IB* III (1954), p. 40.

[2] J. Montgomery (*ICC*) (1951), p. 104. He says that the objection that incense did not reach Palestine until much later is fully disproved by the discovery of incense censers at Tanaach, by the early incense trade in Egypt, and by a name like Keturah. See now the discussion of M. Haran "The uses of incense in the ancient Israelite ritual," *VT* X (1960), pp. 113-29.

[3] Traces of a serpent cult are thought to be found in Num. 21 : 9; 2 Kings 18 : 4 and possibly the seraphim of Is. 6 : 2. Neh. 2 : 13 speaks of a Dragon (or Jackal) Well, but here the word is *tannîm*. See further Montgomery (*ICC*), p. 74.

[4] Solomon is proclaimed by the spring of Gihon (1 Kings 1 : 38). Mowinckel suggests that this was part of the coronation ritual and is reflected in Ps. 110 : 7 "he shall drink of the brook by the way" (*He That Cometh*, pp. 63-64).

[5] See G. von Rad "Das judäische Königsritual," *GS*, pp. 205-13.

Solomon at Gibeon (1 Kings 3 : 4, 3 : 15)

Vss. 2 and 3 may be left aside as redactional (vs. 2), or Deuteronomic (vs. 3), but vs. 4 probably belongs to the old source relating the Gibeon dream (vss. 5-13). It is not certain that vs. 4b in its present form belongs here,[1] but if so *ʿōlôt* of intercession were probably offered for divine assistance.

Vs. 15 which speaks of Solomon returning to Jerusalem after the divine revelation, and offering *ʿōlôt* (*ʿālâ*) and *šelāmîm* (*ʿāśâ*) before the ark of the covenant, is usually struck out as a Deuteronomic addition moving the scene from Gibeon to Jerusalem. Montgomery, however, accepts the sacrificial reference of vs. 15b as concluding the scene at Gibeon. A feast for Solomon's ministers concludes the sacrifice. It is not clear how long Solomon has been on the throne, or whether this was in any sense an initiatory sacrifice.

The Dedication of the Temple (1 Kings 8 : 5, 62-66)

Again at the dedication of the temple there is a clear tradition of sacrifices, but no certainty as to details in the text.[2] The numbers are impossibly large, even for royal hecatombs (22,000 oxen and 120,000 sheep).[3] Hölscher thinks it incredible that the new altar should have been too small on the first occasion it was used.[4]

[1] Montgomery (*ICC*), p. 105 sees no reason to regard vs. 4 as redactoral with Benzinger or partly so with Stade, and asks why a later age should wish to glorify Gibeon. The Hebrew of vs. 4b is, however, difficult. Why the emphatic "on that altar", when only the high place and not an altar had been previously mentioned? Benzinger, *Könige* (*KHC*) (1899), p. 15 suggests a gloss from the Chronicler's addition of the bronze altar in 2 Chron. 1 : 6. Vs. 4b also has no grammatical connection to vs. 4a. The use of the imperfect without waw must be translated with RSV "he used to offer a thousand *ʿōlôt* on that altar." This sounds more like a routine description similar to 9 : 25. Klostermann (*SZ*), p. 276 suggests an emendation of "Solomon" to *šelāmîm* and reads *wayyaʿal ʿōlôt wayyaʿal šelāmîm*. He thinks *ʾelep* "thousand" comes in from Chronicles.

[2] Vs. 5 in the LXX is much shorter and lacks "Solomon," "the congregation" and part of the last clause. Vs. 63 in 2 Chron. 7 : 5 lacks the words "the *šelāmîm* which he offered to the Lord." Vs. 64 in the LXX possibly omitted *minḥâ* in both its occurrences (see BH). In vs. 65 after "our God" LXX adds "in the house which we have built, eating and drinking and rejoicing."

[3] It is possible of course that *ʾelep* might have been used like "hecatomb" in a metaphorical sense for a much smaller number of sacrifices than the literal translation would imply.

[4] G. Hölscher, "Das Buch der Könige, seine Quellen und seine Redaktion," *Eucharisterion* (Gunkel Festschrift), Vol. I, Göttingen (1923), p. 169. He regards the passage as a late midrash-like story.

Snaith points out that there is no record of the construction of this bronze altar and thinks it belonged to the second temple.[1] Mowinckel thinks that the editors had no material, and so pictured the scene as it would have taken place in their own time.[2] This is probably a too pessimistic conclusion, but it must be confessed that scarcely one certain element, except the bare fact of sacrificing on a large scale, remains.[3] Whether the sacrifices were of dedication,[4] or of fellowship, and whether an eating and rejoicing followed is not certain.[5]

The tradition of the vast quantity of victims, both in this incident, and in the previous one, needs some explanation. For the first time in the history we read of sacrifices numbering thousands. It might be possible that the need of providing a sacramental meal for a great assembly would account for the quantity of victims.[6] The use of the verb *zābaḥ* (8 : 62) would support this interpretation,[7] but something more is needed to explain the *ʿōlôt*.[8] It has been suggested that this immense sacrificing reflects a sense of the heavy weight of sin borne by the king on behalf of the people. This might be supported by the fact that the ceremonies probably coincided with the autumn festival, but whether this was so or not a dedication itself was not without its solemn side.[9]

---

[1] N. Snaith, *IB*, pp. 88ff. But see below on 2 Kings 16.

[2] S. Mowinckel, *Psalmenstudien* II, p. 109.

[3] Cf. the vaguer reference in vs. 5. In this verse, however, the Piel is used. In all other instances of the Piel of *zbḥ*, with the exception of the parallel passage in 2 Chron. 5 : 6 and one further passage possibly dependent on it (2 Chron. 30 : 22), apostate worship is being described (so e.g. in the references to "sacrificing and censing" listed on p. 124). As this cannot be the case here, it is suggested that the Piel in vs. 5 means to "offer" in general, "to put something on the altar," while the Qal in vs. 62 comes to the specific sense of "slaughter," although the question of the type of sacrifice remains open (see on 2 Kings 10 : 18ff).

[4] Nothing is said of blood-rites like those of 2 Kings 16 : 13, but these must certainly have taken place (cf. Exod. 24 : 6).

[5] The LXX supplies this in vs. 65, but the mention of rejoicing anticipates that in vs. 66, and is probably not original.

[6] So Snaith, *loc. cit.*

[7] The references to the burning of the fat of the *šᵉlāmîm* imply that the rest was eaten.

[8] MT *ʿōlâ* in vs. 64 must be a collective. In 3 : 4 it is *ʿōlôt*, that are offered by the thousand, and the same is implied in vs. 64b (against Snaith).

[9] H. Gressmann (*SAT*), 2,1 ([2]1921), p. 212 compares present day rites of consecrating a new house by the killing of a sheep or goat on the roof and letting the blood run down.

Solomon's Sacrifices (1 Kings 9 : 25, 10 : 5, 11 : 8)

None of these passages are above question. In 9 : 25 the notice that Solomon sacrificed three times a year *ʿōlôt* and *šᵉlāmîm* is probably from an old source, although scarcely from the "annals."[1] The latter part of the verse "censing it which" (*haqṭêr*) is corrupt.[2] What the three occasions were is a matter for conjecture. One naturally thinks of the three pilgrimage feasts, but in the absence of any other mention of these feasts (except for the feast of the seventh month in 8 : 2) certainty is impossible.

In 10 : 5 an emendation of *ʿōlātô* to *ʿōlōtāw* is necessary to get sacrifice in the text. While this is supported by the LXX, the Chronicler's suggestion of an architectural wonder "the ascent (*ʿᵃlîtāw*) by which he went up into the House of the Lord" also has some support in *ʿōlôtāw* in Ez. 40 : 26.[3] It really becomes a question of what in Solomon's fixtures would have incited the wonder of the Queen of Sheba. Burnt offerings as a subject of wonder might confirm the tradition of the grand scale of Solomon's cult.

In 11 : 8 the Deuteronomic formula for the sin of apostasy "censing and sacrificing" is ascribed to Solomon or his wives.[4]

Jeroboam's Sacrifices (1 Kings 12 : 26-13 : 1)

Again there is a problematical section of which little is left after analysis, and yet which must preserve a genuine tradition.[5] The

---

[1] G. Hölscher, *op. cit.*, p. 172, who thinks that a late source would have had much more frequent royal sacrificing as in Ezekiel, suggests J. Eissfeldt (*HSAT*) (⁴1922), p. 517 assigns it to his ninth century source Sa. Stade, however, in *SBOT* (1904) thought it harmonistic.

[2] Klostermann suggested *ʾiššô* for *ʾitô* which is accepted by BH, but this brings in the further problem of the date of the *ʾiššê*. LXX is also doubtful but probably omits.

[3] In all these passages, however, the text is doubtful.

[4] MT reads feminine participles, but LXX masculine. The grammar of the former has been objected to by Klostermann (*SZ*), Benzinger (*KHC*), Stade (*SBOT*), Eissfeldt (*HSAT*), Hölscher, *op. cit.*, p. 175, and deletion or rearrangement suggested, but is hardly necessary from the Hebrew (cf. Montgomery (*ICC*)).

[5] Montgomery thinks that two sins of Jeroboam are related—that of the high places in vss. 26-31, and that of the king himself officiating at the altar vss. 32ff. Vs. 32, however, with its reference to a feast of the eighth month, seems to belong with the first section, and vs. 31 on improper personnel at the altar, with the latter. It is not certain that Jeroboam was condemned in the latter section for officiating at the altar more than for his other innovations. The repetitions in vss. 32 and 33 suggest compilation, but the

Deuteronomic nature of the passage has long been recognized, but the fact remains that "calves" were made by Jeroboam as the prophets amply imply (Hos. 8 : 5, 10 : 5 etc.), and that some such dedication as that of the text must have taken place.

Jeroboam gives as his motive the prevention of the people going up (*ʿālâ*) to Jerusalem to sacrifice (*ʿāśâ zᵉbāḥîm*). Although to the Deuteronomist the sin of sins for which Jeroboam was responsible was the division of Israel, and this passage might stem directly from this concern, it is not impossible that there was such a going up to Jerusalem to be countered by the new Kingdom. That he consecrated his new altars by sacrifice is also probable. The verbs used are *zābaḥ, haqṭîr* and probably *ʿālâ*. The idea involved would be similar to that in Ch. 8.[1]

Hiel and Jericho (1 Kings 16 : 34)

This incident has been treated in connection with Josh. 6 : 26 see above p. 81. To what was said there may be added the remark, that the occurrence of the passage in a section dealing with Ahab's apostasies, might support the view that child sacrifices of the foundation type are being described.

The Contest on Mt. Carmel (1 Kings 18 : 19ff)

The integrity of this narrative is admitted, except for vss. 31-32, which speak of the construction of a new altar out of twelve stones, where vs. 30 speaks of the repair of an altar already there.[2] Vs. 31 is certainly no proper continuation of vs. 30,[3] and Mont-

ambiguity of the verb *ʿālâ* "went up" or "offered" makes analysis difficult.

[1] J. Morgenstern, *Amos Studies*, Cincinnati (1941), p. 160 (= *HUCA* XII-XIII (1937-1938), p. 34) thinks the original story amplified first by the Deuteronomist, who condemned Jeroboam for setting up sanctuaries outside of Jerusalem, and then by P who charges him with changing the date of the festival. Morgenstern thinks the charges palpably false because nothing would have achieved Jeroboam's object less than the staggering of the dates of the festivals, and allowing the festival-happy crowd from both kingdoms to attend both. His own solution that the time of Jeroboam's feast was the same as that of Solomon's depends on his theory of the Jewish calendar.

[2] "Twelve stones" is thought to be inappropriate in the Northern Kingdom of only ten tribes, while the identification of Jacob by the Gen. 35 formula "Israel shall be your name" is claimed as a P usage.

[3] LXX reads the words "and he rebuilt the altar" after vs. 31. C. F. Burney (*Notes on the Hebrew Text of the Books of Kings*, Oxford (1903), p. 225) thinks the repetitions of the MT due to the diffuse style of the writer, and notes that J in Gen. 32 : 28 records the facts mentioned in vs. 31b, as well as P.

gomery may be right in his suggestion of variant traditions according to one of which, Carmel was already a Yahweh sanctuary, while in the other still under the aegis of Baal. The most illuminating discussion is that of Alt,[1] who argues from the territorial boundaries that Carmel was an undisturbed Canaanite possession, and the symbol of alien worship. David had possibly instituted a parallel Yahweh worship, without eliminating the older Baal cult, but this Yahweh cult was of short duration, because the region probably returned to Phoenicia along with the territories granted by Solomon. It was regained at the latest by the time of Ahab, but remained the stronghold of Baal worship until Elijah suggested this invasion of his domains.

The story no doubt reflects northern sacrificial ritual in the time of Elijah, but shows little difference from that in the south, or apparently for that matter from that of the Baal worship. A stone altar is built, the wood is arranged (*ʿārak*), the bullock killed and cut in pieces (*ntḥ*) and finally the fire applied. The offering is described as an *ʿōlâ* in vss. 34(33) and 38, and the time of the offering is the time of the *ʿᵃlôt ham-minḥâ* (vs. 29, vs. 36).[2] The propitiatory nature of the sacrifice comes out clearly in the activities of the Baal prophets, who lacerate themselves with knives, and dance around the altar (vs. 26ff).[3] Elijah's sacrifice implies communion already established with the deity, but the unique nature of the occasion as an ordeal, in which the sacrifice apparently was merely a tool, renders it an unsuitable example of ordinary sacrifice.[4]

---

[1] A. Alt, "Das Gottesurteil auf dem Karmel," now in *KS* II, pp. 135-49.

[2] That such a time tag was in common use makes it plain that daily offerings were not a post-exilic innovation. It cannot be proved e.g. that this *minḥâ* and that of 2 Kings 3 : 20 were not *ʿōlôt*, or that the twice daily *ʿōlôt* were not pre-exilic, as Wellhausen argued (*Prolegomena*, p. 79).

[3] The verb *psḥ* is thought to refer to the limping dance around an altar. Moslems on *ḥāg* in Mecca must encircle the Kaaba, and such a dance around an altar is well attested. LXX, however, reads "leaped upon the altar." Self-mutilation is referred to in such passages as Hos. 7 : 14; Micah 4 : 14 (5 : 1); Jer. 16 : 6, 41 : 5, 47 : 5, but was forbidden to Israel in Deut. 14 : 1 and Lev. 19 : 28.

[4] Many find rain-making ceremonies involved in the water pouring on the altar and in the context of a time of drought followed by rains. It seems that this aspect of the story is a separate one and better kept distinct from that of the ordeal on Carmel.

The Farewell of Elisha (1 Kings 19 : 21)

This spontaneous act of Elisha of killing (*zābaḥ*) and making a meal of the oxen, with which he had been ploughing raises the question of whether the slaughtering could have taken place at a sanctuary, and have been sacrificial. It is usually understood in this sense, as the verb *zābaḥ* is used, and the flesh is boiled (*bšl*) and eaten,[1] but it has been suggested above that the sacrificial nature of incidents such as these has been too much taken for granted.

The Morning Sacrifice (2 Kings 3 : 20)

Here again the offering of the *minḥâ* (*ʿalôt ham-minḥâ*) is made a time tag, but on this occasion in the early morning. This reference and that of 1 Kings 18 : 33, 38 seem to make it quite plain that twice-daily sacrifices were offered throughout the kingdom period.

Mesha's Sacrifice (2 Kings 3 : 27)

The sacrifice of Mesha's eldest son was almost certainly a desperate attempt to propitiate Chemosh, god of Moab, to turn the tide of battle. The sacrifice is effective, and the Israelites have to go back. G. B. Gray writes: "The sacrifice in this case is a Moabite sacrifice, but the interpreter is a Hebrew interpreter. We need not necessarily infer that a Hebrew interpreter would have approved of a similar sacrifice to Yahweh under any circumstances, but as to the purpose and effect of approved sacrifices to Yahweh also he speaks if indirectly yet clearly enough."[2] Such *ʿōlôt* were propitiatory.

Naaman in Syria (2 Kings 5 : 17)

Naaman in asking for two mules' burden of earth vows to offer no *ʿōlâ* or *zebaḥ* save to Jahweh. He expects to continue to attend the House of Rimmon, but in addition to have a private altar to Yahweh on the transported Jewish soil. To offer *ʿōlâ* and *zebaḥ* seems to be a stereotyped description of sacrifice.

---

[1] LXX omits *bāśār*, which comes in awkwardly after *biššlām*.

[2] G. B. Gray, *Sacrifice in the Old Testament*, p. 86. On the meaning of "wrath" Albright, *Archaeology and the Religion of Israel*, p. 164 compares Josh. 9 : 20 and remarks that Israel considered Mesha's sacrifice a terrible thing.

Jehu in the Baal Temple (2 Kings 10 : 18-27)

The possible over-writing of this old narrative by the Deuteronomist in vss. 19 and 21 does not affect the references to sacrifice. In vs. 19 Jehu professes the desire to offer a great sacrifice (*zebaḥ*) to Baal. In vs. 24, however, it is *ʿōlôt* as well as *zᵉbāḥîm*, that he is going to offer (*ʿāśâ*), and in vs. 25 an *ʿōlâ*, which he has offered (*ʿāśâ*), when the signal is given for the massacre. It is probable, therefore, that the term *zebaḥ* is a general one for sacrifice, and does not in itself settle the question as to the type of sacrifice,[1] or the mood of the offerer. The latter can only be guessed at in the present narrative. The offerer is apparently Jehu himself as ruler.[2] The worshippers are provided with special garments, mentioned only here.

Joash's Ḥaṭṭāʾt and ʾĀšām (2 Kings 12 : 5-17)

In the description of the moneys to be brought into the collection box set up by Joash an exception was made of the *kesep ʾāšām* and the *kesep ḥaṭṭāʾôt*, which were not brought into the house of the Lord, but were for the priests (vs. 17=vs. 16). Money from the *ʾāšām* is referred to in Lev. 5 : 14-16 and Lev. 5 : 24 (6 : 5), but nothing is known of money from the sin offering *ḥaṭṭāʾt*. If some kind of recognition of the priests' services is intended, one would expect mention of *ʿōlâ* and *zebaḥ* money also.[3] It is probable then, that fines were prescribed by the priests as a penance for sin. The question as to whether in addition animal sacrifices like those of Lev. 4-6 were offered, is not raised and deductions as to their

[1] Cf. G. B. Gray, *Sacrifice in the Old Testament*, p. 401: "*Zebaḥ* is used generally if not invariably for a . . . particular class, although etymologically *zebaḥ, slain* (offering) might very suitably have been used for all offerings consisting of slain animals. Curiously enough in Phoenician *zbḥ*, in spite of its obvious etymology, acquired the most general sense of sacred offering, so that in the Marseilles sacrificial tariff we read of *zbḥ šmn*, a *sacrifice of oil*." (See the Conclusion below.)

[2] So in vs. 25 but not necessarily in MT of vs. 24, where the verb "went" is plural. The verb *ʿāśâ* in vs. 25 is used in 1 Kings 18 : 25 for the preparing of a sacrifice, rather than the offering of it, but "offering" is more often the meaning. The variations probably represent an attempt to get around the difficulty of Jehu's officiating in such a place.

[3] The same objection would apply to the suggestion that money was sent to the priests by worshippers at a distance, for the provision of victims. (Montgomery, (*ICC*), p. 432 suggests for *makkārô* in vs. 6 a derivation, not from *nkr* "acquaintance," but from *mkr* "trader").

existence or non-existence can scarcely be made.[1] Even apart from this, the passage is evidence for a sense of sin, and provision for reparation for it, long before the seventh century.

The Sacrifices of Ahaz (2 Kings 16 : 10-16)

Although Ahaz is given the reputation of an innovator, and a "bad" king, who offered his son as a burnt offering (the first of whom this is recorded (16 : 3)), the sacrifices listed in the present passage are not greatly different from what we know from other sources to have been those of Israel.[2] The burning (*qāṭar*) of *ʿōlâ* and *minḥâ*, the pouring out of drink offerings, either alone or as accompaniments of the *ʿōlâ*, the dashing (*zāraq*) of the blood of the *šelāmîm* against the altar (vs. 13) are all otherwise known.[3] It was argued in connection with Exod. 24, that a purificatory significance was to be attached to this blood rite, and this suits the occasion here also better than ideas of communion or of covenant renewal.[4] Ahaz was scarcely concerning himself with covenant renewal. The blood must have signified dedication.

The narrative continues with Ahaz prescribing a further ritual in vs. 15. Upon the great altar are to be burnt the morning *ʿōlâ* and the evening *minḥâ*, the *ʿōlâ* and *minḥâ* of the king and the *ʿōlâ* and *minḥâ* of the *ʿam hā-āreṣ*. The drink offering of the latter is also to be poured out on it (no verb), and the blood of the *ʿōlâ* and *zebaḥ* dashed against it. The relation of vs. 15 to vs. 13 is difficult. Is it a separate order for a regular ritual, or an addition for this occasion, or a doublet? Why are the *ʿōlâ* and *minḥâ* now respectively for "morning" and "evening," why is the drink offering associated only with the offerings of the *ʿam hā-āreṣ* and why is the blood to be dashed against the altar that of the *ʿōlâ* and *zebaḥ* and

---

[1] So G. B. Gray, *Sacrifice in the Old Testament*, p. 62. "It was germane to the story to refer to money; it was not germane to the story to refer to sacrifices."

[2] Ahaz's new altar constructed after the pattern of one seen in Damascus at the time of his meeting with Tiglath-Pileser, probably represents the acceptance of the Assyrian cult that was required from vassals. The ritual employed, however, does not seem un-Israelite.

[3] Drink offerings are referred to in Gen. 35 : 14 and Deut. 32 : 38, and as accompaniments of the *ʿōlâ* in Exod. 29 : 40 and Num. 28-29, but do not figure in Lev. 1-7. The dashing of the blood against the altar occurred also in Exod. 24 : 6.

[4] As favoured e.g. by Schötz, *op. cit.*, p. 78.

not that of the *šᵉlāmîm* as above? It is possible as Snaith supposes that there has been some over-writing by a post-exilic editor, but it is hardly necessary to say that daily morning and evening offerings reflect post-exilic use, when already in 1 Kings 18; 2 Kings 3 this usage seems to be attested.

The final words of vs. 15 "the bronze altar shall be *lᵉbaqqēr*" are usually taken now as a reference to divination "to enquire by,"[1] rather than as previously, "while I consider what should be done with it." The problem of this altar is a little beyond the sphere of this discussion, but is mentioned here because of the theory of Robertson Smith that there was no altar of burnt offering in the temple before Ahaz. On his hypothesis of the late development of the burnt offering, there had been little burning done in the temple and either the pillars Jachin and Boaz (whose tops had cressets for the fat), or a wood fire kindled in the centre of the court sufficed.[2] It is certainly remarkable that the making of the bronze altar is not listed in the bronze equipment made by Hiram in 1 Kings 7 : 13ff., that the later fate of this altar should be unknown and that the various references to the altar of Solomon's temple are attended with difficulty,[3] but the existence of a temple altar seems amply attested by the Psalms.

It must finally be noted on this passage that the king has full charge of the ritual arrangements and himself offers the offerings on special occasions (vs. 13), but for the rest entrusts them to his priest (vs. 15). The priest is quite subservient to him, yet remains

---

[1] S. Mowinckel, *Psalmenstudien* I (1921), p. 146.

[2] W. R. Smith, *Religion of the Semites*, pp. 378, 485-89. Albright accepts Smith's explanation as far as Jachin and Boaz are concerned (*Archaeology and the Religion of Israel*, p. 144), but sees no reason to doubt that an altar of burnt offering was also built by Solomon (pp. 150, 217).

[3] In 1 Kings 8 : 64 it is already too small, as apparently also in the present narrative. In 2 Kings 12 : 9 an altar is referred to "on the right as one goes into the House of the Lord." In the present passage the central altar is moved to the right side—the position occupied by it in 2 Kings 12 : 9. The problem seems not that there was no altar, but that there were too many. De Groot, *op. cit.*, pp. 8-28 agrees with a plurality of altars (cf. Ps. 84 : 4(3)), but the alternative explanation, that the phrase of 2 Kings 12 : 9 is anachronistic for what was to be the position only after 2 Kings 16 : 14, or else belongs rather to one of the "tables" with which Ezekiel is familiar (Ez. 40 : 38-43), seems preferable. See now the very full discussion of W. McKane who favours the last theory in "A Note on 2 Kings 12 : 10," *ZAW* LXXI (1959), pp. 260-65.

the good friend of Isaiah the prophet (Is. 8 : 2). Some support for the sacral kingship theory is thus afforded here.

Josiah's Passover (2 Kings 23 : 21-23)

The ordinance of the "book of the covenant" according to which this Passover was to be kept (vs. 21) was probably that of Deuteronomy. Deut. 16 provides for three changes in practice as against Exod. 12—the sacrifice is to be at the central sanctuary rather than in the home, the victim may be an ox and not just a lamb or goat, and the flesh is to be boiled not roasted. Was the Passover of Josiah unprecedented in the fact that it now observed these rules for the first time, or was it a fact that no Passover had been held since the days of the judges (vs. 23)? To accept the former alternative does not settle all the problems,[1] but is less difficult than the assumption that the Passover began in 621 B.C. Nicolsky, who has tried to illuminate this particular Passover in the light of the history,[2] nevertheless acknowledges the great age of the earlier household rite.[3]

Conclusion

The classification of the eighteen sacrifices in the Books of Kings is less satisfactory than in the earlier chapters. Seven possibly have ideas of propitiation or solemnity, but two of these are non-Israelite. Two cases embracing a meal go into Group B and with these would probably go also 1 Kings 19 : 21, if in fact a sacrifice. Eight cases must go into the unclassifiable category. Several of these

---

[1] In particular that of the relation of Deut. 16 and Exod. 12. The usual analysis which assigns Exod. 12 : 21-23 to an old source, Deut. 16 to the time of Josiah and Exod. 12 : 1-13 to P does not explain why P, having gained the advantages for the priesthood of the centralized rite in Deut. 16, should go back to a house rite in Exod. 12 : 1-13. A. C. Welch, "On the Method of celebrating Passover," *ZAW* XLV (1927), pp. 24-29 suggested that the sources are parallel rather than successive—Exod. 12 : 21-23 being that of the Northern Kingdom until replaced by Deut. 16, and Exod. 12 : 1-13 being that of the Southern Kingdom until Josiah united all the land under the current Northern practice of Deut. 16, now centred on Jerusalem.

[2] M. M. Nicolsky "Pascha im Kulte des jerusalemischen Tempels," *ZAW* XLV (1927), pp. 171-90, 241-53. For him the struggle for independence from Assyria and from Egypt is reflected in the Passover legend of deliverance from Egypt. The destruction of the Passover night is echoed in Zephaniah's "great sacrifice of Yahweh" Zeph. 1 : 7 (p. 188).

[3] *Ibid.*, p. 176.

describe no specific occasion (1 Kings 9 : 25, 10 : 5; 2 Kings 3 : 20, 5 : 17) and those which do are exceptional in one way or another (1 Kings 18 : 23ff; 2 Kings 10 : 18ff, 2 Kings 23 : 2-3). 1 Kings 16 : 35 has been dealt with in an earlier chapter. Most of the sacrifices are those of the kings, but clear proof of these being connected to an expiation of sins is lacking, although possibly to be taken for granted on festival occasions. Examples of regular, individual, Israelite sacrifices are missing,[1] and must be reconstructed from such general considerations as the sense of sin and the place of worship in the life of the people generally.

Any discussion of the sense of sin in this period is complicated by the problem of separating the older sources from their Deuteronomic framework. Beginning from Deuteronomy with its combination of cultic and humanitarian motives, one might be inclined to regard such incidents of social concern as the story of Naboth's vineyard as stemming from this source. A recent investigator, Walker, has concluded, however, that whatever may have been true of Deuteronomy, as far as the Book of Kings is concerned it is only cultic sins that are condemned by the Deuteronomist.[2] This would mean that the sense of social justice in the story of Naboth is pre-Deuteronomic and from the old source itself, as indeed is probable on other grounds. Such incidents are perhaps rare, and against them must be placed the inadequate view of sin revealed in the words of Bathsheba in 1 Kings 1 : 21 "I and my son shall be sinners." She means that they will suffer the condemnation of sinners, although themselves without ethical fault.[3] On the other hand the nature of the sources only rarely lends itself to stories of ordinary morality. Where such stories are recorded, as e.g. in 2 Kings 4 (the woman of Shunem) a fine spirit breathes through the records. In such a story worship at new moons and festivals is also attested (2 Kings 4 : 23), but for the nature of this worship the investigation must turn to the Psalmists and Prophets.

[1] This is due in the main to the nature of the book, as a book of "Kings."

[2] J. C. Walker, "The Axiology of the Books of Kings," *JBR* XXVII (1959), pp. 218-22. It may be questioned, however, whether such cases as the boys and the bears, Shimei's breach of oath, Solomon's prayer for humility and the disobedience of the prophet of Judah are really cultic sins as Walker suggests.

[3] It is possible, however, that *ḥaṭṭāʾîm* is used here in the sense of punishment for sin, as when Abimelech accuses Abraham of bringing a great sin on the people of Gerar (Gen. 20 : 9). *ʾāšām* is used similarly in the doublet of Isaac's wife denying (Gen. 26 : 10).

REFERENCES TO SACRIFICE IN KINGS

Reference	Incident	Terms Used	Primary or Secondary	Israelite or Foreign	National or Individual	Special or Regular
A. Where a sense of sin or solemnity is present						
?1. K. 3 : 4	Solomon at Gibeon	*ʿōlôt zābaḥ ʿālâ*	Primary	Israelite	Royal	?Special
?1. K. 8 : 5, 62-6	Dedication of Temple	*zebaḥ zbḥ* *zebaḥ šᵉlāmîm zābaḥ* *minḥâ ʿōlâ ʿāśâ*	Primary	Israelite	National	Special
?1. K. 12 : 27-13 : 1	Jeroboam's Sacrifices	*zᵉbāḥîm ʿāśâ ʿālâ* *qṭr zbḥ*	?Primary	?Israelite	National	Special
1. K. 18 : 27ff	Baal Prophets	*ʿōlâ*	Primary	Non-Isra.	National	Special
2. K. 3 : 27	Mesha's Sacrifice	*ʿōlâ ʿālâ*	Primary	Non-Isra.	National	Special
2. K. 12 : 5-17	Joash's *Ḥaṭṭāʾt* and *ʾĀšām*	*ʾāšām ḥaṭṭāʾôt*	Primary	Israelite	Individual	Regular
2. K. 16 : 10-16	Ahaz's Sacrifices	*ʿōlâ minḥâ qṭr* *nesek nāsak* *šᵉlāmîm zāraq* *zebaḥ minḥâ ʿōlâ qṭr*	Primary	?Israelite	National Royal	Special Regular
B. Where a sense of sin or solemnity is not present						
1. K. 1 : 9, 19, 25	Adonijah's Accession	*zābaḥ*	Primary	Israelite	Royal	Special
1. K. 3 : 15	Solomon's Banquet	*ʿōlôt šᵉlāmîm ʿālâ ʿāśâ*	?Primary	Israelite	National	Special
?1. K. 19 : 21	Farewell of Elisha	*ʾākal zābaḥ*	Primary	Israelite	Family	Special
C. Doubtful or unclassifiable passages						
1. K. 9 : 25	Solomon's Sacrifices	*šᵉlāmîm ʿōlôt ʿālâ qṭr*	?Primary	Israelite	Royal	Regular
?1. K. 10 : 5	Solomon's Sacrifices	*ʿōlôt*	Primary	Israelite	Royal	Regular
1. K. 16 : 34	Hiel and Jericho (See Joshua 6 : 26)					
1. K. 18 : 19ff	Contest on Carmel	*ʿōlâ minḥâ ʿālâ*	Primary	Israelite	National	Special
2. K. 3 : 20	Morning Sacrifice	*minḥâ ʿālâ*	Primary	Israelite	?	Regular
2. K. 5 : 17	Naaman in Syria	*ʿōlâ zebaḥ ʿāśâ*	Primary	Non-Isra.	Individual	Regular
2. K. 10 : 18-27	Jehu in the Baal Temple	*zebaḥ ʿāśâ* *ʿōlôt zᵉbāḥîm*	Primary	Non-Isra.	National	Regular
2. K. 23 : 21-23	Josiah's Passover	*pesaḥ ʿāśâ*	Primary	Israelite	National	Special

CHAPTER SEVEN

PSALMS

Introduction

Of greatest possible importance to this enquiry is the evidence of the Book of Psalms. Wellhausen's reconstruction of Hebrew religion required a post-exilic Psalter, but present day discussions no longer think this probable. The question of this chapter must therefore be to what extent the earlier dating of much of the Psalter, which is now favoured, affects the position built up by Wellhausen from the later dating.

It is no longer necessary to adduce evidence for the liturgical origin of the Psalter, although this was by no means taken for granted a generation ago.[1] The work of Mowinckel has completely transformed the scene, and has familiarized the method of seeing the psalms in their cultic setting.[2] In some cases the titles of the psalms reflect their employment in connection with particular sacrifices,[3] while in others rubrics of liturgical instructions have

[1] Such works as J. P. Peters, *The Psalms as Liturgies*, New York (1922) and A. C. Welch, *The Psalter in Life, Worship and History*, Oxford (1926) were quite revolutionary as far as the English scene was concerned. In 1916 Peters had argued that the psalms were primarily praise songs to be sung at the time of sacrifice—Psalms 3 and 4 for the morning and evening sacrifice, 5 and 6 for sin offerings, 20 and 21 for offerings before and after battle etc. He suggested the particular point in the psalm when the sacrifice was offered, e.g. 21 : 14, 22 : 26, 27 : 6 ("Ritual in the Psalms," *JBL* XXXV (1916), pp. 143-54).

[2] Mowinckel's *Psalmenstudien* appeared in the years 1921-1924, but from 1916 when his first essay on the Psalms appeared to his *Offersang og sang-offer*, Oslo, (1951) he has steadily maintained this position.

[3] E.g. *Hazkîr* (Ps. 38, 70) is probably to be connected to the *ʾAzkārâ*, and *Tôdâ* (Ps. 100) to the thank offering. B. Jacob, who understood *Hazkîr* as a confession of sins, rather than as connected to the *ʾAzkārâ* sacrifice, nevertheless argued strongly ("Beiträge zu einer Einleitung in die Psalmen," *ZAW* XVII (1897), pp. 48ff) for the sacrificial sense of the Psalter, and the connection of these confessions of sin to sacrifice. "Der Psalter ist ein Gemeindeopfergesangbuch, das hat uns *slh* gelehrt, er ist ein Privat (opfer) gebetbuch, das sollte *lehazkîr* zeigen." (p. 68) "Es ist zu ergänzen *ʾônôtāw* . . . und heisst: Zum Bekennen (seiner Sünde, in Krankheit und Leiden, gesprochen beim Darbringen eines Opfers . . .)" (pp. 63-64).

possibly found their way at points into the text.[1] That sacrifices were accompanied by instrumental music and singing is apparent, not only from pictures of Egyptian and Assyrian rites, but by such Biblical references as Amos 5 : 22-23 and Is. 30 : 29, not to mention the tradition of the Books of Chronicles.

The kind of spoken accompaniment which might accompany a sacrifice is illustrated in Deut. 26 : 1-15, where the liturgy prescribed for use when firstfruits were brought to the sanctuary is undoubtedly very old. Welch has pointed out that the decision as to the form of words to be used could hardly be left entirely to the worshipper, as a sacrifice might have any one of several meanings, unless defined by the particular form appropriate to what was desired.[2] He thinks it probable that models for the various types, with blanks for the worshipper to fill in his own name, were available at the sanctuaries, as in Babylonia and Egypt. For a thank offering in fulfilment of a vow a psalm like Ps. 116 might have been the model, while numbers bringing such offerings at a festival might possibly have been divided into groups corresponding with the different kinds of deliverances described in Ps. 107.

On such a view of the relative places of psalm and sacrifice, it is no longer possible to sharply oppose the material and spiritual elements in the cult, or to trace an evolution from one to the other. Westermann has said that praise was not a substitute for the offering, but had an original significance alongside of it. In a sense it was just as much the deity's food, as was the offering. Just as man needs recognition and "honour" as well as material food, so does God. Praise and sacrifice as existing side by side must therefore be traced back to early times.[3] What then is to be said of the rejection of sacrifice in such psalms as 40 : 7, 51 : 18, 50 : 9ff and 69 : 32? Is such a passage as 40 : 7 to be understood as a spoken repudiation of sacrifice intervening at the point in the ritual where the sacrifice would normally have been offered? Can it be seen as the culmination of Israel's evolution toward a completely spiritualized worship?[4]

---

[1] A. Guillaume, *Prophecy and Divination*, pp. 30-31 thinks, with Thackeray, that the difficult phrase of Ps. 118 : 27 is to be explained in this way "Marshal the festal procession with palm-branches," but see on the passage below.

[2] A. C. Welch, *op. cit.*, p. 76.

[3] C. Westermann, *Das Loben Gottes in den Psalmen*, Berlin (1953), p. 53.

[4] On this view Israel was "distinguished not by the institution but by the

This seems as unlikely for the Psalmists, as it is for the prophets, whose influence is usually to be seen at work in these rejection passages.[1] It is true that the Psalmists' criticisms seem to be more akin to those of the wisdom literature, and to be dictated by indifference to sacrifice, rather than passionate disapproval,[2] but it can hardly be argued from this that sacrifice was now no more than a formal accompaniment from which little was expected.[3] "Guestship" with Yahweh to many a Psalmist meant a mystical experience of eating and drinking, which probably began in the literal eating and drinking of the sacrificial meal (Ps. 36 : 9, 23 : 5-6, 27 : 4, 63 : 6).[4] The frequent thank offerings on the fulfilment of a vow speak of a real joy in sacrificial worship. It is probable that the forgiveness of sins in sacrifice was a chief element in this joy, but it must be admitted that this kind of connection is not well attested.

What is to be made of the fact that sin offerings[5] and guilt offerings are not mentioned, nor the blood of sacrifice, nor atonement through sacrifice?[6] Various constructions could be put on this silence. It could be argued that the silence is accidental, as reference to sacrifice in the Psalms is in any case rather haphazard, or that a sense of sin had not yet developed (but some psalms at least, by their deep sense of sin, contradict this), or that sacrifice, as chiefly directed towards inadvertent sin, was of little relevance to this

---

ultimate abandonment of sacrifice." H. W. Robinson, who quotes this (*Companion to the Bible* (ed.) T. W. Manson, p. 325), clearly recognized, however, the spiritual values of the cult as e.g. when he said on p. 304 "that the Book of Psalms . . . should always be associated with the Book of Leviticus, as though they were written in parallel columns."

[1] See the discussion of the passages concerned below, and for a recent survey of literature dealing with the attitude of the Psalmists to sacrifice, J. J. Stamm, "Ein Vierteljahrhundert Psalmenforschung," *ThR* N.F. XXIII (1955), pp. 61-63.

[2] C. H. Toy, "On some Conceptions of the Old Testament Psalter," *Old Testament and Semitic Studies*, Vol. I, pp. 5-7.

[3] Toy e.g. thinks that it was the temple rather than sacrifice on which the hopes of the people had come to settle (*ibid.*, p. 4).

[4] That this was not purely figurative as the older scholars thought, but began in a real eating has been argued by F. C. N. Hicks, *Fullness of Sacrifice*, London ([3]1946), pp. 93ff., and by G. von Rad, " 'Gerechtigkeit' und 'Leben' in der Kultsprache der Psalmen," *GS*, pp. 238ff.

[5] The *ḥaṭṭāʾt* (MT *ḥᵃṭāʾâ*) is mentioned in Ps. 40 : 7, but only to be rejected.

[6] W. McCullough, *Psalms* (*IB*) IV (1955), p. 13.

deeper sense of sin. This matter will need careful investigation in the sequel.

In this connection the problem of the protestations of innocence in the Psalms needs discussion. How could true worshippers of apparently deeply spiritual insight, nevertheless make such claims to self-righteousness? A succession of explanations have been offered down the years, beginning with the theory that it was the nation, rather than the individual, that was to be seen in the "I" of the Psalms. Then with the study of the comparative materials of Mesopotamia came the suggestion of Gunkel, that such easy penitence, as was customary in the Babylonian cult, was really inferior to the Old Testament worshipper's conviction of his innocence. To be "bloody, but unbowed" was a better attitude than the formalized confessions of Babylon.[1] H. Schmidt investigated the matter more closely and saw in the Israelite professions, the "protestations of falsely accused persons," who were required to thus vindicate their innocence at the sanctuary.[2] Finally the whole discussion has been put on a new footing by von Rad's epoch-making definition of the *ṣaddîq* as the one culticly fit to go through the temple door to worship.[3] In a community consisting of only two classes—the culticly fit (*ṣaddîq*) and the culticly rejected (*rāšāʿ*)—the Psalmist naturally took his place with the former.[4]

In the discussion which follows the specific references to sacrifice in the Psalms will be studied, but obviously the evidence is far more

---

[1] H. Gunkel, *What Remains of the Old Testament*, E.T. London (1928), p. 108.

[2] H. Schmidt, *Das Gebet der Angeklagten im Alten Testament* (*BZAW*) (1928), *Die Psalmen* (*HAT*) (1934), pp. VIff.

[3] G. von Rad, " 'Gerechtigkeit' und 'Leben,' " pp. 225ff.

[4] It is not certain that von Rad's theory has solved all the difficulties of this problem. While Ez. 18 does say that the man who has not eaten upon the mountains, or committed certain other cultic and moral sins listed, is *ṣaddîq*, it is striking that the list given in Ps. 15 does not include the abstaining from unclean meats and forbidden contacts, but lists only moral offences (A. C. Welch, *The Psalter . . .*, p. 58). A. Weiser, *Die Psalmen* (*ATD*) I (^{4}1955), p. 113 writes: "dass in einem Lied, das dem Kultus diente, mit keinem Wort kultische Dinge wie Opfer, Gaben, Reinheitsriten erwähnt werden, sondern nur sittliche Forderungen" is surprising. "Clean hands" in Ps. 24 : 4 perhaps means culticly clean, but then it was for these that the sacrifices were designed, and entry into the temple to offer the sacrifice of expiation must obviously have been possible (cf. B. D. Eerdmans "Sojourn in the Tent of Jahu," *OTS*, I (1942), p. 3).

extensive than this limited selection. In many cases reference is quite accidental, and other psalms might have been included. One has only to think of the great number assigned to the *Thronbesteigungsfest* by Mowinckel—and therefore on his theory cultic—which are scarcely represented in the present list. A study of the forms in which sacrifice is mentioned gives the following results—from Enthronement Psalms (Ps. 96), from Zion Psalms (Ps. 76), from Hymns (Ps. 65), from Royal Psalms (Ps. 20 and possibly 61). The other cases are almost all from individual laments, including the sub-class of Psalms of the Falsely Accused (Ps. 5, 26, 141), and individual thanksgiving (Ps. 54, 56, 66, 107, 116, 119), and in some of these cases crossing over in the course of the Psalm from one to the other (Ps. 22 : 26, 27 : 6, 36 : 9 etc.). The sacrifices of the wicked are mentioned in Ps. 16 : 4, 69 : 23, 106 : 28, 37-38.

Offer Right Sacrifices (Ps. 4 : 6(5))

Opinions differ as to whether this Psalm is to be classified as an individual lament (Kraus),[1] or prayer of confidence (Weiser), or as a royal prayer before battle (Kissane).[2]

Interest centres on the "sacrifices of righteousness" (*zibḥê ṣedeq*) (vs. 6), and whether these are to be understood with most commentators as "with right ritual," or with Delitzsch "with right disposition,"[3] or with Kraus of the help to be expected from Yahweh "salvation bringing". For the first meaning argues one of the two other occurrences of the phrase—Deut. 33 : 19, where the trade agreements of two of the tribes are being described, and a deeper meaning is hardly in view. The other occurrence in Ps. 51 : 21, if regarded as part of a ritualistic appendix, would support this, but if integral to the psalm, would be evidence for the second view. The third view can appeal to the use of "righteousness" for "vic-

[1] H. J. Kraus, *Psalmen* (*BK*) (1958).

[2] E. J. Kissane, *The Book of Psalms*, Vol. I, Dublin (1953). It is possible that Ps. 3 belongs to the royal ritual, and that Ps. 4 is its counterpart, but neither assumption is certain. J. Wellhausen, *Psalms* (*Polychrome*) (1898), p. 165 thought it was a mistake to speak of Ps. 3 and 4 as related to one another as morning and evenings hymns.

[3] F. Delitzsch *Psalms* (*KD*) (E.T. 1871). So A. H. van Weijden (*Die "Gerechtigkeit" in den Psalmen*, Nimwegen (1952), p. 237) "kaum als 'richtige Opfer' in irgend einem technischen Sinn zu verstehen" but "mit innerlicher Gerechtigkeit dargebracht werden."

tory" in such references as Judg. 5 : 11, and the probability that this is the thought in vs. 2 of the psalm "O God of my righteousness." If the sacrifices were indeed thought of as bringing "salvation" in this sense, the reference would be important, but this is only one of the possible interpretations.

Morning Sacrifice (Ps. 5 : 4(3))

This individual lament is usually assigned to the sub-division of Prayers of the Falsely Accused (Schmidt, Kraus). It is probable, therefore that the sins renounced in vss. 5-7 (4-6) are those of the accusers rather than the Psalmist, and cannot be regarded as the purpose of the sacrifice. No word for sacrifice occurs in the text, but the verb *'ārak* is almost universally interpreted as "prepare, arrange or set in order the sacrifice."[1] This is done "in the morning" and is apparently the accompaniment of a morning prayer—its rising smoke perhaps symbolizing, as in so many lands, the wafting of the prayer heavenward. It is apparently this smoke of the sacrifice which is to be understood as the object of the verb *ṣāpâ* "spy out", "watch," rather than the entrails of a sacrificial animal.[2] The behaviour of the smoke is thought to have indicated the acceptance or otherwise of the sacrifice and was therefore "watched."

Blood Libations (Ps. 16 : 4)

The reference is to the offerings of some other group, which are shunned by the Psalmist, but the uncertain state of the text in vs. 4a makes it difficult to state who this group is. With either *māhārû* of MT or *baḥ^a^rû* as suggested by Oesterley,[3] *'aḥr* could be taken in the sense of "another god" (AV, RSV). In this case either a syncretistic Yahweh worship, or a foreign cult might be described. "Drink offerings of blood" are thought to be illustrated in the prohibited

---

[1] Herkenne (*Das Buch der Psalmen* (*HS*) (1936)) and Kissane are exceptions. *'ārak* is used in the cult, of the lamp (Exod. 27 : 21; Lev. 24 : 3) and the shewbread (Exod. 40 : 23; Lev. 24 : 8) besides sacrifice, but sacrifice seems the most suitable meaning here, cf. the use of the verb for the setting of the wood in order, in Gen. 22 : 9. The omission of an object is, however, strange, and lends some support to the suggestion that "words" rather than "sacrifice" be supplied as in Job 33 : 5, 37 : 19.

[2] Mowinckel suggests the addition of *l^e'ôtî* "sign," and thinks of a search for omens (*Psalmenstudien*, I, pp. 146-47). BH's addition of *l^ekā* or *'ēlekā* would take the verb in a spiritualized sense "look up to thee."

[3] W. O. E. Oesterley, *Psalms* (1939).

cult of Is. 57 : 6 and 65 : 11, but blood is not mentioned there as the material of the drink offering, nor anywhere else in the Old Testament. If blood is understood literally, this might be grounds for the repudiation of the offering, as prohibited in Israel,[1] but a metaphorical meaning of "blood" in the sense of bloodshed (see below on Is. 1 : 15) is not impossible—so Delitzsch "as it were of blood". Others suggest "I will not stain my hands with his blood any more than taint my lips with his name," or an emendation with BH *mîyādām*.[2]

The King's Sacrifice (Ps. 20 : 4(3))

This royal psalm is better taken with Gunkel as a prayer before battle, than with Duhm,[3] as for the enthronement of the king, or with Schmidt for the entry of the king on an enthronement of Yahweh festival, or Weiser on a New Year Festival. Welch thinks its lack of colour as to specific situation suggests that the prayer before the campaign was a stereotyped form (from the time of Hezekiah) for a service, which took place in the temple the day before hostilities began.[4] Others would date it much earlier (e.g. Weiser). *Minḥôt* and *ʿōlôt* cannot in this case be distinguished into unbloody and bloody offerings, as with Duhm on his late dating, but *minḥâ* alongside of *ʿōlâ* might possibly be used in the sense of "gifts" (Weiser).[5] "May he find thy *ʿōlâ dšn* (fat)" could mean "accept" but many scholars emend to *drš* (seek favourably) or *rāṣâ* (accept). This prayer for the acceptance of the king's offerings is apparently answered by the oracle of vss. 6ff.[6] The sacrifice has

---

[1] H. Gunkel, *Die Psalmen* (*HK*) (1926), cf. Kraus (*BK*).

[2] Schmidt (*HAT*) thinks *m* a dittography and *dām* an addition.

[3] B. Duhm, *Die Psalmen* (*KHC*) (1899).

[4] A. C. Welch, "Some Misunderstood Psalms III," *ExpT* XXXVII (1925-1926), pp. 408-10. Welch thinks it unlikely that Israel would have been an exception to the usual rule of sacrifice before battle, in view of the fact that her warriors were consecrated for war, and that some of her wars were wars of Yahweh (see above p. 107).

[5] It would be strange to find such a juxtaposition of profane and sacred terms, however, and the two terms may stand in parallelism. MT reads the unusual *meنāḥôt* which survives in Rabbinic usage, but is not otherwise found in the Old Testament. Delitzsch (*KD*) thinks it clear proof that the root was *mnḥ* not *nḥh*.

[6] The oracle sought by Ahab at Ramoth-Gilead—but in this case from the prophets—might be compared.

had a serious purpose and was perhaps in part propitiatory (cf. 1 Sam. 13 : 12).

A Meal for the Poor (Ps. 22 : 26-27(25-26) and 30(29))

Toy does not find any sacrificial reference here, but thinks *'ākᵉlû* of vs. 30 imitated from *y'ōkelû* of vs. 27, which he thinks should read *yir'û* with Ps. 69 : 33(32).[1] He is probably right with regard to vs. 30,[2] but not in his emendation of vs. 27 or in his suggestion of a separate psalm commencing here.[3] An individual lament, which becomes a song of thanksgiving is too frequently found to require a separation into two psalms. In this case the "eating" of the poor in vs. 27 is possibly to be seen as the sequel of the "paying of vows" in vs. 26, and could be a sacrificial meal from the thank offering. This is not, however, completely certain. The occasion is one of thanksgiving, but this does not exclude earlier sacrifices of expiation.

Around the Altar (Ps. 26 : 6-7)

This psalm, when regarded as "a psalm of innocence" raises most starkly the problem of self-righteousness discussed in the introduction, but in the category of a profession of "a falsely accused person" (Schmidt), or of one seeking to establish his cultic "righteousness" (von Rad) much of this difficulty disappears. Three ritual acts are described and each could be understood either figuratively or literally. The "washing of the hands" in innocency might have been a literal washing as with the elders of the city denying guilty knowledge in Deut. 21 : 6. The "going around the altar" (*sābab*) might be the literal *ḥāg* like that in Mecca,[4] or a weakened usage to mean "participate in the ritual."[5] In the third case the *tôdâ*, which is "caused to be heard,"[6] must be the song of

[1] C. H. Toy, *op. cit.*, pp. 8-9.

[2] Most modern commentators agree with the BH suggestion *'ak lô* "yea to him." LXX, however, reads *ephagon*.

[3] The older view of Briggs (*ICC*) (1906), Duhm (*KHC*), Bertholet (*HSAT*) (⁴1923), Schmidt (*HAT*) that the psalm was not a unity is rejected by Staerk (*SAT*) (²1920) and Kraus (*BK*).

[4] Such a festal procession is nowhere explicitly described in the Old Testament, but see above p. 111.

[5] "Stand in a circle" would be possible.

[6] Emending *lašmîa* to *lᵉhašmîaʿ* with BH.

thanksgiving rather than literal sacrifice. (See below on Ps. 50.) Strictly speaking then, no sacrifice is described, but if one is assumed the chief element associated with it must be rejoicing.

Sacrifice of Shouting (Ps. 27 : 6)

This individual psalm is made up of elements of both lament and confidence, but these hardly correspond with the division into two psalms at vs. 6 favoured by Duhm, Bertholet, Briggs and Oesterley. Vs. 6 breathes a note of confidence, which is consummated in the decision to "offer (*zābaḥ*) in his tent sacrifices of shouting (*zibḥê terû'â*.)"[1] The note of rejoicing is again the dominant one, but it is not said whether this joy was the cause, or the result of the sacrifice.

The Mystical Feast (Ps. 36 : 9(8))

In this congregational lament followed by a hymn (Leslie),[2] it is only the latter that requires examination. "They are saturated (*rāwâ*) with the fat (*dešen*) of thy house, from the river of thy delights thou causest them to drink." *Dešen* means the fat pieces of the sacrifices, but Duhm argued for a spiritual, rather than a literal feasting, in view of the figurative drinking in the second half of the verse. Oesterley thought the impersonal "they," referring to men generally, favoured the figurative meaning, but von Rad has sought to identify the "they" with an inner circle of "spirituals," who beginning from the sacramental meal went on to a mystical experience of the vision of God.[3]

Sacrifice Depreciated (Ps. 40 : 7-9(6-8))

This individual thanksgiving for deliverance from the "pit" (? sickness) would normally have been followed by a thank offering, but here surprisingly sacrifice is repudiated as not "desired" by God.[4] The suggestion of Mowinckel[5] that this is a case of a change of accent from offering to song, rather than a complete rejection of

[1] Delitzsch (*KD*) suggests that *zibḥê terû'â* are only a stronger form of *zibḥê tôdâ*. *Terû'â* was at first the battle cry, but becomes frequent for the cultic shout.

[2] E. A. Leslie, *The Psalms*, New York (1949).

[3] See above p. 139 and the work of von Rad cited there.

[4] "Surprisingly" because there is nothing in the context to explain why. There is no deep sense of sin, for which sacrifices were perhaps inadequate as in Ps. 51, nor yet a revulsion from temple worship as artificial, as in the prophets. Rather the psalmist takes his place with the congregation in vs. 10.

[5] S. Mowinckel, *Psalmenstudien*, VI, p. 51.

sacrifice, is not acceptable to Kraus, who notes the prophetic vocabulary in *zebaḥ* and *minḥâ*, "not desire" (*lô ḥāpaṣ*) and the contrast between offering and obedience. This obedience, however, is to the Torah, and illustrates the Torah piety of the post-exilic period.[1]

This is perhaps building too much on the sequence of vss. 7-9. Vs. 7b is regarded as a gloss by Staerk, while it is vss. 8b-9 which is similarly rejected by Schmidt.[2] The possibility of such mutually exclusive solutions, together with the difficulty of making sense of the text—what book is being spoken of,[3] and what is the meaning of "lo I come?"[4]—renders certainty impossible. Almost the full sacrificial vocabulary is contained in vs. 7, only *'āšām* being missing.[5] A number of scholars think the list filled out secondarily in vs. 7b by some one who did not think the list complete enough. *Ḥaṭṭā't* in a logically ordered list would normally come at the beginning, but logical order may not be the determining consideration here.

An Exile's Memories (Ps. 42 : 5(4), 43 : 4)

Elements of false accusation mingle with an exile's sighs in this individual lament, and neither can very well be eliminated. No certainty has been reached between the competing theories of the

---

[1] H. J. Kraus (*BK*), p. 309. K. Koch, however (*Die israelitische Sühneanschauung* (1956), pp. 72-73) thinks the form *ḥᵃṭa'â*, which only occurs in pre-Priestly texts an indication of a pre-exilic date for this psalm and for the sin offering.

[2] Schmidt (*HAT*) thinks that a member of such a group as that of Is. 66 : 1-4 penned the depreciatory vss. 7a and 7b, and an orthodox temple supporter added a contradictory gloss that "in the roll of the book, however, sacrifices were ordered." So C. H. Toy, *op. cit.*, p. 14 "but I say sin offering (*ḥaṭṭā't* for *hinnê bā'tî*) is prescribed."

[3] One naturally thinks of the law, but the sentiments of vs. 7 are those of the prophets, and in particular Jer. 7 : 21-23. Leslie, *op. cit.*, p. 295 says "the book was P, but he read it with prophetic eyes." Wellhausen shrewdly said: "We need not be surprised that it is by means of the Law that the present poet is led to understand JHVH'S preference of obedience to sacrifice. We find, in our books, the thoughts with which we are in sympathy; the rest we pass over." He thinks, however, that the prophets as well as the law must have been included (*Polychrome*), p. 181.

[4] Kraus (*BK*), p. 309 thinks the word order requires the demonstrative force "I myself am the offering."

[5] *Zebaḥ* would include *šᵉlāmîm*, and *ḥᵃṭā'â* (? sin) is, probably to be emended to *ḥaṭṭā't*. (LXX reads *peri hamartias*).

date. Duhm thought the exiled one a Maccabean, but this is certainly too late, Snaith, a priest ejected by Nehemiah,[1] Oesterley, an exile of the Northern Kingdom after 721 B.C. mourning his lost holy places. The Psalmist recalls how he had once gone to worship in the house of God (42 : 5), and looks forward to the time when he will do so again (43 : 4). The text of 42 : 5 has a number of difficulties,[2] but it is clear that the festal crowd is being described and their noisy shouting and songs of *tôdâ*—thanksgiving rather than sacrifice here.

The Covenant Renewal (Ps. 50 : 5, 8-14, 23)

This prophetic liturgy (*Gerichtsrede*) has been widely accepted, since von Rad's demonstration of the existence of such a feast,[3] as the ritual of a covenant renewal feast. The tendency has been to assign the chapter to the post-exilic period on the grounds of its developed sense of law,[4] and its depreciation of sacrifice, but recent investigation into covenant traditions makes probable the assumption of Kraus that it need not be later than Josiah.[5] The references to sacrifice in the chapter need not be post-prophetic as they can hardly be regarded as a rejection of sacrifice.

In vs. 5 the covenant is defined as having been made on the grounds or basis of sacrifice (*ʿᵃlê-zēbaḥ*). This is in line with the position taken above that sacrifice had a place of importance in the amphictyony (see above). In vss. 9ff. the misunderstanding of

---

[1] N. H. Snaith, *Hymns of the Temple*, London (1951), pp. 43ff.

[2] See BH.

[3] G. von Rad, *Das formgeschichtliche Problem des Hexateuch* (1938), *GS*, pp. 30ff. So, also, Mowinckel, Weiser and Kraus.

[4] Part of the Decalogue of Exod. 20 is reflected in vss. 18-20.

[5] The Sinai and Davidic Covenant are completely integrated in vss. 3-4. L. Rost, "Sinaibund und Davidsbund," *ThLZ* LXXII (1947), cols. 129-34 thinks this happened after the fall of the Northern Kingdom, in the centralization festival of Josiah. W. Beyerlin, *Die Kulttraditionen Israels in der Verkündigung des Propheten Micha*, Göttingen (1959), thinks the Davidic Covenant was already transmitted in the covenant renewal feast in the frame of the Sinai tradition before Micah (so Micah 5 : 1-5; cf. Ps. 18 and 89), pp. 76ff. Kraus looks for a much earlier amalgamation in a Zion's festival, which was celebrated from David to Josiah (*Die Königsherrschaft Gottes im Alten Testament*, Tübingen (1951)) but believes the covenant renewal feast to date only from the reforms of Hezekiah and Josiah, when the old covenant tradition was centred on Jerusalem (*BK*), pp. 373-74.

sacrifice as "food of the gods" is scornfully repudiated, but that it is not the institution itself, but only this particular theory of it which is rejected, is plain from the prefatory remark of vs. 8 "I do not reprove (*ʾôkîaḥ*)[1] you for your *zᵉbāḥîm*. Your *ʿōlôt*[2] are continually (*tāmîd*)[3] before me."

In vs. 14 and again in vs. 23 the debate turns on whether a literal or figurative *tôdâ* is to be understood. RSV renders *zōbēaḥ tôdâ* in vs. 23 "he who brings thanksgiving as his sacrifice," but translates the similar words of vs. 14 *zᵉbaḥ tôdâ* "offer a sacrifice of thanksgiving" with the alternative "make thanksgiving your sacrifice" relegated to the margin. There seems no justification for this variation. While *tôdâ* can mean either a sacrifice or a thanksgiving,[4] the use of the verb *zābaḥ* in a metaphorical sense is doubtful,[5] and the literal meaning is probably to be understood. True

---

[1] The rendering of *ʾôkîaḥ* by König (*Die Psalmen*, Gütersloh, (1927)) as "rechtfertigen"—from "justify, approve," rather than "reprove, accuse" is possible from the Hebrew, but is improbable in view of its regular use in the sense of accusation—a use which occurs in vs. 21c of this chapter.

[2] N. H. Snaith, *Hymns of the Temple*, pp. 96-99 seeks a solution of the ambiguous attitude to sacrifice along the lines that it was only the *ʿōlôt*, which the Psalmist rejected. *Zᵉbāḥîm* are approved in vs. 5—the covenant was made concerning *zebaḥ*—and again in vss. 14 and 23—the *tôdôt* being forms of the *zebaḥ*. He thinks therefore that it is *ʿōlôt* which are being condemned in vss. 9-13, and translates vs. 8b in an adversative sense. ("Your *zᵉbāḥîm* I do not reprove") but "your *ʿōlôt* are continually before me." The latter words, however, do not naturally suggest condemnation, and neither this psalm nor any other supports such a distinction between *ʿōlôt* and *zᵉbāḥîm*. Both are condemned in Ps. 51 : 18. Snaith credits the psalmist with a theory of the *zebaḥ* communion meal as a real eating of God, but one may wonder whether this would have been any more acceptable to him than its reverse, which he condemns—that in the sacrifice there was a real eating by God.

[3] *Tāmîd* is a technical term for the daily offering in the late period, but must be rendered non-technically in this adverbial construction.

[4] Snaith gives the following figures (*op. cit.*, p. 99): six times in the Psalms and three times outside the Psalms for a song; always in P and twice elsewhere in the Psalms (Ps. 107 : 22, 116 : 17) for a flesh offering, and so probably here.

[5] König, *op. cit.*, p. 316 lists Pss. 119 : 108a, 51 : 19a and 141 : 2 as instances of sacrificial terminology used metaphorically, but none of these have a parallel use of *zābaḥ*. S. Daiches ("The Meaning of 'Sacrifices' in the Psalms," *Essays in Honour of the Very Rev. Dr. J. H. Hertz*, London (1942), pp. 97ff.) argued that *zābaḥ* here simply means "give," and that "offerings" of thanks were to be understood, instead of animal sacrifices in such references in the Psalms, but this is unlikely. W. Caspari ("Kultpsalm 50," *ZAW* XLV (1927) p. 259) says that in the present instance there is nothing

sacrifices rightly offered are acceptable (vs. 14) and in fact an "honouring of God" (vs. 23).[1] In looking back over this psalm, the impression is received that it is a deeper view of sacrifice which the writer seeks. One naturally thinks of a deeper sense of sin, but "a sacrifice of thanksgiving" suggests rather a deeper—perhaps more sincere—form of praise.

The Great Penitential (Ps. 51 : 18-21(16-19))

This individual lament distinguishes itself from almost all others by its concentration on the sins of the psalmist to the complete oblivion of the faults of others. The sense of personal sin has almost broken the form of individual lament, and neither sickness nor false accusation are an adequate explanation. The post-exilic dating proceeds chiefly from likenesses to Trito-Isaiah,[2] and from the assumption that a deep sense of sin is only to be found late. The former argument is perhaps more valid than the latter. If vss. 20-21(18-19) are an appendix of different tendency from the main psalm, the psalm itself can barely be post-exilic,[3] and earlier drafts of it might lie still further back. One may think at least of the time of Jeremiah and Ezekiel. The sense of sin agrees with the former and the use of "spirit" with the latter.

The depreciation of sacrifice seems more absolute than in any of the psalms so far studied. It cannot be said that sacrifices offered in the right spirit would be accepted, for the Psalmist's statement is that such a right spirit alone needs no sacrifice (vs. 19 (vs. 17)). It is impossible to read the earlier part of the psalm, however, without thinking of the cult. Is it possible that the Psalmist had

---

to suggest that the sacrifice, instead of being made from the usual material, was to be made of words, sounds and thoughts. B. Jacob, *op. cit.*, p. 275 argued similarly that *zābaḥ* (as verb) "heisst unter allen Umständen schlachten in ganz concretem Sinne."

[1] This verse can hardly be understood in the adversative sense of "sacrifice is good, but a good life is better," (cf. Lowther Clarke, *ConciseC* (1952), p. 487). The text of the second clause is uncertain. BH suggests for *śām derek* either *tām derek* or *yšr derek*. Another possibility is *m^e šallēm neder* which would bring the whole verse into parallel with vs. 14, but is rejected by BH as against the metre.

[2] Especially the use of "holy spirit" (vs. 13). Cf. Is. 63 : 10.

[3] The prayer for the rebuilding of the walls of Jerusalem, which commences this appendix is to be dated between 587 B.C. and 458 B.C., but need not be any nearer the latter date than the former. The temple rebuilding began in 520 B.C. or earlier, and the thought of the walls would naturally follow.

already fulfilled the cultic requirements—"the washing," "the purging with hyssop" (vs. 9) and even the sacrificing, and had still not found a cleansing adequate to his deep sin? The present form of vs. 18 implies that no sacrifice had been offered, but the difficulty of the text justifies the raising of a doubt concerning the original form,[1] and with it a doubt as to whether the rejection of sacrifice was absolute, or relative to these particular circumstances.[2] The view of the chapter thus suggested would not rule out the normal use of sacrifice as an expiation for sin, but would show how to some deeply penitent souls at least the inadequacy of such a means of expiation had come to be realized.[3]

The Freewill Offering (Ps. 54 : 8(6))

An individual lament of a falsely accused person becomes a thanksgiving consummated in a freewill offering of gratitude (vs. 8). "With a freewill offering I will sacrifice unto thee" (RSV) *bindābâ ʾezbeḥâ lekā* might just possibly be rendered "I will offer freely" (AV, LXX *hekousiōs*). Kraus thinks the "name" theology of vs. 3 shows the psalm to be post-Deuteronomic, but doubts if this gives an exact date.

Vow and Thank Offering (Ps. 56 : 13(12))

The situation of Ps. 54 : 6 is repeated, but this time *tôdôt* rather than *nedābâ* are promised in fulfilment of a vow.[4] Vows have already

---

[1] It is not certain whether *weʾettēnâ* should be read with vs. 18b against the accent, as RSV "Were I to give a *ʿōlâ*, thou wouldst not be pleased," or with vs. 18a with the accent as AV "Thou desirest not sacrifice, else would I give it," or in the conditional form of the LXX (reading *lû* for *lô*) "if you wished sacrifice I would give it." Textual difficulties continue in vs. 19 where "*zibḥî*" "my sacrifice, O God" is favoured by BH for *zibḥê* "the sacrifices of God" and also in the appendix, where *ʿōlâ* and *kālîl* in vs. 21 are thought an addition by BH. For *zibḥê ṣedeq* see on Ch. 4 above.

[2] As suggested by H. H. Rowley, *The Meaning of Sacrifice*, pp. 98ff.

[3] Rowley rightly suggests that "nothing could be more appropriate than this Psalm to make the offerer of a sin offering realize that the spirit in which he came to the altar was of more importance than his offering, or to call forth from him the spirit of penitence which would make the offering the genuine organ of his approach to God" (*ibid.*, p. 99).

[4] Three kinds of *šelāmîm* are distinguished in the laws—*tôdâ* (thank offering), *neder* (vow) and *nedābâ* (free-will offering). The *tôdâ* was to be eaten the same day, but the *neder* and the *nedābâ* could continue to the next day (Lev. 7 : 15ff). Female victims were permitted (Lev. 3 : 6), but apparently males were preferred for vows (Mal. 1 : 14). A similar restriction on

been met with in Ps. 22 : 26 and Ps. 50 : 14 and 23 and will figure in the majority of the remaining references to sacrifice in the Psalms—61 : 6, 9, 65 : 2, 66 : 13, 76 : 12, 116 : 18 and probably in Ps. 107. The purpose in the present instance is thanksgiving (vs. 14).[1]

Prayer for the King (Ps. 61 : 9(8))

The Psalmist speaks of his vows, which God has heard (vs. 6), and which he will joyfully redeem day after day (vs. 9). The psalm, which is an individual lament by one in exile, is interrupted in vss. 7-8 by a prayer for a king. Gunkel thought this an addition, but Kraus asks if it was not possible that an ordinary individual lament and pilgrimage song could include such a petition for the king. Leslie thinks the Psalmist himself is the king, and vss. 7-8 the congregation's prayer for him. Instead of being in exile, however, he is ill—"the ends of the earth" (vs. 3) being the gate of the underworld. Others have thought of a king in exile (Jehoiachin) praying for the king in Jerusalem (Zedekiah), but it seems unnecessary to complicate the prayer for the king in vss. 7-8 by prayers of a king in the rest of the psalm. No sacrificial word is used.

Praise for the Good Earth (Ps. 65 : 2ff)

This hymn of praise for the good earth belongs to some festival, when vows are paid (vs. 2), and when forgiveness of sins was found in the temple (vss. 3-5). No sacrifice is mentioned, but this use of *kipper*, and the localization of the experience of forgiveness in the temple, suggests forgiveness through sacrifice.[2] If this is well-grounded the question might be asked as to whether this might not have been the case with the other thank offerings following vows. This psalm might be a thank offering liturgy, or a praising of the world creator, or a liturgy of an annual rite for fertility and

---

animals with a defect was made for vows, but not for freewill offerings (Lev. 22 : 23). It is not certain, however, that H knows the same distinctions as P (see below) or for that matter that they obtained in the time of the Psalmists.

[1] See C. H. Toy, *op. cit.*, p. 14 who writes: "though the *quid pro quo* is of the essence of the vow, it is not necessary to suppose that the psalmists' feeling was baldly commercial; it is probable that, along with the belief that success depended upon divine intervention, the vow expressed a simple, devout thankfulness."

[2] Cf. J. J. Stamm, *Erlösen und Vergeben im Alten Testament*, Bern (1940), pp. 134-35.

rain after purgation and expiation. If vs. 5 refers to the offering meal after the sacrifice under the phrase "the goodness of thy house," it is to be noted that such a meal does not rule out an earlier expiation and forgiveness.

Vows and Burnt Offerings (Ps. 66 : 13-15)

The sacrificial reference is more extended than usual, and might be the liturgy which accompanied a thank offering.[1] The vow made in the time of trouble is mentioned in vs. 14,[2] and the redemption of the vow by sacrifice in vs. 13 and 15. It is unusual to find *ʿōlôt* associated with vows, as normally one thinks of *šᵉlāmîm* and the sacrificial meal, and this indeed is P's usage (Lev. 3 and 7). H, however, in Lev. 22 : 18 speaks of vows in connection with *ʿōlôt*, and this was possibly the custom at the popular sanctuaries criticized by the prophets.[3] It is possible of course, that the *ʿōlôt* were additional to the vows.

The Meal Table a Snare (Ps. 69 : 23 (22), 32(31))

In this long individual lament a sick or accused Psalmist invokes on enemies, who have tried to poison him, a retaliation in kind. "Let their table become a snare and their *lišlômîm* a trap." "*Lišlômîm*" seems to be derived from something like "security" or "welfare," but this gives no sense. LXX *antapodosin* presupposes *šillûmîm*. The Targum reads *šalmêhem* and this is accepted by BH and most modern commentators, so RSV "sacrificial feasts."

In vs. 32(31) comes the change of mood, possibly after a priestly oracle. Thanksgiving is now offered, but this does not take the form of sacrifice. The ox and bull with horns and hooves were suitable

---

[1] A separate psalm of individual thanksgiving is usually held to begin at vs. 13. Vss. 1-12 comprise a choir hymn (vss. 1-7), and a national thanksgiving (vss. 8-12). The change of person from plural to singular in vs. 13, and the different type of deliverance in the two halves of the psalm is held to warrant their separation into two psalms. Weiser thinks it an objection to this that vss. 1-12 have no proper ending, and vss. 13-20 no proper beginning.

[2] The verb in vs. 14a *pāṣâ* is that which is used of Jephthah's vow in Judg. 11 : 35.

[3] Several of the sacrificial terms here are parallel to those in Is. 1 : 11ff. *ʿōlôt qᵉṭōret ʿattûdîm ʾêlîm*—the last-named being particularly significant, as in P rams were used only for national offerings, which are apparently not in view in either of these passages.

sacrificial victims,[1] but these do not please the Lord so well as song (*šîr*) and thanksgiving (*tôdâ*). Here *tôdâ* cannot mean sacrifice.

Vows and Presents (Ps. 76 : 12)

This song of Zion (Gunkel) is variously assigned to an historical event (Ewald), an eschatological future (Staerk) and the *Thronbesteigungsfest* (Mowinckel), but the determination of this question is unimportant for the elucidation of the vows and gifts of vs. 12. The worshippers are called to "vow and perform (*nidᵃrû wᵉšalmû*)" and all around about to bring gifts. The latter word *šay* occurs also in Ps. 68 : 30(29) of the gifts brought by the kings to the temple in Jerusalem, and need not have a sacrificial connotation.

Gifts in Worship (Ps. 96 : 8)

This hymn of Yahweh's enthronement also calls the worshipper to bring a gift (*nāśâ minḥâ*)—probably in this case a sacrifice. The call to worship the Lord in *bᵉhadrat qōdeš* (vs. 9) might possibly refer to a special festal dress. Oesterley suggests that the order of service for the festival of Yahweh's enthronement reflected here consisted of the following elements—homage, praise, offerings given to the Levites to prepare and from them to the priests to offer, and then prayer.

Heathen Sacrifices (Ps. 106 : 28, 37-38)

In this long community lament of penitence, the framework of the *Gattung* is probably to be discerned in vss. 1-6, 47-48. Vss. 7-46 are an historical sketch, which seeks to illustrate the theme from some seven or eight sinful episodes in Israel's past.[2] Among these were the sacrifices and festal meal at Baal Peor (Num. 25 : 1-5). The description (vs. 28) differs from that of the Pentateuch by the reference to "sacrifices of the dead (*zibḥê mētîm*)" but this *mētîm* is probably to be seen as descriptive of the gods sacrificed to—they were dead in contrast to Israel's living God—rather than as a

[1] "Parting the hoof" along with "chewing the cud" distinguishes the clean animal in Deut. 14 and Lev. 11.

[2] This sense of sin is not connected to the sacrificial references of the psalm. W. Staerk (*Sünde und Gnade nach der Vorstellung des älteren Judentums, besonders der Dichter der sog. Busspsalmen*, Tübingen (1905), p. 18) speaks of this sense of sin as "churchly" rather than "personal," and more "eine Probe geistlicher Pädagogie als ein Zeugnis lebendiger volkstümlicher Frömmigkeit" (citing Duhm).

reference to the cult of the dead. Phinehas' intervention is described as averting the plague, but the specific rabbinical teaching that "he made atonement" is missing.

The next section of the psalm has the condemnation of child sacrifice. "They sacrificed (*zābaḥ*) their sons and daughters to demons" (vs. 37)[1] . . . "they poured out innocent blood" (vs. 38). The charge is repeated in more detail in vs. 38b, but is possibly to be struck out with BH as a gloss.

Sick Man's Healing (Ps. 107 : 22)

The structure of this song of individual thanksgiving has been mentioned on p. 138 above. It is interesting to note the variations in the refrain, which follows each section of the psalm. The refrain consists in each case of two verses, of which the first appears unchanged in all the stanzas (vss. 8, 15, 21, 31), while the second varies (vss. 9 and 16 summarize the stanza preceding, and vss. 22 and 31 call respectively to sacrifice and praise). The reference to sacrifice in vs. 22 *zābaḥ zibḥê tôdâ* is thus formalized, and could occur equally with the other types of deliverance, for which also presumably sacrifices of thanksgiving were offered. The implication is, that the crying unto the Lord in the time of trouble had included a vow (vs. 6, vs. 13, vs. 19, vs. 28. Cf. Jonah 2 : 9). In the particular case in the third strophe, a sick man's recovery is being celebrated.

Cup of Salvation (Ps. 116 : 18)

This is a further individual thanksgiving, which might well have been a model for those offering the thank offering in fulfilment of vows (see p. 138 above). The paying of vows in vss. 14 and 18 (*šlm nᵉdārîm*) and the offering of "the sacrifice of thanksgiving" (*zebaḥ tôdâ*) (vs. 17) are in the terms already encountered, but what is to be made of the lifting up of the "cup of salvation" (*kôs yᵉšûʿôt*)? Is this phrase to be identified with the libation of wine which normally accustomed animal sacrifice,[2] or is a metaphorical cup

---

[1] For *šēdîm* as demons see on Hos. 12 : 12. Some suggest the Assyrian storm god Shedu.

[2] Such libations are constantly described in the tariffs e.g. Num. 28-29; Exod. 29-40 but somewhat surprisingly do not figure in Lev. 1-7 (see above p. 132). The verb *nāśâ* is hardly appropriate for a libation (unless with

in view, as in almost all similar cases?[1] The word "salvation" suggests the latter, and might imply a saving value in the whole sacrificial process.

Binding to the Altar (Ps. 118 : 27b)

Most modern commentators, with the exception of König, find no sacrificial reference in this obscure verse. While König may be right in thinking that *ḥāg* can mean festal offering (cf. Exod. 23 : 18; Mal. 2 : 3),[2] no offering was "bound with cords" *'isᵉrû baᶜᵃbōtîm* to "the horns of the altar." The horns were probably a mere ledge to which nothing could be tied, and in any case the living victim was not placed on the altar, but sacrificed away from the altar and only the blood brought to the altar.[3] Some scholars follow the versions in taking *ᶜᵃbōtîm* in the sense of "leafy branches." While the adjective *ᶜbt* "leafy" would possibly justify this, the word *ᶜᵃbōtîm* occurs usually in the sense of "cords" in the Old Testament. Others suggest for "bind" *'āsar*, "begin" (the festal procession) on the analogy of "binding" or "beginning a war" in 1 Kings 20 : 14, but Toy points out that there the joining of the two armies in battle would justify the use of *'āsar* but with only one object this would not be the case. He doubts if the psalm is really about a festival and concludes that although *ḥāg* means festival, "the psalm has nothing to do with a festival; that the verb *'āsar* yields no satisfactory sense in the connection; that the expression *ᶜad qarnôt ham-mizbēaḥ* is unintelligible" and therefore the verse is to be rejected as a gloss made up of fragments of several contradictory rubrics.[4]

Oesterley we think of a "raising" similar to the "heaving" of the offerings) but would suit the treatment of the wine in the Passover ritual.

[1] The "cup of wrath" is referred to in Jer. 25 : 15; Is. 51 : 17; Ps. 75 : 9(8), and the cup in a good sense in Ps. 16 : 5(4), 23 : 5.

[2] This is denied by Toy *op. cit.*, pp. 11-12. Toy examines the relevant passages in the Old Testament and the Mishna and concludes that neither "offering" nor yet "procession" or "dance" is satisfactory in the Old Testament. The meaning can only be "festival."

[3] The name *mizbēaḥ* for altar, the instructions of Exod. 20 : 24 and the story of Gen. 22 imply, however, that at one time sacrificing took place on the altar. The Targum suggests a binding of the animals until the time came for them to be sacrificed, but this is not what the text implies.

[4] For a recent attempt at elucidation of the text see J. Meysing, "A Text-reconstruction of Ps. cxvii (cxviii) 27," *VT* X (1960), pp. 130-37.

Offerings of the Mouth (Ps. 119 : 108)

The freewill offerings (*nidbôt*) of the mouth might come into the category of a sacrificial term used metaphorically as König claimed (see above p. 148). *Neḏāḇâ* may, however, be used non-sacrificially (Hos. 14 : 5(4); Ps. 110 : 3) and this may be the case here. The use of *rāṣâ* and "holding his life in his hand" in the next verse might support a solemn meaning, but thanksgiving is more probable.

Prayer as Sacrifice (Ps. 141 : 2)

This lament of a falsely accused person speaks of prayer, not sacrifice. Prayer, is, however, likened to both incense, and the evening *minḥâ*. Whether the usage is purely metaphorical and implies no contrast (Briggs), or whether prayer is thought of as an inferior substitute for sacrifice by one who was prevented from sacrificing, or a superior substitute by one who had grown beyond sacrifice, as most others think, is uncertain.

Conclusion

Contrary to what one may have expected from a book assigned to the second temple by Wellhausen, explicit instances of expiatory sacrifice in the Psalms are almost non-existent.[1] The three cases assigned to Group A—Ps. 20 : 4, 51 : 18-21 and 65 : 2ff perhaps do not belong there. Ps. 51, where the sense of sin is really deep, actually repudiates sacrifice, and only on a particular interpretation supplies evidence for sacrifice as normally expiating. Ps. 65 : 2ff. refers to a forgiveness of sins, which apparently takes place in the temple, but the connection to sacrifice is not clearly made. The only sacrifice in the context is a vow. Other psalms which speak of forgiveness of sins mention neither sacrifice nor temple (e.g. Ps. 32).

Much has been made of the fact that the element of expiation is missing from individual laments,[2] and the conclusion drawn that

[1] So S. Herner (*Sühne und Vergebung in Israel*, Lund (1942), p. 105): "Am bemerkenswertesten an der Anschauung des Psalters über die Opfer ist, dass er niemals die sichere Gewissheit der Priesterschrift über die Kraft der Opfer, Sühne zu schaffen, zum Ausdruck bringt. Es wurde schon gesagt, dass "Sühne" dem Psalter ein fast völlig unbekannter Begriff ist und dass dieser statt dessen von Vergebung spricht. Das Opfer wird indessen im allgemeinen als etwas Gottwohlgefälliges hingestellt."

[2] Psalm 20 is a royal psalm and Ps. 65 a congregational hymn.

this type of psalm must have become loosed from the cult.[1] Against this, however, must be set the large number of cases (see C (e)), where the individual lament becomes a thanksgiving. In thanksgiving psalms, the sacrificial reference is much more frequently found. One must ask the question as to what brought about the change of mood in these psalms. Was it that a *Heilsorakel* had been given, assuring the worshipper of his acceptance? If so, did this assurance arise merely from a priestly word in answer to a verbal catechism, or did it not more likely spring from the knowledge that an offering had been accepted (cf. 5 : 4)? A number of references, which reflect the belief in the power of sacrifice to attain its end, support this—4 : 6, 66 : 13-15, and possibly 116 : 18 and 141 : 2. These are perhaps evidence also for the solemn view.

In coming to Group B, it is not sufficient to look only for the note of joy or thanksgiving, because of the fact just noted, that in most cases a lament preceded the thanksgiving. On the other hand these laments cannot be automatically classified as confessions of sin, because they are so often accompanied by protestations of innocence. If the Law Codes are any guide, the vow and thanksgiving should have been accompanied by sacrificial meals, but references to such meals are rare in these psalms. They are probably to be seen in the mystical feasting of Ps. 36 : 9, and possibly in the eating of Ps. 22 : 27 and the corrupt text of 69 : 23.

The large number of cases in Group C may be further classified as follows (a) lacking explicit reference to sacrifice (26 : 6-7, 42 : 5, 43 : 4, 118 : 27), (b) merely formal reference to sacrifice (76 : 12, 96 : 8, 119 : 108, 141 : 2), (c) the sacrifices of the wicked (16 : 4, 106 : 28, 37-38), (d) rejection of sacrifice (40 : 7-9, 69 : 32), (e) laments which become thanksgiving (22 : 26-27, 27 : 6, 36 : 9, 40 : 7-9, 54 : 8, 56 : 13, 66 : 13-15, 107 : 22, 116 : 18), (f) explicit mention of vows redeemed by sacrifice (22 : 26-27, 50 : 14, 23, 56 : 13, 61 : 6, 9, 65 : 2, 66 : 13, 76 : 12, 116 : 18), (g) other cases (4 : 6, 5 : 4, 50 : 5, 8-14).

[1] So H. Gunkel and J. Begrich, *Einleitung in die Psalmen*, Göttingen (1933), pp. 261ff. and J. J. Stamm, *Erlösen und Vergeben im Alten Testament*, p. 134, who writes: "Es ist zu bemerken, dass keiner der angeführten Psalmen, die alle zur Gattung der "Klagelieder des Einzelnen" gehören, eine kultische Sühneleistung erwähnt, wie dies im Gesetz selbstverständlich ist. Zur Erklärung dafür ist zu bedenken, dass die genannte Psalmengattung sich in besonderem Masse vom Kult und seinen Bräuchen gelöst hat."

The mood of the sacrifices in all these doubtful cases must be determined in the light of what is probable concerning the nature of the cult in general. Quell thought Mowinckel's description of the cult as "Fest," and concerned with "die grossen und schönen Stunden des Lebens"[1] as one-sided. For a vegetation cult this may have been true, but cult in its higher stages embraced a wider circle of feelings. "Auch die bitteren Stunden, auch Schmerz und Klage, auch die menschlichsten Gefühle gehören dem Kultus . . . Die Stimmung ist eine ehrfürchtige, mag sie als Freude oder Trauer, Hoffnung oder Angst, auftreten."[2] Mowinckel, however, also recognized this, when he said that the attitude of the worshipper fluctuated between the two poles of "fear of Yahweh" and "joy in Yahweh," and that the former was more normal.[3] This joy of forgiveness rightly marked the great festivals, but this too had its more solemn side: "there is forgiveness with Thee, that thou mayest be feared." (Ps. 130 : 4).

[1] S. Mowinckel, *Psalmenstudien* II, pp. 19ff.
[2] G. Quell, *Das kultische Problem der Psalmen*, Berlin (1926), p. 38.
[3] Mowinckel, *Psalmenstudien* II, p. 130.

Reference	Incident	Terms Used		Primary or Secondary	Israelite or Foreign	National or Individual	Special or Regular
A. Where a sense of sin or solemnity is present							
Ps. 20 : 4	The King's Sacrifice	*minḥâ ʿōlōt*		Pre-exilic	Israelite	Royal	Special
?Ps. 51 : 18-21	The Great Penitential	*zebaḥ ʿōlâ z^{e}bāḥîm*		?exilic	Israelite	Individual	Regular
		ʿōlâ kālîl		Secondary			
?Ps. 65 : 2, 4	Praise for Good Earth	*neder*	*šlm kipper*	?	Israelite	Community	Regular
B. Where a sense of sin or solemnity is not present							
Ps. 36 : 9 (cf. Ps. 63 : 6)	The Mystical Feast	*dešen*		?	Israelite	Individual	Regular
Ps. 22 : 26-27, 30	Meal for the Poor	*n^{e}dārîm*	*šlm ʾākal*	?Primary	Israelite	Individual	Special
?Ps. 69 : 23	Meal Table a Snare	*?š^{e}lāmîm*			(Wicked)	Individual	Regular
C. Doubtful or unclassifiable passages							
a. Lacking explicit reference to sacrifice							
Ps. 26 : 6-7	Around the Altar	*?tôdâ*		?	Israelite	Individual	Regular
Ps. 42 : 5	An Exile's Memories	*?tôdâ*		?	Israelite	Community	Regular
43 : 4							
?Ps. 118 : 27	Binding to Altar	*ḥāg*					
b. Merely formal reference to sacrifice							
Ps. 76 : 12	Vows and Presents	*šay*	*šlm nādar*		?Israelite	Individual	Regular
Ps. 96 : 8	Gifts in Worship	*minḥâ*	*nāśâ*	?	Israelite	Individual	Regular
Ps. 119 : 108	Offerings of Mouth	*nidbôt*		?	Israelite	Individual	Regular
Ps. 141 : 2	Prayer as Sacrifice	*minḥâ q^{e}ṭōret*		?	Israelite	Individual	Regular
c. The sacrifice of the wicked							
Ps. 16 : 4	Blood Libations	*n^{e}sākîm*	*nāsak*	?exilic	?	?	?
Ps. 106 : 28	Heathen Sacrifices	*z^{e}bāḥîm*	*ʾākal*	?exilic	Non-Isra.	National	Special
37-38			*zābaḥ*				
d. Rejection of sacrifice							
Ps. 40 : 7-9	Sacrifice Depreciated	*zebaḥ minḥâ*		?	Israelite	Individual	Regular
		ʿōlâ ḥ^{a}ṭāʾâ		?Secondary			
Ps. 69 : 32	Sacrifice Depreciated				Israelite	Individual	Regular

REFERENCES TO SACRIFICE IN THE PSALMS (Continued)

Reference	Incident	Terms Used		Primary or Secondary	Israelite or Foreign	National or Individual	Special or Regular
C. (Continued)							
e. Laments which become thanksgiving							
Ps. 27 : 6	Sacrifice of Shouting	*zᵉbāḥîm*	*zābaḥ*	?	Israelite	Individual	Special
Ps. 54 : 8	Freewill Offering	*nᵉdābâ*	*zābaḥ*	?exilic	Israelite	Individual	Special
Ps. 56 : 13	Vows and Thank Offerings	*nᵉdārîm tôdôt*	*šlm*		Israelite	Individual	Special
Ps. 66 : 13-15	Vows and Burnt Offerings	*ʿôlôt nᵉdārîm*	*šlm*				
		qᵉṭōret ʿôlôt	*ʿālâ ʿāśâ*	?	Israelite	Individual	Special
Ps. 107 : 22	Sick Man's Healing	*zibḥê tôdâ*	*zābaḥ*	?	Israelite	Individual	Special
Ps. 116 : 18	Cup of Salvation	*nᵉdārîm*	*šlm*	?late	Israelite	Individual	Regular
		zebaḥ tôdâ	*zābaḥ*				
(Also Ps. 22 : 26-27, 36 : 9, 40 : 7-9 above)							
f. Vows redeemed by sacrifice							
Ps. 50 : 14, 23	The Covenant Renewal	*tôdâ*	*zābaḥ*	?Middle	Israelite	National	Festival
Ps. 61 : 6, 9	Prayer for the King	*nᵉdārîm*	*šlm*	?pre-exilic	Israelite	Individual	?Regular
(Also Ps. 22 : 26, 56 : 13, 65 : 2, 66 : 13, 76 : 12, 116 : 18 above)							
g. Other cases							
Ps. 4 : 6	Offer Right Sacrifice	*zᵉbāḥîm*	*zābaḥ*	?early	Israelite	Individual	Regular
Ps. 5 : 4	Morning Sacrifice		*ʿārak*	early	Israelite	Individual	Regular
Ps. 50 : 5	The Covenant Renewal	*zebaḥ*		?Middle	Israelite	National	Festival
Ps. 50 : 8-14	Sacrifice Depreciated	*zᵉbāḥîm ʿōlôt*		?Middle	Israelite	National	Special

CHAPTER EIGHT

THE EIGHTH CENTURY PROPHETS

Introduction

Nowhere has the reaction from Wellhausen and Robertson Smith been more acute than on the question of the attitude of the great prophets to the cultus. These scholars saw in the prophetic criticism of the cultus a total rejection in the interests of spiritual religion. After reviewing the evidence, Robertson Smith concluded, that to the prophets "sacrifice is not necessary to acceptable religion,"[1] and Skinner "sacrificial worship was at best an irrelevance and at worst an offence."[2]

This extreme verdict came to be called in question by a series of scholars in this century, who asked whether such a spiritual religion, divorced from institutions, was really credible in the men of that age.[3] This swing of the pendulum was in part due to a liturgical and sacramentarian revival, and the charge was made that it was as much dictated by a predisposition in favour of the cult, as Wellhausen had been by his antipathy against it. It is true that representatives of the liturgical tradition took their part in the debate,[4] but remarkably enough the chief spokesmen were from non-liturgical churches.[5]

---

[1] W. R. Smith, *The Old Testament in the Jewish Church*, London ([2]1902), p. 294.

[2] J. Skinner, *Prophecy and Religion*, Cambridge (1922), p. 182.

[3] E.g. A. C. Welch, *Prophet and Priest in Old Israel*; H. W. Robinson, *Inspiration and Revelation in the Old Testament*, Oxford (1946), pp. 222ff, "Theology of the Old Testament," *Record and Revelation*, pp. 340ff; A. Johnson, *The Cultic Prophet in Ancient Israel*, Cardiff (1944); H. H. Rowley, "The Religious Value of Sacrifice," *ExpT* LVIII (1946-1947), pp. 69-71.

[4] See especially F. N. Hicks, *The Fullness of Sacrifice*, and the works of Phythian-Adams, O. Quick, and A. G. Hebert. To these scholars the prophets' message was defective in its view of sin and repentance. Their offer of pardon on mere repentance, without the costly and demanding ritual of sacrifice was branded "Pelagian." So O. Quick, *The Gospel of the New World*, London (1944), p. 46.

[5] Robinson, Johnson and Rowley were all Baptists. When N. H. Snaith, "Prophets and Sacrifice and Salvation," *ExpT op. cit.*, pp. 152-53 traced the change of front to liturgical interests, and a desire to establish a particular

Now the reaction itself has gone to the extreme in the suggestion that the great prophets also were cult specialists, perhaps deriving their revelation from the inspection of the omens in the carcases of sacrificial victims.[1] This view is quite impossible, when reasonable but not excessive weight is given to those five passages in which the greatest of the prophets spoke in criticism of the cult (Amos 5 : 21-25; Hos. 6 : 6; Is. 1 : 11-15; Mic. 6 : 6-8; Jer. 7 : 21-22).

What is to be made of these passages? First it must be said that this is not all that these prophets had to say about the cult.[2] It is a salutary discipline to first collect the positive statements of the prophets to the cult, as Roubos has done,[3] and then in the light of these come to the study of the critical passages.[4] It is hardly

---

view of the atonement in the New Testament, Rowley replied ("Prophets and Sacrifice," *ibid.*, pp. 305-307) that the opposite was true in his case. He came from the least liturgical of churches and a study of the Old Testament had forced him to revise long held views on the atonement. In 1932 he had argued for the prophetic rejection of sacrifice, but continued study of the evidence had compelled him to see that their rejection was not absolute. See, also his *Re-Discovery of the Old Testament*, London (1945), pp. 98, 109ff, *The Meaning of Sacrifice*, Manchester (1950), *The Unity of the Bible*, London (1953), pp. 30-61, "Ritual and the Hebrew Prophets," *Myth, Ritual, and Kingship* (1958), pp. 236-60, "Sacrifice and Morality," *ExpT* LXX (1959), pp. 341-2, replying to a detailed criticism of the above works by R. Dobbie, *ibid.*, pp. 297-300.

[1] So A. Haldar, *Associations of Cult Prophets Among the Ancient Semites*, Uppsala (1945) who thinks even Amos a cult prophet. N. W. Porteous, "Ritual and Righteousness," *Interpretation* III (1949), p. 402 rightly comments "here we are right back in the jungle of primitive superstition out of which Israel was the first to hack a way." See further S. Lehming, "Erwägungen zu Amos," *ZThK* LV (1958), pp. 145-69.

[2] Nor is it all that the prophets as a whole had to say. Oesterley, *Sacrifices* . . ., p. 191 points out that there were eighteen prophets. Of these only five are claimed as opponents of the cult. He thinks that this number should be reduced to four, and that of the four only Jeremiah is really against it.

[3] K. Roubos, *Profetie en Cultus*, Wageningen (1956), pp. 116-17 summarizing Ch. II. He shows that each of the prophets in question accepts, approves and even joins in the cult—Amos by the use of phrases from cult-liturgy and the categories of "clean and unclean," Hosea in his assertion that it is a judgment of Yahweh, that in the future the people will have to do without the sacrificial service, Micah by the value he attaches to cultic consecration, and Isaiah and Jeremiah by the place they give to the holy city and the temple in their visions of the future. On Amos see A. Bentzen, "The Ritual Background of Amos i 2-ii 16," *OTS* VIII (1950), pp. 85-99, and on the other points the exegesis below.

[4] Roubos concludes that the prophets were not totally against the cult,

possible to say with Mowinckel that sacrifice and cult are not the same thing, and that one might be approved while the other is condemned,[1] for as Hentschke replied sacrifice is at the heart of the cult and the cult must stand or fall with the verdict on sacrifice.[2] Is it possible then that it was only an apostate cult that was condemned? This seems probable, but in seeking this way out several problems must be met.

Was it the same type of worship which was being condemned by all the prophets? Had only the prophecies of Amos and Hosea survived it might be possible to conclude, that it was the Baalizing of the cult begun in the Northern Kingdom by Jeroboam I that was being condemned by the prophets and that the south was exempt,[3] but Isaiah and Micah make an equally strong attack on Jerusalem itself. Again, had it been only Amos, Isaiah and Micah, it might be a possible explanation, that it was the insincerity of the Yahweh worshippers, who used worship as a cover for social injustice, that was the subject of these condemnations, but Hosea speaks of a Baal cult, with its attendant fertility rites.[4] Most scholars believe that it is the same syncretistic cult, which is being spoken of, and that the difference in language, is to be put down to the theological outlook of the prophets concerned.[5] It is not impossible, however, that chronological considerations may be an explanation, and that there was a deterioration between Amos and

---

and were certainly not champions of spiritual religion, but as preachers of the dynamic element they criticized the cult as static. He quotes "capturing God in a cult is a pagan practice" (p. 123).

[1] S. Mowinckel, *Psalmenstudien* VI, p. 51, I, p. 137.

[2] R. Hentschke, *Die Stellung der vorexilischen Schriftpropheten zum Kultus*, Berlin, (1957), pp. 75-76.

[3] Amos and Hosea do not condemn the Jerusalem cult. Amos, however, includes Beersheba along with Bethel, Gilgal and Samaria in his condemnations. Hosea can hardly be seen as the heir to the Elijah anti-Baal tradition, when his strictures on the house of Jehu are remembered.

[4] For these see H. G. May, "The Fertility Cult in Hosea," *AJSL* XLVIII (1932), pp. 73-98 (an extreme statement) and G. Östborn, *Yahweh and Baal*, Lund (1956). To Hosea the cult is addressed to Baal, while to the other prophets to Yahweh.

[5] L. Rost ("Sinaibund und Davidsbund," *ThLZ* LXXII (1947), cols. 131ff.) thinks of a difference of theological heritage—Amos and Isaiah were influenced by the Davidic Covenant, Hosea by the Sinaitic. (Also in "Erwägungen zu Hos. 4; 13f," *Festschrift Alfred Bertholet*, Tübingen (1950), p. 460.)

Hosea,[1] like the deterioration in the south between Isaiah-Micah, and Jeremiah-Ezekiel.[2]

It may well be that the prophetic criticism of the cult is to be understood against the background of the complete break-down of the covenant relation, which the prophets thus witnessed in their day.[3] If in fact for Amos, as for Jeremiah, the doom of the state was writ, suggestions for the improvement of the cultus could hardly be expected. One need only recall Amos 3 : 14 "I will punish the altars of Bethel," and Amos 9: 1 "Smite the capitals until the thresholds shake." This is not to say, however, that the condemnation extended only to an "eschatological cult" and not normal sacrificial practice, as Press has argued.[4] While there is abundant evidence for the heightening (*Steigerung*) of the cult of which Press speaks,[5] there is little for his view that this was due to the people taking the prophetic message seriously, and multiplying their sacrifices to turn away the wrath of God. It is the prophets' complaint that the people were heedless of their message. There is little evidence that they were attempting to propitiate a coming wrath,[6] or that the prophets blamed them for this. C. R. North, who agrees that the prophets' rejection of the cult of their day was absolute, asks if a more favourable verdict might not have been given, had the prophets seen "the pathetically eager and sin-conscious sacrificial exercises of post-

---

[1] F. Dumermuth, "Zur deuteronomischen Kulttheologie," *ZAW* LXX (1958), pp. 84-85 thinks of a "push" made by the Baal cult between these two prophets.

[2] It is assumed that Hosea may have been as much as twenty years later than Amos. The deterioration in the south was retarded by the "deuteronomic" movement, and was much less rapid.

[3] So J. D. W. Watts, *Vision and Prophecy in Amos*, Leiden (1958), p. 79: "Sin was judged as having broken the bonds of the covenant and invalidated covenant institutions." Cf. A. Guillaume, *Prophecy and Divination*, pp. 89ff, who speaks of Amos as the victim of circumstances: "in this matter of sacrifice he had the misfortune to live in a vacuum."

[4] R. Press, "Die Gerichtspredigt der vorexilischen Propheten und der Versuch einer Steigerung der kultischen Leistung," *ZAW* LXX (1958), pp. 181-84.

[5] This "*Steigerung*" is evidenced in the vast offerings of which Micah speaks, in the increased frequency of sacrifice attested by Amos and the innovation of rare incense in the time of Jeremiah.

[6] Press thinks Jer. 6 : 19 and Hos. 6 : 1ff. prove that the punishment has already begun.

exilic times, with their emphasis on *ḥaṭṭāʾt*, *ʾāšām* and expiation."[1]

Of even greater moment than the question of the prophets' view of the future is their estimate of the past, particularly of Israel's wilderness period. It seems impossible to maintain that Israel had not sacrificed in the wilderness in the face of the evidence of the Yahwist and Elohist adduced in Chapters II and III above,[2] but it does not necessarily follow, as Maag supposes, that Amos has an inaccurate picture of the history when he asks in 5 : 25 if Israel had brought sacrifices in the wilderness.[3] Hosea also has been supposed to have inherited a non-sacrificial tradition,[4] but had he done so he would certainly have made something of the absence of sacrifice in his idealized wilderness period.[5] No writer before Jere-

---

[1] C. R. North, "Sacrifice in the Old Testament," *ExpT* XLVII (1935-1936), pp. 252-53. G. B. Gray, *Sacrifice in the Old Testament*, p. 43 thinks otherwise when he remarks "in repudiating the popular theory of sacrifice as gifts, the prophets never made the slightest attempt to recall or establish the claims of any other theory of sacrifice in its place."

[2] In the Book of the Covenant the first law deals with the building of altars (Exod. 20 : 24ff.), another speaks of "the blood of *my* sacrifice" (23 : 18), and yet a third gives the rule "not to appear before me empty" (23 : 15). While the present form of the Code is thought to reflect conditions in Canaan, it belongs to the pastoral rather than the agricultural stage, and along with the tradition of covenant-making in the wilderness, must go back to the earliest days of Israel's life. This covenant was consummated in sacrifice (Exod. 24 : 3-8; Ps. 50 : 5).

[3] V. Maag, *Text, Wortschatz und Begriffswelt des Buches Amos*, Leiden (1951), pp. 221-22. For the difficulties of this view see H. H. Rowley, *The Unity of the Bible*, p. 42 and for variations the works of Burkitt, Kennett and Kraus. F. C. Burkitt, "The Prophets of Israel," *GoreC* (1928), p. 423a argued that there had been no sacrifice in the wilderness because it was not Yahweh's land. Guillaume, *op. cit.*, pp. 88-89 replied that Sinai, the covenant sacrifice there and the travelling ark were all Yahwistic. H. J. Kraus, *Gottesdienst in Israel*, p. 120 suggests that there was an ancient tent festival tradition, which did not include sacrifice in the wilderness. Kennett maintained that non-sacrificial worship was retained in Israel until almost the exile, but this depends upon datings for the Pentateuchal books which are impossibly late. ("The Conflict between Priestly and Prophetic Ideas in the church of Israel," *Interpreter* XIV, pp. 104ff. and elsewhere).

[4] E. Sellin, *Mose* . . ., Leipzig (1922), pp. 40ff. thought that the E Decalogue with its emphasis on moral requirements, and its silence as to sacrifice, was typical of the whole E tradition which Hosea took over. O. Procksch, *Jesaia* I (*KAT*) (1930) p. 39 remarks that Wellhausen thought the prophets created a cult-less religion, but Sellin shows Moses did. A similar view is expressed by P. Volz, "Die radikale Ablehnung der Kultreligion durch die alttestamentlichen Propheten," *ZSTh* XIV (1937), pp. 63-85.

[5] S. Jellicoe, "The Prophets and the Cultus," *ExpT* LX (1949), pp. 256-58.

miah does this. Amos asks a rhetorical question, which need only mean that sacrifice was not the main business of the forty years in the wilderness.[1] This is another matter from saying that the prophets knew of no tradition of the Mosaic origin of sacrifice.[2] They certainly knew J and E, the Book of the Covenant, the ritual Decalogue, and possibly some of the materials of D, if not of P. In all of these sacrifice has its place.

It is probable therefore that those scholars are right, who see in the passages under discussion the employment of a Hebrew speech idiom which must not be taken too literally, when translated into another language. Guillaume has spoken of "Semitic emphasis by negation" by which a negative statement preceding a positive is not to be taken seriously. "No God but Allah" means that Allah is the only God.[3] Lattey speaks of "the relativity of the negative" as meaning "less of this" rather than "not this."[4] Rowley has elaborated this argument in the articles and works referred to above.[5] It is possible that this is not wholly satisfactory, but opportunity will be given to test it in the examination which follows.

AMOS

The Wine of Fines (Amos 2 : 6-8)

The question here is whether the "wine of fines" in vs. 8 is to be understood in a cultic or a civil sense. On 2 Kings 12 : 17 it was

[1] Jellicoe asks whether Amos was concerned at all with the question of whether Yahweh desired sacrifices. In Ch. 5 : 21-26 the subject under discussion is the disobedience of the people. For other discussions see E. Würthwein, "Amos 5, 21-27," *ThLZ* LXXII (1947), cols. 143-52; H. W. Hertzberg, "Die prophetische Kritik am Kult," *ibid.*, LXXV (1950), cols. 219-26; R. Rendtorff, "Priesterliche Kulttheologie und prophetische Kultpolemik," *ibid.*, LXXXI (1956), cols. 339-42.

[2] This might be said to be the starting point of higher criticism ancient and modern. Anastasius the Sinaite, Patriarch of Antioch in the seventh century A.D. describes the objection of certain heretics that "when He had given order for the complicated Levitical meat-offering, God says afterward through Isaiah and Jeremiah that he had given no commandment unto Israel concerning sacrifices or concerning burnt offerings," J. P. Migne, *Patrologia, series graeca*, LXXXIX, p. 286. Graf wrote in similar strain on Jer. 7 : 22-23 in 1862, *Der Prophet Jeremia*, Leipzig (1862), p. 123. See the writer's "Rise and Decline of the Grafian Hypothesis," p. 1ff.

[3] Guillaume, *op. cit.*, pp. 369-81.

[4] C. Lattey, "The Prophets and Sacrifice," *JTS* XLII (1941), pp. 155-65.

[5] See also now H. Kruse, "Die 'dialektische Negation' als semitisches Idiom," *VT* IV (1954), pp. 385-400.

suggested that the priests collected money, as a penance for sin, and this could be the meaning here.[1] A cultic interpretation may be given of both 8a and 7b, but neither verse requires it,[2] and vss. 6b and 7a rather support the view that civil and social offences are being condemned throughout. The fines are those prescribed by the corrupt judges, which have been paid in kind rather than money, or which having been paid in money are now turned into provisions for a sacrificial banquet. This banquet is a sacrificial meal of the wealthy, held at a sanctuary, which is caustically described by Amos as "the house of *their* god."[3] It is probable therefore that neither sin offering nor sense of sin is in view here.

Bethel and Gilgal (Amos 4 : 4-5)

The extravagant worship of the sanctuaries at Gilgal and Bethel is here satirized by Amos: "to worship is to transgress, and to intensify worship is to multiply transgression." It is probable that an intensification of normal worship requirements is, therefore, to be seen in the list. "Bring your sacrifices every morning, your tithes every three days." It is not the daily sacrifice of the morning *ʿōlâ*, which is referred to, but a *zebaḥ*, perhaps like that of Elkanah (1 Sam. 1) offered once a year. Similarly the tithe under the Deuteronomic rule (Deut. 14 : 28) was offered in the third year,[4] but here a *zebaḥ* is brought every morning and a tithe every third day.[5] A

---

[1] Cf. P. Volz, *Die biblischen Altertümer*, Stuttgart (1914), p. 133.

[2] M. A. Beek, "The Religious Background of Amos II 6-8," *OTS* V (1948), pp. 135-36 thinks that ordinary incest rather than temple prostitution is referred to in vs. 7b. Amos does not elsewhere speak of cultic immorality as Hosea does.

[3] The rejection of the cult is reflected in the words "in the house of *their* god."

[4] This passage and Gen. 28, which also links tithes to Bethel, are the only references to tithes before Deuteronomy. (The LXX reading of 1 Sam. 1 : 20 was rejected on p. 97 above.)

[5] So Harper (*ICC*), pp. 92; cf. T. H. Robinson, *Die Zwölf Kleinen Propheten* (*HAT*), p. 86. This seems preferable to the explanation of Wellhausen, *Die Kleinen Propheten*, Berlin (1892), p. 78 that *lab-bōqer* must be "in the morning" and therefore *lišlōšet yāmîm* "after three days, on the third day." It is true that *lab-bōqer* in all its uses in the Psalms means "early in the morning" (except Ps. 49 : 15 which is corrupt) and also that "three days" as the festival period seems implied in Exod. 19 : 10-15. Marti (*Das Dodekapropheton* (*KHC*) (1904), p. 181) thinks "every morning" would require a plural or the repetition of the noun, "morning by morning." The suggestion, however, that sacrifices were brought on the morning of the second day

similar extravagance may be present in the call in vs. 5 to burn (*qṭr*) the *tôdâ* with (or without)[1] leaven, and to ostentatiously proclaim and publish "freewill offerings" (*nᵉdābôt*).

The full list of sacrificial terms here, and particularly the division of the *zebaḥ* into two of the three catagories of the P law—*tôdâ* and *nᵉdābôt*[2] show how far from primitive ritual and how near the full development of P the cult was in the time of Amos.[3]

It remains to ask, whether a sense of sin was present in these sacrifices. Sellin's view that "zur Entsündigung zog man zu diesen Heiligtümern hinauf vgl. Gen. 35, 2, zur Mehrung der Sünde gereicht es, sagt Amos in bittrer Ironie,"[4] is rejected by Weiser who finds little evidence for a sense of sin.[5] Maag thinks no more than the *do ut des* formula to be present and this seems probable.[6]

Sacrifice in the Wilderness (Amos 5 : 21-25)

The historical and religious problem raised by this passage has been treated in the introduction. The form of the text also presents

---

after arrival at the sanctuary and tithes on the third day, is pure conjecture. More might be said for Snaith's view (*The Book of Amos* Vol. II, London (1946), p. 72) that the three days were those of the three feasts of Unleavened Bread, Weeks and Tabernacles. There seems no point, however, in Amos simply stating normal procedure. Only something hopelessly extravagant suits the satire.

[1] *Min* in *mēhāmēṣ* may be understood either as a privative "without leaven" (with T. H. Robinson (*HAT*) and N. H. Snaith), or as a partitive "of, or from leaven." It is not known what the normal practice was in the Northern Kingdom at this time, but probably it differed from place to place. The codes which have come down to us in Exod. 23 : 18, 34 : 25; Lev. 2 : 11, 6 : 10 forbid leaven in altar sacrifices, although allowing it in certain cakes that did not come near the altar (Lev. 7 : 13, 23 : 17).

[2] Cf. S. Oettli, "Der Kultus bei Amos und Hosea," *Greifswalder Studien*, Gütersloh (1895), pp. 12-13. The third category of vows *nᵉdārîm* is also well attested for the early time e.g. 2 Sam. 15 : 8.

[3] Harper (*ICC*), p. 94 noted that "this vocabulary of religious worship is noteworthy for its size and scope, its definiteness," and showed a fully developed cultus, constantly expanding.

[4] E. Sellin, *Das Zwölfprophetenbuch*, (*KAT*) (1922), p. 183.

[5] A. Weiser, *Die Profetie des Amos*, Giessen (1929), p. 163. Weiser agrees, however, that "Das Sühnemotiv hat wohl da und dort in vorexilischer Zeit schon eine Rolle im Opferkultus gespielt, denn Sühneopfer gibt es, seit es Opfer gibt."

[6] V. Maag, *op. cit.*, pp. 224-25. Maag writes: "Der Kult zur Zeit des Amos hat nichts zu tun mit Sündbewusstsein, Vergebung und Heiligung. Sein Ziel ist die Erwirkung göttlicher Wohltaten und die magische Bannung von Unglück." It was morally indifferent, and proceeded from the theology that God and man owed nothing to each other.

difficulties—*ʿōlôt* in vs. 22, because it lacks the suffix of the following terms, *šelem* in vs. 22, because it is unparalleled in the singular, and *minḥâ* in vs. 25, because it is singular, where the accompanying *zᵉbāḥîm* is plural.

The difficulty of *šelem* and *minḥâ* may be overcome by reading the plurals *šalmê* and *minḥôt*,[1] but that of *ʿōlôt* is hardly met by Harper's suggestion that *ʿōlôt* and *minḥôt* go so closely together that the suffix of the first serves also for the second. The attempt to connect the phrase "even though you offer me burnt offerings" with what follows is far from smooth,[2] and it seems better to assume that something has fallen out after it (BH), or that the phrase itself is an addition, by some redactor, who missed *ʿōlôt* from the list (Guthe (HSAT), Sellin, Hentschke). On the determination of this point will turn the decision as to whether the *minḥâ* is a third kind of sacrifice in addition to the *ʿōlôt* and *šᵉlāmîm*, and so a cereal offering,[3] or as in vs. 25 a second kind over against the *zᵉbāḥîm*, and so probably a burnt offering.

The force of Amos' rejection of the sacrifices of these worshippers is reflected in the suffix "your" for the "my" of the Book of the Covenant. Nothing in the text suggests a sense of sin, and general considerations seems to make it improbable that there was one. The music and songs of the cult are, however, mentioned (vs. 23).

HOSEA

As noted above, Hosea speaks of the apostate cult as a worship of Baal, rather than Yahweh. His use of the plural Baalim is probably to be understood in the sense of "Baal and all his works," "the whole Baal pantheon" (cf. "other gods" 3 : 1), rather than of separate local numina. The Ugaritic literature gives the picture of one powerful god, Baal, son of Dagon, who tends to displace El as supreme. The Baals of Carmel, Samaria, Hermon etc. might be compared to the Madonnas of Lourdes and elsewhere. The Baal worship described in Hosea seems to have been of an orgiastic

---

[1] There is LXX support for the plural in vs. 25.

[2] C. Orelli, *Die zwölf kleinen Propheten* (*SZ*) ([3]1908) suggests "If you offer me burnt offerings, to your meal-offerings I have no favour," and T. H. Robinson (*HAT*) "If you bring me burnt offerings then I have no pleasure in your gifts."

[3] RSV; H. W. Robinson, *Amos* (*AbingdonC*) (1929); R. S. Cripps, *A Critical and Exegetical Commentary on the Book of Amos* ([2]1955).

character, centring in sacral prostitution (4 : 14) and self-mutilation (7 : 14).

The Joy of the Feast (Hos. 2 : 13-15 (11-13))

The light-hearted joyousness of the cultus is abundantly in evidence here, but little of any more solemn note. Feasts and mirth are synonymous (vs. 13 (11)). A "burning" is made to the Baals (*qṭr*) vs. 15 (13). Ring and jewelry are included in the festal attire (vs. 15 (13)). The festal calendar embraces feasts, new moons, sabbaths and appointed feasts (vs. 13 (11)). No other sacrificial terminology is used.

The Removal of Sacrifice (Hos. 3 : 4)

The reference to sacrifice here is too brief for classification, but the passage as a whole would be important, if it could be established, as claimed by some, that Hosea sees the removal of sacrifice, as a necessary stage in Israel's salvation. Sacrifice could not then be to him a legitimate means of grace. In the analogy in vs. 3, however the sinning wife is deprived, not only of the illegitimate sexual relations with her lovers, but apparently also of the relation with her own husband, which in other circumstances would have been legitimate. The possibility therefore, remains open that legitimate as well as illegitimate things are condemned in vs. 4, and that the condemnation of the former, e.g. the monarchy and sacrifice, was relative to these circumstances, and not absolute.[1]

The Sin of the Priests (Hos. 4 : 8)

The "*ḥaṭṭāʾt* of my people" eaten by the priests suggested to older commentators "sin offering," as the sin offerings of the people were to be eaten by the priests (Lev. 6 : 19 (26) ff). Wellhausen, to whom the sin offering was of post-exilic origin, rejected this rendering, and translated "they eat the sin of my people."[2] A literal eating of the sin offering was no sin, but metaphorical "eating" or "feeding" is a common charge against leaders (cf. Is. 56 : 11; Ez.

[1] So A. C. Welch, *Kings and Prophets of Israel*, London (1952), p. 180. For a new estimate of Hosea's attitude to the monarchy see G. Östborn, *op. cit.*, pp. 55ff who thinks the "king" references are to be referred, not to the earthly king, but to Baal.

[2] J. Wellhausen, *Prolegomena*, p. 73.

34 : 10), and gives a better parallel to the following line "they are greedy for their iniquity (*'āwôn*)." It seems better, therefore, to leave offerings out of the picture,[1] and to think of this priestly sin, as their condoning or joining in the people's sin for the sake of gain, and living off this gain. Penance payments in cash, or in offerings would not then be in view.

Sacrifices of the Baal Cult (Hos. 4 : 13-19)

The sacrificial references are in vs. 13 "they *zbḥ* (piel) on the tops of the mountains and (*qṭr*) upon the hills," in vs. 14 "they *zbḥ* (piel) with cult prostitutes (*qᵉdēšôt*)" and vs. 19 "they shall be ashamed of their sacrifices." In the last verse the anomalous plural *zibḥôtām* is best emended to *mizbᵉḥôtām* "altars" with LXX.[2] This passage hardly throws light on normal Yahweh worship.

Seeking the Lord (Hos. 5 : 6)

"Seeking the Lord with flocks and herds" implies extravagant sacrificial worship. There has been no real turning back to the Lord, however (vs. 4), —and sacrifice is of no avail. The verse is thus parallel to Amos 5 : 22 and 4 : 4-5 in its rejection of the sacrifices of a people so sadly compromised. The motives actuating these worshippers were so hopelessly mixed, that their worship could not be accepted. Penitence, if among them, could not have been very deep.[3]

Mercy not Sacrifice (Hos. 6 : 6)

Read in the light of the preceding section, it would seem that the sacrifice condemned here is that which has not been the vehicle

---

[1] Some modern commentators have returned to the translation "sin offering." Weiser e.g. (*Das Buch der zwölf Kleinen Propheten* I (*ATD*) (1949), p. 33) suggests "the more the sin, the more rich the sin offering, the flesh of which fell to the priests."

[2] H. S. Nyberg, *Studien zum Hoseabuche*, Uppsala (1935), p. 35 prefers to retain MT and thinks the form an old North Hebrew peculiarity.

[3] In this connection the problem passage 6 : 1-3 should perhaps be discussed. It can hardly be a prophetic call to repentance in view of its connection to what goes before "they seek me, saying" (5 : 15), nor can it be a confession of genuine penitence in view of what follows (6 : 4ff). An increasing number of scholars accept the view that it is a hymn of the fertility cult, to which vs. 4ff. is reply. So A. C. Welch, *Prophet and Priest in Old Israel*, p. 108; *Kings and Prophets of Israel*, London (1952), pp. 145ff, 172, who notes that Yahweh here is closer to nature than to moral processes. His coming is assumed as automatic, where for Hosea repentance must come first, and sacrifice, which lacks repentance, must be rejected.

of repentance. Linguistic considerations alone cannot determine, whether more weight is to be given to the negative in 6a "and not sacrifice," or the comparative in 6b "more than burnt offerings."[1] The latter alternative is favoured by those who think Hosea's condemnation of the cult to be relative, and not absolute.

The Sin of Ephraim (Hos. 8 : 11-13)

In vs. 11 the repetition of the words *laḥᵃṭāʾ* "for sinning" in both parts of the verse, where they occur only in the second part in the LXX, have led to their deletion from one member or another by most scholars. Orelli retained the words in the sense of "to un-sin, to expiate (*lᵉḥaṭṭēʾ*)" in 11a. This rendering was rejected by Marti, as implying a consciousness of guilt in the people, where Hosea shows the direct opposite was the case.[2] It has been revived by Nyberg, but is not very probable.

In vs. 13, as also in vs. 12, the text is corrupt, but most render with RSV "they love sacrifice, they sacrifice flesh and eat it."[3] Sellin (*KAT*) thinks this the most absolute word of Hosea's book against sacrifice, reducing it to nothing more than slaughtering and flesh-eating.

Sacrifices in Exile (Hos. 9 : 4-6)

If vs. 4 connects to the preceding and following verses predicting exile in Assyria, an emendation of the sacrificial reference appears necessary. The "unclean food" which will be eaten in Assyria (vs. 3) is apparently that which has not been consecrated by sacrifice (vs. 4b). Libations of wine will no longer be poured to Yahweh (vs. 4a) and feast days will pass, without proper observance (vs. 5). It is surprising then to read in vs. 4ab "they shall not please him (*ʿārab*) with their sacrifices." Most scholars accept Kuenen's emendation of *ʿārab* to *ʿārak* "they shall not set in order (prepare),

---

[1] Cf. H. Kruse, *op. cit.*, pp. 391ff; E. König, "On the Meaning and Scope of Jeremiah vii 22, 23," *Exp* 6th series VI (1902), pp. 208-18, "Der Jeremiaspruch 7, 21-23," *ThStKr* LXXIX (1906), pp. 362ff.

[2] K. Marti, *Das Dodekapropheton* (*KHC*) (1904).

[3] For *zibḥē habhābay* Delitzsch sought a derivation connected to "to roast" (cited by Orelli (*SZ*)), others thought of *yāhab* "to give," but more probable is *ʾāhab* "to love," which has some support in LXX *ēgapēmena* in vss. 12 and 13.

sacrifice."[1] Both are good sacrificial terms, but *ʿārab* of the MT, apart from the context, would be the more natural (cf. Jer. 6 : 20; Mal. 3 : 4).[2]

The Apostasy of Israel (Hos. 11 : 2)

The falling away of Israel after the deliverance of the exodus is described "they kept sacrificing (*zbḥ* piel) and burning incense (*qṭr*) to images." With this may be compared two other passages which have not been given separate consideration—3 : 1 "the Lord loves the people of Israel though they turn to other gods and love cakes of raisins," 10 : 1 "Israel is a luxuriant vine . . . the more his fruit increased, the more altars he built."

Sacrifice in Gilgal (Hos. 12 : 12(11))

The difficult form *šᵉwārîm* has given rise to various emendations. The simplest is that of AV and RSV, now reintroduced by Nyberg, "bulls,"[3] but this could only be a sin on the theory that all animal sacrifice was a sin to Hosea. The LXX rendering *archontes* presupposing *śārîm* is favoured by Sellin, who thinks of a murder of princes in Gilgal (cf. 6 : 8, 9 : 15). This seems far-fetched. Since Hitzig a favourite emendation has been *laš-šēdîm* "to demons,"[4] (cf. Deut. 32 : 17; Ps. 106 : 37). The connection of such sacrifice to Gilgal, is not otherwise known. 9 : 11-17 possibly refers to child sacrifice at Gilgal, but this also is not certain.[5] The verb is again *zbḥ* in the piel.

Kissing the Calves (Hos. 13 : 2)

The kissing of the calves presumably refers to devotion to the golden "calves" set up by Jeroboam (cf. 10 : 5, 8 : 5), but what is

[1] A. Kuenen, *National Religions and Universal Religions*, London (1882), pp. 312-13.

[2] It is accepted by Weiser and Nyberg. LXX reads it with vs. 4aa and "their sacrifices" with vs. 4ba (so AV). This suits the Hebrew accent, but not the parallelism. *Lāhem* of vs. 4b is usually emended to *laḥmām* "their bread."

[3] Reading *šôrîm* for MT. Nyberg notes that the LXX read these consonants.

[4] Supplying *l* which may have dropped out after the final *l* in Gilgal. This is accepted by Wellhausen, Guthe (*HSAT*), Nowack (*HK*), Gressmann (*SAT*), Robinson (*HAT*), Procksch (*BH*), Weiser (*ATD*) and many others.

[5] Harper thinks, however, that there was no child sacrifice until the time of Ahaz. Melville Scott replies that this is the time of Ahaz (*The Message of Hosea*, London (1921)).

the meaning of *zōbḥē 'ādām*. Orelli argued that such a phrase could only mean "sacrificers of men,"[1] and found proof that child sacrifice was already current in the north at least in the time of Hosea. It was felt by others, however, that Hosea would hardly have passed by such a practice without comment, and that the grammatical arguments were not completely convincing.[2] The alternative of pointing *zbḥu* as an imperative with the LXX has been favoured by an increasing number of scholars,[3] and gives a place to the difficult *'ōmrîm* "(sacrifice to them!) they say." Sellin suggests that this had been the formula since the days of Jeroboam.[4]

The Sacrifices of the Lips (Hos. 14 : 3(2))

The MT reading *pārîm* "bulls of our lips" is not entirely impossible,[5] despite the almost universal preference for the LXX *karpon* (*pᵉrî*). The verb *šlm* is common in the cult. Sellin suggests that a new cult is being founded in which prayer will take the place of sacrifice, but this possibly implies a degree of spiritualization beyond the capacity of the men of that time. Hosea might think of the "sacrifices of the lips," as the accompaniment of sacrifice for the future. "Take with you words and return to the Lord" implies penitence as the requisite of worship. The lack of it will then have been the reason for the prophet's rejection of the old sacrifice. This perhaps alone of the verses examined suggests the prophet's view of what a true cult should be.[6]

ISAIAH

It is quite improbable that Isaiah, whose inaugural vision had taken place in the temple, amid the smoke of sacrifice[7] and whose

---

1 He claimed that the participle of this verb can only be connected genitively with the object of the sacrifice (*SZ*), p. 39.

2 A. B. Davidson, *Hebrew Syntax*, Edinburgh (³1901), p. 32 says that Hebrew has various circumlocutions for adjectives e.g. the genitive and its construct, when the two things are identical as e.g. the thing and its name, or its class "a wonder of a counsellor," (Is. 9 : 6) so "men who sacrifice." Similarly Gesenius-Kautzsch, *Hebrew Grammar*, Oxford (²1910), p. 416 "sacrificing men." Oesterley, *Sacrifices* . . ., p. 121 compares Prov. 15 : 20 "a fool of a man."

3 Gressmann (*SAT*), Sellin (*KAT*) and now RSV.

4 So in vs. 4 it is Yahweh not the bull god that brought them out of Egypt.

5 Cf. the Targum "And may the words of our lips be received before thee like bullocks, as an acceptable offering on the altar."

6 In view of the present trend to accept this chapter as genuine, discussion of this point has been omitted.

7 N. H. Snaith, *Mercy and Sacrifice*, London (1953), p. 96.

hopes for the future centred in the holy city, should have completely rejected the cult. Lods has pointed out how typical it is that the call narrative should contain a cleansing of the lips—the cleansing of uncleanness in the temple showing his interest in the ritual, and the fact that it is the lips that are cleansed, showing the moral emphasis on speech and thought, rather than on ceremonial acts.[1] The cleansing by a hot coal, rather than by sacrifice is admittedly unusual, but Boutflower is surely right, when he stresses that the coal was from the fire of the expiatory offering.[2]

A number of attempts have been made to make the chapter entirely cultic,[3] but these fall into the opposite extreme. Isaiah gave to the cult a subordinate place and criticized those who substituted cultic conformity for moral obligation. The people who drew near with the lips while their hearts were far distant come in for his condemnation (29 : 13), but this no more implies a total rejection of the cult, than his awareness of the presence of such "unclean lips" at the time of his own call in the temple (Is. 6 : 7).[4]

The references to sacrifice in Isaiah are therefore of two types—on the one hand there is his acceptance of the regular ritual as an integral part of the religious life (29 : 1 ff, 30 : 29), and on the other his famous attack on the temple worshippers in Ch. 1 : 11-21. This latter passage is important as evidence that the faults which disfigured the northern cultus and called forth the rebuke of Amos and Hosea, were by no means absent from Jerusalem.[5] There is little to choose between Amos and Isaiah in the strength of their criticism.

Rejected Sacrifices (Is. 1 : 11-15)

The sacrificial terminology is found in vss. 11 and 13 and again

---

[1] A. Lods, *The Prophets and the Rise of Judaism*, p. 101.

[2] C. Boutflower, *The Book of Isaiah*, London (1930), p. 30; J. J. Stamm, *Erlösen und Vergeben*, p. 117; J. Köberle, *Sünde und Gnade*, pp. 162-63.

[3] Ph. Béguerie, "La Vocation d'Isaie," *Études sur les prophètes d'Israël*, *Lectio Divina* 14, Paris (1954), pp. 11-51, esp. pp. 27ff, 41ff. thinks of the Babylonian *bît rimki* (House of Ablution) with its purification of the lips, the Egyptian ceremonies of the opening of the mouth and the touching of the tongue with knives, the *qōdeš* chant, the glory, the "how long" and the sacred tree.

[4] N. H. Snaith, *Mercy and Sacrifice*, pp. 96ff.

[5] L. G. Rignell's attempt ("Isaiah Chapter I," *Studia Theologica* XI (1958), pp. 140-58, esp. p. 147) to prove that it is the unclean cult introduced by Ahaz (2 Kings 16: 15), rather than the Yahweh cult, which is condemned by Isaiah, is hardly successful.

constitutes a comprehensive list[1]—in vs. 11 *zᵉbāḥîm*, *ʿōlôt* of rams, the fat of fatlings, and the blood of bulls, lambs and he-goats, and in vs. 13 *minḥâ* and *qᵉṭôret*.[2] The ram as a sacrificial victim is known in the later ritual only in connection with the expiatory offerings,[3] but this can hardly be assumed here in view of its more general use earlier (Gen. 15 : 9, 22 : 13; 1 Sam. 15 : 22; Micah 6 : 7; Ps. 66 : 15). Duhm and Herntrich imply that the hands full of blood, which are rejected (vs. 15), are full of the blood of sacrifice,[4] but blood here must stand for bloodshed, or blood-red sin as in Is. 5 : 7; Hab. 2 : 8 etc. It is this blood that is rejected, not the blood of sacrifice.[5] It is because there has been no true penitence and putting away of sin (vss. 16-18) before coming to sacrifice, that sacrifice has been ineffective.[6] Isaiah's own experience in Ch. 6 in which sin was expiated (*kipper*) at the altar, after his confession, must be allowed to interpret the promise of pardon in vs. 18 "though your sins be as scarlet, they shall be as white as snow."[7]

The Call of Isaiah (Is. 6 : 5-7)

See above pp. 174-175.

---

[1] H. W. Hertzberg, *Der Erste Jesaja* (*Bibelhilfe*), Kassel (²1952) remarks that all kinds of offerings are condemned—the burnt offerings of the fore-court, the incense offering of the inner house and the cereal offering of the fruits of the field (p. 22). LXX also decides for the cereal meaning of *minḥâ* in vs. 13 by rendering *semidalis* and reads *šāwʾ* as a predicative adjective.

[2] *Qᵉṭôret* is now frequently rendered "incense" instead of "sacrificial smoke" with Wellhausen. So RSV. Cf. Procksch, *Jesaia* I (*KAT*) (1930); Hertzberg (*Bibelhilfe*) and others.

[3] T. K. Cheyne in the 1880 edition of his *Prophecies of Isaiah*, Vol. I, London (1880), p. 6 therefore suggested that the *ʿōlôt* were trespass offerings here.

[4] B. Duhm, *Jesaia* (*HK*) (⁴1922), p. 31: "weg mit dem Opferblut und weg mit dem Unrecht!" V. Herntrich, *Der Prophet Jesaja*, Kapitel 1-12 (*ATD*) (1950), p. 14: "'the blood of atonement' is revealed through the prophetic word as the blood of accusation."

[5] Gray (*Isaiah* (*ICC*) (1912), pp. 19-20) thinks the MT reading of *ʾāwen* "iniquity" in vs. 13 for LXX *ṣôm* "fast," an attempt to soften an earlier absolute condemnation of sacrifice by the suggestion that it was sin, rather than sacrifice which was condemned, but sacrifice in itself is no more condemned by Isaiah, than prayer in itself (cf. vs. 15).

[6] The writer is not convinced by E. Robertson, "Isaiah Chapter I," *ZAW* LII (1934), pp. 231-36 and others that there is no proper connection between vss. 11-15 and vss. 16ff.

[7] The sharp break between vss. 17 and 18 favoured by many commentators is not necessary, nor is the interpretation of the question of the latter as ironical.

Sacrifice in Egypt (Is. 19 : 19-21)

This passage with its prophecy of the conversion of Egypt, the erection of altar and *maṣṣēbâ* to Yahweh there, and the offering of *zebaḥ* and *minḥâ* is a remarkable one, whatever its date.[1] Cheyne long ago thought the passage "the swan-song of Isaiah,"[2] and many modern scholars while not acknowledging Isaianic authorship, are prepared to go back nearly as far, and to link it as closely as possible to the prophet.[3] The connection of such a prophecy to the Isaiah school or to Isaiah himself is further evidence that Isaiah did not absolutely reject sacrifice. The sacrifices are apparently of supplication, and when accompanied by true repentance will be heard and answered "he will heed their supplications and heal them," (the verb *ʿātar* as in 2 Sam. 24 : 25 and 21 : 14).

The Round of the Feasts (Is. 29 : 1ff.)

This passage and the two which follow use sacrificial terminology in the metaphorical sense as the vocabulary of prophecy. "Ariel" is probably an altar-hearth,[4] and the point of the comparison is that Jerusalem in the coming siege and victory will become a place of carnage, as blood-stained as any altar-hearth. More germane to this investigation is the reference to the yearly round of the feasts

---

[1] Duhm (*HK*), Marti (*KHC*) (1900), and Gray (*ICC*) tried to connect it with the building of the Leontopolis temple in 160 B.C., but this verdict is now rendered quite impossible by the Qumran Isaiah scrolls. Guthe (*HSAT*) thought it was from the third century B.C. and Procksch (*KAT*) from the Persian age, but again it was difficult to place so large-hearted a vision in the post-exilic period. The reference to Assyria would also then be pointless. Some have suggested a connection to the founding of the Elephantine temple, but a prophet with the spiritual genius of the author of this prophecy hardly needed this particular historical stimulus to induce his vision. The older critics thought of a date before Josiah's Reform and Deuteronomy, i.e. before the condemnation of the *maṣṣēbâ* and sacrifice outside of Jerusalem. See G. A. Smith (*ExpB*) (Rev. ed. 1927), pp.281-82; W. R. Smith, *The Prophets of Israel*, ([2]1895), pp. 335ff, 436; T. K. Cheyne, *op. cit.*, Vol. I, p. 110 (an opinion later revised, cf. G. A. Smith, *in. loc.*).

[2] Cheyne, *ibid.*

[3] E. König, (*Das Buch Jesaja* (1926), p. 206) thinks this ascription not impossible. Hertzberg thinks the prophecy depends upon Isaiah; Fischer, (*Das Buch Isaias* (*HS*) Vol. I (1937)) that the differences in style are due to a disciple and Kissane, (*The Book of Isaiah*, Vol. I (1941)), that it is Isaianic.

[4] As in the Moabite Stone, but cf. now W. F. Albright, *Archaeology and the Religion of Israel*, pp. 151, 218 who thinks of a "denizen of the underworld" from the Accadian cosmic mountain Arallu.

in vs. 1.[1] Oesterley comments "that Isaiah takes for granted, that for the present the feasts, of which the sacrifices formed the central part of the celebration, would continue."[2]

Assyria as a Sacrifice (Is. 30 : 27-33)

The authenticity of this passage has been denied by a long line of critics including Marti, Cheyne, Gressmann and Mowinckel, but has been defended by Duhm, Procksch, Peake,[3] Binns[4] and now in part by Scott.[5] Skinner felt[6] the passage too gloating for Isaiah, and somewhat different in style and thought and suggested an Isaianic disciple. Some make a division between vss. 27-30 and 31-33, but Schmidt,[7] Auvray[8] and Hertzberg see a unity in the sacrificial metaphor of Assyria on the offering table and in the offering fire. Sacrificial terminology is possibly to be discerned in the "waving" of vss. 28 and 32 (*nûp*), in the feast of vs. 29 and in the *Topheth* (? burning place) and *melek* (*moloch*) of vs. 33.[9]

Interest will again centre on the feast. It is a night celebration, and is accompanied by song and gladness, and the sound of the flute, as the worshippers go to the holy mountain. Such a night celebration suggests the Passover,[10] but many hold there is insufficient evidence for its celebration before Josiah. Duhm thinks that what evidence there is —that of Deuteronomy would suggest a house festival, not a *ḥāg* to the temple, but Procksch thinks the impulse to centralization which Deuteronomy enforced to have begun under Hezekiah. The slaughter of the Assyrians under the

[1] It seems more natural to think of the round of the years, and then of the round of the feasts within the year, rather than of each year having but one feast. This would then be the first evidence, outside the codes for the keeping of a plurality of feasts.

[2] Oesterley, *Sacrifices . . .*, p. 198.

[3] A. S. Peake, "Isaiah," *PeakeC*, p. 457.

[4] L. Elliott Binns, "Isaiah," *GoreC*, p. 454.

[5] R. B. Y. Scott, *Isaiah* (*IB*) V (1956).

[6] J. Skinner, *Isaiah* (*CamB*) ([2]1915), p. 248.

[7] H. Schmidt, *Die grossen Propheten* (*SAT*) II, 2 (1915).

[8] R. Auvray, *Isaie* (*JerusB*) (1951), pp. 125ff.

[9] O. Eissfeldt, *Molk als Opferbegriff*, p. 58 thinks this verse contains a reference to Ahaz's sacrifice of his child as a Molech-offering in the difficult "*gam-hû*" ("even he"). On Eissfeldt's theory see p. 75f. above and the next chapter. Here the "king" may, however, be the "king of Assyria" (RSV).

[10] A. Dillmann, *Der Prophet Jesaia* (*KEH*) ([5]1890), p. 278 thought the absence of the article with *ḥāg* favoured Passover rather than Tabernacles which was *hā-ḥāg* par excellence.

walls might then be paralleled to the scene in Egypt (but cf. p. 134 above).[1] Others think the festival more likely to have been Tabernacles, which in later times also had night rites. Evidence for nightly cultic activity is found in Ps. 134 : 1.

The Sacrifice of Edom (Is. 34 : 6)

A slaughter rather than a sacrifice is spoken of here. "The Lord hath a *zebaḥ* in Bozrah, and a great slaughter (*ṭebaḥ*) in Edom." *Zebaḥ* and *ṭebaḥ* are parallel. The passage is not from Isaiah.[2]

MICAH

Somewhat surprisingly Micah has only one sacrificial reference—Ch. 6 : 6-8.

What shall I offer? (Micah 6 : 6-8)

The unity and early date of this passage are increasingly being recognized. T. H. Robinson thought that vss. 6-8 did not continue vss. 1-5, but Weiser and Anderson[3] stress the connection between the two parts. Among scholars favourable to Micah's authorship are Sellin, Schmidt, Weiser, Wolfe,[4] and Beyerlin.[5] Robinson sees no objection to the time of Micah, but thinks the style not that of the prophet.[6]

The ineffectiveness of extravagant sacrifice is depicted under the description of *ʿōlôt*, calves of a year old, thousands of rams and ten thousand of rivers of oil and the first-born. The lack of justice, mercy, and walking humbly with God prevents the acceptance of the sacrifice. A sense of sin is implied in vs. 7 in the words "for the sin of my soul," but it led to no penitence and amendment of life.[7]

[1] Some think this historical connection was not made so soon, but this cannot be proved.

[2] Its connections are with Ch. 35 and Deutero-Isaiah and with the exilic attitude to Edom.

[3] G. W. Anderson, "A Study of Micah 6 : 1-8," *SJT* IV (1951), pp. 191-97.

[4] R. Wolfe, "Micah," (*IB*) VI, New York (1956).

[5] W. Beyerlin, *Die Kulttraditionen Israels in der Verkündigung des Propheten Micha*, Göttingen (1959), pp. 69ff.

[6] F. C. Burkitt, "Micah 6 and 7 a Northern Prophecy," *JBL* XLV (1926), pp. 159-61 apparently saw no difficulty in the early date when he argued for the northern origin of the prophecy after the fall of Samaria.

[7] The prophet himself is the speaker, and it is his own vocabulary which he puts into the mouth of those whom he caricatures. He speaks of "sin", but this is not to say these worshippers did.

Conclusion

Twenty-two instances of sacrifice have been examined in the above survey. In view of the polemizing nature of so many of the references, particularly in Hosea where more than half the occurrences are to be found, it is necessary to note whether the reference is favourable or unfavourable.

In Group A there are three favourable references, which imply a connection of sin and sacrifice, but with the exception of Is. 6 : 5-7, which speaks only of the prophet's personal experience, they refer to a future cult, rather than to that of the present. They are Is. 19 : 19-21, which is possibly not by the prophet, Is. 6 : 5-7, which speaks of cleansing by the altar rather than specifically by sacrifice and Hos. 14 : 2, which envisages sacrifice replaced by penitence and prayer. The last reference is possibly unfavourable, and the others not clear, but it has been suggested above that they may serve to indicate the kind of cult, of which the prophets would have approved.

For the cult of the present, only one doubtful passage speaks of a connection of rejected sacrifice to sin (Micah 6 : 6-8). The sacrifices in the other rejection passages—Is. 1 : 11-15; Amos 4 : 4-5, Amos 5 : 21-25; Hos. 5 : 6—can hardly have been actuated by a sense of sin in view of the calls to penitence in the same contexts. They are therefore assigned to Group C.

In Group B are the references to the meals in the sanctuary in Amos 2 : 8, and Hos. 8 : 11-13 and to the joyous feasts of Hos. 2 : 13-15 (11-13) (all unfavourable). Hos. 9 : 4-6 probably also refers to sacramental eating and Is. 30 : 27-33 to a festal rejoicing, but these passages are not so clear and are therefore put, together with Hos. 4 : 8, into Group C.

Also in Group C are the formal references to sacrifice, which imply nothing as to its motive, Hos. 3 : 4, 6 : 6; Is. 29 : 1, 34 : 6, and the condemnations of the Baal cult, Hos. 4 : 13-19, 11 : 2, 12 : 12(11), 13 : 2.

The results reached seem to bear out the conclusion of Hempel in his investigation of the "fear of God" in the Old Testament, that the "Festfeiern der bäuerlichen Gemeinde des 7. Jahrhunderts und der grossen Heiligtümer des Kulturlandes" lacked the element of fear. The contrast with his findings in the earlier period (but not in the cult) led him to conclude that "dieser Kultus nicht aus der genuin-israelitischen, sondern aus einer anderen Frömmigkeit stammt."[1] Not all Hempel's findings correspond with those presented here,[2] but his basic principle, that the relation of man to God was characterized by both fear and confidence, by both repulsion and attraction, is also that of the present work. The change in this period may be put down in part to a confidence arising from the new economic order and way of life, and in part to the influence of ideas of the magical efficacy of sacrifice in the Canaanite fertility cult.

---

[1] J. Hempel, *Gott und Mensch im Alten Testament*, Stuttgart (^{2}1936), pp. 13ff.

[2] He finds a similar lack of fear in some Yahwistic narratives, particularly that of Gen. 18, which can hardly have any connection to the Canaanized eighth century cult, and seems to too sharply distinguish "cult" from "piety." The complexity of the evidence is, however, fully conceded by him.

REFERENCES TO SACRIFICE IN THE EIGHTH CENTURY PROPHETS

Reference	Incident	Terms Used	Primary or Secondary	Israelite or Foreign	National or Individual	Special or Regular
A. WHERE A SENSE OF SIN OR SOLEMNITY IS PRESENT						
Micah 6 : 6-8	What Shall I Offer	*ʿôlôt* *qdm* *šemen bekôr*	?Primary	Israelite	Individual	?Regular
?Hos. 14 : 3(2)	Sacrifices of Lips	*šlm*	?Primary	Israelite	Individual	Regular
?Is. 6 : 5-7	Call of Isaiah	*kipper*	Primary	Israelite	Individual	Regular
?Is. 19 : 19-21	Sacrifice in Egypt	*zebaḥ minḥâ* *ʿābad* *neder* *nādar*	?Secondary	?	National	Regular
B. WHERE A SENSE OF SIN OR SOLEMNITY IS NOT PRESENT						
Amos 2 : 8	Wine of Fines	*šātâ*	Primary	Israelite	Individual	Regular
Hos. 2 : 13-15 (11-13)	Joy of the Feast	*qṭr*	Primary	?Israelite	Festival	Regular
Hos. 8 : 11-13	Sin of Ephraim	?*zebaḥ* *zābaḥ* *ʾākal*	Primary	Israelite	Individual	Regular
C. DOUBTFUL OR UNCLASSIFIABLE PASSAGES						
a. Doubtful passages						
?Hos. 9 : 4-6	Sacrifices in Exile	*zebāḥîm* *nāsak* *ʾākal*	Primary	Israelite	Individual	Regular
?Is. 30 : 27-33	Assyria as Sacrifice		?Primary	Israelite	Festival	Regular
?Hos. 4 : 8	Sin of the Priests	?*ḥaṭṭāʾt* *ʾākal*	Primary	Israelite	Individual	Regular
b. Formal references						
Hos. 3 : 4	Removal of Sacrifice	*zebaḥ*	Primary	Israelite		
Hos. 6 : 6	Mercy not Sacrifice	*zebaḥ ʿōlôt*	Primary	Israelite		
Is. 29 : 1	Round of the Feasts		Primary	Israelite	Festal	Regular
Is. 34 : 6	Sacrifice of Edom	*zebaḥ*	Secondary	Israelite	Individual	Regular
c. Rejection passages						
Amos 4 : 4-5	Bethel and Gilgal	*zebāḥîm* *hēbîʾ* *nedābôt tôdâ* *qṭr*	Primary	Israelite	Individual	Regular
Amos 5 : 21-25	Sacrifice in Wilderness	*ʿōlôt minḥôt šelem* *ʿālâ* *zebāḥîm minḥâ* *nāgaš*	Primary	Israelite	Individual	Regular
Is. 1 : 11-15	Rejected Sacrifices	*zebāḥîm ʿōlôt minḥâ* *qeṭōret* *hēbîʾ*	Primary	Israelite	Individual	Regular
Hos. 5 : 6	Seeking the Lord		Primary	Israelite	?National	Regular
d. Condemnations of Baal cult						
Hos. 4 : 13-19	Sacrifices of Baal Cult	*qṭr zbḥ*	Primary	?Israelite	Individual	Regular
Hos. 11 : 2	Apostasy of Israel	*qṭr zbḥ*	Primary	?Israelite	Individual	Regular

CHAPTER NINE

THE SEVENTH CENTURY PROPHETS

Introduction

The introductory problems of the last chapter are intensified in the study of Jeremiah, Ezekiel and Zephaniah. Again there is much sacrificing both of a legitimate and an illegitimate kind. Again there is strong rejection of the cult, and irreconciliably juxtaposed with it, favourable references. The solutions proposed are even more radical.

That the cult should have still further degenerated in the direction of Canaanite worship is consistent with the Biblical theory of the decline under Manasseh, but less so with that of the reform of Josiah. Only a few of the passages to be considered can be dated before the reform. The remainder, which must come from the years between 626 and 586, indicate a relapse not much behind that of the Manasseh period. The burning of incense to or worship of "false gods" is described, not only in such formal references as Jer. 1 : 16, 11 : 13, 11 : 17, 18 : 15, and 44 : 3, but in more extended passages treating of the Baal cult (Jer. 19, 32 : 29ff.), the worship of the Queen of Heaven (Jer. 44 : 17-18, cf. 7 : 18), child sacrifice (Jer. 7 : 31; Ez. 16 : 18-21, 20 : 26-31, 23 : 39), and the "mysteries" of Ez. 8.[1] The prevalence of animal sacrifice is evidenced by Ezekiel's comparison of the crowded cities of a repopulated land, to the temple flocks awaiting sacrifice (Ez. 36 : 37-38), by Jeremiah's frequent use of the expression "a lamb led to the slaughter" (Jer. 11 : 19, 12 : 3, 51 : 40),[2] and by the popularity of the sacrificial metaphor for judgment (Jer. 46 : 10; Zeph. 1 : 7-8; Ez. 39: 17-19).[3]

---

[1] On Ez. 8 cf. T. H. Gaster, "Ezekiel and the Mysteries," *JBL* LX (1941), pp. 289-310.

[2] These verses are not further treated in the sequel, but the view of F. A. Farley, "Jeremiah and 'The Suffering Servant of Jehovah' in Deutero-Isaiah," *ExpT* XXXVIII (1926-1927), pp. 521-24, which connects Jer. 11 : 19 with Is. 53 and identifies Jeremiah with the Suffering Servant should perhaps be noted.

[3] On these references see O. Schmitz, *Die Opferanschauung des späteren Judentums*, pp. 50-52.

It is again difficult to separate the legitimate use of the cult from the illegitimate. All the references belong to Judah and many to the temple itself.

There is no question that Jeremiah has passages in which the cult is sharply repudiated. Whether these are to be taken absolutely will depend in part on the view taken of the attitude of Jeremiah to Deuteronomy. If Jeremiah and Deuteronomy are to be dated from the same period as criticism has long assumed, they must have stood in some relation to each other. If Jeremiah knew Deuteronomy and approved of it, he could not have absolutely rejected the sacrifice which Deuteronomy enjoins. Few today hold the view once favoured, that Jeremiah was the author of Deuteronomy (and of Kings), but many scholars think that he was at first in favour of Josiah's Reform and deeply influenced by Deuteronomy. Driver found traces of this influence on nearly every page of Jeremiah,[1] but Kennett and his successors in the "Cambridge School," which makes Deuteronomy exilic or later, thought the influence the other way round.[2] Jeremiah was the inspirer of Deuteronomy. Schofield, in the Wheeler Robinson Festschrift, therefore argued that Jeremiah did not know Deuteronomy,[3] while Rowley in the Theodore Robinson Festschrift, replied that he did.[4]

Hyatt has sought a solution in a theory of a Deuteronomic edition of Jeremiah, in which the editors are responsible for the echoes of Deuteronomic phraseology, the passages favourable to the reform and the whole chronology, which places Jeremiah before the reform.[5] In actual fact he began to prophesy after Deuteronomy,

[1] S. R. Driver, *Deuteronomy* (*ICC*) ([3]1902), p. xlvii.

[2] R. H. Kennett, "The Origin of the Book of Deuteronomy," *Deuteronomy and the Decalogue*, Cambridge (1920), pp. 1-33.

[3] J. N. Schofield, "The Significance of the Prophets for Dating Deuteronomy," *Studies in History and Religion* (ed.) E. A. Payne, London (1942), pp. 44-60.

[4] H. H. Rowley, "The Prophet Jeremiah and the Book of Deuteronomy," *Studies in Old Testament Prophecy* (ed.) H. H. Rowley, Edinburgh (1950), pp. 157-74. Rowley cited (p. 169) Jeremiah's appeal to a law for the release of slaves, which must have included females, and pointed out that such a law was only found in Deuteronomy. A. Puukko, "Jeremias Stellung zum Deuteronomium," *Alttestamentliche Studien Rudolf Kittel*, Leipzig (1913), p. 146 drew the opposite conclusion from the verbal citation in vs. 14, but left out of account the context on which Rowley relies.

[5] J. P. Hyatt, "Jeremiah and Deuteronomy," *JNES* I (1942), pp. 156-73, also "Jeremiah", (*IB*) V, (1956), pp. 788-89, and "The Peril from the North in Jeremiah," *JBL* LIX (1940), pp. 511-13 (esp. for the dating).

not in 626 B.C. but more than a decade later, and was always against both reform and cult, as Ch. 2 : 8, 8 : 8-9 and the temple sermon prove. Many will feel that this radical solution of Hyatt is less satisfactory than the older view of these passages it seeks to replace, viz. that Jeremiah began as a supporter of Deuteronomy in the reform (cf. Ch. 11 : 1ff.), but later, when he realized that it did not go deep enough, turned from it.[1] On either view no clear case can be made for the interpretation of Jeremiah's sacrificial references in the light of Deuteronomy.[2]

Along with the decision on Deuteronomy, also of importance for Jeremiah's view of sacrifice, is the question of the prophecies of restoration, which include references to a reinstituted cult. On this matter no agreement has been reached. Although not many scholars are now prepared to make the sharp distinction, which Duhm made between the poetic and prose sections of Jeremiah,[3] perhaps the majority favour the theory of an over-working of the original oracles by an editor—Baruch, or a Deuteronomist,[4] or a "Biographer."[5] To this editor, who may be dated about 550 B.C. or later, is due the repetitious, conventionalized theological style, the restoration passages, the hopes for the Davidic dynasty and the favourable attitude to the cult.[6]

A similar view of Ezekiel is also favoured by a number of writers, following the cue of Hölscher.[7] Most radical of these is Irwin, who leaves only a fragment of the prophecy—250 out of 1,273 verses—to Ezekiel.[8] To him Ezekiel was not interested in ritual,[9] and was

[1] J. Skinner, *Prophecy and Religion*, pp. 89ff; F. A. Farley, "Jeremiah and Deuteronomy," *ExpT* XXXVII (1925-1926), pp. 316-18.

[2] See the article of R. S. Dobbie further treated in the next chapter. "Deuteronomy and the Prophetic Attitude to Sacrifice," *SJT* XII (1959), pp. 68-82.

[3] He allowed only the former—some sixty in number—to the prophet (B. Duhm, *Jeremia* (*KHC*) (1901), pp. XIIIff).

[4] J. P. Hyatt, *op. cit.*

[5] H. G. May, "Towards an Objective Approach to the Book of Jeremiah: the Biographer," *JBL* LXI (1942), pp. 139-55.

[6] So May, *ibid.* He thinks the Biographer responsible for the twenty references to "covenant" including those of Chs. 30-31. He was interested in post-exilic psalmody, and to him the injunction to bring psalms and *tôdôt* in Jer. 33 : 11 is to be traced.

[7] G. Hölscher, *Hesekiel, der Dichter und das Buch*, Giessen (1924).

[8] W. A. Irwin, *The Problem of Ezekiel*, Chicago (1943).

[9] See his edition of J. M. P. Smith's *The Prophets and their Times*, Chicago (^{2}1941), pp. 214-16.

not of course, the author of Chs. 40-48,[1] or the other references favourable to sacrifice. One feels that whatever the verdict may be on Jeremiah, at least for Ezekiel this surgery is too radical, and that Rowley has certainly right on his side, when he insists that the book gives throughout the impression of one personality.[2]

Further discussion of these issues is perhaps better handled in connection with the study of the individual passages.

JEREMIAH

Exotic Sacrifices (Jer. 6 : 20)

In similar vein to the older prophets, Jeremiah in vs. 20b rejects *ʿōlôt* as not acceptable (*rāṣâ*), and *zᵉbāḥîm* as not pleasing (*ʿārab*). His scorn in vs. 20a of the special importation of frankincense (*lᵉbônâ*) from Sheba and of the sweet cane (used in the making of incense) from a distant land, is parallel to his predecessor's satires on the heightening of sacrifice, but the elements involved are new. Incense itself was probably not an innovation,[3] but explicit mention of its foreign origin is not found earlier.[4]

The significance of Jeremiah's rejection of sacrifice has been variously estimated. Skinner[5] and Schmidt (*SAT*) think this passage post-Deuteronomic and in opposition to Deuteronomy, but this can hardly be proved. Weiser sees a continuation of the old amphictyonic tradition subordinating the cultic to the moral,[6]

---

[1] These chapters are also rejected by Snaith, "The Priesthood and the Temple," *A Companion to the Bible* (ed.) T. W. Manson, Edinburgh (1939), pp. 423ff. and by many others.

[2] H. H. Rowley, "The Book of Ezekiel in Modern Study," *BJRL* XXXVI (1953-1954), pp. 146-90. The unanimity of critics that this was so during the first century of Biblical criticism, when all was so closely investigated, is an impressive witness which cannot be lightly set aside.

[3] So Volz, *Jeremia* (*KAT*) ([2]1928), p. 82; Nötscher, *Jeremia* (*HS*) (1934), p. 77. For the contrary view see J. Wellhausen, *Prolegomena*, p. 65 and the discussion above on p. 124.

[4] Some scholars have noted that it is the sole exception to the custom of offering only indigenous products and domesticated animals, into the life of which man's labour might have been thought of as having entered.

[5] Skinner, *Prophecy and Religion*, p. 124.

[6] One of the clearest statements of his view occurs at this point in his Jeremiah commentary (*ATD*) I (1952), p. 63. He finds an opposition between two basically different kinds of piety—the theocentric Yahweh cult and the anthropocentric offering cult. In the centre of the covenant cult was an act of God, while in the offering cult an act of man. Jer. 9 : 13, which speaks of the forsaking of the law, is a reference to the rejection of the covenant cult.

and Volz of a primitive Mosaic religion without sacrifice. That neither of these views are probable has been adequately shown in earlier chapters. It is not clear from the present passage, that the sacrifice is specifically directed to turning away the wrath of Yahweh or that it goes beyond Is. 1 : 11ff., to which it is closely similar in construction (e.g. *lāmmâ* . . ?)

The Temple Sermon (Jer. 7)

The references to sacrifice belong to sections which are possibly appendices (cf. the very much shorter form in Ch. 26 : 2-6) and possibly in part Deuteronomic. Deuteronomic influence is usually seen in the condemnation of the Queen of Heaven cult in vss. 16-20 and the Topheth cult in vss. 31ff. These passages will be dealt with in connection with Ch. 44 and Ch. 19, and attention here confined to the famous rejection passage in vss. 21-28.

The passage begins with the taunt "add your *ʿōlôt* to your *zᵉbāḥîm* and eat flesh," which probably means, not so much "multiply your sacrifices" (cf. Is. 29 : 1 "add ye year to year"), as "eat *ʿōlôt* equally with *zᵉbāḥîm*"—a violent breach of the law that *ʿōlôt* were sacred to Yahweh and on no account to be eaten. Yahweh has lost all interest in such *ʿōlôt* and they might just as well be eaten, as offered to him (cf. Is. 1 : 11ff). This is reinforced by the appeal to the history of the exodus period,

> for in the day that I brought them out of the
> land of Egypt, I did not speak to your fathers
> or command them concerning *ʿōlâ* and *zebaḥ*, but
> this command I gave them "obey my voice."

How is this verse to be understood?

Agreement has now been fairly generally reached, that the verses cannot be understood in Graf's sense[1] that no law codes associating sacrifice with Moses existed in Jeremiah's time.[2] Nor need it be assumed that Jeremiah knew of such laws, and by this verse sought to combat them —such a refutation would need to be made explicit,

[1] Already in his Jeremiah commentary in 1862 (*Der Prophet Jeremia*, Leipzig (1862), pp. 121-23).

[2] That this was an illegitimate inference from the verse is acknowledged by most recent commentators. So Volz (*KAT*); Rudolph (*HAT*, 1947); Hyatt (*IB*) and others.

if intended as an attack on such venerable documents as those of J and E. Still less can he have meant that no sacrificing took place in the time of Moses—it would be open to his objectors to simply refer to the traditions of J and E.

Difficult as it may seem, one or other of the moderating explanations of the verses must be adopted[1]—either that which beginning from "in the day" limits the non-mention of sacrifice to a particular occasion (such as that of Exod. 19 and 20),[2] or that which, identifying "your fathers" with the congregation, distinguishes between the fundamental laws like the decalogue, given to the public assembly, which were non-sacrificial, and others which might have been sacrificial,[3] or that which, rendering *ʿal-dibrê* "in the interest of, out of concern for," thinks the meaning only that sacrifice was not the main purpose of the law,[4] or that which taking the final words, "that it may be well with thee" as determinative, argues that, the commandment to which this kind of promise was attached in the earlier literature was concerned with obedience, not sacrifice,[5] or that which falls back again on the "not this but that" formula as meaning only "more of this and less of that."[6]

Nothing is said of the purpose of sacrifice in the passage.

Holy Flesh (Jer. 11 : 15)

The RSV rendering of this verse "can vows and sacrificial flesh

---

[1] A modified rejection is favoured by Rothstein (*HSAT*); Nötscher (*HS*); Gelin (*JerusB*) (1951), p. 61; Allis, *The Five Books of Moses* ([2]1949), Philadelphia, pp. 169-73; Guillaume, *Prophecy and Divination*, pp. 373, 378. Absolute rejection is favoured among others by G. A. Smith, *Jeremiah*, New York ([4]1929), pp. 155-59; Hyatt and Hopper (*IB*); Volz; Micklem *Prophecy and Eschatology*, London (1926), p. 200 and others.

[2] It is more probable, however, that the whole period of the exodus events is intended.

[3] So E. König, "Meaning and Scope of Jeremiah vii 22, 23," and "Der Jeremiaspruch 7, 21-23," *op. cit.*, who says "This sets aside only the primary rank, but not the existence, of the laws concerning sacrifice." ("Meaning and Scope," p. 373).

[4] So O. Allis, *op. cit.*, p. 172, who lists all the uses of the term, and argues from the preceding verse for the sense that Yahweh's interest was not in sacrificial food.

[5] Cf. S. R. Driver, *The Book of the Prophet Jeremiah*, London (1906), p. 44.

[6] So H. H. Rowley, *The Unity of the Bible*, p. 41. He points out that Jeremiah's words echo the covenant formula of Exod. 19 : 5. For the view that this is the oldest of the covenant formulas see J. Muilenburg, "The form and structure of the covenantal formulations," *VT* IX (1959), pp. 347-65.

avert your doom? Can you then exult?" suggests propitiatory sacrifices, but the AV, unintelligible as it is, is nearer the MT "many and the holy flesh is passed from thee, when thou doest evil, then thou rejoicest."[1] The emending of *ha-rabbîm* to "vows" is supported by the LXX *euchai*,[2] but Hyatt thinks *ha-beriyîm* "fatlings" nearer to the Hebrew.[3] The emendation of *ya'abrû* to Hiphil *ya'abīrû* involves only the vowels and is not impossible, but the omission of *kî* as a dittography and the deletion or emendation of *'āz ta'alōzî* is less certain.[4] RSV may be on the right lines,[5] but it would be unsafe to draw any inferences from so corrupt a text.

Ineffective Sacrifice (Jer. 14 : 12)

This passage, like the two preceding (7 : 16, 11 : 14), follows a prohibition laid on Jeremiah (vs. 11) not to pray for the people. Neither his prayers, nor the people's fasting and sacrifices will avail. *'ōlâ* and *minḥâ* might be the daily morning and evening sacrifices here, but this is not certain. The passage might be Deuteronomic as Hyatt thinks, but need not be so. The sacrifices are apparently intended to supplicate Yahweh.

Sabbaths and Offerings (Jer. 17 : 26)

Few scholars can be found to defend Jeremiah's authorship of the section vss. 19-27, or of vs. 26 in particular. The emphasis on keeping the sabbath is thought to be impossible to one of Jeremiah's outlook, and is usually assigned to the time of Neh. 13 : 15-22. In Trito-Isaiah, however, there is the combination of Sabbath emphasis and the prophetic preference for ethics above ritual (e.g. Is. 58),

---

[1] S. R. Driver, *op. cit.*, p. 68, 355 says, however, that it is no real translation of the Hebrew text. The use of the Aramaic pronominal suffix *kî* is unlikely in Jeremiah. Orelli on the other hand thinks this a North Israelite usage like Ps. 103 : 3-5, 116 : 7, 19, and Ps. 24 : 4, 3, 7.

[2] *Euchē* and *euchesthai* are more often "vows" than "prayers" in the LXX (Cornill, *Das Buch Jeremia*, Leipzig (1905), p. 148).

[3] J. P. Hyatt, "The Original Text of Jeremiah 11 : 15-16," *JBL* LX (1941), pp. 57-60. One Old Latin mss reads *adipes*, but this may stand for *ha-ḥalābîm* (BH) rather than *ha-beriyîm*.

[4] LXX "by these escape" is favoured by G. A. Smith.

[5] *Rā'â*, however, may be interpreted of sin rather than doom (both usages occur together in vs. 17), and in this case the sacrifices would be expiatory not propitiatory.

but even on the early date for this passage favoured by McCullough[1] this would be later than Jeremiah. The problem of vs. 26 is a separate one, as it appears to break the connection between vs. 27 and the rest of the section. It predicts the coming of the inhabitants of many districts of south and central Palestine to the house of the Lord with *ʿōlâ, zebaḥ, minḥâ, lᵉbônâ* and *tôdâ*.[2] Whether such a verse was possible to Jeremiah, depends on the view taken of his ministry as a whole. May finds in the verse the typical repetitious style of his "Biographer."

Child Sacrifice (Ch. 19, 7 : 31, 32 : 35)

The story of Jeremiah's purchase and breaking of a potter's earthen jar is interrupted by a long condemnation of the Baal cult[3] in terms similar to those of Ch. 7 : 31ff. The passage could either be a duplicate of 7 : 31ff. or its original, and its author either the Deuteronomic editor (Hyatt), or the prophet himself. A similar passage is found in 32 : 35. The relations between the three passages may be set out as follows:

7 : 31	19 : 5	32 : 35
they have built the high place of Topheth to burn in the fire (*śārap bāʾēš*) their sons and daughters	they have built high places of Baal to burn in the fire (*śārap bāʾēš*) their sons *ʿōlōt* to Baal	they have built high places of Baal to cause to pass through (*haʿᵃbîr*) their sons and daughters to Molech

which I did not command, nor did it enter my mind.

It is clear that *haʿᵃbîr* is to be interpreted by *śārap bāʾēš*, and that a real sacrifice is in view. What is not clear is that this is a first-born offering, in view of the reference to the sacrifice of daughters also, or that it was addressed to Yahweh, as Eissfeldt

---

[1] W. S. McCullough, "A Re-examination of Isaiah 56-66," *JBL* LXVII (1948), pp. 27-36. He thinks Is. 56-66 is to be dated between 586 and 562 B.C.

[2] The last term may be an addition, as the repetition of *mᵉbiʾê* suggests.

[3] Volz separates the Topheth discourse from the jar incident and gives to it vss. 2ab, 3-6, 11b and 12ff, while Hyatt gives it vss. 2b-9, 11b-13. Possibly the location of the two stories was the same.

assumes, instead of to "other gods."[1] Albright thinks that there was indeed a god Muluk in the Mesopotamian region,[2] but allows this much of Eissfeldt's thesis, that a derivative from the name of this deity may have come to be used for "promise, vow or pledge,"[3] and that children might have been sacrificed to Muluk as patron of vows. Albright suggests that "Ahaz was one of the first to borrow the Syrian custom of sacrificing children to confirm a solemn vow or pledge." On this view the sacrifice was not propitiatory, but in confirmation of the sanctity of a promise.

Thank Offerings after the Return (Jer. 33 : 11)

Whether Jeremiah could have said this will depend on the view taken of his restoration prophecies, and of his attitude to sacrifice. On the view taken here it is not impossible that Jeremiah could have prophesied a return, and have given sacrifices of thanksgiving (*tôdâ*) a place in that return. Weiser, however, who accepts the verse, finds the reference to the offerings superfluous stylistically.[4] Others find the whole of vs. 11 interpolated in imitation of the oft recurring Jeremianic formula for depopulation in 7 : 34, 16 : 9 and 25 : 10. Hyatt regards the formula itself as Deuteronomic in each of its appearances. Volz rejects the whole chapter.

The Levitical Ministry (Jer. 33 : 18)

This verse is universally rejected as inconsistent with Jeremiah's outlook, and as missing from the LXX. Whatever may be the reason for the LXX omission which runs from vss. 14-26, and forms the longest single omission in the book, it cannot be that the passage is later than the LXX. Its hope of a continuing Davidic

---

[1] Eissfeldt, *Molk als Opferbegriff*, p. 43 argues that 7 : 31 is primary, and that 19 : 5 and 32 : 35 secondarily introduce Baal and Moloch to avoid the implication that the sacrifices were to Yahweh. For the view that the sacrifices were not to Yahweh, but to a god Moloch see A. Bea, "Kinderopfer für Moloch oder für Jahwe?" *Biblica* XVIII (1937), pp. 95-107, and on the whole question K. Dronkert, *De Molochdienst in het Oude Testament*, Leiden (1953).

[2] W. F. Albright, *Archaeology and the Religion of Israel*, pp. 162ff.

[3] So the Syriac *mulkânâ* means "promise." Cf. "swearing by Milcom" (Zeph. 1 : 5).

[4] It is made doubly suspect by the addition of a liturgical section for Ps. 136 : 1. If the reference to the thank offering goes along with this insertion it can hardly be from Jeremiah. For *tôdâ* LXX reads *dōra*.

line naturally brings it near to the time of the monarchy, but its association of the Davidic ruler with the Levitical priest would better suit the time of the restoration under Haggai and Zechariah. This time would also suit the Deuteronomic terminology of "the priests the Levites" better than the later time favoured by some scholars. The participles of the Hebrew require the translation "offering (*maʿaleh*) *ʿōlâ*, burning (*maqṭîr*) *minḥâ* and sacrificing (*ʿōśeh*) *zebaḥ*." One cannot imagine the circumstances under which Jeremiah himself could have promised that a Levitical priesthood performing these tasks should not cease for ever.

The Cutting of a Covenant (Jer. 34 : 18)

See on Gen. 15.[1]

The Offerings of the Pilgrims (Jer. 41 : 5)

In this reference eighty pilgrims bring sacrifice to the house of the Lord, which is undoubtedly in Jerusalem, rather than in Mizpah, where Gedaliah ruled. The time of the incident is apparently some little time after the fall of Jerusalem—possibly as long as five years, if this be the length of Gedaliah's term as governor. The worshippers certainly knew that the temple had been destroyed, as their mourning garb indicates.[2] They come nevertheless in the seventh month with *minḥâ*[3] and *lebônâ*. Does this mean that the altar of the ruined temple still continued to function, as Welch supposes,[4] or had they confined their offerings to the cereal *minḥâ* because there was no possibility of animal sacrifice, as Orelli suggests?[5]

Of interest is the fact, that the regions from which the pilgrims come to Jerusalem (Shechem, Shiloh (LXX Salem), Samaria), are all in nominally Northern Kingdom territory. These cities may have been taken into Judah under Josiah (Hyatt), and have worshipped in Jerusalem since the Josianic reform of 621 B.C., or may have

[1] The fact that Jeremiah calls down a fate like that of the slaughtered calf on the defaulting covenant members, would support the view that the original rite was a symbolic self-imprecation, but it is not certain, that this is the original text here. LXX omits the element of "cutting" and a slight emendation is needed in the MT to bring in the comparison (*kāʿēgel* for *hāʿēgel*).

[2] Shaved beards, rent garments and bodies gashed.

[3] LXX reads *manna* as in 17 : 26.

[4] A. C. Welch, *Post-Exilic Judaism*, Edinburgh (1935), pp. 160ff.

[5] C. Orelli, *Jeremia* (*SZ*) (^{3}1905), p. 166.

recommenced the annual pilgrimage to Jerusalem after 721 B.C. (Nötscher) or perhaps had never completely stopped it at the disruption (Gelin). Weiser thinks Deuteronomic centralization the hallowing of this old custom of an autumn pilgrimage to Jerusalem. The offerings on this occasion were certainly accompanied by mourning and possibly by the confession of sin.

Worship of the Queen of Heaven (Jer. 44 : 15-19, 7 : 18)

The Queen of Heaven cult, which had been condemned by Jeremiah in Ch. 7 : 16-20 is described with some additional details on its resumption in Egypt. The worship involved the burning of incense (*qṭr*), as well as the offering of libations and figured cakes, and was a matter of solemn vows.[1] The misfortune of the ruin of the state, and the calamity of the exile is interpreted as the wrath of the goddess at the intermission of her cult. The resumed sacrifices are to propitiate her. In normal worship they had been for food and prosperity and such like (vs. 17).

Judgment a Sacrifice (Jer. 46 : 10)

This passage from its connection to the similar exilic passage in Is. 34 : 6 is probably later than Jeremiah. For the metaphor see on Is. 34 : 6 and Zeph. 1 : 7-8.

Sacrifice in Moab (Jer. 48 : 35)

It is not certain if this should read with RSV "him who offers sacrifice in the high place" (MT literally "the offerer of") or with the LXX "he that going up to the high places." The reference is quite formal and says nothing of the purpose of sacrifice.

ZEPHANIAH

Judgment a Sacrifice (Zeph. 1 : 7-8)

The metaphor of the coming judgment as a banquet probably makes its first appearance in the Old Testament here.[2] In its other

[1] The words "that which goeth out of the mouth" also describe Jephthah's vow in Judg. 11 : 36.

[2] J. Gray in "The Hebrew Conception of the Kingship of God," *VT* VI (1956), p. 270 thinks the metaphor possibly connected to Anat's massacre of her adversaries, who were apparently lured for this purpose to a banquet in her temple (Gordon, *UH*, ʿnt II).

occurrences, which are all probably later than Zephaniah, it appears in foreign oracles with the enemies of Israel as the victim. In Zephaniah, however, it is a judgment against Israel that is being announced, and Israel herself is apparently the victim with her enemies the guests, who will feed upon her at the meal.[1] Whether such a meal is rightly called a sacrifice has been questioned by Gaster, who says *zebaḥ* properly means "the slaughtering of an animal," and does not necessarily denote a sacrifice. Moffatt's translation "The Eternal hath ready a victim for sacrifice" thus obscures the point. The verse should read "Yahweh hath prepared a meal."[2]

Sacrifices of Ethiopia (Zeph. 3 : 10)

The translation of the verse is far from certain, but the first and last phrases are unobjectionable "from beyond the rivers of Cush . . . they shall bring my *minḥâ*."[3] *Minḥâ* in this passage could possibly mean "tribute," for which the verb *yābal* "lead along in procession"[4] would be more appropriate,[5] but the context speaks of a conversion of the heathen, like that of Is. 19, and this would imply "offerings."[6]

---

[1] Unless vs. 7 belongs with vss. 14-18 (as Sellin (*KAT*) and Horst (*HAT*)), and not with vss. 8-13, or 2-12. J. M. P. Smith (*ICC*) and C. Taylor (*IB*), however, consider rearrangement unnecessary.

[2] T. H. Gaster, *Thespis* (1950), p. 209. The use of *qᵉrûʾîm* "the ones called" for guests at a meal has already been encountered (see on 2 Sam. 15 : 11, 9 : 24; 1 Sam. 16 : 5; 1 Kings 1 : 9). The consecrating of guests is referred to in 1 Sam. 16 : 5 (cf. 1 Sam. 20 : 26), but is omitted in 1 Sam. 9. In the present context the consecration may just possibly be of warriors for war.

[3] This is all that is read by the best texts of the LXX (Rahlfs), except that the plural of *minḥâ* is read.

[4] *Yābal* is not elsewhere used of an offering in the Old Testament, but the picture of offerings in procession is common in ancient pictures (cf. Ps. 76 : 12(11)).

[5] Cf. Is. 18 : 7 and Ps. 68 : 30 (in both of which Ethiopia is in the context) where kings "bear along" (*yābal*) gifts (*šay*).

[6] The rendering of the problematic middle clause as "my suppliants, the daughter of my dispersed ones" would bring in a reference to the Jewish exiles, who are not otherwise in the context. The context may not, however, be original. Elliger (*ATD*), who accepts vss. 9-13 as from the prophet, doubts vs. 10, while the whole passage is doubted by most scholars. It is not certain, however, that a conversion of the heathen need be late, in view of the presence of this element in the Psalms, or that such a prophecy of salvation could not belong side by side with prophecies of judgment.

NAHUM

The Feasts of Judah (Nah. 2 : 1(1 : 15))

This call to Judah to keep her feasts (*ḥāgî ḥaggîm*) and fulfil her vows (*šlm nᵉdārîm*), if by Nahum, refers to the freedom of Judah from further interruption by foreign invasion "never again shall the wicked come against you." On a later date the reference could be to the resumption of the festal calendar after the exile.

HABAKKUK

Sacrifice to a Net (Hab. 1 : 16)

The Chaldean tyrant, "whose own might is his god," (vs. 10 RSV), offers worship (*zbḥ* (Piel) *qṭr*) to the instruments—which have brought him victory—the "nets" by which he has gathered men "like fish of the sea." Sacrifice to weapons, like that to a standard (cf. on Exod. 17 : 15), is known from classical antiquity, but is not otherwise mentioned in the Old Testament.[1]

EZEKIEL

Child Sacrifice (Ez. 16 : 15-21, 20 : 25-31, 23 : 36-39)

The authenticity of these three passages is doubted by some scholars, but apart from their connection with the present contexts, and some redactional elements, the passages need not be impugned.[2] They may be set out comparatively as follows:

---

[1] But cf., however, the placing of Goliath's sword in the sanctuary at Nob (1 Sam. 21 : 9).

[2] 16 : 16-21 is rejected by Hölscher, *op. cit.*, p. 93, but assigned to a second strand by A. Bertholet (*HAT*, [1]1936) and G. Fohrer (*HAT*, [2]1955). Rothstein (*HSAT*) queries "fine flour, oil and honey" in vs. 19, but although the list is parenthetical, these were not impossible in an intensified cult. 20 : 25-31 is rejected by May (*IB*) VI (1956) and Hölscher. Irwin omits vss. 27-29. "Blasphemed," "provocation of your offering," "poured out libations" and the pun on *bāmâ* are thought to be non-Ezekielian traits. 23 : 36-39 comes in awkwardly as a further prophecy against Oholah and Oholibah together, after each has been judged separately in the earlier verses, and is rejected by Fohrer. Cooke (*ICC*, 1936), however, thinks it may have been uttered on another occasion.

16 : 15-21	20 : 25-31	23 : 36-39
20	26	37
you took your sons and your daughters	their first-born	their sons
whom you had borne to me		whom they had borne to me
these you sacrificed (*zābaḥ*)	to cause to pass through (*ha‘abîr*)	to cause to pass through (*ha‘abîr*)
to them		to them
to be devoured (*lekôl*)		for food (*le’oklâ*)
21	31	39
my sons	your sons	their sons
you slaughtered (*šāḥaṭ*)		they slaughtered (*šāḥaṭ*)
to cause to pass through (*ha‘abîr*)	to cause to pass through (*ha‘abîr*) the fire (*bā’ēš*)	
to them	(with your idols)	to their idols

As in the case of the Jeremiah references, daughters as well as sons are sacrificed (16 : 20), although the sacrifice in 20 : 26 is of first-born. The words "for food" in 23 : 37 hardly bear the sense of "food for the gods," but should be taken as in 16 : 20 of the "devouring" of the fire (cf. Is. 5 : 24). LXX read *bā’ēš* for them in 20 : 37, but does not read this, where the MT has it, in 20 : 31. The verb *šāḥaṭ* is surprising, and, if the verbs of 16 : 21 are in order, would imply that the children were first killed, and then burnt, and not burnt alive, as the Greek tradition has it. From 23 : 39, which speaks of the worshippers slaughtering children and coming in to Yahweh's sanctuary on the same day, it is usually deduced that the child sacrifice was also thought of as offered to Yahweh. The prophet, however, thought quite otherwise by his use of "to them," "to their idols" and the analogy of harlotry after other gods.

What is to be made then of 20 : 25-26, and the statement that Yahweh had given them commands which were not good and defiled them in making them offer their first-born? If vs. 26 stood alone it could be explained as an instance, for which there are other parallels, of the working of the principle of "hardening," by which, what God allows to happen, is ascribed to his volition—men being incited to sin so that the punishment of sin, which they deserve, will come upon them—"I defiled them by their very gifts in making them offer by fire, all their first-born, that I might horrify them." As a continuation of vs. 25, however, the case becomes a matter of commandment. The "statutes which were not good by which they could not have life" which Yahweh had given are apparently the basis of the defiling of vs. 26.

Bewer argues that vs. 27 which speaks of a blasphemy of the people, is out of place before vss. 28ff. which contain no blasphemy, and should be read as an introduction to vs. 25.[1] The blasphemy then consists in the assertion that Yahweh had given them commandments which were not good, and the passage reads:

> moreover your fathers uttered this blasphemy against me—when they dealt treacherously with me—that I had given them statutes that were not good... and that I had defiled them in their gifts...

Bewer supports this surgery by noting that the true introduction to vs. 28, which should be parallel to vs. 9 and vs. 14, must have been displaced by the insertion of the present section. Ezekiel's position is like that of Jeremiah (Jer. 7 : 31, 19 : 5) "it never came into my mind," as is clear from vs. 11, 16 : 20ff., 23 : 26. "The people had misinterpreted the law of Exod. 22 : 29 as demanding the sacrifice of their first-born children (cf. Micah 6 : 7) in spite of Exod. 34 : 20, 13 : 13."[2]

Vs. 28 describes the Israelites in Canaan at any high hill or leafy tree sacrificing (*zābaḥ*) their *zebāḥîm*, presenting (*nātan*) the provocation of their offering (*qorbān*), setting their soothing odours (*rēaḥ niḥôaḥ*) and pouring out their drink offerings (*nesākîm*).

Sacrifices in Jerusalem (Ez. 20 : 40-41)

If the occasion is still the same as in the previous instance, Bewer may be right in seeing in the present passage and in vss. 29 and 31, the prophet's repudiation of a plan to build a high place in Babylon.[3] His answer is that in Jerusalem alone should men bring offerings. Only on the view of his radical rejection of the cult (and

---

[1] J. A. Bewer, "Textual and Exegetical Notes on the Book of Ezekiel," *JBL* LXXII (1953), pp. 159-61, also in *The Prophets* (*Harper's Annotated Bible*), New York (1955), p. 381.

[2] J. A. Bewer, *The Prophets*, p. 381.

[3] Bewer, "Beiträge zur Exegese des Buches Ezechiel," *ZAW* LXIII (1951), pp. 195-97.

non-authorship of Chs. 40-48) can it be argued that he could not have given this favourable place to sacrifice.[1]

Yahweh will seek (*dāraš*) their *tᵉrûmôt* and the *rēʾšît* of their gifts.[2] Israel will be accepted (*rāṣâ* vss. 40, 41) and will herself be a *rēaḥ niḥôaḥ* (vs. 41).[3] Nothing can be deduced from the fact that the acceptance of Israel precedes her bringing of offerings (vs. 40) (as for example that sacrifice could not therefore be the ground of acceptance) because *rāṣâ* occurs again in vs. 41 after the reference to offerings. The "acceptance" is neither the cause nor the result of the sacrifices, but a state of divine openness in which offerings, when they are brought, can be accepted.

Judgment a Sacrifice (Ez. 39 : 17-20)

The majority of commentators regard the Gog and Magog prophecies of Chs. 38-39 as later than Ezekiel, but this view is not shared by Bewer,[4] who not only accepts the prophet's authorship of the whole, but even allows that several drafts of his on the subject are represented here. Vss. 17-19 do not logically follow vss. 14-16, but may be read either as parallel to them (Bewer) or preceding them, or independently as a separate apocalypse (Cooke).

The victims which provide this feast are probably the enemies of Israel. The guests are the birds and beasts of the field (vs. 17), rather than Israel. The horror of the occasion is accentuated by the fact, that the fat and blood, which would normally have been sacrosanct to Yahweh, are consumed by the guests. The passage is longer than the similar examples already examined in Is. 34 : 6; Jer. 46 : 10 and Zeph. 1 : 7-8.

EZEKIEL 40-48

This section, if by Ezekiel, would be decisive for his thought, but as it is really a code, comparable with H and P, it has been excluded from this investigation.

---

[1] So W. Zimmerli (*BK*) (1959), p. 453.

[2] On this word see BH. If "gifts" be read, *rēʾšît* must then be rendered non-technically as a construct "the choicest of" (RSV) rather than as "first-fruits."

[3] Understanding *b* as *b* essentiae, or emending to *k* as BH. Another possibility is to read it as *b* pretii "the sacrificial performance for the sake of which the offerer has been accepted by God" (Zimmerli), p. 458.

[4] J. A. Bewer, *The Prophets*, pp. 327ff.

Conclusion

Twenty-four references to sacrifice in the Books of Jeremiah, Zephaniah, Nahum, Habakkuk and Ezekiel have been studied. Half of these are unfavourable and come in the category either of "sacrifices rejected by the prophets" (Jer. 6 : 20, 7 : 21, 11 : 15, 14 : 12), or of condemnations of the apostate cult (Jer. 7 : 18, 44 : 15, 7 : 31, 19 : 4, 32 : 35; Ez. 16 : 15-21, 20 : 25-31, 23 : 36-39 —all but two child sacrifice).

The remaining twelve include five in prophecies of restoration, where the question of date arises and seven in formal references, which indicate little of the purpose of sacrifice. There are virtually no straightforward cases, except possibly Jer. 41 : 4. This has been assigned to Group A. Also to Group A should possibly go some of the "rejected sacrifices"—e.g. Jer. 14 : 12 and 44 : 15-19, which seem to imply propitiatory ideas.

Group B is also poorly represented. Only the doubtfully authentic Jer. 33 : 11 seems to qualify for this group. The sacrificial meals, which form the background to the judgment metaphor in Jer. 46 : 10; Zeph. 1 : 7-8 and Ez. 39 : 17-19 are also possibilities, but are used only in a metaphorical sense.

In Group C come the great majority of cases—the six which are too formal for anything to be deduced from them (the judgment scenes and Jer. 34 : 18, 43 : 35; Nah. 2 : 11 (1 : 15), Hab. 1 : 16), the six child sacrifice passages, the other unfavourable passages and the four prophecies of restoration of doubtful date.

In their view of the evolution of expiatory sacrifice, Wellhausen and Robertson Smith laid weight on this century as the time when "earnestness superseded the old joyousness of the cultus [which] now had reference principally to sin and its atonement."[1] The present chapter provides little evidence for this view. The emergence of child sacrifice is usually relied on for proof, but before this could be seen as a step towards the solemnity of P's cult, it would need to be proved that child sacrifice belonged to the Yahweh cult, rather than to an apostate worship, that it arose in the troubles of the seventh century, rather than in the luxurious cult of the preceding century, and that it expressed a sense of sin.

The first of these assumptions has been seen to be questionable

[1] J. Wellhausen, *Prolegomena*, p. 486. Cf. *ibid.*, p. 421 and pp. 1-5 above.

and the same may also be true of the second. Wellhausen based his case on the fact that child sacrifice was condemned by Jeremiah and Ezekiel, but not by the earlier prophets.[1] If, however, Micah 6 belongs to the prophet, and the possible allusions to child sacrifice in Hosea are allowed, and Is. 30 is understood as a condemnation of Ahaz's sacrifice of his son,[2] the position becomes different. Whether a "sense of sin" is expressed in these sacrifices will depend on the content given to this term. What sense of sin there was, was a disease of morbid minds, rather than any achievement of the moral consciousness. It is possible that this is what Wellhausen meant. He seems to have shared the Romantics' scorn of the sin-conscious priestly ritual, which cramped the uninhibited freedom of the natural man.[3]

---

[1] J. Wellhausen, *Die Kleinen Propheten*, p. 144.

[2] Viz. that the "promise" of Ahaz to the king of Assyria, which had been sealed by sacrifice, had brought doom, in which the king of Assyria also shared. Cf. A. Bea *op. cit.*, pp. 101ff.

[3] On Wellhausen's debt to Romanticism see F. Boschwitz, *Julius Wellhausen, Motive und Massstäbe seiner Geschichtsschreibung*, Dissertation, Marburg (1938), and the present writer's *The Rise and Decline of the Grafian Hypothesis*, pp. 35-36.

Reference	Incident	Terms Used	or Secondary	or Foreign	or Individual	or Regular
A. Where a sense of sin or solemnity is present						
Jer. 41 : 4	Offerings of the Pilgrims	*minḥâ l^{e}bônâ* *hēbî᾽*	Primary	Israelite	Individual	?Regular
?Jer. 14 : 12	Ineffective Sacrifice	*ʿōlâ minḥâ* *ʿālâ*	Primary	Israelite	Individual	Regular
?Jer. 44 : 15-19 7 : 18	Worship of Queen of Heaven	*n^{e}sākîm* *nāsak qṭr*	Primary	?Israelite	?	?Regular
B. Where a sense of sin or solemnity is not present						
?Jer. 33 : 11	Thank Offerings after Return	*tôdâ* *hēbî᾽*	?Secondary	Israelite	Individual	Regular
C. Doubtful or unclassifiable passages						
a. Formal References						
?Zeph. 1 : 7-8	Judgment a Sacrifice	*zebaḥ*	Primary	Israelite	?	Regular
?Jer. 46 : 10	Judgment a Sacrifice	*zebaḥ*	?Secondary		?	
?Ez. 39 : 17-20	Judgment a Sacrifice	*zebaḥ* *᾽ākal zābaḥ*	Primary	Israelite	?	Regular
Jer. 34 : 18	Cutting a Covenant	*kārat*	Primary	Israelite	?	?
Jer. 48 : 35	Sacrifice in Moab	*qṭr ʿālâ*	Primary	Non-Isra.	Individual	Regular
Nah. 2 : 1(1 : 15)	Feasts of Judah	*ḥāg n^{e}dārîm* *ḥāgag*	Primary	Israelite	Festal	Regular
Hab 1 : 16	Sacrifice to a Net	*qṭr zbḥ*	Primary	Non-Isra.	National	Special
b. Rejected Sacrifices						
Jer. 6 : 20	Exotic Sacrifice	*l^{e}bônâ ʿōlôt z^{e}bāḥîm*	Primary	Israelite	Individual	Regular
Jer. 7 : 21-22	The Temple Sermon	*ʿōlôt z^{e}bāḥîm* *᾽ākal* *ʿōlâ zebaḥ*	Primary	Israelite	Individual	Regular
?Jer. 11 : 15	Holy Flesh	*b^{e}śar qōdeš*	Primary	Israelite	?	Regular
c. Condemnations of the Apostate Cult						
Jer. 7 : 31	Child Sacrifice	*śārap*	?Primary	?Israelite	Individual	?Special
Jer. 19 : 4		*ʿōlôt* *śārap*	?Secondary			
Jer. 32 : 35		*haʿabîr*	?Secondary			
Ez. 16 : 15-21	Child Sacrifice	*šāḥaṭ* *zābaḥ haʿabîr*	?Primary	?Israelite	Individual	?Special
Ez. 20 : 25-31		*z^{e}bāḥîm* *haʿabîr* *n^{e}sākîm qorbān*	?Primary	?Israelite	Individual	?Special
Ez. 23 : 36-39		*šāḥaṭ* *haʿabîr*	Secondary	?Israelite	Individual	?Special
d. Prophecies of Restoration						
Jer. 17 : 26	Sabbaths and Offerings	*ʿōlâ zebaḥ minḥâ* *l^{e}bônâ tôdâ* *hēbî*	?Secondary	Israelite	Individual	Regular
Jer. 33 : 18	The Levitical Ministry	*ʿôlâ minḥâ zebaḥ* *ʿālâ* *qṭr ʿāśâ*	Secondary	Israelite	Cultic	Regular
Ez. 20 : 40-41	Sacrifices in Jerusalem	*t^{e}rûmôt*	?Primary	Israelite	Individual	Regular
Zeph. 3 : 10	Sacrifices of Ethiopia	*minḥâ* *yābal*	?Primary	?	?	?

CHAPTER TEN

DEUTERONOMY

Introduction

The consideration of the Book of Deuteronomy is of fundamental importance, but is attended by correspondingly great difficulties. Where in the history of Israel's religion does it belong? Is it post-prophetic, and evidence for a prophetic attitude? Is it from the Jerusalem priesthood and a forerunner of P, or is it in part at least from a country priesthood in north Israel at an earlier time?

For over a century the scholarly view of the religion of Israel has turned upon the pivot of the Josianic dating of Deuteronomy. With its origin in the seventh century the book could at one and the same time be both prophetic and priestly—the heir of the prophets and the forerunner of P. In its ethical and humanitarian interests, and its campaign for a purified cult it was thought to be prophetic, while in its centralization of all worship in Jerusalem, it enhanced the prestige of the priesthood there, and prepared for P.[1] On the whole it was the prophetic element in the book that was chiefly emphasized, Merx being almost alone in his view that the book had a better claim to be called the "priestly writing" than P.[2] It was therefore the more surprising that Deuteronomy appeared to reflect nothing of the prophetic depreciation of sacrifice.[3] It has been appealed to by Rowley and others as evidence that the prophetic rejection of sacrifice could not therefore have been complete.[4]

---

[1] So A. Lods, *The Prophets and the Rise of Judaism*, E.T. (1937), p. 149ff., who instanced the increase in the dues of the priests in D, and the approval of sacrifice, which the prophets had rejected.

[2] For P he preferred the title "The Law of the Tabernacle" (A. Merx, *Die Bücher Moses und Josua*, Tübingen (1907), pp. 44ff).

[3] Unless one says with O. H. Gates, "The Relation of Priests to Sacrifice before the Exile," *JBL* XXVII (1908) pp. 84-85 that Deuteronomy agreed with the prophets that the multitude of sacrifices everywhere throughout the land was injurious, and sought by centralization to "legislate them out of existence."

[4] See the works of Rowley cited on p. 162.

Dobbie in his attack on this latter view has devoted special consideration to the sacrificial witness of Deuteronomy,[1] and has concluded that the appeal to this book as a witness to prophetic views is illegitimate. Deuteronomy was not actuated by prophetic principles,[2] its moral maturity need not be post-prophetic,[3] its condemnation of the cult is wholly other than that of the prophets,[4] it neither develops prophecy by incorporating sacrifice into a prophetic ethical system,[5] nor regulates sacrifice in the light of prophetic criticism by eliminating undesirable elements,[6] but is to be seen with von Rad and recent investigators as more priestly than prophetic.

Von Rad's view[7] begins from a theory of the origin of Deuteronomy quite different from that of the older critics. With Welch[8] and Alt,[9] he looks for a north Israelite origin of the book in the circles of the country Levites. This goes for the bulk of the material, but does not rule out a Josianic setting to the overlaid demand for centralization,[10] and it is generally in the passages dealing with centralization

---

[1] R. Dobbie, "Deuteronomy and the Prophetic Attitude to Sacrifice," *SJT* XII (1959), pp. 68-82.

[2] Its conception of "clean" e.g. is not that of the prophets (*ibid.*, p. 81).

[3] Not the prophets, but J and E, were the creators of Israel's ethics (*ibid.*, p. 71).

[4] Deuteronomy objects only to "other gods" while the prophets have a world view, which cannot admit sacrifice at all (*ibid.*, p. 81).

[5] *Ibid.*, p. 72.

[6] *Ibid.*, p. 77. G. B. Gray, *Sacrifice*, p. 47 is cited for the view that the non-mention of *minḥâ* and *qorbān* in Deuteronomy indicated the recession of the "gift" idea before the prophetic preaching. Dobbie's answer (p. 78) that "it is not cogent to sustain an argument for the regulation of sacrifices in Deuteronomy by references to practices which emerge only in a later generation" strangely overlooks the earlier use of *minḥâ* to which Gray refers.

[7] G. von Rad, *Studies in Deuteronomy*, E.T. London (1953).

[8] A. C. Welch, *The Code of Deuteronomy*, London (1924).

[9] A. Alt, "Die Heimat des Deuteronomiums," *KS* II, pp. 250-75.

[10] Alternatively it is possible that centralization belonged also to the earlier form of the book, but applied to a northern sanctuary—perhaps Shechem or Bethel. F. Dumermuth, in his extensive article, "Zur deuteronomischen Kulttheologie und ihren Voraussetzungen," *ZAW* LXX (1958), pp. 59-98 points out that such phrases as "the place Yahweh chooses," and "where he places his name" are used of Shiloh (Jer. 7 : 12), and of Gilgal or Gibeon (Josh. 9 : 27, cf. 9 : 23). In fact centralization was no new thought in Israel at any time after the Judges (p. 62)—a statement that Wellhausen would never have made. Cf. the statement of H. J. Kraus ("Zur Geschichte des Passah-Massot-Festes im Alten Testament," *EvTh*

that the sacrificial references occur. It is doubtful then if Robertson Smith's summary of the teaching on sin and sacrifice, based on the unitary origin of the book, can still be held. It may be true, as he says, that the idea of sin was never connected with the ritual,[1] but this is of less significance, when it is seen that the passages on which he draws for his definition of sin are not the sacrificial passages, but come from an earlier civil code.[2] It remains a question how much of the present Book of Deuteronomy figured in Josiah's Reform—whether Chs. 12-26, which have the best right to be considered the Code proper, or these together with Chs. 5-11 as introduction and 28 as conclusion,[3] or the whole of Chs. 1-30 (Driver), or some smaller portion of Chs. 12-26 such as the cultic section in Chs. 12-18.[4]

XVIII (1958), p. 60 that Deut. 16 deals with "nicht eine umstürzende Zentralisierung, sondern eine Wiederherstellung alter, amphiktyonischer Kultordnungen in gereinigter ("entmagisierter") Gestalt." He warns that "es sollte der Begriff der "Zentralisierung" in Zukunft nur mit grösster Vorsicht benutzt werden." Welch in his articles "When was the worship of Israel centralised at the Temple?" *ZAW* XLIII (1925), pp. 250-55 and "The Problem of Deuteronomy," *JBL* XLVIII (1929), pp. 291-306 finds from the analogy of 1 Kings 11 : 32, 14 : 21 and 2 Kings 21 : 7 that Deuteronomy 12 : 5 must refer to Jerusalem, but thinks the usage in 12 : 14 and the rest of the Code different and applicable to any sanctuary. He limits the demand for centralization to 12 : 1-7 and regards this as an interpolation. Further on the whole problem see V. Maag ("Erwägungen zur deuteronomischen Kultzentralisation," *VT* VI (1956), pp. 10-18) who sees two distinct strands, one centralizing from the Jerusalem of Josiah, and another non-centralizing from country Levite circles.

[1] He points out that in Deuteronomy sin is a crime, an offence against law and justice (19 : 15, 21 : 22, 22 : 26, 24 : 16), and an act of heathenism (20 : 18), a breach of faith toward Yahweh (23 : 21, 22), or lack of kindliness to the poor (24 : 15), and that such offences are not expiated by sacrifice, but by punishment at the hand of man or God (W. Robertson Smith, *The Old Testament in the Jewish Church* ([2]1892), p. 372).

[2] Robertson Smith recognized that Deuteronomy was not a full sacrificial code, but negative rather than positive in its ritual details. It was concerned to condemn heathen worship, and to divert sacrifice from the old local sanctuaries to the central, without otherwise changing the old usage (*ibid.*, p. 371).

[3] Chs. 1-4 might be a general introduction to the Deuteronomic Work of History and Ch. 34 displaced from the end of Numbers, when Deuteronomy was brought into the Tetrateuch (cf. M. Noth, *Überlieferungsgeschichtliche Studien* I (1943), Halle, pp. 54(12) ff).

[4] J. P. Hyatt, "Jeremiah and Deuteronomy," *JNES* I (1942), pp. 158-59 notes that all the reforms of 2 Kings 22-23 except the action against the *qᵉdešîm* are in Chs. 12-18. This is also the most important section for sacrifice.

What was the effect of centralization? Wellhausen has some eloquent pages over the strait jacket effect of the reform in cutting religion off from its roots in nature and everyday life. It was a backward movement from the life of the green tree to the dead wood of legalism,[1] by which "life and worship fell apart."[2] These statements need not be taken too seriously,[3] for by the same type of argument one could reach the opposite conclusion that centralization, by depriving the worshipper of the local and outward expression of the cult, saved him from parochialism, helped inward spirituality and prepared for the exile,[4] and by the requiring of sacrifice only rarely favoured the religion of the heart, rather than outward forms, which the prophets had proclaimed.[5]

Of greater importance is the question as to why the Deuteronomist needs to emphasize "rejoicing before the Lord" at the central sanctuary as he is in the habit of doing. Was it that he feared that the new worship would be less attractive than the old, or is there evidence here that the old worship was uniformly joyful, or alternatively that it was not? No certain answer can be given to this question. The references to sacrifice in Deuteronomy are few, and with the exception of Deut. 21 : 1-9 and a few fragmentary prohibitions of apostate worship (12 : 31, 18 : 10, 14 : 21), are concerned only with centralization (Deut. 12 : 1-27) and its conse-

---

He agrees that the code is a unity, but thinks that the reform stressed only Chs. 12-18, while Jeremiah was more interested in the section on family life in Chs. 19-26.

[1] Cf. J. Wellhausen, *Prolegomena*, p. 81.

[2] *Ibid.*, p. 77.

[3] There is some truth in the remark of A. Harper, (*ExpB* I, Grand Rapids, Mich. 1947 (repr.) p. 564), that centralization did not take religion away from the people, but merely substituted a long day's walk to Jerusalem for a half a day's walk to a local sanctuary. Palestine was not a large country, the Judah of Josiah was still smaller, and pilgrimage to a shrine was customary early as well as late. The Book of the Covenant did not authorize worship at every place, but only such sanctuaries as Yahweh selected.

[4] J. M. P. Smith, *The Origin and History of Hebrew Law*, Chicago (1931), pp. 55-56. Smith also, like Wellhausen, lists among the results the secularization of country life and the increase of the power and wealth of temple and priests.

[5] G. A. Barton, *The Religion of Israel*, New York (1918), pp. 114-15. Cf. V. Maag, "Erwägungen zur deuteronomischen Kultzentralisation," p. 18. Maag sees the significance of centralization to lie in the removal of the *zebaḥ* sacrifice to Jerusalem and the permission for non-sacrificial slaughter elsewhere. See Ch. 1 above.

quences (15; 19-23, 16 : 1-8, 18 : 1-8), and give no picture of the cultus as a whole.

In the survey which follows the references to sacrifice in the two old poems appended to the rear of the book (Deut. 32 and 33) are also included, but are to be kept separate from the references in the Code.

Sacrifice at the Sanctuary (Deut. 12 : 1-27)

The repetitions of the chapter suggest that it consists of a collection of laws dealing with centralization. The usual analysis divides the chapter into the four sections, vss. 1-7, 8-12, 13-19, 20-27. These sections may come from four sources,[1] from three sources,[2] or from two.[3] There does not seem to be any principle in the slight variations between the lists of sacrifices, which for convenience may be set out as follows—

v6 *hēbîʾ, ʿōlôt, zᵉbāḥîm, mᵃʿaśrôt, tᵉrûmôt, nᵉdārîm, nᵉdābôt, bᵉkōrōt*
v11 *hēbîʾ, ʿōlôt, zᵉbāḥîm, mᵃʿaśrôt, tᵉrûmôt, nᵉdārîm mibḥar*
v13 *ʿālâ, ʿōlôt*
v17 *maʿśar, tᵉrûmôt, nᵉdārîm, nᵉdābôt, bᵉkōrōt*
v26 *qᵉdāsîm nᵉdārîm*
v27 *ʿāśâ, ʿōlôt, zᵉbāḥîm*

These terms have all been met before, with the exception of *tᵉrûmôt*, which is not certainly attested before Deuteronomy.[4] The

---

[1] So F. Horst, *Das Privilegrecht Jahves*, Göttingen (1930), pp. 4ff. Cf. A. Bertholet (*KHC*) (1899) who thought the first and second belong respectively to the authors of Chs. 5 : 1-30 and 1-4.

[2] Vss. 20-27 are sometimes seen as a doublet of vss. 13-19. Horst, however, regards vss. 26-27 as the original nucleus.

[3] The second and fourth may be doublets of the first and third, or the first and second which use the plural verb may be younger than the third and fourth which use the singular.

[4] The AV renderings of "heave offering" for *tᵉrûmôt* and "wave offering" for the parallel *tᵉnûpâ* derived from *rûm* "to lift up" and *nûp* "to wave" and understanding a vertical and horizontal movement at the altar, as a token presentation to God, are questionable. "Waving" is not an intelligible procedure, when applied to rams, he-goats and even Levites (Num. 8 : 11). G. R. Driver has accordingly argued, ("Three Technical Terms in the Pentateuch," *JSS* I (1956), pp. 100ff) from a root "height" to which both the Arabic "what exceeds" and the Babylonian "balance of a tax" are related, to the rendering of *tᵉnûpâ* as "additional gifts" or "special contribution." A similar meaning seems likely for *tᵉrûmâ*, and may be derived from the verb *rûm* in the sense of "lifted off" or "separated" (cf. LXX *aphorisma*, which is sometimes used instead of *aparchē* to translate it). Driver, however,

sections 1-7, 8-12 and 13-19 each consist of a negative command followed by a positive command. Centralization is clearer in the positive commands (vss. 5-6, 10-11, 14),[1] than in the negative, which in vss. 2-3 speak of *Kultusreinheit*, rather than *Kultuseinheit*,[2] and in vss. 8-9 of some unspecified cultic practice of Israel in the wilderness, which is not to be continued in the Promised Land. Vss. 14-15 and 20ff. make provision for non-sacrificial slaughter. The problem of the relation of these verses to the law of H in Lev. 17, which withdraws the permission granted here,[3] and to the passages suggesting non-sacrificial slaughter noted above[4] cannot be gone into here.

It is thought to be significant for the Wellhausen-Robertson

---

connects it to an Assyrian root TRM used for a levy or tax on land (*ibid.*, pp. 102-103). This comes close to the meaning suggested by *BDB* for the term in the present passage "a product of the soil." Both *terûmâ* and *tenûpâ* were separated off for the priest's use. The precise difference between the two terms seems beyond recovery. Driver suggests that both were in common use in Babylonia, and were perhaps borrowed by the Hebrew exiles without a clear understanding of their meaning. The Deuteronomic use, however, seems too early for this. On the terms see also A. Vincent, "Les rites du balancement . . ." *Mélanges Syriens* (Dussaud Festschrift (1939) Vol. 1, pp. 267-72).

[1] It is not certainly present, however, in vss. 10-11. Welch has argued also that the phrase "in one of your tribes" in vs. 14 is different from "out of all your tribes" in vs. 5.

[2] The heathen sanctuaries, which are to be destroyed, are simply described as "places" (*meqōmôt*). Neither here, nor elsewhere in Deuteronomy is the term "high places" (*bāmôt*) used.

[3] The following possibilities may be listed—H follows D and revokes the permission given, because local slaughter had led to offering to field spirits (Lev. 17 : 7)—or H precedes D and allows a multiplicity of sanctuaries (Lev. 26 : 31) but has been over-written with centralization by P—or H, as a projection back into the wilderness, was purely an idealization and never intended to be carried out. It is difficult to see how the H law of centralization could ever have operated at any time after Israel had entered the land. Welch thinks that profane slaughter had been a necessity from the entry onwards, and accordingly takes Deuteronomy far back in time. Eating meat was, of course, not an every day happening (cf. vs. 20), but eating that which was taken in hunting was permitted from the beginning (vs. 22) and would have helped to familiarize the custom.

[4] E. König (*KAT*, 1917), pp. 120-21 thinks these passages cannot stand against 1 Sam. 14 : 32-35, and raises the question as to whether the blood in such cases could not have been consecrated by the housewife to the deity. Although adhering to the view that "all slaughter was sacrifice," he firmly rejects its complement that there was no sacrifice without a meal (*Geschichte der alttestamentlichen Religion*, Gütersloh (1912), p. 501).

Smith view, that eating and rejoicing are almost a synonym for sacrifice in this passage, and neither sin offering, trespass offering nor sense of solemnity are to be found. G. A. Smith writes:

> it has been rightly emphasised... that in so elaborate a list of offerings, apparently meant to be complete, there is no mention of the sin and guilt offerings which are enforced in P; these, therefore, were unknown, or disregarded, by the deuteronomists. The worship to which Israel is commanded in D is, in spite of D's rigorous ethical teaching and sense of Israel's sins, one only of joyous communion with Jehovah and thankfulness for the material blessings which He annually provides.[1]

Against this position it may be objected that the lists are stereotyped and take no great care to be precise,[2] as the omission in the third section of the *zebaḥ* itself, with which the chapter is mainly concerned, shows.[3] The Deuteronomist for reasons of his own, emphasized the joy of the festival, but it cannot be proved that this joy was not (as in the Psalms) preceded by or even occasioned by expiation and forgiveness[4] or that it was all there was to the festival, or that this kind of festival was all there was to the cult,[5] or that such a cult was ever that of Israel as a whole.[6]

Firstlings (Deut. 15 : 19-23)

This is the first of several passages applying the principle of centralization to older institutions. The older law requiring the bringing of the firstling males is given in vs. 19 and the modifications required by centralization in vss. 20-23.[7] The basic law is

---

[1] G. A. Smith (*CamB*) (1918), pp. 165-67.

[2] Cf. K. Galling, *Der Altar . . .*, p. 74: "Die Argumentation e silentio kann jedoch nicht als stichhaltig angesehen werden, da es dem Verfasser hier nicht auf eine vollständige Aufzählung der verschiedenen Opfer ankommt."

[3] Marti (*HSAT*) thinks the end of vs. 13 has fallen out, but this is doubtful. Vss. 15-16, which interrupt the connection between vss. 14 and 17 may, however, be an insertion. F. Horst who accepts them (*op. cit.*, p. 5) argues that the section comes from a source where profane slaughter has completely secularized the *zᵉbāḥîm*.

[4] Cf. E. König, *Geschichte der alttestamentlichen Religion*, p. 501.

[5] Cf. the remark of L. Köhler, *Old Testament Theology*, p. 195 that the regulations of Deuteronomy are for the great feasts and do not touch the essence of the cult.

[6] The prior question here is that of the date of the legislation and whether it belonged to the earlier or later strata of the book, to a northern sanctuary or to Jerusalem, to an actual practice, or to an ideal programme.

[7] F. Horst, *op. cit.*, pp. 78-81. Cf. G. von Rad, *Studies in Deuteronomy*, p. 17.

similar to that in Exod. 22 : 20 and Exod. 34 : 19-20, Exod. 13 : 12-15. There, however, firstlings were to be brought at eight days old (Exod. 22 : 30), while here from year to year (vs. 20)—a change necessitated by the substitution of the central sanctuary for the local. For the same reason human first-born, who figure also in the earlier laws, drop out of sight here. The sacrificial victim now provides a meal for the worshipper and his family (vs. 20)—a fact not mentioned in the earlier laws, and in apparent contradiction to the provisions of P.[1] Blemished firstlings may not be sacrificed but may be eaten for food at home (vss. 21-22)—a further advance on J and E, but consistent with P's requirement that sacrifices be perfect. The passage concludes like 12 : 23 with a prohibition of eating the blood.

The Passover (Deut. 16 : 1-8)

This law for the centralized passover has independent attestation in the narrative of Josiah's Passover (see above p. 134).[2] The differences from the P law of Exod. 12 noted there—the celebration to be in the central sanctuary rather than the home, the victims to be from the herd as well as the flock, and the flesh to be boiled and not roasted—cannot be accounted for by a simple evolution from D to P. Boiling is not obviously an earlier practice than

---

[1] In Num. 18 : 18 the flesh of the firstlings is for the priests.

[2] The chapter is usually analysed into a Passover source in vss. 1-2 and 5-7 and an Unleavened Bread source in vss. 3-4 and 8. However, if the prohibition of leaven with the Passover is primitive, as argued above, vss. 3a and 4a could belong to the Passover source, along with vs. 4b with its requirement that the flesh of the sacrifice not remain until the morning. When from vss. 3b and 8b are deducted the traces of P, scarcely sufficient remains to be a separate source. (Cf. G. B. Gray, "Passover and Unleavened Bread," *JTS* XXXVII (1936), pp. 251ff. who pointed out that the Passover references could stand alone, but not the rest.) This would seem to dispose of Beer's theory mentioned on pp. 60f. that Passover belonged to the south and Unleavened Bread to the north, and also of the view discussed on pp. 79f. that the two feasts were separate down to the time of the Deuteronomist, as Deuteronomy and E together as northern books attest both (cf. Gray, *ibid.*, p. 253). The discrepancy between the worshippers returning to their tents on the morning after the Passover (vs. 7), and remaining for seven days (vss. 3, 4, 8) may possibly be met by the assumption that the "tents" were the temporary dwellings of the festival (H. J. Kraus, "Zur Geschichte des Passah-Massot-Festes . . .," p. 59; J. Pedersen, *Israel* III-IV, p. 388, who compares Hos. 12 : 10(9). Against this, however, see E. Kutsch, "Erwägungen zur Geschichte der Passahfeier . . .," p. 13).

roasting (see pp. 99f. above), large cattle for victims are not likely to be earlier than small,[1] and the reversion of P to a domestic rite, after D had achieved the gain of centralization, has been remarked above (p. 134) to be not very intelligible. Kraus rightly warns against seeing "die priesterlichen Kultordnungen als ritualisierende Weiterentwicklung der durch das Deuteronomium ins Leben gerufenen "Zentralisierung"" in Wellhausen's sense, and says that "P ist eine sehr eigenständige Quelle, die ihrerseits auf alte Traditionen zurückgreift."[2]

The Maintenance of the Ministry (Deut. 18 : 1-8)

This passage, like the foregoing, adds little to the discussion of the motive of sacrifice, but speaks rather of the provision to be made for the displaced clergy consequent upon centralization,[3] and the priestly portions of the sacrificial meal. In vs. 1 they are to receive the *'īššê*,[4] and in vs. 3 the shoulder, cheeks and stomach.

---

[1] J. Henninger, "Les fêtes de printemps . . .," p. 412; H. Haag, "Ursprung und Sinn der alttestamentlichen Paschafeier," *Das Opfer der Kirche* (*Luzerner Theologische Studien* I), Luzern (1954), p. 31.

[2] H. J. Kraus, "Zur Geschichte des Passah-Massot-Festes . . .," p. 62.

[3] The various terms used for the priestly ministry are one of the puzzling features of the book—Levites (12 : 12, 12 : 18, 14 : 27, 29, 16 : 11, 16 : 14, 18 : 6), priests (17 : 12, 18 : 3, 19 : 17, 20 : 2, 26 : 3, 4), the priests the Levites (17 : 9, 17 : 18, 18 : 1, 24 : 8, 27 : 9), the priests the sons of Levi (21 : 5, 31 : 9) and all the tribe of Levi (18 : 1). Wellhausen's view that in the time of Deuteronomy no differentiation within the priestly tribe had yet emerged, has been challenged by Manley and Wright. G. T. Manley, (*The Book of the Law*, Grand Rapids (1957), pp. 104-107) argues that the priest (and "the priest the Levite") always occupies an honourable position in Deuteronomy (e.g. sits with the judges Ch. 17 : 9), while the position of the Levite is always subordinate and dependent (e.g. he is to be the object of charity Ch. 12 : 12). G. E. Wright ("The Levites in Deuteronomy," *VT* IV (1954), pp. 325-30, *Deuteronomy* (*IB*) II (1953)) makes the same distinction and regards the Levites proper as the teachers to whom we owe the Book of Deuteronomy, and "the priests the Levites" as the altar clergy, the priests proper of P, but has to concede—and perhaps this is a fatal concession —that the distinction does not hold for the crucial verse, 18 : 6.

[4] The term *'īššê*, which occurs 63 times in P, and only elsewhere in the doubtful passages Josh. 13 : 14; 1 Sam. 2 : 28 is usually derived from "fire," so "fire offerings" RSV. Against the connection with fire stands its use for the shewbread (Lev. 24 : 9), which was certainly not burnt and for the cakes and flour of the *minḥâ* (W. B. Stevenson, "The Hebrew 'Olah and Zebach Sacrifices," *Bertholet Festschrift* (1950), p. 488. Stevenson thinks it a general word for offering like *qorbān*). Another derivation has therefore been sought in the Arabic *'anaš* "to be sociable or friendly" and so "an

This is different from the breast and thigh prescribed by P, and possibly also from the earlier use (see p. 99) above but the difference may be geographical rather than chronological. Parallel codes are appealed to by Wright in place of the straight-line evolution favoured by Wellhausen.[1]

Child Sacrifice Forbidden (Deut. 12 : 31, 18 : 10)

Among the abominable things, which the heathen do for their gods, and which Israel is not to follow is "the burning of sons and daughters in the fire to their gods." Wright suggests some kind of trial by ordeal.[2] This is not very probable for the phrase *maʿabîr* "passed through the fire" (18 : 10), and seems ruled out by *śārap bāʾēš* (12 : 31).

The Apostate City (Deut. 13 : 17 (16))

The execution of the ban on an apostate city is described by the term *kālîl.* The fact that a "burning in the fire" is involved has led a number of commentators to translate *kālîl* by "whole burnt offering" (so RSV). It is true that *kālîl* along with *ʿōlâ,* or as a substitute for it has this meaning (see above p. 104), but it can also mean quite simply "wholly" as in Exod. 28 : 31, and as understood by the LXX *pandēmei.*[3]

Kid in Mother's Milk (Deut. 14 : 21)

This has been discussed on p. 61 above.[4]

Unblemished Offerings (Deut. 17 : 1)

This general law that only animals without defect should be offered in sacrifice has found particular illustration in the law of

---

offering which establishes friendly relations with the deity, an atonement" (Cf. E. König, *Theologie des Alten Testaments*, Stuttgart (¹ & ²1922), p. 297). Gray in a judicious discussion, finds little evidence for the latter meaning in the Old Testament, (*Sacrifice in the Old Testament*, pp. 9-13), and thinks the objection to a connection with fire a misunderstanding. The term served for an offering any portion of which was burned—the frankincense with the shewbread and *minḥâ,* the fat from the *šelāmîm,* the *ʿōlâ* in its entirety. It was from the remainder that was not burnt, that the priests received their portion in the present verse.

[1] G. E. Wright (*IB*).

[2] Wright (*IB*), pp. 417 and 447ff.

[3] Cf. H. Cazelles "entière" (*JerusB*) (1950); C. Steuernagel (*HK*) Göttingen (²1923), p. 104 and E. König (*KAT*), p. 124 who remarks that in 1 Sam. 15 offering (vs. 15) and ban (vs. 33) are opposed to each other.

[4] For a different interpretation see F. Horst, *op. cit.*, pp. 47ff.

firstlings in 15 : 21. It is there included in the interpretative additions to an old command, but in the present case probably has claim to be regarded as old in its own right. It is independent of what follows, but may go with the two immediately preceding laws (16 : 21, 22).[1]

Ritual for an Untraced Murder (Deut. 21 : 1-9)

From the use of *kipper* twice in vs. 8 "expiate O Lord thy people ... let the blood be expiated," one might judge this to be a crucial passage for this enquiry. This prayer has been preceded by the slaughtering of an animal, apparently in the stead of the unknown murderer. This looks like support for the theory of substitution, and was appealed to as such by older scholars.[2] On the other side it is argued that this killing is not a sacrifice, and can hardly be used to illuminate the sacrifices of the Levitical cult. The method of killing by "breaking the neck" was that which was resorted to for the firstling ass, which could not be sacrificed (Exod. 13 : 13), and the Deuteronomist would hardly have included the passage if a sacrifice away from the central altar was involved. It is the Deuteronomist's habit, however, to adapt older material to his own theology and this has very probably happened here. No one will deny that the material is old—as old as anything in the book—and there are hints to suggest that a sacrifice was described in the older version.

Vss. 1-2 in which the responsibility for the ritual of expiation is assigned to the nearest city is illustrated in many ancient sources.[3] Vss. 3-4 list a series of qualifications in the victim, and the place of slaughter, which are similar to those required in other cultic in-

---

[1] The first of these prohibiting an *ʾᵃšērâ* beside the altar of the Lord can scarcely refer to Jerusalem as Marti (*HSAT*) supposes, but must predate centralization.

[2] So C. F. Keil (*KD*), E.T. (repr. 1949), pp. 404ff; A. Dillmann, *Die Bücher Numeri, Deuteronomium und Josua*, Leipzig (²1886), p. 338; G. Oehler, *Theologie des Alten Testaments*, Stuttgart (²1882), p. 430.

[3] In the Code of Hammurabi a householder reporting a robbery must first swear that the robbery was not with his connivance. In Arabia the local residents must similarly swear that they are not guilty of the murder. In I *Aqhat* 151-69 (*UL*, pp. 98ff., *UH*, pp. 180ff.) Danel curses, not only the unknown assassin of Aqhat but also the nearest cities (cf. T. H. Gaster, *Thespis*, pp. 302-304).

struments.[1] The requirement of running water (cf. Amos 5 : 24) was probably not so much because streams were popular sanctuaries (Bertholet (*KHC*)), as that the water was conceived of, as like the scapegoat (Lev. 16 : 22), the bird (Lev. 14 : 5-7) and the ephah (Zech. 5 : 5-11), as carrying away the guilt.[2] If blood had been shed in the earlier form of the rite,[3] this would have been symbolically portrayed in the blood of the sacrifice being washed away down the stream to reappear no more.[4] The concern was to free the survivors from guilt, rather than to appease the spirit of the dead (Marti (*HSAT*) and Bertholet (*KHC*)) for if the latter had been intended the ritual should have taken place at the scene of the murder (Junker).[5]

Vs. 5 which introduces the priests is usually judged an intrusion, but this is not certain.[6] Vss. 6ff. describe the negative confession

---

[1] Like the altar of Exod. 20 : 25, which must be of unhewn stones the victim must be an unbroken heifer, which has not worked or pulled in the yoke, and the place of slaughter a valley that has been neither ploughed or sown.

[2] Cf. R. Press, "Das Ordal im alten Israel II," *ZAW* LI (1933), pp. 236ff.

[3] Possibly *ʿārap* has this meaning. *BDB* regard it as a denominative from "neck," so to "break the neck," but Köhler, *Lexicon* connects it to the Arabic *ʿrp* "to cut in pieces." W. R. Smith, *Religion of the Semites*, p. 371 speaks of the heifer as "sacrificed by breaking (or perhaps, severing) its neck," and A. Bertholet (*KHC*) compares the sacrificing to the Greek Chthonians by bending back the head of the animal toward the earth, and cutting the throat. Even if no blood was shed, as with the scapegoat, the rite could still signify the transference of guilt and be significant for the total view of sacrifice.

[4] It is possible that the rough ground chosen was not only unploughed, but also unploughable, so that the poured out blood should never be uncovered by cultivation.

[5] H. Junker, *Das Buch Deuteronomium* (*HS*).

[6] The phraseology is that of the Deuteronomist, but he can scarcely be responsible both for the form of the story, which removes the sacrificial reference, and for the insertion of a reference to priests to validate it as a sacrifice. The priests are introduced too late for the latter, but their association with the elders and judges in a supervisory capacity (vs. 2), like that with the judges in Ch. 17 is not impossible. Wright (*IB*) finds the verse unobjectionable, and thinks only vs. 1, part of vs. 2 and vs. 9 reworked from the old source. Welch who agrees in the main with Elhorst's suggestion (*ZAW* XXXIX (1921), pp. 58ff.) that an old Canaanite ritual had been taken over by Israel, suggests that the legislators, unable to follow their usual method of transferring old rituals to the Yahweh shrine, introduced the priests "to prevent any acknowledgement of another god than Yahweh slipping in" and to "see to it that nothing grossly offensive to higher religion takes place" (*ZAW* XLII (1924), pp. 163-64).

which accompanies the hand-washing in connection with the ceremony. It is true that this cannot be cited for a sense of sin, but if the rite was at all frequent, as it might well have been, it must have helped condition more normal sacrifice. It might be expected *a fortiori* that where sin had been committed and sacrifice was offered for it, confession and prayer for pardon accompanied it. At least the witness of this passage cannot be dismissed out of hand as having no bearing on sacrifice.[1]

Deut. 27 : 1ff.

For this passage see pp. 81ff. above.

The Song of Moses (Deut. 32 : 17, 38)

The criticism of this chapter has entered a new era with Eissfeldt's acceptance of a date in the eleventh century.[2] This opinion, held also by Albright,[3] is in marked contrast to the exilic or seventh century date favoured by almost all other critics,[4] and represented most recently in Baumann's description of it as post-prophetic and a prophecy rather than a song.[5] Baumann thinks vs. 17 which describes Israel as sacrificing to demons and to gods not known before, can only refer to the apostasy under Manasseh,[6] but on the earlier dating a parallel may be found in Judg. 5 : 8 (see above pp. 86f.). Sacrificing to *šēdîm* has already been encountered in Ps. 106 : 37 (see p. 154) and Hos. 12 : 12 (see p. 173) and need not be further treated here.[7]

---

[1] G. von Rad, *Das Gottesvolk im Deuteronomium*, Stuttgart (1929), p. 32 speaks of the passage as the only one in Deuteronomy dealing with expiation but remarks that it was not the ceremony itself that expiated but the grace of God forgiving the guilt. Could this not also be said of sacrifice?

[2] O. Eissfeldt, *Einleitung in das Alte Testament* ([2]1956), pp. 271-72 and *Das Lied Moses*, Berlin (1958).

[3] W. F. Albright, "Some Remarks on the Song of Moses in Deuteronomy xxxii," *VT* X (1959), pp. 339-46.

[4] Steuernagel (*HK*) (only in the exile); Bertholet (*KHC*) (end of the exile); König (*KAT*) (late, because of the monotheism in vs. 39); Marti (*HSAT*) (dependent on Jer., Ezek. and Deutero-Is.); Sellin (c 500 B.C. from the parallels to Trito-Isaiah ("Wann wurde das Moselied Dtn 32 gedichet?" *ZAW* XLIII (1925), pp. 161-73)).

[5] E. Baumann, "Das Lied Mose's (Dt. XXXII 1-43) auf seine gedankliche Geschlossenheit untersucht," *VT* VI (1956), pp. 414-24.

[6] *Ibid.*, p. 422.

[7] Albright's article (p. 342) may be consulted on some difficulties in the text. The wholly unattested *seʿārûm*, for which a meaning has been sought in

Vs. 38 in similar strain taunts the false gods, which the apostates among the people have chosen "let the gods, who ate the fat of their sacrifices (*zᵉbāḥîm*), and drank the wine of their drink offering (*nesek*), rise up and help you." This bald statement of the "food for the gods" theory of sacrifice need not be taken as a serious description of the understanding of sacrifice. Interesting on the early date theory is the reference to drink offerings of wine, which are not elsewhere attested so early.[1] The use of *kipper* in vs. 43, with Yahweh as subject, is also striking in an early document.

The Blessing of Moses (Deut. 33 : 10, 19)

An early date for this chapter occasions less surprise. While Eissfeldt is content to say "before 721," Marti (*HSAT*), and Steuernagel (*HK*) think of the time of Jeroboam II, Bewer of that of Jeroboam I[2] and Sellin of the time of the Judges.[3] The argument for eleventh or tenth century dating has been put on a new footing by the orthographic study of Cross and Freedman,[4] and has been accepted by Wright. The threatened state of Judah (vs. 7) might be due to the difficulties of the conquest, rather than the disruption. The priestly function of the Tribe of Levi (vss. 8-11) may be later than Gen. 49, but Gen. 49 itself need not be as late as J. Cross and Freedman, however, except this Levi oracle from their conclusion and regard it as later than the rest of the poem.[5]

While this may be true, the sacrificial references in vs. 10b seem

---

"dread" (RSV, cf. Jer. 2 : 12) or "know" (LXX, cf. Arabic *šaʿara*) he thinks should be vocalized as *śeʿîrîm* "demons" and read for *šēdîm* in the first cola of the verse. *Bāʾû* is a transparent dittography, *ḥᵃdāšîm* "new" should be emended to be read as *ḥērešîm* "deaf" and the whole phrase rendered on the analogy of Hab. 1 : 13 "who are too deaf to approach."

[1] Apart from Gen. 35 : 14, they first figure in 2 Kings 16 : 13 (see pp. 154, 132).

[2] J. A. Bewer, *The Literature of the Old Testament*, New York (Rev. ed. 1933), p. 18.

[3] E. Sellin, *Introduction to the Old Testament*, E. T. London (1923), pp. 38ff.

[4] F. M. Cross and D. M. Freedman, "The Blessing of Moses," *JBL* LXVII 1948), pp. 191-210.

[5] They write (p. 203): "in 8-10 there is a complete break in style, metre and content with the rest of the poem. The relative pronoun (*ʾᵃšer*), the sign of the definite accusative (*ʾet*), and the article, all suspicious in ancient poetry, occur in these lines." The tenth century spellings and archaic forms which abound in the surrounding verses are also absent. "How much, if any, of vss. 8-10 belong to the original blessing must remain a question" (p. 204).

archaic enough "to put *qeṭôrâ* in thy nostrils and *kālîl* upon thy altar." In the light of 1 Sam. 26 : 19 and Gen. 8 : 20 it can hardly be denied that there is a propitiatory sense here. LXX reads "in thy nostrils" (*be'appekā*) as "in thy wrath" (*en orgē sou.*) G. A. Smith speaking of the piacular force of the later burnt offering says:

> its smoke symbolized to Israel the confession of their sin and their surrender of the lives He was pleased to accept in place of their guilty and forfeit selves. No sacrament could be more adequate than this, which proved at once the death deserved by the guilty, the blackness and bitterness of their sin, and its disappearance in the infinite purity of the skies, the unfathomable mercy of Heaven. It is this piacular meaning which is behind the LXX *en orgē sou* "in thy wrath" for *in thy nostrils.*[1]

How much of this description Smith would apply to the early time is dubious (see his comment on p. 208), but the fact that he can make this note on the present verse shows that it is not altogether inappropriate.

Sacrifice of Zebulon (Deut. 33 : 19)

The blessing of Zebulon and Issachar precedes a description of their trade "they suck the affluence of the seas, and the hidden treasures of the sand," by a reference to a "calling of the peoples (*'ammîm*) to the mountain," and "the offering of right sacrifices." The implication seems to be of a sacrifice sealing the trade agreements. If so, the "peoples" are most probably Gentiles, (Marti (*HSAT*); Bertholet (*KHC*); Steuernagel (*HK*)) and the mountain, Carmel, which was situated by the seas (Marti (*HSAT*); Cazelles (*JerusB*)). It is remarkable in such a case that the sacrifice is specifically described as "right" and in no way irregular,[2] and one must ask whether Gentiles need really be imported into the text. "Peoples" is not impossible to Israelites, and it may be a union of the two tribes that is being described. The mountain in this case might be Tabor at the border of the two tribes,[3] as Carmel hardly was.

---

[1] G. A. Smith (*CamB*).

[2] But see pp. 141f. above.

[3] O. Eissfeldt, "Der Gott des Tabor," *ARW* III (1934), pp. 14-41 thinks a God Tabor was worshipped there, and remarks that the worship was not regarded as idolatrous, but this is perhaps to build too much on *har*, which is missing in the LXX.

Conclusion

The seventeen references to sacrifice occur in twelve passages in the Book of Deuteronomy. The references are in most cases incidentally introduced and scarcely furnish material for a complete picture.

To Group A are assigned one passage from the Code (Deut. 21 : 1-9), and one from the Songs (Deut. 33 : 8-11). The first is not, however, certainly a sacrifice and the date of the second is debated.

To Group B are assigned the important Ch. 12 from the Code and two slighter references in the Songs (Deut. 32 : 38, 33 : 19). What has been said on p. 208 concerning Ch. 12 must, however, be borne in mind.

Group C comprising nine doubtful or unclassifiable references may be further sub-divided as follow—a. not a sacrifice (13 : 17), b. merely formal reference to sacrifice (17 : 1), c. condemnations of apostate worship (12 : 31, 18 : 10, 14 : 21, 32 : 17) and regulations consequent upon centralization (15 : 19-23, 16 : 1-8, 18 : 1-8). The last three cases all involve "eating" and possibly should go with the master-passage (Ch. 12) into Group B. On the other hand it has been suggested in an earlier chapter, that firstlings and passover might have had solemn connections.

The conclusion of Herner, that the offerings in Deuteronomy are brought only at joyful feasts and never atone, and that to the Deuteronomic school the relation to God is restored by prayer and conversion, without sacrifice,[1] is questionable, to say the least. Joy is not mentioned in 12 : 26, 15 : 20 or 16 : 7, and where it is, it does not exclude atonement. For the latter, Deut. 21 : 1-9 also has something to say.

---

[1] S. Herner, *Sühne und Vergebung in Israel*, pp. 22-23.

REFERENCES TO SACRIFICE IN DEUTERONOMY

Reference	Incident	Terms Used	Primary or Secondary	Israelite or Foreign	National or Individual	Special or Regular
A. WHERE A SENSE OF SIN OR SOLEMNITY IS PRESENT						
The Code						
Deut. 21 : 1-9	Ritual for Untraced Murder	*kipper*	Primary	?Israelite	Local	Special
The Songs						
Deut. 33 : 8-11	The Blessing of Levi	*kālîl q^{e}ṭôrâ* *śîm*	?Primary	Israelite	Cultic	Regular
B. WHERE A SENSE OF SIN OR SOLEMNITY IS NOT PRESENT						
The Code						
Deut. 12	Sacrifice at Sanctuary		Primary	Israelite	Individual	Regular
v 6		*b^{e}kōrōt n^{e}dābōt n^{e}dārîm t^{e}rûmôt ma^{c}aśrôt z^{e}bāḥîm ^{c}ōlôt hēbî$^>$*				
v 11		*mibḥar n^{e}dārîm t^{e}rûmôt ma^{c}aśrôt z^{e}bāḥîm ^{c}ōlôt hēbî$^>$*				
v 13		*^{c}ōlôt ^{c}ālâ*				
v 17		*b^{e}kōrōt n^{e}dābōt n^{e}dārîm t^{e}rûmôt ma^{c}śar*				
v 26		*n^{e}dārîm q^{e}dāšîm*				
v 27		*z^{e}bāḥîm ^{c}ōlôt ^{c}āśâ*				
The Songs						
Deut. 32 : 38	Sacrifice to False Gods	*nesek z^{e}bāḥîm* *$^>$ākal*	Primary	?Israelite	Individual	Regular
33 : 19	Sacrifices of Zebulon	*z^{e}bāḥîm* *zābaḥ*	Primary	?Israelite	Tribal	Regular
C. DOUBTFUL OR UNCLASSIFIABLE PASSAGES						
The Code						
a. Not Sacrifice						
Deut. 13 : 17(16)	The Apostate City	?(*kālîl*)				
b. Formal References						
Deut. 17 : 1	Unblemished Offerings	*zābaḥ*	Primary	Israelite	Individual	Regular
c. Condemnations of Apostate Worship						
Deut. 12 : 31	Child Sacrifice Forbidden	*śārap*	Primary	?Non-Isra.	Individual	?Special
18 : 10	Child Sacrifice Forbidden	*ha^{ca}bîr*	Primary	?Non-Isra.	Individual	?Special
Deut. 14 : 21	Kid in Mother's Milk	*bšl*	Primary	?Non-Isra.	Individual	?
d. Regulations Consequent Upon Centralization						
Deut. 15 : 19-23	Firstlings	*$^>$ākal zābaḥ*	Primary	Israelite	Family	Regular
Deut. 16 : 1-8	Passover	*^{c}āśâ zābaḥ*	Primary	Israelite	Family	Regular
Deut. 18 : 1-8	Maintenance of Ministry	*$^>$iššê zebaḥ* *zābaḥ*	Primary	Israelite	Cultic	Regular
The Songs						
Deut. 32 : 17	Sacrifice to Demons	*zābaḥ*	Primary	?Israelite	Individual	?

CHAPTER ELEVEN

THE EXILE AND AFTER

Before gathering together the results of this enquiry into the sense of sin in pre-exilic sacrifice, it will be useful to carry the investigation into the later materials in a summary fashion. Space precludes a similar detailed discussion of each passage, but the results arrived at by the application of the same method of classification may be briefly recorded. The remaining Old Testament books outside the Priestly Code—the Holiness Code, Ezekiel's Code, the exilic and post-exilic prophets, the Wisdom Literature, Ezra-Nehemiah and Chronicles—will be surveyed in this chapter.

The Holiness Code

The sacrificial references are found chiefly in Chs. 17, 22 and 23 and to a lesser extent in Chs. 19 and 21. In Chs. 18 and 20 they are represented only by the prohibitions of sacrifice to Molech, and in Ch. 24 by the law for the shewbread and in Ch. 26 by the indirect reference in vs. 31. Most scholars find strong P overwriting in Ch. 23 and also in some crucial references elsewhere.

To Group A is assigned 17 : 11 with its theory of sacrifice. The precise meaning of the verse is hotly debated, but Kennedy's cautious verdict that "the substitutionary theory of the atonement, the principle of a life for a life, is not explicitly taught in this passage, although the thought lies near"[1] justifies the assignation of the verse to Group A. The other references to offerings for sin—19 : 21-22 (*'āšām*), 23 : 19 (*ḥaṭṭā't*), 23 : 26 (Day of Atonement), 23 : 24-36 (Tabernacles)—are almost universally regarded as P additions, and can only doubtfully be included here. The passage with the best claim to inclusion is perhaps 19 : 21-22. It is suspect on the ground, that a casuistic law of this kind in the third person among a series of apodictic commandments in the second person, cannot be in place, but this is not to say, that it does not belong to the Holiness

[1] A. R. S. Kennedy, *Leviticus and Numbers* (*CB*), Edinburgh, n.d., p. 123. K. Koch in *Die israelitische Sühneanschauung*, p. 14 goes further. See the quotation on p. 18 above.

Code. Failing a more convincing argument for its deletion it has been left in A. If the *'āšām* was known to H in 19: 21-22, it is probable that the mention of the addition of a fifth in 22 : 10-16 refers also to the *'āšām* (cf. Lev. 5 : 14-16). It is not certain, however, that an offering is referred to in addition. The case for the deletion of *ḥaṭṭā't* in 23 : 19 is stronger. It is claimed that vss. 18-19 breaks the connection from vss. 17-20 and that the numbering of the set sacrifices for the Feast of Firstfruits is derived from Num. 28 : 27-30. The Numbers passage, however, is not identical, nor is vs. 20 impossible as a continuation of vs. 19, but when the strong P overwriting of the chapter is taken into account, it is probable that these verses come from this source.

Material of the B type may possibly be seen in the remainder of Ch. 17, in Ch. 19 : 5-8 and in Ch. 23 : 39-43. The various prohibitions in Ch. 17—against profane slaughter (vss. 1ff., vss. 8ff.), against sacrifice to field spirits (vss. 5ff.), against eating blood (vss. 10ff.), against eating blood of domestic animals (vss. 13ff.), and against eating carrion (vs. 15)—all have to do with the sacrificial meal. The note of joy is not, however, included, but mention is made rather of the sprinkling of the blood on the altar and the burning of the fat for the *reaḥ niḥôaḥ* (vs. 6).[1] A similar emphasis is found in the law for the acceptable (*rāṣâ*) *zibḥê šᵉlāmîm* in 19 : 5-8. The eating of it may not continue beyond the second day. "Rejoicing before the Lord" is referred to in the law for the Feast of Tabernacles in 23 : 39-43, but in this passage eating or sacrifice is not mentioned.

In Group C come the two prohibitions of child sacrifice (18 : 21, 20 : 1-5), the formal references to the unblemished priesthood as offering *'îššê*, as the bread of God (21 : 6, 8, 17, 21, 22), and eating of the sacrifices, the H references to the Feasts of Firstfruits (23 : 9-12) and Weeks (23 : 16-18, 19b), the redactional materials on the shewbread (24 : 5-9) and the feasts (Passover 23 : 4-8, Firstfruits 23 : 13-14, Weeks 23 : 18b-19, Trumpets 23 : 23-25, Atonement 23 : 26-32 and Tabernacles 23 : 34-36). Of the H materials the passage 22 : 18-25 is of interest because of its distinction between the *'ōlôt* for freewill and vowed offerings (vs. 18), and the *zibḥê šᵉlāmîm* for the same purpose.[2] In both unblemished offerings

[1] Unless this verse is a P addition.

[2] In P vows and freewill offerings together with *tôdôt* make up the *zibḥê šᵉlāmîm*. The *'ōlâ* as a vow is not, however, unparalleled (Ps. 66 : 13), while a

are required to be accepted (*rāšâ*). The passage is followed by some isolated laws—the sacrificial victim to be not less than eight days old (22 : 27), a calf and its mother not to be sacrificed on the same day (22 : 28), the *tôdâ* not to be left to be eaten until the morning (22 : 29-30). A final reference, which speaks of the rejection of the *reaḥ niḥôaḥ* in the time of disaster (26 : 31) does not specifically mention sacrifice, but no doubt refers to it.

While the tone of the Code is solemn, specific references to expiation are less than one would expect from such a statement as that of Lods, that atonement was the chief purpose of sacrifice in H.[1] However, if Lev. 17 : 11 is understood in an expiatory sense and taken as stating H's theory of sacrifice, the other references will need to be read in this light, even where explicit mention of expiation is missing.

Ezekiel's Code

The sacrificial references are probably all to be assigned to Group A. Some passages which would otherwise go into Group B include also formal reference to sin and guilt offerings, while others which lack these and perhaps should go into Group C, may be assumed to share the expiatory view evident elsewhere in this Code. The references occur chiefly in three main blocks of material—in connection with the furnishings of the temple (40 : 38-43, 42 : 13-14, 43 : 18-27, 46 : 19-24), the personnel of the temple (44 : 1-45 : 17), and in the festal calendar (45 : 18-46 : 24).

The *temple furnishings* are to include tables for slaughtering the offerings (40 : 38-43), rooms for the eating of the offerings by the priests (42 : 13-14), and kitchens for the cooking of the sacrifices by the priests for themselves (46 : 20) and for the people (46 : 24). The offerings listed are, in 40 : 38ff.—*ʿōlâ*, *ḥaṭṭāʾt* and *ʾāšām* (vs. 39),[2] *ʿōlâ* and *zebaḥ*,[3] and *qorbān*[4] (vss. 42-43), in 42 : 13-14—*minḥâ*,

---

freewill *ʿōlâ* is mentioned in Ez. 46 : 12. *Tôdôt* are mentioned separately in vs. 29, as if in an independent category, but the passage need not be consecutive.

[1] A. Lods, *The Prophets and the Rise of Judaism*, pp. 263-64.

[2] LXX^{B} omits *ʿōlâ*, but *ʿōlâ* is present in the section in any case in vss. 38 and 42.

[3] *Zebaḥ* is possibly to be deleted in vs. 42, but supplied with the LXX in vs. 41.

[4] *Qorbān* which is not found elsewhere in Ezekiel's Code, and is otherwise only in P, is not read by the LXX and is suspect here.

ḥaṭṭā't and *'āšām* to be eaten by the priests in a holy place, in 46 : 20 —*'āšām* and *ḥaṭṭā't* to be boiled by the priests (*bšl*) and *minḥâ* to be baked, and in 46 : 24—*zebaḥ* of the people to be boiled (*bšl*) by those who minister in the sanctuary. These passages would belong respectively to formal references indicating nothing of the mood of the offerer (Group C) or to the sacrificial meal category (Group B), but in each case *'āšām* and *ḥaṭṭā't* are listed.

Among the temple furnishings, an altar is to be constructed. The rules for its dedication in 43 : 18-27 include an initial *ḥaṭṭā't* of a bull (vs. 19), the blood of which is to be put (*nātan*) on the four horns and corners to cleanse (*ḥiṭṭē'*) and expiate (*kipper*). Similar rites with goats, bulls and rams are repeated for seven days (vss. 22-26), the goats being apparently for a *ḥaṭṭā't* and the bulls and rams for an *'ōlâ,*[1] if indeed any distinctions can be made. This altar is then ready for use for *'ōlôt* and *šᵉlāmîm* that the worshippers may be accepted (*rāṣâ*) vs. 27. The altar's use is generally described in the opening verse (vs. 18) as "for offering burnt offerings upon it and for throwing blood against it (*zāraq*)." It is possible, but not probable, that the whole passage is secondary. The change from second to third person implies some earlier history.

The second main block of material deals in Ch. 44 with the functions of the *temple personnel*. Vs. 3 permits the prince to sit in the special gate to "eat bread before the Lord" i.e. the sacrificial meal (a B Group reference). In vss. 4-14 foreigners are excluded from sanctuary service ("offering (*qrb*) food (*leḥem*), fat and blood" vs. 7) and are replaced by the de-graded Levites. The Levites are to slay the *'ōlâ* and *zebaḥ* of the people (vs. 11)—a variation from the normal slaying by the worshippers which prevailed both earlier and later, except in one or two doubtful references in Chronicles. The approach to the altar and the offering (*qrb*) of the fat and blood are reserved for the Levitical priests, the sons of Zadok (vs. 15). The passage thus far is a C Group formal reference, but vs. 27 provides for the priest to offer a *ḥaṭṭā't* when he goes in to minister—a provision otherwise unmentioned in the laws. Vss. 28-31 provide dues for the priests. They are to eat the *minḥâ,* the *'āšām* and the *ḥaṭṭā't* (vs. 29)—the same list as in 42 : 13 and 46 : 20—and shall

[1] The salting of the sacrifice, although known from such references as Mark 9 : 49, is mentioned only here in the Old Testament (but cf. Lev. 2 : 13).

have in addition the *rē'šît* of the *bikkûrîm*, the *terûmâ* and the *rē'šît* of the dough[1] (vs. 30), but may not eat anything that has died of itself (vs. 31). Somewhat surprisingly nothing is said of the priests eating the *zebaḥ* or the *šelāmîm*.

The passage 45 : 13-17 assigns the responsibility for the offerings to the people (vs. 16) and to the prince (vs. 17). The offerings are listed variously as *minḥâ, ʿōlâ, šelāmîm* (vs. 15), *ʿōlôt, minḥâ, nesek* (vs. 17a) and *ḥaṭṭā't, minḥâ, ʿōlâ, šelāmîm* (vs. 17b). The reason for the variations and for the omission of the *'āšām* is unknown. Of interest is the repeated reference (vss. 15, 17) to the expiatory purpose (*kipper*) of all these offerings—even of the *minḥâ* and the *šelāmîm*. This goes beyond P, which speaks of the *ʿōlâ* as atoning (Lev. 1 : 4), but not of the *šelāmîm* and the *minḥâ*.

The third type of material giving the regulations for the various festivals of the *festal calendar* runs from 45 : 18-46 : 13. The half-yearly expiations are first provided for (45 : 18-20). The blood of a young bull sacrificed for a *ḥaṭṭā't* is to be used to expiate the sanctuary. It is not certain whether the second expiation is six months later (the first of the seventh month with the LXX), or only seven days later (the seventh of the (first) month with MT and RSV) (vs. 20). In this case the sacrifices are said to be for those who have sinned "through error or ignorance" (*šōgeh ûmippetî*). Next the half-yearly festivals of Passover and Unleavened Bread and Tabernacles (45 : 21-25) are to include similar sin offerings provided by the prince. The Sabbath and New Moon offerings of the prince follow (46 : 1-5, 6 - 8). Both he and the people are onlookers while the *ʿōlâ, šelāmîm* and *minḥâ* are offered. At other feasts the prince provides similar offerings (46 : 11-12), *nedābâ* of *ʿōlâ* or *šelāmîm* being particularly mentioned, and for daily offerings (46 : 13-14) a lamb for the morning burnt offering and with it a *minḥâ* including *sōlet* for an *ʿōlâ tāmîd*. *'Āšām, ḥaṭṭā't* and *kipper* are not included in this part of Ch. 46, which could thus go into Group C.

E. L. Allen's summary of the Code's provisions for sacrifice draws attention to the following particular emphases.[2] Revisions of the traditional system were—"first, in his scheme for the great annual feasts (45 : 21-25) he seems determined to get away from the old

[1] First mentioned here.

[2] E. L. Allen, *Ezekiel* (*IB*) VI, New York (1956), pp. 314-16.

agricultural associations. He passes over Pentecost altogether and concentrates upon Passover and Tabernacles . . . The festivals . . . are no longer to be the joyful occasions they were in the past. Instead they are burdened with a sense of the nation's sin, and are to be opportunities for an earnest reckoning with God in repentance and atonement . . . Second . . . religion must be built into the daily life of the community [cf. the institution of the daily sacrifice], not just reserved for certain special occasions (46 : 13-15) . . . Third, the purpose of sacrifice throughout is to make atonement . . ." Despite this revision defects remained. "Access to God is indirect . . . the common people can draw near to him only in the person of . . . priest or prince. They stand and look on while these offer worship on their behalf (46 : 1-3) . . . Sacrifice is impermanent in its results. The act of cleansing the sanctuary or making atonement for the temple has to be renewed every six months (45 : 18-20) . . . It is also inadequate, since it only covers sins of inadvertence" (45 : 20).

In view of the fact on the one hand, that all these elements were probably not new to Ezekiel, and on the other, that his Code did not come into practice as temple usage, it is difficult to estimate to what extent his views represent the sentiments of his contemporaries.

Exilic and Post-exilic Prophets

Sacrifice is referred to in Deutero-Isaiah, Trito-Isaiah, Malachi, Jonah, Joel, Deutero-Zechariah and Daniel, but somewhat surprisingly not in Haggai or First-Zechariah. Of the thirty-two instances only a handful permit of classification in either of the major groups A and B. To Group A is assigned Is. 52 : 13-53 : 12. Many scholars would dispute the sacrificial application of *yazzeh*, *śeh* and *'āšām*, but an increasing number are now willing to acknowledge it.[1] The difficult passage, Is. 43 : 23-25 (*'ōlâ*, *minḥâ*, *zebaḥ*, *lebônâ*),

[1] See H. H. Rowley, *The Unity of the Bible*, pp. 55ff; J. Muilenburg, "Isaiah," (*IB*) V (1956), pp. 614ff; L. G. Rignell, "Is lii : 13-liii : 12," *VT* III (1953), pp. 87-92. Rignell writes: "The conceptions, and even the terminology itself, which are used to make clear the mission of the Servant are influenced by the Pentateuchal description of sacrifice in ancient Israel. E.g. lii : 15 *yzh*, besprinkle with the blood of the victims, expiate. The Servant was as a lamb (*śeh*) led to the slaughter, liii : 7. *Śeh* is used of the paschal lamb. The Servant should give himself as a guilt offering (*'āšām*) liii : 10" (p. 89). For the interpretation of *yzh* in this sense see J. Lindblom,

which can hardly be taken in Volz's sense of a rejection of pre-exilic sacrifice,[1] or in Elliott Binns' of offerings offered to Babylonian gods,[2] or emended as desiderated by M. Scott by the omission of the three "nots" in vss. 23-24,[3] might also support the expiatory meaning, if taken in the sense that Israel had burdened Yahweh with sins, instead of with sacrifices which take away sin. This is, however, doubtful. Jon. 1 : 16 (*zᵉbāḥîm*), where the heathen sailors offer sacrifices and vow vows, after the pacifying of the storm, could be also understood as a thanksgiving, but the fact that the men "feared Yahweh with a great fear" seems to favour a propitiatory sense.

To Group B belong the joyous offerings (*ʿōlôt* and *zᵉbāḥîm*) of the house of prayer in Is. 56 : 7, and the sacrifices boiled by the worshippers for eating in Zech. 14 : 21 (*zebaḥ*). A sacrificial meal is also implied in Is. 62 : 9, where there is no sacrificial reference, and Is. 65 : 3-4 and 65 : 11, where the reference is to an apostate cult.

In Group C similar references to the apostate cult occur in Is. 57 : 6[4] and 66 : 17. Is. 66 : 3, if the parallel clauses in apposition are taken in the comparative sense "he who slaughters an ox is like him who kills a man,"[5] reducing the regular cultus to the level of the apostate cult, would imply a rejection of sacrifice unequalled in any pre-exilic prophet.[6] That this can hardly be the case is indicated by the favourable reference to sacrifice in Is. 66 : 20. A further passage, which on the surface might seem to imply a rejection of the cult by Deutero-Isaiah (40 : 16) "Lebanon would not suffice for fuel, nor are its beasts enough for a burnt offering (*ʿōlâ*)," is to be understood with Chary[7] as a witness to the impor-

---

The Servant Songs in Deutero-Isaiah, Lund (1952), pp. 40-41; E. J. Young, *Studies in Isaiah*, Grand Rapids (1954), pp. 199ff.

[1] P. Volz, *Jesaia II* (*KAT*) (1932), pp. 45ff.

[2] L. Elliott Binns (*GoreC*), p. 464.

[3] M. Scott, "Is. xliii : 22-25," *ExpT* XXXVII (1925-1926), pp. 270-71.

[4] Here (vs. 5) and 66 : 3 human sacrifice is included.

[5] This has some support in the DSS reading *kmkh* and in the LXX *hōs*.

[6] The verse belongs, however, to the condemnation of a temple building project, the identification of which is obscure (vss. 1ff).

[7] Th. Chary, *Les prophètes et le culte à partir de l'exil*, Tournai (1955), pp. 86-87. This work may be consulted with profit for the whole of this chapter.

tance of the cult. God is so great that even the highest form of adoration is not sufficient.[1] Volz treats this as an addition.

The importance of the cult is further attested in the next two groups of references—those of Malachi and Jonah, and of Joel and Daniel. In Mal. 1 : 7ff. the complaint is made that inferior offerings were being brought and in 3 : 8ff. that tithes and offerings (*maʿaśēr ûtᵉrûmâ*) are being withheld. The altar is described uniquely as a table, and the offerings as food (1 : 7, 1 : 13, 3 : 10), but the reference is to the "food of God," rather than to a shared sacrificial meal. Such an emphasis is not inconsistent with the threat of the rejection of unworthy sacrifices (1 : 10, 2 : 3,[2] 2 : 12, 2 : 13) nor with the promise of the acceptance of the offerings of a purified cult (3 : 3-4), as even now the offerings of the Gentiles are accepted (1 : 11).[3] Jon. 2 : 9 speaks of a sacrifice of thanksgiving in fulfilment of a vow. The value of the cult is further witnessed by the numerous references in Joel and Daniel to the cutting off of the daily sacrifice as a calamity (Joel 1 : 9, 1 : 13, 2 : 14—in each case *minḥâ* and *nesek*; Dan. 8 : 11, 12, 13, 11 : 31, 12 : 11—in each case *tāmîd*; 9 : 27—*minḥâ* and *zebaḥ*). The evening *minḥâ* as a note of time is also referred to in Dan. 9 : 21, but this reference like the others to the daily offering must be classed as a "formal reference" which indicates nothing of the mood of the offerer. A further reference in Daniel which is quite exceptional in nature is 2 : 46, where divine honours including sacrifice, are offered to Daniel by Nebuchadnezzar, and apparently not refused (*nesek, minḥâ, niḥôaḥ*).[4]

Other references which probably refer to sacrifice, but imply nothing concerning its nature are Is. 60 : 7, where flocks and rams are to come up (*ʿālâ*) with acceptance (*rāṣôn*) on the altar, Zech. 9 : 11 "the blood of my covenant" and Zech. 9 : 15, where there is a possible reference to blood on the corners of the altar. The fountain open for uncleanness in Zech. 13 : 1 is not sacrificial,[5] and the

---

[1] It remains a difficulty, however, that the "beasts of Lebanon," naturally understood as wild animals, were not permitted in Israelite sacrifice.

[2] But here the term is *ḥaggîm*.

[3] For the numerous interpretations of this remarkable verse see the commentaries.

[4] The Apocrypha also adds a detailed sacrificial reference in 3 : 38-40 (Prayer of Azariah 15-17).

[5] The connection of 13 : 1 to the suffering shepherd of 11 : 4 favoured by W. Nowack, (*Die kleinen Propheten* (*HK*) (^{3}1922), p. 392), and Horst' sinter-

reference to *ḥaṭṭā't* in 14 : 19 is probably to be taken in the sense of punishment rather than a sin offering.

Although this exhausts the references to sacrifice in these books, it is realized that many other passages, where confession of sin and expiation are mentioned, have a bearing on the theme. The great prayer of Dan. 9 is full of the sense of sin and speaks of the seventy weeks as appointed for atonement (*kipper* vs. 24), but this atoning is not related to sacrifice. Similarly in First-Zechariah the taking away of sin is referred to in Ch. 3 (the Vision of Joshua) and in Ch. 5 : 5ff. (the Vision of the Ephah), but in neither case explicitly through sacrifice. This again occasions surprise in view of what is commonly understood of the place of sacrifice for sin in post-exilic Judaism. In fact there is little trace of expiation in this whole section, although evidence comes from the sixth, fifth, fourth, third and second centuries B.C. The most frequent sacrificial term is *minḥâ* (thirteen times) but there is little to show that it is used in P's sense of a cereal offering, where it chiefly occurs in Malachi, although this may be the case in Is. 43 : 23-25 and 66 : 20.

Wisdom Literature

The twelve references to sacrifice scattered throughout Job, Proverbs and Ecclesiastes represent each of the three categories.

The sacrifices of the Prologue and Epilogue of the Book of Job in 1 : 5 and 42 : 8 are sacrifices to expiate sin and belong to Group A.[1] *'Ōlâ* rather than "sin offering" may be in keeping with the patriarchal setting given to the story.[2] Sins of thought (1 : 5) and word (42 : 8) are in view.

To Group B are assigned the three references to feasting in the Book of Proverbs. The adulterous woman in 7 : 14ff. invites the youth to her home with promises of a repast from *zibḥê šᵉlāmîm*, which she had offered for vows that day (and had to be eaten at

pretation of 12 : 9 of the offering of the innocent appeasing Yahweh's wrath (*HAT*, p. 248, cf. J. J. Stamm, *Das Leiden des Unschuldigen in Babylon und Israel*, Zürich (1946), p. 75), could only be established if the identity of the enigmatic shepherd was known.

[1] G. Fohrer, finds it an evidence of an old tradition, that these sacrifices "nach alter Anschauung den Zorn Gottes beschwichtigen" ("Überlieferung und Wandlung der Hioblegende," *Festschrift Friedrich Baumgärtel*, Erlangen (1959), p. 51).

[2] LXX, however, reads *peri hamartias* "sin offering."

least by the next day). 17 : 1 contrasts "a dry morsel with quiet" with "a house full of sacrifices (*zᵉbāḥîm*) with strife."

The Group C references are in the main in repudiation of sacrifice as inferior to conduct. In Prov. 15 : 8 the *zebaḥ* of the wicked, which is an abomination is contrasted to the prayer, which is acceptable (*rāṣâ*). In 21 : 3 judgment and justice are more acceptable than sacrifice (*zebaḥ*), and in Eccles. 4 : 17 (5 : 1) "hearing" is better than "to give the sacrifice (*zebaḥ*) of fools."[1] These verses do not reject the cult as such, but sacrifices offered as a cover by the wicked. This is probably the meaning of Prov. 21 : 27, where the first phrase is the same as 15 : 8, but *yᵉbîʾennû bᵉzimmâ* in the second phrase is obscure. Some suggest "when he brings it for wickedness" i.e. "to atone for wickedness," but others prefer "with wickedness."

Two references to vows (Job 27 : 27, Eccles. 5 : 4ff.), and the inclusion of sacrificing and not sacrificing in the list of the activities of men in Eccles. 9 : 2, indicate that the cult is functioning normally, although not often referred to. This comparative silence is in keeping with the nature of the Wisdom Literature, which takes the distinctive institutions of Israel for granted.[2] Caution is also needed in the use of this literature as evidence for the exilic and post-exilic period in view of the recent tendency to date much, at least of the Book of Proverbs, early.

Ezra-Nehemiah

The many tangled questions of the criticism of these books, and their relation to the work of the Chronicler cannot be treated in this brief survey. While no agreement has been reached on the historical worth of the Aramaic documents and the memoirs of Nehemia and Ezra, these sources are at least older than the rest of the books and are here classified as "primary," while the remaining sections—whether from the pen of the Chronicler or not—are classed as "secondary." A further difficulty is the crossing over of categories with sin offerings and rejoicing appearing in the same

---

[1] The verb "give" is unusual. LXX renders "gift of" (*doma*) reading *mimmattat* for MT *mittēt*.

[2] One may contrast the frequent references to sacrifices in the Accadian Wisdom literature published in *ANET* Part VI, Princeton (1950), cf. pp. 427a, 435a, 437b, 438b, 439b.

passages. Such passages partake of both A and B elements and are grouped together as a new intermediate category A-B.

The three passages assigned to Group A, because of the presence of *niḥôaḥ*, *'āšām* and *ḥaṭṭā't* (Ezra 6 : 9-10, 10 : 19; Neh. 10: 32-39), do not otherwise reflect a sense of sin and are not from unimpeachable sources. Ezra 6:9-10 in the Aramaic source is not impossible as a general provision from the Persian king,[1] but is possibly coloured in details by Jewish ritual terminology.[2] *'ōlôt* are to be provided for by the supply of the sacrificial animals, the materials required for cereal offerings and drink offerings are also to be supplied, and *niḥōaḥ* are to be offered (*qrb*), presumably as propitiatory sacrifices, for the life of the king and his sons. Ezra 10 : 19, which appropriately describes the offering of a guilt offering (*'āšām*) of a ram by the priests for the (? inadvertent) sin of mixed marriages, need not be a late passage. Neh. 10 : 33-40 (32-39) lists the sacrifices for which the people agreed to be responsible annually, and includes along with the third shekel, the shewbread, the *minḥâ tāmîd*, the *'ōlôt tāmîd*, the wood offerings,[3] the firstlings, firstfruits, tithes and *t^erûmôt*, also *ḥaṭṭā'ôt* to *kipper* for Israel. The question of the date of the passage is complicated by its differences from the P law at a number of points, but it can hardly be late.

The A-B Group comprises several passages which, while containing formal references to sin offerings, or purificatory rites, nevertheless reflect joyful worship. These are Ezra 6 : 16-18, 6 : 19-22; Neh. 12 : 30-43. Ezra 6 : 16-18 from the Aramaic source is the concluding summary describing the dedication of the temple and the offerings and sin offerings (*ḥaṭṭā't*) which accompanied it. The occasion is one of joy (vs. 16). Similar joy marks the feast of Passover and Unleavened Bread of 6 : 19-22 (secondary), but the celebrations are preceded by purificatory rites which are not further described. The dedication of the walls in Neh. 12 : 43 (source doubtful) is likewise an occasion of joyful sacrifice (*z^ebāḥîm*), but purificatory rites, again unspecified, have preceded it in 12 : 30.

---

[1] Cf. the similar interest in the Elephantine ritual (A. Cowley, *op. cit.*, pp. 112ff.).

[2] R. A. Bowman, *Ezra-Nehemiah* (*IB*) III (1954), pp. 617-18, thinks this use of the Chronicler's terminology in his way makes the verses suspect.

[3] Otherwise unmentioned.

Passages of a similar nature, but lacking mention of the sin offering are assigned to Group B. Neh. 8 : 9-13 (secondary), which calls the people to joy instead of mourning, does not mention sacrifice, but implies the sacrificial meal in the "eating and drinking and sending portions" of vs. 12. The succeeding narrative of the keeping of the Feast of Booths (vss. 13-18 secondary) also stresses the rejoicing, but does not mention sacrifice.

C passages comprise formal references, and also the more extended narrative of Ezra 3, which does not permit of easy classification. This chapter, from a secondary source of doubtful value, describes the rebuilding of the altar (vss. 2-3), the celebration of the Feast of Tabernacles (vs. 4) and the restoration of the cultus (vss. 5-6). Burnt offerings and freewill offerings (*neḏāḇâ*) are mentioned, but not sin offerings. Esdras suggests that the motive was thanks for the safe protection of the road, but more probably the rites were of dedication.[1] A similar passage in 8 : 35 (primary) is given a like motive by Esdras, but here sin offerings are mentioned along with burnt offerings, but the reference seems formalized. Ezra 7 : 16ff., from the Aramaic source, which speaks of the provision of revenue for *minḥôt, niskâ* and apparently for burnt offerings, is parallel to Ezra 9 : 10, but lacks the reference to prayer for the king. Formal references to the remanent population of the land as sacrificing (*zāḇaḥ*) to the God of Israel,[2] (Ezra 4 : 2 secondary), to the rebuilding of the temple as the place of sacrifices and fire offerings[3] (Ezra 6 : 3 primary), to the evening sacrifice (*minḥat ʿereb*) as a time tag (Ezra 9 : 4-5 primary), to the "feeble Jews" wishing to sacrifice—*zebaḥ* (Neh. 3 : 34 (4 : 2) primary), to the priestly dues and their disposal (Neh. 12 : 44-47 secondary), to the chamber of Tobiah as the place of the *minḥâ* and the *lebônâ* (Neh. 13 : 5-9 secondary) add nothing to the discussion.

This investigation does not support the contention that the joyful sacrificial meal disappeared under the "permanent sense of guilt" in the post-exilic period. The note of joy seems rather to be the dominant one. The rejoicing is spontaneous, while the references to sin offerings seem somewhat formal.

---

[1] Unless they are to be thought of as propitiatory arising from the fear of vs. 3.

[2] Reading *to him* for "not" with Q.

[3] Emending with RSV.

Chronicles

To do anything like justice to the Chronicler's considerable materials on the cultus would require a separate volume. It is probably unwise to attempt a survey, but for the sake of completeness a superficial classification without claim to exactness may be given. Sacrifice occupies a much larger place in these books than in those of their predecessors, but this is in keeping with the plan of the writer. Some thirty-six references fall to be considered. The writer's interest in sacrifice is indicated by his introduction of sacrificial references, where they are missing in the Books of Samuel and Kings.[1] On the other hand many of the sacrificial narratives in the earlier books are omitted, possibly on dogmatic grounds.[2] In a third class of references the materials of Samuel and Kings are reproduced with little change. This type of reference, although listed here, is of little value for the thought of the Chronicler and will be designated by "parallel," while the Chronicler's own material will be designated "peculiar."

In Group A comes, first, the description of the functions of the Aaronites in 1 Chron. 6 : 34(49) (peculiar) as including "making atonement." The reference is quite formal. Next come three "parallel" references—Ornan's threshing-floor (1 Chron. 21 : 23-30), Solomon at Gibeon (2 Chron. 1 : 6) and the dedication of the temple (2 Chron. 7 : 4ff.), which retain the classification of A assigned to them earlier, but do not present any new elements in Chronicles. Ahaz's sacrifices to the gods of Damascus (2 Chron. 28 : 22) are more briefly described than in 1 Kings 16, and are attributed a propitiatory purpose.

Group A-B, like the passages in Ezra-Nehemiah, combine joyous thanksgiving with purificatory rites. Long descriptions involving the offering of sin offerings for atonement are given of Hezekiah's Reform (2 Chron. 29 esp. vss. 21-24 peculiar) and the following joyous worship, and of Hezekiah's Passover gladness and its preceding purificatory rites (2 Chron. 30 peculiar).

Group B includes 1 Chron. 29 : 20-22 (peculiar)—a joyous offering and meal arranged by David at the occasion of the desig-

---

[1] E. g. Solomon's Temple is now specifically defined as a place of sacrifice (2 Chron. 2 : 4-6, 7 : 12).

[2] E.g. the story of Ahaz's altar.

nation of Solomon as king, and 2 Chron. 23 : 18 (peculiar), where the functions of Jehoiada's Levites are the offering of *ʿōlôt* with rejoicing. Perhaps to be included here as a change of emphasis from Kings is the account of Joash's temple reform in 2 Chron. 24 : 8-14, with its remarkable omission of the *ʾāšām* and *ḥaṭṭāʾt* references, which stood in the text of Kings.

Group C includes such unclassifiable narratives as that of the removal of the ark (1 Chron. 15 : 26-16 : 3 parallel and 2 Chron. 5 : 6 peculiar), the consecration of Jeroboam's priests (2 Chron. 13 : 9 peculiar), Asa's thank-offering (2 Chron. 15 : 10 peculiar), Uzziah's presumption (2 Chron. 26 : 16-19 peculiar, possibly expiatory offering of Day of Atonement), Manasseh's Reform (2 Chron. 33 : 16 peculiar) and Josiah's Passover (2 Chron. 35 parallel but extended). The other references are formal—the functions of the Levites (1 Chron. 9 : 29-32 peculiar), a psalmist's offering (1 Chron. 16 : 29=Ps. 96 : 8), the tabernacle of Gibeon (1 Chron. 16 : 40 peculiar), the altar of burnt offering (1 Chron. 22 : 1 peculiar), the functions of the Aaronites (1 Chron. 23 : 13 peculiar), the functions of the Levites (1 Chron. 23 : 27ff. peculiar), the function of the temple (2 Chron. 2 : 4-6 peculiar), the washing of the offering (2 Chron. 4 : 6 peculiar), the fire from heaven (2 Chron. 7 : 1 peculiar), the function of the temple (2 Chron. 7 : 12 peculiar), Solomon's sacrifices (2 Chron. 8 : 12 and 9 : 4 parallel), the function of Judah's priests (2 Chron. 13 : 10-11 peculiar), Ahab's hospitality (2 Chron. 18 : 2), Hezekiah's provision (2 Chron. 31 : 2-4 peculiar), Manasseh's apostasy (2 Chron. 33 : 6 peculiar), and Amon's apostasy (2 Chron. 33 : 24 and 34 : 4 peculiar).

From this evidence it must be concluded that, although numerous additional references to sacrifice were introduced by the Chronicler, only in the first case in A and in the two cases in A-B, do they make the expiatory aspect prominent. Neither in his new material nor his reproduction of old sources does the Chronicler lay weight on this aspect. As with Ezra-Nehemiah his emphasis is rather on the joyous nature of worship.

Conclusion

It must be emphasised again as said at the outset of this chapter that the detailed discussion of the post-exilic cult lies outside this enquiry, and much further material would need to be studied before certain conclusions could be drawn for this period. In particular the dating of the Psalms and the "secondary" materials encountered above in the earlier sources would need to be gone into, the total theological position of each of the post-exilic writers studied, and above all the data of P fully investigated. Nothing of this is attempted here, and the conclusions arrived at in the absence of this kind of investigation can at best be partial and inadequate, and may even be misleading. Nevertheless some judgment must be expressed on the post-exilic period in view of the common assumption, that it was in this period that the sense of sin came to be associated with Israelite sacrifice.

The materials studied in this chapter cover a wide period reaching approximately from the seventh to the second centuries B.C. Despite this no clear pattern of a developing sense of sin in connection with sacrifice emerges. The documents which lay most stress on this aspect—the Holiness Code and Ezekiel's Code—are the ones most difficult to date. They belong to the type of material described in the Introduction (p. 19) as unsatisfactory for evidence in an historical enquiry. Different scholars will date them differently according to a preconceived idea of when this accentuated sense of sin was most likely to have developed. Three possible periods may be distinguished — before the exile in the seventh century, during the exile in the sixth century, after the exile in the fifth century.

That the Babylonian exile was interpreted as a punishment for Israel's sins is apparent from a passage like Is. 40 : 2. The message of the prophet, however, was that this sin had been more than paid for, and God was now willing to forgive. His prophecy reflects no great concern for cultic expiation. His successor, possibly back in Palestine, spoke of Israel's sin as separating them from God (Is. 59 : 2), but the passage is a typical prophetic condemnation of contemporary social injustice, and does not mirror the "leaden pressure of sin and wrath" of which Wellhausen spoke. Haggai, Zechariah and Malachi have a sense of sin and also a keen cultic interest, but do not bring the two into close connection. Ezra-Nehemiah and Chronicles do speak of cultic expiation, but even more of the joy of forgiveness which follows it. Some of the late Psalms are usually adduced as further evidence, but this would be a *petitio principii* in the present instance, as the chief argument for their late date is their sense of sin.[1]

Other arguments have been brought forward on general grounds. Harper thought, that Israel's contact with a vast sacrificial system centring in propitiation in Babylon, brought this element to the fore in her own cult,[2] but the evidence would seem to suggest that resistance rather than receptivity characterized the exile's reaction to the Babylonian cult (cf. Is. 46). Oesterley thinks "the teaching of both Ezekiel and Deutero-Isaiah on the transcendental character of God, with the inevitable recognition of the insignificance of man in His sight must have generated the sense of unworthiness" and that "the exaltation of the divine Law with its ever-increasing demands tended to make many feel their inability to fulfil its requirements adequately."[3] A further factor was the growing sense of individual responsibility attested by Ezekiel. To these it may be replied that emphasis on the law has more often induced spiritual pride than humility,[4] that the sense of individual responsibility was also taught by Jeremiah and earlier,[5] and that divine transcendence and human insignificance is also the teaching of Isaiah and the eighth century prophets (cf. Is. 2 : 22) and was scarcely so revolutionary a discovery in the exile.

If the exilic and post-exilic periods do not supply the required evidence, what of the pre-exilic period? Exile was not a new factor in 586 B.C. Already in 597 B.C. in Judah and in 721 B.C. in Samaria its bitter lesson had been brought home. The long Deuteronomic judgment on the fall of the Northern Kingdom in 2 Kings 17 : 7ff. may be from the sixth century in its literary form, but must have had currency in Deuteronomic preaching much earlier. The covenant blessings and cursings in Deut. 28 and Lev. 26 already threaten

---

[1] This applies also to some "late" passages adduced by Oesterley, *Sacrifices . . .* as evidence for post-exilic cultic interest—Is. 19; Micah 6-7; Jer. 33 : 17-18.

[2] W. R. Harper, *The Priestly Element in the Old Testament*, Chicago (Rev. ed. 1902), p. 45.

[3] He cites Neh. 8 : 9 "the people wept when they heard the words of the law" (W. O. E. Oesterley and T. H. Robinson, *Hebrew Religion*, p. 333).

[4] Oesterley admits that this was the case later on, but thinks that it was not so at the first (*ibid.*, p. 333).

[5] See H. H. Rowley, *The Faith of Israel*, London (1956), Ch. IV; G. E. Wright, *The Biblical Doctrine of Man in Society*, London (1954), pp. 22ff; and J. Hempel, *Gott und Mensch im Alten Testament*, pp. 189ff.

exile as a judgment upon sin. How far back this element reaches cannot be positively affirmed, but one is tempted to ask in the light of the results reached in the earlier chapters of this work, whether there was ever a time when such an emphasis was impossible in Israel.[1] For the present chapter, however, it is sufficient that it be shown that no revolutionary new element entered the thought of Israel in the later period,[2] through inattention to which conclusions drawn for the earlier period might be invalidated. This, it is hoped has been demonstrated.

---

[1] Cf. the remarks of S. A. Cook cited on pp. 11 and 13 above.

[2] Ezekiel's Code, which alone would contradict this statement is not held to establish a contrary position for the reasons stated on p. 224—namely its ideal nature, the fact that it never operated as temple usage, the uncertainty as to the extent to which it expressed the sentiments of the prophet's contemporaries or was new to the prophet, if he was the author, or to which period it belongs, if he was not.

REFERENCES TO SACRIFICE IN THE HOLINESS CODE

Reference	Incident	Terms Used		Primary or Secondary	Israelite or Foreign	National or Individual	Special or Regular
A. Where a sense of sin or solemnity is present							
Lev. 17 : 11	Life in Blood		*kipper*	Primary	Israelite		Regular
19 : 21-22	Intercourse with Slave	*ʾāšām*	*hēbīʾ*	?Primary	Israelite	Individual	Special
? 22 : 10-16	Eating Holy Thing	*tᵉrûmâ qᵃdāšîm*		Primary	Israelite	Individual	Special
B. Where a sense of sin or solemnity is not present							
Lev. 17 : 1ff.	Against Profane Slaughter	*qorbān*	*qrb*	Primary	Israelite	Individual	Regular
17 : 5ff.	Against Field Spirits	*zibhê šᵉlāmîm*	*zābaḥ*	Primary	Israelite	Individual	Regular
		zebaḥ ʿōlâ ʿālâ	*qṭr*				
17 : 10ff.	Against Eating Blood			Primary	Israelite	Individual	Regular
19 : 5-8	Unfinished Sacrificial Meal	*zebaḥ šᵉlāmîm zābaḥ*	*ʾākal*	Primary	Israelite	Social	Regular
23 : 39-43	Feast of Tabernacles			Primary	Israelite	Festal	Regular
C. Doubtful or unclassifiable passages							
Lev. 18 : 21	Children to Molech	*haʿᵃbîr*	*nātan*	Primary	?Non-Isra.	Individual	?Special
20 : 1-5	Children to Molech		*nātan*				
21 : 6, 8	Unblemished Priesthood	*leḥem ʾīššê*	*qrb*	Primary	Israelite	Priestly	Regular
17, 21, 22							
23 : 9-12	Feast of Firstfruits	*ʿōlâ*	*ʿāśâ*	Primary	Israelite	Festal	Regular
23 : 15-	Feast of Weeks	*minḥâ*	*qrb*	Primary	Israelite	Festal	Regular
18a, 19b		*zebaḥ šᵉlāmîm*					
24 : 5-9	The Shewbread	*ʾīššê ʾazkārâ lᵉbôna*		Secondary	Israelite	?	Regular
23 : 4-8	Feast of Passover	*ʾīššê*	*qrb*	Secondary	Israelite	Festal	Regular
23 : 13-14	Feast of Firstfruits	*niksâʾīššê minḥâ qorbān*	*hēbīʾ*	Secondary	Israelite	Festal	Regular
23 : 18b-19	Feast of Weeks	*niksâ ʾīššê minḥâ ḥaṭṭāʾt*	*ʿāśâ*	Secondary	Israelite	Festal	Regular
23 : 23-25	Feast of Trumpets	*ʾīššê*	*qrb*	Secondary	Israelite	Festal	Regular
23 : 26-32	Day of Atonement	*kippûrîm kipper ʾīššê*	*qrb*	Secondary	Israelite	Festal	Regular
23 : 34-36	Feast of Tabernacles	*ʾīššê*	*qrb*	Secondary	Israelite	Festal	Regular
22 : 18-25	Unblemished Offerings	*nᵉdābâ neder qorbān*	*qrb*	Primary	Israelite	Individual	Regular
	Unblemished Offerings	*zebaḥ šᵉlāmîm ʿōlâ*	*qrb*	Primary	Israelite	Individual	Regular
		nᵉdābâ ʿāśâ ʾīššê	*qrb*				
22 : 27	Eight Days Old	*ʾīššê qorbān*		Primary	Israelite	Individual	Special
22 : 28	Calf and Mother		*šāḥaṭ*				
22 : 29-30	Toda Not left Over	*zebaḥ tôdâ zābaḥ*	*ʾākal*	Primary	Israelite	Individual	Regular
26 : 31	Rejected Sacrifice	*rēaḥ niḥôaḥ*		?Primary	Israelite		Special
23 : 37-38	Summary of Offerings	*minḥâ ʿōlâ ʾīššê*	*qrb*	Secondary	Israelite	Festal	Regular

Reference	Incident	Terms Used		Primary or Secondary	Israelite or Foreign	National or Individual	Special or Regular
A. WHERE A SENSE OF SIN OR SOLEMNITY IS PRESENT							
The Temple Furnishings—A or C, A or B							
Ez. 40 : 38-43	Sacrificial Tables	*ʾāšām ḥaṭṭāʾt ʿōlâ šāḥaṭ* ?*qorbān zebaḥ*		Primary	Israelite	Individual	Regular
42 : 13-14	Chambers for Priests	*ʾāšām ḥaṭṭāʾt minḥâ nûaḥ*		Primary	Israelite	Individual	Regular
46 : 20	Kitchens for Priests	*ʾāšām ḥaṭṭāʾt minḥâ bšl*		Primary	Israelite	Individual	Regular
46 : 24	Kitchens for People	*zebaḥ*	*bšl*	Primary	Israelite	Social	Regular
43 : 18-27	Dedication of Altar	*ḥaṭṭāʾt ḥiṭṭēʾ* *ʿōlâ ʿāśâ ʿālâ*	*kipper* *qrb*	?Primary	Israelite	National	Special
18	Use of the Altar	*ʿōlâ*	*ʿālâ*	Primary	Israelite		Regular
27	Use of the Altar	*šelāmîm ʿōlôt*	*ʿāśâ*				
The Temple Personnel—A or C							
Ez. 44 : 1-3	Prince's Meal	*leḥem*	*ʾākal*	Primary	Israelite	National	Regular
44 : 7	Foreign Servants Excluded	*leḥem*	*qrb*	Primary		Priestly	Regular
44 : 11	Duties of Levites	*ʿōlâ zebaḥ*	*šāḥaṭ*	Primary	Israelite	Priestly	Regular
44 : 15-27	Duties of Zadokites	*ḥaṭṭāʾt leḥem*	*qrb*	Primary	Israelite	Priestly	Regular
44 : 29-31	Priestly Dues	*ʾāšām ḥaṭṭāʾt minḥâ ʾākl* *rēʾšît bikkûrîm terûmâ*		Primary	Israelite	Individual	Regular
45 : 13-17	Responsibility for Offerings						
	— people	*terûmâ* *šelāmîm ʿōlâ minḥâ kipper*	*rûm*	Primary	Israelite	Individual	Regular
	— prince	*nesek ʿōlôt minḥâ* *šelāmîm ʿōlâ minḥâ ḥaṭṭāʾt*	*ʿāśâ*	Primary	Israelite	National	Regular
The Festal Calendar—A (Ch. 45), C (Ch. 46)							
Ez. 45 : 18-20	Two Annual Cleansings	*ḥaṭṭāʾt ḥiṭṭēʾ*	*kipper*	Primary	Israelite	National	Special
45 : 21-24	Feast of Passover	*ḥaṭṭāʾt ʿōlâ minḥâ*	*ʿāśâ*	Primary	Israelite	National	Special
45 : 25	Feast of Tabernacles	*ḥaṭṭāʾt ʿōlâ minḥâ*	*ʿāśâ*	Primary	Israelite	National	Special
46 : 1-5	Prince's Sabbath Offering	*šelāmîm ʿōlâ minḥâ qrb*	*ʿāśâ*	Primary	Israelite	National	Regular
46 : 6-8	Prince's New Moon Offering	*minḥâ*	*ʿāśâ*	Primary	Israelite	National	Regular
46 : 11-12	Prince's Other Offerings	*nedābâ minḥâ* *šelāmîm ʿōlâ*	*ʿāśâ*	Primary	Israelite	National	Regular
46 : 13-15	Daily Offering	*ʿōlâ minḥâ* *ʿōlâ tāmîd*	*ʿāśâ*	Primary	Israelite	National	Regular

REFERENCES TO SACRIFICE IN THE EXILIC AND POST-EXILIC PROPHETS

Reference		Incident	Terms Used	Primary or Secondary	Israelite or Foreign	National or Individual	Special or Regular
A. Where a sense of sin or solemnity is present							
Is.	52 : 13-53 : 12	The Suffering Servant	*'āšām hizzâ*	Prim. 6th C	Israelite	Individual	Special
?	43 : 23-25	Sacrifice not Brought	*zebāḥîm ʿōlôt hēbī' lebônâ minḥâ*	Prim. 6th C	?Israelite	Individual	Regular
?Jon.	1 : 16	Sailors' Sacrifice	*zebaḥ zābaḥ*	Prim. 5th C	?Non-Isra.	Individual	Special
B. Where a sense of sin or solemnity is not present							
Is.	56 : 7	House of Prayer	*ʿōlôt zebāḥîm*	Prim. 5th C	All Peoples	Individual	Regular
Zech.	14 : 21	The Pots of Jerusalem	*bšl zābaḥ*	Prim. 4th C	All Peoples	Individual	Regular
?Is.	62 : 9	Feasting in Sanctuary	*'ākal*	Prim. 5th C	Israelite	Individual	Regular
Is.	65 : 3-4(65 : 11)	Apostate Cult	*mesāk ʿārak zābaḥ qṭr*	Prim. 5th C	?Non-Isra.	Individual	Regular
C. Doubtful or unclassifiable cases							
Is.	57 : 5-7	Apostate Cult	*nesek šapak šāḥaṭ minḥâ zebaḥ zābaḥ ʿālâ*	Prim. 5th C	?Non-Isra.	Individual	Regular
	66 : 17	Apostate Cult	*'ākal*	Prim. 5th C	?Non-Isra.	Individual	Regular
	66 : 3	Degenerate Yahweh Worship	*minḥâ ʿālâ zābaḥ šāḥaṭ lebônâ zkr*	Prim. 5th C	?Israelite	Individual	Regular
	66 : 20	Gentiles' Offering	*minḥâ hēbī'*	Prim. 5th C	Gentile	Individual	Regular
	40 : 16	Lebanon not Sufficient	*ʿōlâ*	Prim. 6th C	?Israelite		
Mal.	1 : 7ff.	Inferior Offerings	*leḥem zābaḥ nāgaš*	Prim. 5th C	Israelite	Individual	Regular
	3 : 8ff.	Tithes and Offerings	*terûmâ maʿašēr hēbī'*	Prim. 5th C	Israelite	Individual	Regular
	1 : 10, 2 : 3	Rejected Sacrifice	*minḥâ ḥaggîm*	Prim. 5th C	Israelite	Individual	Regular
	2 : 12, 13	Rejected Sacrifice	*minḥâ nāgaš*	Prim. 5th C	Israelite	Individual	Regular
	3 : 3-4	Acceptable Offerings	*minḥâ nāgaš*	Prim. 5th C	Israelite	National	Regular
	1 : 11	Gentiles' Offering	*minḥâ muqṭār nâgaš*	Prim. 5th C	?Gentile		Regular
Jon.	2 : 9	Jonah's Vow	*tôdâ nedārîm šlm zābaḥ*	Prim. 5th C	Israelite	Individual	Special
Formal References							
Joel	1 : 9, 13, 2 : 14	Offerings Cut Off	*nesek minḥâ*	Prim. 4th C	Israelite		Regular
Dan.	8 : 11, 12, 13, 11 : 31, 12 : 11		*tāmîd*	Prim. 2nd C	Israelite		Regular
Dan.	9 : 27	Offerings Cut Off	*zebaḥ minḥâ*	Prim. 2nd C	Israelite		Regular
	9 : 21	Evening Oblation	*minḥâ ʿereb*	Prim. 2nd C	Israelite		Regular
	2 : 46	Daniel Worshipped	*minḥâ niḥôah nāsak*	Prim. 2nd C	Gentile	Royal	Special
Is.	60 : 7	Flocks on Altar		Prim. 5th C	Israelite		Regular
Zech.	9 : 11	Blood of Covenant		Prim. 4th C	Israelite	National	
	9 : 15	Blood on Altar		Prim. 4th C	Israelite	?	?
Not Sacrifice							

REFERENCES TO SACRIFICE IN THE WISDOM LITERATURE

Reference	Incident	Terms Used		Primary or Secondary	Israelite or Foreign	National or Individual	Special or Regular
A. Where a sense of sin or solemnity is present							
Job 1 : 5	Job's Offering for Sons	*ʿōlôt*	*ʿālâ*	Archaizing	?Non-Isra.	Individual	Regular
42 : 8	The Offering of Friends	*ʿōlâ*	*ʿālâ*	Archaizing	?Non-Isra.	Individual	Special
B. Where a sense of sin or solemnity is not present							
Prov. 7 : 14	Adulterous Woman's Feast	*zibḥê šelāmîm* *nedārîm*	*šlm*	?	?Israelite	Individual	?Special
17 : 1	House of Feasting	*zebāḥîm*		Early	Israelite	Individual	Regular
C. Doubtful or unclassifiable cases							
Prov. 15 : 8	Sacrifice Depreciated	*zebaḥ*		Early	Israelite	Individual	Regular
21 : 3	Sacrifice Depreciated	*zebaḥ*		Early	Israelite	Individual	Regular
Eccl. 4 : 17(5 : 1)	Sacrifice Depreciated	*zebaḥ*	*nātan*	Late	Israelite	Individual	Regular
?Prov. 21 : 27	The Offering of Wicked	*zebaḥ*	*hēbîʾ*	Early	Israelite	Individual	Regular
Job 22 : 27	Vows Accepted	*nedārîm*	*šlm*	Archaizing	Israelite	Individual	Special
Eccl. 5 : 3(5 : 4)	Against Rash Vows	*neder*	*šlm nādar*	Late	Israelite	Individual	Regular
9 : 2	One Fate to All		*zābaḥ*	Late	Israelite	Individual	Regular

REFERENCES TO SACRIFICE IN EZRA-NEHEMIAH

Reference	Incident	Terms Used		Primary or Secondary	Israelite or Foreign	National or Individual	Special or Regular
A. WHERE A SENSE OF SIN OR SOLEMNITY IS PRESENT							
?Ezra 6 : 9-10	The Royal Edict	*ʿōlôt niḥôaḥ*	*qrb*	?Primary	?Israelite	?National	?Regular
? 10 : 19	Foreign Wives	*ʾāšām*		?Primary	Israelite	Priestly	Special
?Neh. 10 : 33-40	The Compact	*ʿōlôt tāmîd minḥâ tāmîd*					
(32-39)		*haṭṭaʿôt*	*kipper*				
		qorbān ʿēṣîm	*hēbîʾ*	?Primary	Israelite	Individual	Regular
		maʿᵃśrōt rēʾšît					
		bᵉkōrôt tᵉrûmot					
A-B. WHERE BOTH A AND B ELEMENTS ARE PRESENT							
Ezra 6 : 16-18	Dedication of the Temple	*ḥaṭṭāʾâ*	*qrb*	?Primary	Israelite	National	Special
6 : 19-22	Passover and Unleavened Bread	*pesaḥ*	*šāḥaṭ ʾākal*	?Secondary	Israelite	National	Special
Neh. 12 : 30-43	Dedication of Wall	*zᵉbāḥîm*	*zābaḥ*	?	Israelite	National	Special
B. WHERE A SENSE OF SIN OR SOLEMNITY IS NOT PRESENT							
?Neh. 8 : 9-13	Joy of Strength	*(mānôt)*	*ʾākal*	Secondary	Israelite	National	Special
? 8 : 13-18	Feast of Tabernacles			Secondary	Israelite	National	Special
C. DOUBTFUL OR UNCLASSIFIABLE CASES							
Ezra 3							
vss 2-3	Rebuilding of Altar	*ʿōlôt*	*ʿālâ*	Secondary	Israelite	National	Special
4	Feast of Tabernacles	*ʿōlôt*		Secondary	Israelite	National	?
5-6	Restoration of Cultus	*ʿōlâ tāmîd*	*nādab*	Secondary	Israelite	National	Regular
		nᵉdābā ʿōlôt	*ʿālâ*				
Ezra 8 : 35	Offerings on Arrival	*ḥaṭṭāʾt ʿōlôt*	*qrb*	Primary	Israelite	National	Special
7 : 16ff.	Revenues for Ezra	*nᵉdābôt*		Primary	?Israelite	National	Special
		minḥôt niskâ	*qrb*				
Formal References							
Ezra 4 : 2	Sacrifices of Remanent		*zābaḥ*	Secondary	?Non-Isra.		Regular
6 : 3	Place of Sacrifice	*ʾīššê zᵉbāḥîm*	*zābaḥ*	Primary	?Israelite	National	Regular
9 : 4-5	Evening Offering	*minḥâ ʿereb*		Primary	Israelite	National	Regular
Neh. 3 : 34(4 : 2)	Feeble Jews		*zābaḥ*	Primary	?Israelite		
12 : 44-47	Priestly Revenues	*maʿᵃśrōt rēʾšît tᵉrûmôt*		Secondary	Israelite		Regular

Reference	Incident	Terms Used	Primary or Secondary	Israelite or Foreign	National or Individual	Special or Regular
A. WHERE A SENSE OF SIN OR SOLEMNITY IS PRESENT						
1. Chr. 6 : 34(49)	Function of Aaronites	*qeṭôret ʿōlâ* *kipper qṭr*	Peculiar	Israelite	Priestly	Regular
? 21 : 23-30	Ornan's Threshing Floor	*minḥâ ʿōlôt šelāmîm* *zābaḥ ʿālâ*	Parallel	Israelite	National	Regular
?2. Chr. 1 : 6	Solomon at Gibeon	*ʿōlôt* *ʿālâ*	Parallel	Israelite	Royal	Special
? 7 : 4ff.	Dedication of Temple	*zebaḥ šelāmîm minḥâ ʿōlôt* *zābaḥ ʿāśâ*	Parallel	Israelite	National	Special
2. Chr. 28 : 3, 23 (29 : 7)	Ahaz's Sacrifices	*haabîr* (*ʿōlôt* *ʿālâ*)	?	?Israelite	Royal	Special
A-B. WHERE BOTH A AND B ELEMENTS ARE PRESENT						
2. Chr. 29 : 17ff.	Hezekiah's Reform	*ḥaṭṭāʾt ʿōlâ* *ʿālâ*	Peculiar	Israelite	National	Special
29 : 25ff.	Hezekiah's Worship	*ʿōlâ* *ʿālâ*	Peculiar	Israelite	National	Special
30 : 15ff.	Hezekiah's Passover	*ʿōlôt zibḥê šelāmîm* *hēbîʾ zbḥ*	Peculiar	Israelite	National	Special
B. WHERE A SENSE OF SIN OR SOLEMNITY IS NOT PRESENT						
1. Chr. 29 : 20-22	Designation of Solomon	*zebāḥîm ʿōlôt ʿōlâ nesākîm* *zābaḥ ʾākal*	Peculiar	Israelite	National	Special
2. Chr. 23 : 18	Function of Levites	*ʿōlôt* *ʿālâ*	Peculiar	Israelite	Priestly	Regular
?2. Chr. 24 : 8-14	Joash's Temple Repairs	*ʿōlôt* *ʿālâ*	?	Israelite	?National	Special Regular
C. DOUBTFUL OR UNCLASSIFIABLE CASES						
Unclassifiable Narratives						
1. Chr. 15 : 26-16 : 3	Removal of the Ark	*šelāmîm ʿōlôt qrb* *zābaḥ*	Parallel	Israelite	National	Special
2. Chr. 5 : 6	Removal of the Ark	*zbḥ*	Peculiar	Israelite	National	Special
13 : 9	Consecration of Jeroboam's Priests	*mallê*	Peculiar	?Israelite	Priestly	Special
15 : 10	Asa's Thank Offering	*zābaḥ*	Peculiar	Israelite	National	Special
26 : 16-19	Uzziah's Presumption	*qeṭôret* *qṭr*	Peculiar	Israelite	Royal	Special
33 : 16	Manasseh's Reform	*zibḥê šelāmîm tôdâ* *zābaḥ*	Peculiar	Israelite	National	Special
35	Josiah's Passover	*pesāḥîm pesaḥ ʿōlâ* *šāḥaṭ ʿālâ*	?	Israelite	National	Special
Formal References						
1. Chr. 9 : 29-32	Functions of Levites (continued next page)	(*lebônâ sōlet*)	Peculiar	Israelite	Priestly	Regular

REFERENCES TO SACRIFICE IN CHRONICLES (continued)

Reference	Incident	Terms Used		Primary or Secondary	Israelite or Foreign	National or Individual	Special or Regular
C. (continued)							
1. Chr. 16 : 29	A Psalmist's Offering	*minḥâ*	*nāśâ*	Parallel	Israelite	Individual	Regular
16 : 40	Tabernacle at Gibeon	*ʿōlôt*	*ʿālâ*	Peculiar	Israelite	National	Regular
22 : 1	Altar of Burnt Offering	(*ʿōlâ*)		Peculiar	Israelite		
23 : 13	Functions of Aaronites		*qṭr*	Peculiar	Israelite	Priestly	Regular
23 : 27ff.	Functions of Levites	*minḥâ sōlet ʿōlôt*	*ʿālâ*	Peculiar	Israelite	Priestly	Regular
2. Chr. 2 : 4-6	Function of Temple	*qᵉṭôret ʿōlôt*	*qṭr*	Peculiar	Israelite		Regular
4 : 6	Washing of Offering	*ʿōlâ*		Peculiar	Israelite		Regular
7 : 1	Fire from Heaven	*zᵉbāḥîm ʿōlâ*		Peculiar	Israelite	National	Special
7 : 12	Function of Temple	*zebaḥ*		Peculiar	Israelite	National	Regular
8 : 12	Solomon's Sacrifices	*ʿōlâ*	*ʿālâ*	Parallel	Israelite	Royal	Regular
9 : 4	Solomon's Sacrifices	? *ʿōlôt*		Parallel	Israelite	Royal	Regular
11 : 16	Sacrificing at Jerusalem		*zābaḥ*	Parallel	Israelite	Individual	Regular
13 : 10-11	Function of Judah's Priests	*qᵉṭôret ʿōlôt*	*qṭr*	Peculiar	Israelite	Priestly	Regular
18 : 2	Ahab's Hospitality		*zābaḥ*	Peculiar	Israelite	Social	Regular
31 : 2-4	Hezekiah's Provision	*šᵉlāmîm ʿōlâ*		Peculiar	Israelite	Royal	Regular
33 : 6	Manasseh's Apostasy		*haʿᵃbîr*	Peculiar	Israelite	Royal	Special
33 : 24 (34 : 4)	Amon's Apostasy		*zābaḥ zbḥ*	Peculiar	Israelite	Royal	Special

CONCLUSION

Summary of Results

In drawing together the results of this enquiry, one is made aware of the provisional nature of conclusions based upon such fragmentary data. On the whole the probabilities of the case must be allowed the chief weight, and the statistics only employed as subsidiary supporting evidence. The probabilities look different today from what they did to Wellhausen nearly a century ago. In particular the recognition of the closer co-operation of priest and prophet in the cult, the expiatory nature of the seasonal festivals, the centralizing tendencies in early Israel, the developed state of neighbouring cults, and the higher character which is now accorded early Israelite faith, all combine to suggest the probability of an earlier connection between sin and sacrifice than Wellhausen allowed. With this the statistics arrived at in this work agree.

Of the references to sacrifices studied in the early material the results are—

Group A	Group B	Group C	Total
43	21	115	179

There is no discernible difference in proportion in the late period—

Group A	Group B	Group C	Total[1]
42	22	83	147

It might be held to invalidate the method that so large a number of references were unclassified (Group C). While it is true that the distribution of these cases could completely alter the picture, it will be found on examination that formal references account for about half this third group and no classification of these could possibly be made. The rest would naturally be classified according to the dominant theory and would have little value as independent evidence. When deductions are made for secondary narratives and non-Israelite sacrifices the figures are in the same proportion—but six less in both A and B groups in the early period.

[1] Actually 141 passages. The six A-B cases are counted in both A and B groups, and twice in the total.

Closer examination of these A instances is necessary if a sense of sin or solemnity is to be established for regular Israelite sacrifice, and this is provided by the divisions made throughout into individual and national, and regular and special categories.

The A cases in the early period divide as follows—

	Total	Regular	Special
Individual	16	9	7
National	18	9	9

In the late period the proportion is similar—

	Total	Regular	Special
Individual	13	8	5
National	18	8	10

B Group sacrifices not reflecting a sense of sin or solemnity are chiefly social, rather than individual, and in the early period give—

Regular	Special
14	6

and in the late period—

Regular	Special
11	10

When the distribution of the types of sacrifice —*ʿōlâ, minḥâ, zebaḥ* and *šᵉlāmîm*—is investigated, it is found that all types appear in Group A.

The results are[1]—

		Group A	Group B	Group C	Total
ʿŌlâ	Early	20	3	24	47
	Late	23	5	19	47
Minḥâ	Early	8	1	14	23
	Late	14		21	35
Zebaḥ	Early	11	13	48	72
	Late	8	10	25	43
Šᵉlāmîm	Early	7	3	6	16
	Late	7	4	5	16

1 The difference between these small numbers and the much larger figures obtained by a lexical count is due chiefly to the omission of the P statistics, to the deletion of secondary and non-Israelite references and to the count here being by passages rather than individual instances, (several occurrences of

Survey of some Theories

In the light of these figures a number of the theories mentioned in the Introduction can now be reviewed.

It will be recalled that Gray arrived at the conclusion that "while propitiation and expiation as the end of sacrifice were in the earlier periods . . . anything but unknown or even exceptional, it was also far from being constant or even relatively frequent."[1] He thought such sacrifices were chiefly offered on special occasions and in national crises, but the figures show almost as many individual, regular instances of the more solemn type of sacrifice as national and special.

Robertson Smith's theory of the late origin of the *ʿōlâ* does not appear to be true for the Old Testament period. The *ʿōlâ* appears an equal number of times in early and late sources (47) and this remains true, even if the dividing line is made at the time of the beginning of the kingdom (20 times before Samuel, and 27 times in the rest of the pre-exilic material). For the early use of the *ʿōlâ*, and for its probable atoning value, speaks also the Ras Shamra evidence. A *šrp* "burnt offering" is found in the list of sacrifices in I : 4,[2] and in a passage dealing with "forgiveness of soul" (*slḥ npš*) in IX : 7.[3] The ritual in the latter passage is for the king in Tishri, and Gray suggests the comparison to the Hebrew Day of Atonement.[4]

The Israelite *ʿōlâ* seems to have been the most widely used and typical of the Israelite sacrifices, and in no way inferior to the *zebaḥ*. With this agrees the researches of Rendtorff into P's offerings

---

a term in a passage being counted only once). A lexical count based on Lisowsky's concordance yields the following results—

	Early	Late	P	Total
ʿŌlâ	85	84	120	289
Minḥâ	35	46	97	212*
Zebaḥ	83	34	45	162
Zābaḥ (vb)	95	37	1	133
Šᵉlāmîm	23	18	46	87

*includes "gift" 34.

[1] G. B. Gray, *Sacrifice in the Old Testament*, p. 95.
[2] C. H. Gordon, *UH*, p. 129, *UL*, p. 111.
[3] *UH*, p. 132, *UL*, pp. 113-14.
[4] J. Gray, *Legacy of Canaan*, pp. 141ff.

and their pre-history.[1] More than half his space is devoted to the discussion of this one sacrifice, and the conclusion reached that from beginning to end it was the *'ōlâ* that played the decisive role in the Israelite cult.[2]

Wellhausen's theory of the *'ōlâ* as one of the *zebaḥ* victims set aside from the communal meal to be wholly burnt, and therefore occurring in the singular to *zᵉbāḥîm* in the plural[3] is also not borne out by the evidence.[4] *'ōlâ* stands alone 11 times,[5] with only *minḥâ* 5 times and with only *zᵉbāḥîm* 6 times and with only *šᵉlāmîm* 9 times. Wellhausen's statement that

> as a rule, the *'Olah* occurs only in conjunction with *Zebāḥîm*, and when this is the case the latter are in a majority and are always in the plural, while on the other hand the first is frequently in the singular

is not supported even by the 16 passages which he lists as evidence. In only two instances—and both where the text is in question (Exod. 18 : 12 and 1 Kings 8 : 63)—does *'ōlâ* stand in the singular with *zᵉbāḥîm* in the plural. Of two more where *'ōlâ* is singular, in one *zebaḥ* is also singular (2 Kings 5 : 17) and in the other does not occur at all (1 Sam. 13 : 9-12). Only two of the other instances have *'ōlâ* in the singular, but the same context has the plural also (1 Sam. 6 : 14; 2 Sam. 6 : 17). The remaining ten instances all have *'ōlôt* in the plural (Exod. 10 : 25, 24 : 5, 32 : 6; Josh. 8 : 31; Judg. 20 : 26, 21 : 4; 1 Sam. 10 : 8; 2 Sam. 24 : 23-25; 1 Kings 3 : 15; 2 Kings 10 : 24-25).[6]

In 8 cases cited by Wellhausen in his list of 16 it is with *šᵉlāmîm*

---

[1] R. Rendtorff, *Studien zur Geschichte des Opfers im alten Israel*, Habilitationsschrift in Typescript, Göttingen (1953). (Announced for publication in *Wissenschaftliche Monographien*).

[2] Rendtorff thinks 1 Kings 9 : 25 witness to the fact that the *'ōlâ* was already firmly established in the temple ritual at the beginning of the monarchy. Cf. also A. S. Herbert, *Worship in Ancient Israel*, London (1959), pp. 17ff.

[3] J. Wellhausen, *Prolegomena*, p. 70.

[4] This was pointed out long ago by W. Baxter, *Sanctuary and Sacrifice*, London (1895), pp. 364ff.

[5] Wellhausen agreed that there were 11 such references (*Prolegomena*, p. 69), but regarded them as "extraordinary or mythical in their character" (p. 70).

[6] 23 other passages Wellhausen could have cited have *'ōlôt* (pl) 16 times and *'ōlâ* (sing) only 7 times. The latter is probably to be understood as a collective when it occurs in the singular. Further on the *'ōlâ* see p. 53 above.

not *zᵉbāḥîm* that *ʿōlôt* stands, and it cannot be assumed for the early period that *šᵉlāmîm* were a type of *zᵉbāḥîm*. In the Ugaritic literature the *šᵉlāmîm* (*šlmm*) are connected with the burnt offering (*šrp*) in the contexts already cited (I : 4, and IX : 7).[1] A similar position is found in the early Israelite references, where the connections of *šᵉlāmîm* are chiefly with *ʿōlôt*. It was noted on pp. 72, 85 and 107 that the connections with *zᵉbāhîm* were such as to suggest that separate sacrifices were spoken of. This view has been elaborated by Rendtorff,[2] who notes that *šᵉlāmîm* never occur alone, but always with *ʿōlâ*, that they were not brought on joyful occasions, and were probably not a meal at all but a special burnt offering for a festival.[3] This would explain their apparently expiatory or propitiatory character in the passages discussed above,[4] and in the Ugaritic references.[5]

For the theory of Maag, the evidence presents no decisive verdict. There is some decline in the use of the *zebaḥ* in the late period, but

---

[1] In Young's *Concordance of Ugaritic* more than half the total 46 occurrences of the *šlm* root refer to "peace" or "welfare" (frequently in epistles), but 14 refer to an offering. These occur in 8 contexts—in lists of offerings in 3 : 17, 52; 5 : 7; 9 : 7, 15 and 1 : 4, 8 (with *šrp* in the last two), and in narrative contexts only in *ʿnt* III : 13; IV : 53, 74 "pour a *šlm* into the midst of the earth" and *krt* 130, 131, 275 "take *šlmm* in peace." In the former of the narrative passages the offerings are liquid and can be poured. The following words *ʾarbdd* are rendered by Gordon (*UH*, p. 188, *UL*, pp. 19-21) "libation," but by Driver, *Canaanite Myths and Legends*, Edinburgh (1956), p. 89 and Glossary, p. 135 "honey (from a pot)." Driver also renders *Baal* V, ii : 32 (*ʿnt* 2 : 31-32) by "poured out (like) the oil of a peace-offering from a bowl" (*ibid.*, p. 85), but Gordon leaves the text of *šlm* incomplete (*UH*, p. 187, *UL*, p. 18). It is suggested that pipes found upright in the ground with pots beneath were probably used for this rite as part of a fertility ritual. (See A. S. Kapelrud, *Baal in the Ras Shamra Texts*, Copenhagen (1952), pp. 19-20, and also for the justification of the translations.)

[2] In the work cited. (Cf. also his article "Opfer," *EKL* II, col. 1693.)

[3] *Ibid.*, pp. 68ff. The relation of this *šᵉlāmîm* offering to P's *zibḥê šᵉlāmîm* remains a matter for investigation.

[4] Pp. 72, 93.

[5] This seems the best explanation of Keret 130, 275. V. Maag, *Text, Wortschatz und Begriffswelt des Buches Amos*, p. 254 "soothing offering." Urie (*op. cit.*, pp. 75-77) argued for this meaning in all the references. N. H. Snaith, however, ("Sacrifices in the Old Testament," p. 314) claims that the miscellaneous objects listed in this context—silver, gold, a share of an estate, slaves, three horses and a chariot—are given as a bribe to Keret, and that since no slaughter was involved the translation of *šᵉlāmîm* should be "recompense" as in Deut. 32 : 35 and Is. 59 : 18. It is not certain, however, that the *šᵉlāmîm* are not additional to the other gifts.

nothing like its total discontinuance (the noun occurs 34 times and the verb 37 times in late sources against 83 and 95 times in the earlier). What is remarkable, is the almost complete non-occurrence of the verb *zābaḥ* in P (only once), although the noun occurs 45 times. The reasons for this belong to the study of P, but the fact must be noted for the support it gives to the suggestion that the *zebaḥ* lost its old character of a communion meal at Josiah's Reform.

At a number of points above attention was drawn to pre-Josianic references, which seemed in contradiction to the principle that all slaughter up to that time was sacrifice. Although their number is small in comparison with the regular usage (5 out of 95 uses of the verb *zābaḥ* in the early literature—Num. 22 : 40; 1 Sam. 28 : 24; 1 Kings 19 : 21; Ez. 34 : 3, 39 : 17 (also the noun in 1 Sam. 9 : 13; Is. 34 : 6; Jer. 46 : 10; Zeph. 1 : 7) and in some other incidents without this verb—Gen. 18 : 6, 27 : 9; Exod. 22 : 1; 1 Sam. 25 : 11) they should not be lost sight of in view of the possibility of a secular use of the verb in the Canaanite literature.[1]

It was not found possible to exclude the solemn note from the *zebaḥ* in the early period (11 with, and 13 without) any more than the late (8 with, 10 without). A similar use of *dbḥ* in an expiatory sense is found in Ugaritic (Text 2 : 15, 24, 32, 33).[2] Despite this it remains true that the instances where the solemn element is lacking are chiefly *zᵉbāḥîm*.[3]

---

[1] A. van Selms argues for the rendering of *dbḥ* as "meal" not "sacrifice" in 51, III, 17-22 (*UH*, p. 140, *UL*, p. 30) on the grounds that a reference to a sacrifice of shame could only mean sacrificial prostitution, which would be out of place (*Marriage and Family Life in Ugaritic Literature*, London (1954), pp. 79-80). Snaith thinks that "the verb has to do with slaughtering and the noun with food and a feast." He continues "there are roughly 20 instances, most of which refer in a general way to a slaughtered victim. But there are some cases which definitely refer to a feast. These are Keret II i 40, II i 60, III iv 27 and 28, III vi 5; Rephaim I i 10; Baal VI iv 28ff. There are three references to sacred meals, two of them definitely in a temple (Aqhat II i 32 and II ii 21), and one probably in a temple . . ." ("Sacrifices in the Old Testament," p. 313 (references as in Driver, *Canaanite Myths and Legends*)).

[2] *UH*, p. 129, *UL*. pp. 110-11.

[3] Further on *zebaḥ* see above pp. 56, 57, 74, 105, 108f., 126, 131, 207, and for other sacrificial terms as follows—*minḥâ* p. 50, *kālîl* p. 104, *ʾāšām* p. 102, *ḥaṭṭāʾt* p. 131, *qᵉṭōret* p. 124, *tᵉrûmâ* pp. 206f., *ʾiššê* pp. 210f..

Limits of the Enquiry

On the question of the origin of sacrifice, the limitations of this work prevent any pronouncement. The chief modern theories—those of Wilhelm Schmidt, Meuli and Jensen are surveyed by Vorbilcher.[1] While this survey shows just how far the discussion has moved since Robertson Smith, the material cannot be directly applied to Israel in the historic period without caution. It is with the rites of Israel as they appear in the Old Testament, rather than with their origin, or the original meaning of their terms that the study of Old Testament sacrifice must chiefly deal.[2] The task of separating elements from the nomadic and sedentary inheritances of Israel is interesting, but speculative and has not been attempted.

No theory of the nature of Israelite sacrifice is offered here. The element of solemnity in the approach to the deity, which has been underlined would support expiatory or propitiatory ideas, but to draw a distinction between expiation and propitiation would require a theological precision which the fragmentary nature of the material could hardly sustain.[3] It is readily admitted that for the theory of sacrifice resort must be made to the Priestly Code.[4] The exclusion of this work from the present treatment is not because it is not important to the subject, but because its importance for earlier times could only be established by showing independently that its chief allegedly late element is not late but early.[5] If this much at least has been gained, enquiry into the pre-history of P's laws on sacrifice can proceed, and in this way finally a more satisfactory picture of Israelite sacrifice, agreeable to all the evidence, can be drawn.

---

[1] A. Vorbilcher, *op. cit.*

[2] So G. B. Gray, *Sacrifice in the Old Testament,* pp. 1ff., 55ff. cf. also L. Köhler, *Old Testament Theology,* pp. 182, 186 and A. C. Welch, *Prophet and Priest in Old Israel,* pp. 139ff.

[3] This involves a total "theology" of the nature of man and God in the Old Testament and the relation between them.

[4] See the writer's article "Sacrifice and Offering," *New Bible Dictionary,* IVF, London (1962) pp. 1113-1122.

[5] The dating of the P Code itself is a much more complicated question, to the elucidation of which the study of sacrifice is only one of a number of enquiries, which must be undertaken.

APPENDIX I

ABBREVIATIONS

General

AV	Authorized Version (King James, 1611)
BH	Biblia Hebraica (ed.) R. Kittel ([3]1937)
(ed.)	Editor
esp.	especially
E.T.	English Translation
GS	Gesammelte Studien
KS	Kleine Schriften
LXX	Septuagint (ed.) A. Rahlfs ([3]1949)
MT	Massoretic Text
N.F.	Neue Folge
N.S.	New Series
RSV	Revised Standard Version (1952)

Periodicals

AJSL	*American Journal of Semitic Languages and Literature*, Chicago
ARW	*Archiv für Religionswissenschaft*, Leipzig
BASOR	*Bulletin of the American Schools of Oriental Research*, New Haven
Bibl.	*Biblica*, Rome
BJRL	*Bulletin of the John Rylands Library*, Manchester
EvTh	*Evangelische Theologie*, München
Exp	*Expositor*, London
ExpT	*Expository Times*, Edinburgh
HTR	*Harvard Theological Review*, Cambridge (Mass)
HUCA	*Hebrew Union College Annual*, Cincinnati
JBL	*Journal of Biblical Literature*, New York
JBR	*Journal of Bible and Religion*, Boston
JLH	*Jahrbuch für Liturgik und Hymnologie*, Kassel
JNES	*Journal of Near Eastern Studies*, Chicago
JRAI	*Journal of the Royal Anthropological Institute*, London
JSS	*Journal of Semitic Studies*, Manchester
JTS	*Journal of Theological Studies*, Oxford
MGWJ	*Monatschrift für Geschichte und Wissenschaft des Judentums*, Breslau
OTS	*Oudtestamentische Studiën*, Leiden
PEQ	*Palestine Exploration Quarterly*, London
RB	*Revue Biblique*, Paris
RHLR	*Revue d'histoire et de littérature religieuses*, Paris
RHPhR	*Revue d'histoire et de philosophie religieuses*, Strassburg
RHR	*Revue de l'histoire des religions*, Paris
RThPh	*Revue de théologie et de philosophie*, Lausanne

SJT	*Scottish Journal of Theology*, Edinburgh
ThLZ	*Theologische Literaturzeitung*, Leipzig
ThR	*Theologische Rundschau*, Tübingen
ThStKr	*Theologische Studien und Kritiken*, Berlin
ThT	*Theology Today*, Princeton
ThZ	*Theologische Zeitschrift*, Basel
VT	*Vetus Testamentum*, Leiden
VTSuppl.	*Supplements to Vetus Testamentum*, Leiden
ZÄS	*Zeitschrift für Ägyptische Sprache und Altertumskunde*, Leipzig
ZAW	*Zeitschrift für die Alttestamentliche Wissenschaft*, Giessen
ZDPV	*Zeitschrift des Deutschen Palästina-Vereins*, Leipzig
ZSTh	*Zeitschrift für Systematische Theologie*, Gütersloh
ZThK	*Zeitschrift für Theologie und Kirche*, Freiburg

Encyclopaedias, Dictionaries etc.

ANET	*Ancient Near Eastern Texts* (ed.) J. B. Pritchard, Princeton ([2]1955)
CathEnc	*Catholic Encyclopedia*, London
BDB	*A Hebrew and English Lexicon of the Old Testament* by F. Brown, S. R. Driver and C. A. Briggs, Oxford (1907)
Davidson	*Hebrew Syntax* by A. B. Davidson, Edinburgh ([3]1901)
DB	*Dictionary of the Bible* (ed.) James Hastings, 5 vols, Edinburgh
DB(One Vol.)	*Dictionary of the Bible* (ed.) James Hastings, One Volume, New York (1909)
EB	*Encyclopaedia Biblica* (ed.) T. K. Cheyne and J. Black, London
EBrit	*Encyclopaedia Britannica*
EKL	*Evangelisches Kirchenlexikon* (ed.) H. Brunotte and O. Weber, Göttingen (1955)
ERE	*Encyclopaedia of Religion and Ethics* (ed.) James Hastings, Edinburgh
Gesenius-Kautzsch	*Hebrew Grammar* (ed.) A. Cowley, Oxford ([2]1910)
ISBE	*International Standard Bible Encyclopaedia* (ed.) James Orr, Grand Rapids
Köhler	*Lexicon in Veteris Libros* by L. Köhler and W. Baumgartner, Leiden (1953)
Lisowsky	*Konkordanz zum hebräischen Alten Testament* by G. Lisowsky, Stuttgart (1958)
PRE	*Realencyklopädie für protestantische Theologie und Kirche*, 24 vols, Leipzig ([3]1896-1913)
RGG	*Die Religion in Geschichte und Gegenwart*, Tübingen ([2]1927-1932)
UH	*Ugaritic Handbook* by C. H. Gordon, Rome (1947)
UL	*Ugaritic Literature* by C. H. Gordon, Rome (1949)

Commentaries (Series)

ATD *Das Alte Testament Deutsch* (ed.) V. Herntrich and A. Weiser, Göttingen

Genesis	G. von Rad ([5]1958)

Exodus	M. Noth (1959)
Joshua-Judges	H. W. Hertzberg (1953)
Samuel	H. W. Hertzberg (1956)
Psalms	A. Weiser (^{4}1955)
Isaiah I	V. Herntrich (1950)
Jeremiah	A. Weiser (1952-1955)
Ezekiel	W. Eichrodt (1959-)
Minor Prophets I	A. Weiser (1949)
Minor Prophets II	K. Elliger (1950)

Bibelhilfe *Bibelhilfe für die Gemeinde* (ed.) E. Stange, Kassel

Isaiah I	H. W. Hertzberg (^{2}1952)

BK *Biblischer Kommentar* (ed.) M. Noth, Neukirchen

Psalms	H. J. Kraus (1958-1960)
Ezekiel	W. Zimmerli (1959-)
Minor Prophets	H. W. Wolff (1956-)

CB *Century Bible* (ed.) W. F. Adeney, Edinburgh

Leviticus-Numbers	A. R. S. Kennedy (n.d.)
Samuel	A. R. S. Kennedy (1905)

CamB *Cambridge Bible* (ed.) A. F. Kirkpatrick, Cambridge

Leviticus and Numbers	A. T. Chapman and A. W. Streane (1914)
Deuteronomy	G. A. Smith (1918)
Isaiah	J. Skinner (^{2}1915-1917)

ClarB *Clarendon Bible* (ed.) T. Strong, H. Wild and G. H. Box, Oxford

Genesis (In the Beginning)	S. H. Hooke (1947)

ExpB *Expositor's Bible* (ed.) W. R. Nicoll

Deuteronomy	A. Harper (repr. Grand Rapids, 1947)
Isaiah	G. A. Smith (Rev. ed. New York, 1927)

HAT *Handbuch zum Alten Testament* (ed.) O. Eissfeldt, Tübingen

Exodus	G. Beer (1939)
Joshua	M. Noth (^{2}1953)
Psalms	H. Schmidt (1934)
Jeremiah	W. Rudolph (1947)
Ezekiel	A. Bertholet (1936)
	G. Fohrer (1955)
Minor Prophets	T. H. Robinson (1938)
	F. Horst (1938)

HK *Handkommentar zum Alten Testament* (ed.) W. Nowack, Göttingen

Genesis	H. Gunkel (^{5}1922)
Exodus-Numbers	B. Baentsch (1933)
Deuteronomy	C. Steuernagel (^{2}1923)
Joshua	C. Steuernagel (^{2}1923)
Judges-Samuel	W. Nowack (1902)
Psalms	H. Gunkel (^{4}1926)
Isaiah	B. Duhm (^{4}1922)
Minor Prophets	W. Nowack (^{3}1922)

HS *Die Heilige Schrift des Alten Testamentes* (ed.) F. Feldmann and H. Herkenne, Bonn

Genesis	P. Heinisch (1930)

Deuteronomy	H. Junker (1933)
Psalms	H. Herkenne (1936)
Isaiah	J. Fischer (1937-1939)
Jeremiah	F. Nötscher (1934)

HSAT *Die Heilige Schrift des Alten Testaments* (ed.) E. Kautzsch and A. Bertholet, Tübingen ([4]1922-1923)

Deuteronomy	K. Marti
Judges	R. Kittel
Samuel	R. Kittel
Kings	O. Eissfeldt
Psalms	A. Bertholet
Isaiah	H. Guthe
Jeremiah	J. Rothstein
Amos, Hosea, Micah	H. Guthe

IB *The Interpreter's Bible* (ed.) G. A. Buttrick, New York

Exodus	J. Rylaarsdam (I, 1952)
Deuteronomy	G. E. Wright (II, 1953)
Joshua	J. Bright (II, 1953)
Judges	J. M. Myers (II, 1953)
Samuel	G. B. Caird (II, 1953)
Kings	N. H. Snaith (III, 1954)
Ezra-Nehemiah	R. A. Bowman (III, 1954)
Psalms	W. McCullough (IV, 1955)
	W. R. Taylor (IV, 1955)
Isaiah I	R. B. Y. Scott (V, 1956)
Isaiah II	J. Muilenburg (V, 1956)
Jeremiah	J. P. Hyatt (V, 1956)
	S. R. Hopper
Ezekiel	H. G. May (VI, 1956)
	E. L. Allen
Micah	R. Wolfe (VI, 1956)
Zephaniah	C. Taylor (VI, 1956)

ICC *The International Critical Commentary* (ed.) S. R. Driver, A. Plummer and C. A. Briggs, Edinburgh

Genesis	J. Skinner ([2]1930)
Numbers	G. B. Gray (1903)
Deuteronomy	S. R. Driver ([3]1902)
Judges	G. F. Moore (1895)
Samuel	H. P. Smith (1899)
Kings	J. A. Montgomery (1951)
Psalms	C. A. Briggs (1906-1907)
Isaiah I	G. B. Gray (1912)
Ezekiel	G. A. Cooke (1936)
Amos-Hosea	W. R. Harper (1905)
Micah, Zephaniah	J. M. P. Smith (1911)

JerusB *La Sainte Bible en francais sous la direction de l'École Biblique de Jérusalem*, Paris

Deuteronomy	H. Cazelles (1950)
Samuel	R. de Vaux (1953)
Isaiah	R. Auvray (1951)
Jeremiah	A. Gelin (1951)

KAT *Kommentar zum Alten Testament* (ed.) E. Sellin, Leipzig

Genesis	O. Procksch (^{2} & ^{3}1924)
Deuteronomy	E. König (1917)
Samuel	W. Caspari (1926)
Isaiah I	O. Procksch (1930)
Isaiah II	P. Volz (1932)
Jeremiah	P. Volz (^{2}1928)
Minor Prophets	E. Sellin (1922)

KD *Biblischer Commentar über das Alte Testament* (ed.) C. F. Keil and F. Delitzsch, Leipzig, repr. Grand Rapids

Deuteronomy	C. F. Keil (repr. 1949)
Psalms	F. Delitzsch (repr. 1949)

KEH *Kurzgefasstes exegetisches Handbuch zum Alten Testament*, Leipzig

Numbers-Joshua	A. Dillmann (^{2}1886)
Isaiah	A. Dillmann (^{5}1890)

KHC *Kurzer Hand-Commentar zum Alten Testament* (ed.) K. Marti, Tübingen

Genesis	H. Holzinger (1898)
Exodus	H. Holzinger (1900)
Deuteronomy	A. Bertholet (1899)
Joshua	H. Holzinger (1901)
Samuel	K. Budde (1902)
Kings	I. Benzinger (1899)
Psalms	B. Duhm (1899)
Isaiah	K. Marti (1900)
Jeremiah	B. Duhm (1901)
Ezekiel	A. Bertholet (1897)
Minor Prophets	K. Marti (1904)

Polychrome *Polychrome Bible* (ed.) P. Haupt (E.T. of *Sacred Books of O.T.*)

Psalms	J. Wellhausen (1898)

Proph. *Prophezei* (*Schweizerisches Bibelwerk für die Gemeinde,*) Zürich

Genesis I	W. Zimmerli (1943)

SAT *Die Schriften des Alten Testaments* (ed.) H. Gressmann, Göttingen

Die Anfänge Israels	H. Gressmann (1, 2, ^{2}1922)
Die älteste Geschichtsschreibung und Prophetie Israels	H. Gressmann (2, 1, ^{2}1921)
Lyrik (Psalmen, usw)	W. Staerk (3, 1, ^{2}1920)
Die grossen Propheten	H. Schmidt (2,2, 1915)

SBOT *The Sacred Books of the Old Testament* (ed.) P. Haupt, Leipzig

Samuel	K. Budde (1894)
Kings	B. Stade (1904)

SZ *Kurzgefasster Kommentar zu den heiligen Schriften Alten und Neuen Testamentes* (ed.) Strack and Zöckler, Nördlingen, München

Samuel-Kings	A. Klostermann (1887)
Jeremiah	C. Orelli (^{3}1905)
Minor Prophets	C. Orelli (^{3}1908)

WC *The Westminster Commentaries* (ed.) W. Lock and D. C. Simpson, London

Genesis	S. R. Driver (^{15}1948)

Commentaries (One Volume)

AbingdonC *The Abingdon Bible Commentary* (ed.) F. C. Eiselen, E. Lewis and D. G. Downey, New York (1929)
Judges — W. O. E. Oesterley
Amos — H. W. Robinson

CatholicC *A Catholic Commentary on Holy Scripture,* London 1953.
Exodus — E. Power

ConciseC *Concise Bible Commentary* (ed.) W. K. Lowther Clarke, London (1952)

GoreC *A New Commentary on Holy Scripture* (ed.) C. Gore, H. L. Goudge and A. Guillaume, London (1928)
The Prophets of Israel — F. C. Burkitt
Isaiah — L. Elliott Binns

PeakeC *A Commentary on the Bible* (ed.) A. S. Peake, London ([2]1937)
Isaiah — A. S. Peake

APPENDIX II

BIBLIOGRAPHY

Commentaries (on Individual Books)

(For One Volume Commentaries and Commentaries in Series see Appendix I)
Bewer, J. A. *The Prophets* (*Harper's Annotated Bible*) New York, 1955.
Boutflower, C. *The Book of Isaiah. Chapters I-XXXIX*, London, 1930.
Burney, C. F. *Notes on the Hebrew Text of the Books of Kings*, Oxford, 1903.
— *The Book of Judges*, London, 1918.
Cheyne, T. K. *Prophecies of Isaiah*, 2 vols, London, 1880.
Cornill, C. H. *Das Buch Jeremia*, Leipzig, 1905.
Cripps, R. S. *A Critical and Exegetical Commentary on the Book of Amos*, London, [2]1955.
Delitzsch, F. *Commentar über die Genesis*, Leipzig, [4]1872.
Driver, S. R. *The Book of the Prophet Jeremiah*, London, 1906.
— *Notes on the Hebrew Text and the Topography of the Books of Samuel*, Oxford, [2]1913.
Graf, K. H. *Der Prophet Jeremia*, Leipzig, 1862.
Hertz, J. H. (ed.) *The Pentateuch and Haftorahs*, 5 vols, London, 1929-1935.
Hölscher, G. *Hesekiel, der Dichter und das Buch*, Giessen, 1924.
Irwin, W. A. *The Problem of Ezekiel*, Chicago, 1943.
Kissane, E. J. *The Book of Isaiah*, 2 vols, Dublin, 1941-1943.
— *The Book of Psalms*, 2 vols, Dublin, 1953-1954.
König, E. *Die Genesis*, Gütersloh, [2] & [3]1918.
— *Das Buch Jesaja*, Gütersloh, 1926.
— *Die Psalmen*, Gütersloh, 1927.
Leslie, E. A. *The Psalms*, New York, 1949.
Maag, V. *Text, Wortschatz und Begriffswelt des Buches Amos*, Leiden, 1951.
Nyberg, H. S. *Studien zum Hoseabuche*, Uppsala, 1935.
Oesterley, W. O. E. *The Psalms*, London, 1939.
Schulz, A. *Die Bücher Samuel*, Vol. I, Münster, 1919.
Scott, M. *The Message of Hosea*, London, 1921.
Skinner, J. *Prophecy and Religion*, Cambridge, 1922.
Smith, G. A. *Jeremiah*, New York, [4]1929.
Snaith, N. H. *Book of Amos*, London, 1946.
Tuch, F. *Commentar über die Genesis*, Halle, [2]1871.
Weiser, A. *Die Profetie des Amos*, Giessen, 1929.
Wellhausen, J. *Der Text der Bücher Samuel*, Göttingen, 1871.
— *Die kleinen Propheten übersetzt, mit Noten*, Berlin, 1892.

General

Albright, W. F. "Archaeology and the Date of the Hebrew Conquest of Palestine," BASOR No. 58, 1935, pp. 10-18.
— *From the Stone Age to Christianity*, Baltimore, [2]1946.
— *Archaeology and the Religion of Israel*, Baltimore, [3]1953.
— *Archaeology of Palestine*, Middlesex (Penguin Books), [3]1956.
— "Some Remarks on the Song of Moses in Deuteronomy xxxii," *VT* X, 1959, pp. 339-46.

Allis, O. *The Five Books of Moses*, Philadelphia, ²1949.
Alt, A. *Kleine Schriften zur Geschichte des Volkes Israel*, 2 vols, München, 1953.
— "Der Gott der Väter," 1929, now in *ibid.*, Vol. I, pp. 1-78.
— "Die Wallfahrt von Sichem nach Bethel," *ibid.*, pp. 79-88.
— "Die Staatenbildung der Israeliten in Palästina," *ibid.*, Vol. II, pp. 1-65.
— "Das Gottesurteil auf dem Karmel," *ibid.*, pp. 135-49.
— "Die Heimat des Deuteronomiums," *ibid.*, pp. 250-75.
— "Zum Gott der Väter," *PJB* XXXVI, 1940, pp. 100-103.
Anastasius the Sinaite, *Viae Dux*, Ch. XXII in Migne J. P. (ed.) *Patrologia Series graeca*, LXXXIX, 1865, p. 286.
Anderson, G. W. "A Study of Micah 6 : 1-8," *SJT* IV, 1951, pp. 191-97.
Anderson, R. "The Role of the Desert in Israelite Thought," *JBR* XXVII, 1959, pp. 41-44.
Auerbach, E. "Die grosse Überarbeitung der biblischen Bücher," *Congress Volume Copenhagen* 1953 (*VTSuppl.* I), 1953, pp. 1-10.
Barclay, W. *Letter to the Hebrews*, Philadelphia, ²1957.
Barton, G. A. *A Sketch of Semitic Origins*, New York, 1902.
— *The Religion of Israel*, New York, 1918.
— "A Comparison of Some Features of Hebrew and Babylonian Ritual," *JBL* XLVI, 1927, pp. 79-89.
— *Hamitic and Semitic Origins*, Oxford, 1934.
Baumann, E. "Das Lied Mose's (Dt XXXII 1-43) auf seine gedankliche Geschlossenheit untersucht," *VT* VI, 1956, pp. 414-24.
Baumann, H. "Nyama, die Rachemacht," *Paideuma* IV, 1950, pp. 191-230.
Baumgartner, W. "Ras Schamra und das Alte Testament I," *ThR* XII, 1940, pp. 163-88, II, *ibid.*, XIII, 1941, pp. 1-20, 85-102, 157-183.
— "Ugaritische Probleme und ihre Tragweite für das Alte Testament," *ThZ* III, 1947, pp. 81-100.
Baxter, W. L. *Sanctuary and Sacrifice*, London, 1895.
Bea, A. "Kinderopfer für Moloch oder für Jahwe?" *Biblica* XVIII, 1937, pp. 95-107.
Beek, M. A. "The Religious Background of Amos II: 6-8," *OTS* V, 1948, pp. 132-41.
Beer, G. "Die Bitterkräuter beim Paschafest," *ZAW* XXXI, 1911, pp. 152-53.
— *Pesachim: Die Mischna*, Giessen, 1912.
Béguerie, Ph. "La vocation d'Isaie," *Études sur les prophètes d'Israël* Lectio Divina 14, Paris, 1954, pp. 11-51.
Bennett, W. H. "Sin (Hebrew and Jewish)," *ERE* XI, 1920, pp. 556-60.
Bennewitz, F. *Die Sünde im alten Israel*, Leipzig, 1907.
Bentzen, A. "The Cultic Use of the Story of the Ark," *JBL* LXVII, 1948, pp. 37-53.
— "The Ritual Background of Amos i 2-ii 16," *OTS* VIII, 1950, pp. 85-99.
Benzinger, I. *Hebräische Archäologie*, Tübingen, ³1927.
Berguer, G. "Les origines psychologiques du rite sacrificiel," *RThPh* N.S. XVII, 1929, pp. 5-27.
Berry, G. R. "The Ritual Decalogue," *JBL* XLIV, 1925, pp. 39-43.
Bertholet, A. *A History of Hebrew Civilization*, E. T. London, 1926.
— "Opfer: I Religionsgeschichtlich," *RGG* IV, ²1930, cols. 704-711.
— "Zum Verständnis des alttestamentlichen Opfergedankens," *JBL* XLIX, 1930, pp. 218-233.
— *Der Sinn des Kultischen Opfers*, Berlin, 1942.

Bewer, J. A. "Critical Notes on Old Testament Passages," *Old Testament and Semitic Studies in Memory of W. R. Harper* Vol. II, Chicago, 1908, pp. 211-14.
— "The Composition of Judges, Chaps 20, 21," *AJSL* XXX, 1913-1914, pp. 149-65.
— *The Literature of the Old Testament*, New York, Rev. ed. 1933.
— "Beiträge zur Exegese des Buches Ezechiel," *ZAW* LXIII, 1951, pp. 193-201.
— "Textual and Exegetical Notes on the Book of Ezekiel," *JBL* LXXII, 1953, pp. 158-68.
Beyerlin, W. *Die Kulttraditionen Israels in der Verkündigung des Propheten Micha*, Göttingen, 1959.
Böhl, F. M. T. de L. "Das Zeitalter Abrahams," *Opera Minora*, Groningen, 1953, pp. 26-49.
Boschwitz, F. *Julius Wellhausen, Motive und Massstäbe seiner Geschichtsschreibung*, Dissertation, Marburg, 1938.
Brandt, W. "Zur Bestreichung mit Blut", *ZAW* XXXIII, 1913, pp. 80-81.
Brekelmans, C. "Exodus XVIII and the Origins of Yahwism in Israel," *OTS* X, 1954, pp. 215-24.
Bright, J. *A History of Israel*, Philadelphia, 1959.
Brinker, R. *The Influence of Sanctuaries in Early Israel*, Manchester, 1946.
Brock-Utne, A. "Eine religionsgeschichtliche Studie zu dem ursprünglichen Passahopfer," *ARW* XXXI, 1934, pp. 272-78.
— "Die religionshistorischen Voraussetzungen der Kain-Abel-Geschichte," *ZAW* LIV, 1936, pp. 202-39.
Buber, M. *Moses*, Oxford, 1946.
— "Die Erzählung von Sauls Königswahl," *VT* VI, 1956, pp. 113-73.
Buren, E. D. van. "Places of Sacrifice," *Iraq* XIV, 1952, pp. 76-92.
Burkitt, F. C. "Micah 6 and 7 a Northern Prophecy," *JBL* XLV, 1926, pp. 159-61.
— "The Prophets of Israel," *GoreC*, 1928, pp. 419-32.
Burney, C. F. "A Theory of the Developement of Israelite Religion in Early Times," *JTS* IX, 1908, pp. 321-52.
— *Israel's Settlement in Canaan*, London, 1918.
Caspari, W. "Kultpsalm 50," *ZAW* XLV, 1927, pp. 254-66.
Chapman, A. T. *Introduction to the Pentateuch*, Cambridge, 1911.
Chary, Th. *Les prophètes et le culte à partir de l'exil*, Tournai, 1955.
Cheyne, T. K. *Jewish Religious Life after the Exile*, New York, 1898.
— "Hiel," *EB* II, 1901, cols. 2062-63.
Closen, G. E. "Der Dämon Sünde," *Biblica* XVI, 1935, pp. 431-42.
Cook, S. A. (ed.) W. Robertson Smith, *Lectures on the Religion of the Semites*, London, [3]1927.
— "The Theophanies of Gideon and Manoah," *JTS* XXVIII, 1927, pp. 368-53.
— *The "Truth" of the Bible*, Cambridge, 1938.
Cooke, G. A. *A Textbook of North-Semitic Inscriptions*, Oxford, 1903.
Cowley, A. *Aramaic Papyri of the Fifth Century B.C.*, Oxford, 1923.
Cross, F. M. and Freedman, D. M. "The Blessing of Moses," *JBL* LXVII, 1948, pp. 191-210.
Cross, L. B. "Sacrifice in the Old Testament," Grensted, L. W. (ed.) *The Atonement in History and in Life*, London, 1929, pp. 33-64.
Curtiss, S. I. *Primitive Semitic Religion Today*, Chicago, 1902.

Curtiss, S. I. "Discoveries of a Vicarious Element in Primitive Semitic Sacrifice," *Exp* 6th series, VI, 1902, pp. 128-34, "The Semitic Sacrifice of Reconciliation," VI, 1902, pp. 454-62, "Some Religious Usages of the Dhîâb and Ruala Arabs and their Old Testament Parallels," IX, 1904, pp. 275-85, "The Origin of Sacrifice among the Semites as deduced from Facts gathered among Syrians and Arabs," X, 1904, pp. 461-72, "Survivals of Ancient Semitic Religion in Syrian Centres," XI, 1905, pp. 415-431.

Daiches, S. "The Meaning of 'Sacrifices' in the Psalms," Epstein, I., Levine, E. and Roth, C. (ed.) *Essays in Honour of the Very Rev. Dr. J. H. Hertz,* London, 1942, pp. 97-109.

Dalman, G. *Arbeit und Sitte in Palästina,* 7 vols, Gütersloh, 1928-1942.

Davidson, A. B. "Covenant," *DB* I, 1898, pp. 509-515.

— "The Word "Atone" in the Extra-Ritual Literature," *Exp* 5th series X, 1899, pp. 92-103.

— *The Theology of the Old Testament,* Edinburgh, 1904.

Dewar, L. "The Biblical Use of the Term 'Blood'," *JTS* N.S. IV, 1953, pp. 204-208.

Dhorme, E. "Le sacrifice accadien à propos d'un ouvrage récent," *RHR* CVII-CVIII, 1933, pp. 107-125.

— *L'évolution religieuse d'Israël.* Vol. I *La religion des Hébreux nomades,* Bruxelles, 1937.

Dobbie, R. "Deuteronomy and the Prophetic Attitude to Sacrifice," *SJT* XII, 1959, pp. 68-82.

— "Sacrifice and Morality in the Old Testament," *ExpT* LXX, 1959, pp. 297-300.

Driver, G. R. *Canaanite Myths and Legends,* Edinburgh, 1956.

— "Three Technical Terms in the Pentateuch," *JSS* I, 1956, pp. 97-105.

Driver, S. R. "Offer, Offering, Oblation," *DB* III, 1900, pp. 587-89.

— "Expiation and Atonement (Hebrew)," *ERE* V, 1912, pp. 653-59.

Dronkert, K. *De Molochdienst in het Oude Testament,* Leiden, 1953.

Dumermuth, F. "Zur deuteronomischen Kulttheologie und ihren Voraussetzungen," *ZAW* LXX, 1958, pp. 59-98.

Dupont-Sommer, A. *Les inscriptions araméennes de Sfiré* (Stèles I & II), Paris, 1958.

Dussaud, R. *Le sacrifice en Israël et chez les Phéniciens,* Paris, 1914.

— *Les origines cananéennes du sacrifice israélite,* Paris, 1921. The Ugaritic material referred to in the text is incorporated in the second edition, 1941.

— "Les trois premiers versets de la Genèse," *RHR* C, 1930, pp. 123-41.

— "Israël, d'après un livre récent," *ibid.*, CIII-CIV, 1931, pp. 201-20.

— "La mythologie phénicienne d'après les tablettes de Ras Shamra," *ibid.*, pp. 353-408.

— "Le sanctuaire et les dieux phéniciens de Ras Shamra," *RHR* CV-CVI, 1932, pp. 245-302.

— *Les découvertes de Ras Shamra (Ūgarit) et l'Ancien Testament,* Paris, 1937.

Eerdmans, B. D. "Have the Hebrews been nomads?" *Exp.* 7th series, VI, 1908, pp. 118-31.

— "The Nomads Again: A reply to Prof. G. A. Smith," *ibid.*, pp. 345-48.

— "The Book of the Covenant and the Decalogue," *ibid.*, VIII, 1909, pp. 21-33, 158-67, 223-30.

— "Sojourn in the Tent of Jahu," *OTS* I, 1942, pp. 1-16.

Eerdmans, B. D. *The Religion of Israel*, E. T. Leiden, 1947.
Ehrenzweig, A. "Kain und Lamech," *ZAW* XXXV, 1915, pp. 1-11.
Eissfeldt, O. *Hexateuch-Synopse*, Leipzig, 1922.
— "Opfer: II A. Im A.T." *RGG* IV, ²1930, cols. 711-17.
— "Der Gott des Tabor und seine Verbreitung," *ARW* XXXI, 1934, pp. 14-41.
— *Molk als Opferbegriff im Punischen und Hebräischen und das Ende des Gottes Moloch*, Halle, 1935.
— "Der geschichtliche Hintergrund der Erzählung von Gibeas Schandtat (Richter 19-21)," *Festschrift Georg Beer*, Stuttgart, 1935, pp. 19-40.
— "Lade und Stierbild," *ZAW* LVIII, 1940-1941, pp. 190-215.
— *Geschichtsschreibung im Alten Testament*, Berlin, 1948.
— "El and Yahweh," *JSS* I, 1956, pp. 25-37.
— *Einleitung in das Alte Testament*, Tübingen, ²1956.
— *Das Lied Moses Deuteronomium* 32 1-43 *und das Lehrgedicht Asaphs Psalm* 78 *samt einer Analyse der Umgebung des Mose-Liedes*, Berlin, 1958.
Elhorst, H. J. "Eine verkannte Zauberhandlung (Dtn 21. 1-9)", *ZAW* XXXIX, 1921, pp. 58-67.
Elmslie, W. A. L. *How Came Our Faith*, Cambridge, 1948.
Engnell, I. *Studies in Divine Kingship in the Ancient Near East*, Uppsala, 1943.
— "Paesaḥ-Maṣṣōt and the Problem of 'Patternism,' " *Orientalia Suecana* Vol. I, Uppsala, 1952, pp. 39-50.
Erman, A. *Die ägyptische Religion*, Berlin, ²1909.
Fairman, H. W. "The Kingship Rituals of Egypt," Hooke, S. H. (ed.) *Myth, Ritual, and Kingship*, Oxford, 1958, pp. 74-104.
Farley, F. A. "Jeremiah and Deuteronomy," *ExpT* XXXVII, 1925-1926, pp. 316-18.
— "Jeremiah and the Suffering Servant of Jehovah in Deutero-Isaiah," *ibid.*, XXXVIII, 1926-1927, pp. 521-24.
Feuchtwang, D. "Das Wasseropfer und die damit verbundenen Zeremonien," *MGWJ*, LIV N.F. 18, 1910, pp. 535-52, 713-29, LV N.F. 19, 1911, pp. 43-63.
Flight, J. W. "The Nomadic Idea and Ideal in the Old Testament", *JBL* XLII, 1923, pp. 158-226.
Fohrer, G. "Überlieferung und Wandlung der Hioblegende," *Festschrift Friedrich Baumgärtel*, Erlangen, 1959, pp. 41-62.
Frankfort, H. *Kingship and the Gods*, Chicago, 1948.
Frazer, J. G. *Totemism and Exogamy*, 4 vols, London. 1910.
— *The Golden Bough*, One Volume Edition, New York, repr. 1948.
Gall, A. F. von. *Zusammensetzung und Herkunft der Bileam-Perikope in Num* 22-24, Giessen, 1900.
Galling, K. *Der Altar in den Kulturen des alten Orients*, Berlin, 1925.
— "Bethel und Gilgal," *ZDPV* LVI, 1943, pp. 140-55.
Gardiner, A. H. and Peet, T. E. *The Inscriptions of Sinai*, Part II (ed.) J. Černý, London, 1955.
Gaster, T. H. "The Service of the Sanctuary: A Study in Hebrew Survivals," *Mélanges Syriens* (M. René Dussaud), Vol. II, Paris, 1939, pp. 577-82.
— "Ezekiel and the Mysteries," *JBL* LX, 1941, pp. 289-310.
— *Thespis*, New York, 1950.
— *Festivals of the Jewish Year*, New York, 1952.
Gates, O. H. "The Relation of Priests to Sacrifice before the Exile," *JBL* XXVII, 1908, pp. 67-92.

Gayford, S. C. *Sacrifice and Priesthood* (*Jewish and Christian*), London, 1924.
Gemser, B. "God in Genesis," *OTS* XII, 1958, pp. 1-21.
George, A. "Fautes contre Yahweh dans les Livres de Samuel," *RB* LIII, 1946, pp. 161-84.
Ginsberg, H. L. "A Punic Note," *AJSL* XLVII, 1930-1931, pp. 52-53.
Glasson, T. "The 'Passover', a Misnomer: The Meaning of the Verb *Pasach*," *JTS* N.S. X, 1959, pp. 79-84.
Gray, G. B. *Sacrifice in the Old Testament*, Oxford, 1925.
— "Passover and Unleavened Bread: The Laws of J, E and D," *JTS* XXXVII 1936, pp. 241-53.
Gray, J. "Cultic Affinities between Israel and Ras Shamra," *ZAW* LXII, 1949-1950, pp. 207-20.
— "Canaanite Kingship in Theory and Practice," *VT* II, 1952, pp. 193-220.
— "The Hebrew Conception of the Kingship of God," *VT* VI, 1956, pp. 268-85.
— *The Legacy of Canaan* (*VTSuppl.* V), Leiden, 1957.
Green, W. H. *The Hebrew Feasts*, New York, 1886.
Groot, J. de. *Die Altäre des Salomonischen Tempelhofes*, Berlin, 1924.
Guillaume, A. *Prophecy and Divination*, London, 1938.
Gunkel, H. *What Remains of the Old Testament*, E.T. London, 1928.
— and Begrich, J. *Einleitung in die Psalmen*, Göttingen, 1933.
Gurney, O. R. *The Hittites*, Middlesex (Penguin Books), 1952.
Gusdorf, G. *L'expérience humaine du Sacrifice*, Paris, 1948.
Haag, H. "Ursprung und Sinn der alttestamentlichen Paschafeier," *Das Opfer der Kirche* (Luzerner Theologische Studien I), Luzern, 1954, pp. 17-46.
Hahn, H. F. *The Old Testament in Modern Research*, Philadelphia, 1954.
Haldar, A. *Associations of Cult Prophets Among the Ancient Semites*, Uppsala, 1945.
Hammershaimb, E. "On the Ethics of the Old Testament Prophets," *Congress Volume Oxford* 1959 (*VTSuppl.* VII), Leiden, 1960, pp. 75-101.
Haran, M. "The Uses of Incense in the ancient Israelite Ritual," *VT* X, 1960, pp. 113-29.
Harper, W. R. *The Priestly Element in the Old Testament*, Chicago, Rev. ed. 1902.
Harrelson, W. "Worship in Early Israel," *Biblical Research* (Papers of the Chicago Society of Biblical Research) III, 1958, pp. 1-14.
Haupt, P. "Babylonian Elements in the Levitic Ritual," *JBL* XIX, 1900, pp. 55-81.
Heidel, A. *The Gilgamesh Epic and the Old Testament Parallels*, Chicago, ^{2}1949.
Hempel, J. *Gott und Mensch im Alten Testament*, Stuttgart, ^{2}1936.
— "The Literature of Israel," Robinson, H. W. (ed.), *Record and Revelation*, Oxford, 1938, pp. 28-73.
Hengstenberg, E. W. *Egypt and the Books of Moses*, E. T. Edinburgh, 1845.
Henninger, J. "Les fêtes de printemps chez les arabes et leurs implications historiques," *Revista do Museu Paulista* N.S. IV, 1950, pp. 389-432.
— "Was bedeutet die rituelle Teilung eines Tieres in zwei Hälften," *Bibl.* XXXIV, 1953, pp. 344-53.
Hentschke, R. *Die Stellung der vorexilischen Schriftpropheten zum Kultus*, Berlin, 1957.

Herbert, A. S. *Worship in Ancient Israel*, London, 1959.
Herner, S. *Die Opfermahle nach dem Priesterkodex*, Lund, 1911.
— *Sühne und Vergebung in Israel*, Lund, 1942.
Herrmann, J. *Die Idee der Sühne im Alten Testament*, Leipzig, 1905.
Hertzberg, H. W. "Die prophetische Kritik am Kult," *ThLZ* LXXV, 1950, cols. 219-26.
Hesse, F. *Die Fürbitte im Alten Testament*, Mikrodruck, Hamburg, 1951.
Hicks, F. N. *The Fullness of Sacrifice*, London, [3]1946.
Hölscher, G. "Das Buch der Könige, seine Quellen und seine Redaktion," *Eucharisterion* (Gunkel Festschrift) I, Göttingen, 1923, pp. 158-213.
Hommel, F. *The Ancient Hebrew Tradition* (as illustrated by the Monuments), E.T. London, 1897.
Hooke, S. H. *The Origins of Early Semitic Ritual*, London, 1938.
— "The Early Background of Israelite Religion," Manson, T. W. (ed.) *A Companion to the Bible*, Edinburgh, 1939, pp. 271-86.
— "The Theory and Practice of Substitution," *VT* II, 1952, pp. 1-17.
— *Babylonian and Assyrian Religion*, London, 1953.
— Review of R. K. Yerkes, "Sacrifice in Greek and Roman Religions and Early Judaism," *JTS* V, 1954, pp. 240-42.
— *The Siege Perilous*, London, 1956.
— (ed.), *Myth, Ritual, and Kingship*, Oxford, 1958.
Hopkins, E. W. *Origin and Evolution of Religion*, New Haven, 1923.
Horst, F. *Das Privilegrecht Jahves*, Göttingen, 1930.
Hubert, H. and Mauss, M. "Essai sur la nature et la fonction du sacrifice," *L'Année Sociologique* II, 1897-1898, pp. 29-138.
Hyatt, J. P. "The Peril from the North in Jeremiah," *JBL* LIX, 1940, pp. 511-13.
— "The Original Text of Jeremiah 11 : 15-16," *JBL* LX, 1941, pp. 57-60.
— "Jeremiah and Deuteronomy," *JNES* I, 1942, pp. 156-73.
— "The Ras Shamra Discoveries and the Interpretation of the Old Testament," *JBR* X, 1942, pp. 67-75.
— "Yahweh as the "God of my Father," " *VT* V, 1955, pp. 130-36.
Irwin, W. A. (ed.) J. M. P. Smith, *The Prophets and their Times*, Chicago, [2]1941.
Jack, J. W. *The Ras Shamra Tablets: Their Bearing on the Old Testament*, Edinburgh, 1935.
Jacob, B. "Beiträge zu einer Einleitung in die Psalmen," II *ZAW* XVII, 1897, pp. 48-80, III *ibid.*, pp. 262-79.
Jacob, E. *The Theology of the Old Testament*, E.T. London, 1958.
James, E. O. *Primitive Ritual and Belief* (An Anthropological Essay), London, 1917.
— "Sacrifice, (Introductory and Primitive)," *ERE* XI, 1920, pp. 1-7.
— *Sacrifice and Sacrament*, London, 1927.
— *The Origins of Sacrifice*, London, 1933.
— "After 50 Yrs: Aspects of Sacrifice in the Old Testament," *ExpT* L, 1938-1939, pp. 151-55.
— *The Nature and Function of Priesthood*, London, 1955.
— *History of Religions*, London, 1956.
— *Myth and Ritual in the Ancient Near East*, London, 1958.
— *The Ancient Gods*, London, 1960.
James, F. *Personalities of the Old Testament*, New York, 1939.
Jastrow, M. "Religion of Babylonia and Assyria," *DB* Extra Vol. 1904, pp. 531-84.

Jellicoe, S. "The Prophets and the Cultus," *ExpT* LX, 1949, pp. 256-58.
Jenni, E. "Vom Zeugnis des Richterbuches," *ThZ* XII, 1956, pp. 257-74.
Jensen, A. E. "Über das Töten als kulturgeschichtliche Erscheinung," *Paideuma* IV, 1950, pp. 23-38.
Jeremias, A. *The Old Testament in the light of the Ancient East*, 2 vols. E.T. London, [2]1911.
Jeremias, J. "Ritual (Assyrio-Babylonian Ritual)," *EB* IV, 1903, cols. 4114-4125.
Jevons, F. B. *Introduction to the History of Religion*, London, [3]1904.
Johnson, A. *The Cultic Prophet in Ancient Israel*, Cardiff, 1944.
— "Divine Kingship in the Old Testament," *ExpT* LXII, 1950-1951, pp. 36-42.
— *Sacral Kingship in Ancient Israel*, Cardiff, 1955.
— "Old Testament Exegesis, Imaginative and Unimaginative" *ibid.*, LXVIII, 1956-1957, pp. 178-79.
— "Hebrew Conceptions of Kingship," Hooke, S. H. (ed.) *Myth, Ritual, and Kingship*, Oxford, 1958, pp. 204-35.
Junker, H. "Die Schlacht — und Brandopfer im Tempelkult der Spätzeit," *ZÄS* XLVIII, 1911, pp. 69-77.
Kapelrud, A. S. *Baal in the Ras Shamra Texts*, Copenhagen, 1952.
— "King and Fertility: A discussion of II Sam. 21 : 1-4," *Interpretationes ad Vetus Testamentum pertinentes Sigmundo Mowinckel*, Oslo, 1955, pp. 113-22. (Also *ZAW* LXVII, 1955, pp. 198-205.)
Kaufmann, Y. *The Biblical Account of the Conquest of Palestine*, E.T. Jerusalem, 1953.
— *The Religion of Israel*, E.T. Chicago, 1960.
Kautzsch, E. "The Religion of Israel," *DB* Extra Vol., 1904, pp. 612-734.
Keller, C. A. "Über einige alttestamentliche Heiligtumslegenden I," *ZAW* LXVII, 1955, pp. 141-68, II, *ibid.*, LXVIII, 1956, pp. 85-97.
— "Von Stand und Aufgabe der Moseforschung," *ThZ* XIII, 1957, pp. 430-41.
Kelso, J. A. "The Water Libation in the Old Testament," *Exp* 8th series XXIV, 1922, pp. 226-40.
Kennedy, A. R. S. "Sacrifice and Offering," *DB* One Volume, 1909, pp. 810-18.
Kennett, R. H. "The Conflict between Priestly and Prophetic Ideas in the Church of Israel," *Interpreter* XIV, pp. 104-15.
— "The Origin of the Book of Deuteronomy," *Deuteronomy and the Decalogue*, Cambridge, 1920, pp. 1-33.
— *The Church of Israel*, Cambridge, 1933.
Kent, C. F. *Israel's Laws and Legal Precedents*, London, 1907.
King, L. W. *Legends of Babylon and Egypt in relation to Hebrew Tradition*, London, 1918.
Kittel, R. *A History of the Hebrews*, 2 vols., E.T. London, 1895-1896.
— *Studien zur hebräischen Archäologie und Religionsgeschichte*, Leipzig, 1908.
Knudson, A. C. *The Religious Teaching of the Old Testament*, New York, 1918.
Koch, K. *Die israelitische Sühneanschauung und ihre historischen Wandlungen*, Habilitationsschrift Typescript, Erlangen, 1956.
— "Die Eigenart der priesterschriftlichen Sinaigesetzgebung," *ZThK* LV, 1958, pp. 36-51.
— *Die Priesterschrift von Exodus 25 bis Leviticus 16*, Göttingen, 1959.

Köberle, J. *Sünde und Gnade im religiösen Leben des Volkes Israel bis auf Christum*, München, 1905.
Köhler, L. *Hebrew Man*, E.T. London, 1956.
— *Old Testament Theology*, E.T. London, 1957.
König, E. *Die Hauptprobleme der altisraelitischen Religionsgeschichte*, Leipzig, 1884.
— "On the Meaning and Scope of Jeremiah vii 22, 23," *Exp* 6th series VI, 1902, pp. 135-54, 208-18, 366-77.
— "Der Jeremiaspruch 7, 21-23," *ThStKr* LXXIX, 1906, pp. 327-93.
— "The Significance of the Patriarchs in the History of Religion," *Exp* 7th series X, 1910, pp. 192-207.
— *Geschichte der alttestamentlichen Religion*, Gütersloh, 1912.
— "The Burning Problem of the Hour in Old Testament Religious History," *Exp* 8th series XXI, 1921, pp. 81-106.
— *Theologie des Alten Testaments*, Stuttgart, [1] & [2]1922.
Kraus, H. J. *Die Königsherrschaft Gottes im Alten Testament*, Tübingen, 1951.
— "Gilgal," *VT* I, 1951, pp. 181-99.
— *Gottesdienst in Israel* (Studien zur Geschichte des Laubhüttenfestes), München, 1954.
— "Zur Geschichte des Passah-Massot-Festes im Alten Testament," *EvTh* XVIII, 1958, pp. 47-67.
Kruse, H. "Die 'dialektische Negation' als semitisches Idiom," *VT*, IV, 1954, pp. 385-400.
Kroeber, A. L. "Totem and Taboo: an Ethnologic Psychoanalysis," *American Anthropologist* XXII, 1920, pp. 48-55.
Kuenen, A. *The Religion of Israel to the Fall of the Jewish State*, 3 vols., E.T. London, 1874-1875.
— *National Religions and Universal Religions*, London, 1882.
— *An Historico-Critical Inquiry into the Origin and Composition of the Hexateuch*, E.T. London, [2]1886.
Kutsch, E. "Gideons Berufung und Altarbau Jdc 6, 11-24," *ThLZ* LXXXI, 1956, pp. 75-84.
— "Erwägungen zur Geschichte der Passafeier und des Massotfestes," *ZThK* N.F. LV, 1958, pp. 1-35.
Kyle, M. G. *Moses and the Monuments*, Oberlin, 1919.
Lagrange, M. J. *Études sur les religions sémitiques*, Paris, 1905.
Langdon, S. "The History and Significance of Carthaginian Sacrifice," *JBL* XXIII, 1904, pp. 79-93.
Lattey, C. "The Prophets and Sacrifice: A Study in Biblical Relativity," *JTS* XLII, 1941, pp. 155-65.
Leeuw, G. van der. "Die *do-ut-des*-Formel in der Opfertheorie," *ARW* XX, 1920-1921, pp. 241-53.
— *Religion in Essence and Manifestation*, E.T. London, 1938.
Lehming, S. "Erwägungen zu Amos," *ZThK* LV, 1958, pp. 145-69.
— "Versuch zu Ex. XXXII," *VT* X, 1960, pp. 16-50.
Lesêtre, H. "Sacrifice," Vigouroux, F. (ed.) *Dictionnaire de la Bible* 50, Paris, [2]1928, cols. 1311-1337.
Leslie, E. *Old Testament Religion in the Light of its Canaanite Background*, New York, 1936.
Lewis, E. "Propitiation," *Harper's Bible Dictionary* (ed.), Miller M. S. and Miller, J. L. New York, 1952, pp. 585-86.
Lewy, I. *The Growth of the Pentateuch*, New York, 1955.

Lewy, J. "Les textes paléo-assyriens et l'Ancien Testament," *RHR* CX, 1934, pp. 29-65.
Lindblom, J. *The Servant Songs in Deutero-Isaiah*, Lund, 1952.
Lindhagen, C. *The Servant Motif in the Old Testament*, Uppsala, 1950.
Lods, A. "Eléments anciens et éléments modernes dans le rituel du sacrifice israélite," *RHPhR*, 1928, pp. 399-411.
— "Israelitische Opfervorstellungen und — bräuche," *ThR* N.F. III, 1931, pp. 347-66.
— *Israel from its Beginnings to the Middle of the Eighth Century*, E.T. London, 1932.
— *The Prophets and the Rise of Judaism*, E.T. London, 1937.
— "The Religion of Israel I: Origins," Robinson, H. W. (ed.) *Record and Revelation*, Oxford, 1938, pp. 187-215.
Loisy, A. "La notion du sacrifice dans l'antiquité israélite," *RHLR* N.S. I, 1910, pp. 1-30.
— *Essai historique sur le sacrifice*, Paris, 1920.
Luther, B. "Die Persönlichkeit des Jahwisten," Meyer, E. (ed.) *Die Israeliten und ihre Nachbarstämme*, Halle, 1906, pp. 105-73.
— "David's Passahopfer," *ibid.*, pp. 170-73.
Maag, V. "Zum Hieros Logos von Beth-El," *Asiatische Studien* (Zeitschrift der Schweizerischen Gesellschaft für Asienkunde) V, 1951, pp. 122-33.
— "Erwägungen zur deuteronomischen Kultzentralisation," *VT* VI, 1956, pp. 10-18.
— "Der Hirte Israels," *Schweizerische Theologische Umschau* XXVIII, 1958, pp. 2-28.
— "Malkût Jhwh," *Congress Volume Oxford* 1959 (*VTSuppl* VII), Leiden, 1960, pp. 129-53.
MacCulloch, J. A. "Firstfruits (Introductory and Primitive)," *ERE* VI, 1913, pp. 41-45.
McCullough, W. S. "A Re-examination of Isaiah 56-66," *JBL* LXVII, 1948, pp. 27-36.
— "Israel's Kings, Sacral and Otherwise," *ExpT* LXVIII, 1956-1957, pp. 144-48.
McKane, W. "A Note on 2 Kings 12 : 10," *ZAW* LXXI, 1959, pp. 260-65.
Malamat, A. "Doctrines of Causality in Hittite and Biblical Historiography: A Parallel," *VT* V, 1955, pp. 1-12.
Manley, G. T. *The Book of the Law*, Grand Rapids, 1957.
Marti, K. *Religion of Old Testament*, E.T. London, 1907.
Masson, O. "A propos d'un ritual pour la lustration d'une armée," *RHR* CXXXVII, 1950, pp. 5-25.
May, H. G. "The Fertility Cult in Hosea," *AJSL* XLVIII, 1932, pp. 73-98.
— "The Relation of the Passover to the Festival of Unleavened Cakes," *JBL* LV, 1936, pp. 665-82.
— "The Patriarchal Idea of God," *JBL* LX, 1941, pp. 113-28.
— "The God of my Father: A Study of Patriarchal Religion," *JBR* IX, 1941, pp. 155-58.
— "Towards an Objective Approach to the Book of Jeremiah: the Biographer," *JBL* LXI, 1942, pp. 139-55.
Médebielle, A. *L'Expiation dans l'Ancien et le Nouveau Testament*, Rome, 1924.
— "Expiation" *Dictionnaire de la Bible Suppl* III, 1938, cols. 1-262.

Meek, T. J. "Monotheism and the Religion of Israel," *JBL* LXI, 1942, pp. 21-43.
— *Hebrew Origins*, New York ²1950.
Mendenhall, G. E. *Law and Covenant in Israel and the Ancient Near East*, Pittsburgh, 1955.
Menes, A. "Tempel und Synagoge," *ZAW* L, 1932, pp. 268-76.
Merx, A. *Die Bücher Moses und Josua*, Tübingen, 1907.
Metzinger, A. "Die Substitutionstheorie und das alttestamentliche Opfer," *Bibl* XXI, 1940, pp. 159-87, 247-72, 353-77.
Meuli, K. "Griechische Opferbräuche," *Phyllobolia für Peter von der Mühll*, Basel, 1946, pp. 185-288.
Meyer, E. *Die Israeliten und ihre Nachbarstämme*, Halle, 1906.
Meysing, J. "A Text-Reconstruction of Ps. cxvii (cxviii) 27," *VT* X, 1960, pp. 130-37.
Micklem, N. *Prophecy and Eschatology*, London, 1926.
Mitchell, H. G. *The Ethics of the Old Testament*, Chicago, 1912.
Möhlenbrink, K. "Die Landnahmesagen des Buches Josua," *ZAW* LVI, 1938, pp. 238-67.
— "Josua im Pentateuch," *ZAW* LIX, 1942-1943, pp. 14-58.
Money-Kyrle, R. *The Meaning of Sacrifice*, London, 1930.
Montgomery, J. A. *Arabia and the Bible*, Philadelphia, 1934.
Moore, G. F. "Sacrifice," *EB* IV, London, 1903, cols. 4183-4233.
Moraldi, L. *Espiazione sacrificale e riti espiatori nell'ambiente biblico e nell' Antico Testamento*, Rome, 1956.
Moret, A. "Du sacrifice en Égypte," *RHR* LVII, 1908, pp. 81-101.
Morgenstern, J. "The Oldest Document of the Hexateuch," *HUCA* IV, 1927, pp. 1-138.
— "A Chapter in the History of the High-Priesthood," *AJSL* LV, 1938, pp. 1-24, 183-97, 360-77.
— *Amos Studies* I-III, Cincinnati, 1941, pp. 3-124, 127-79, 183-428 = *HUCA* XI, 1936, pp. 18-140, XII-XIII, 1937-1938, pp. 1-53, XV, 1940, pp. 59-304.
— "The King-God," *VT* X, 1960, pp. 138-97.
Morris, L. "The Biblical Use of the Term 'Blood'," *JTS* N.S. III, 1952, pp. 216-27.
— *The Apostolic Preaching of the Cross*, Grand Rapids, 1955.
Mowinckel, S. *Psalmenstudien* I-VI, Kristiana, 1921-1924.
— "Der Ursprung der Bilᶜāmsage," *ZAW* XLVIII, 1930, pp. 233-71.
— *The Two Sources of the Pre-deuteronomic Primeval History(JE) in Gen.* 1-11, Oslo, 1937.
— *Offersang og Sangoffer*, Oslo, 1951.
— *He That Cometh*, E.T. Oxford, 1956.
Muilenburg, J. "The Site of Ancient Gilgal," *BASOR*, CXL, 1955, pp. 11-27.
— "The form and structure of the covenantal formulations," *VT* IX, 1959, pp. 347-65.
Nagel, G. "Sacrifices," Allmen, J-J. von (ed.), *A Companion to the Bible*, E.T. New York, 1958, pp. 375-80.
Naville, E. *The Old Egyptian Faith*, E.T. London, 1909.
Nicolsky, M. M. "Pascha im Kulte des jerusalemischen Tempels," *ZAW* XLV, 1927, pp. 171-90, 241-53.
Nielsen, E. *Shechem*, Copenhagen, 1955.

Nielsen, E. "Some Reflections on the History of the Ark," *Congress Volume Oxford* 1959 (*VTSuppl.* VII), Leiden, 1960, pp. 61-74.
Nötscher, F. *Biblische Altertumskunde* (*Die HS*), Bonn, 1940.
North, C. R. "The Religious Aspects of Hebrew Kingship," *ZAW* L, 1932, pp. 8-38.
— "Sacrifice in the Old Testament," *ExpT* XLVII, 1935-1936, pp. 250-54.
Noth, M. *Das System der zwölf Stämme Israels*, Stuttgart, 1930.
— "Bethel und Ai," *PJB* XXXI, 1935, pp. 7-29.
— *Überlieferungsgeschichtliche Studien* I, Halle, 1943.
— *Überlieferungsgeschichte des Pentateuch*, Stuttgart, 1948.
— "Gesetze im Pentateuch," *GS*, München, 1957, pp. 9-141.
— "Jerusalem und die israelitische Tradition," *ibid.*, pp. 172-87.
— *The History of Israel*, E.T. London, 1958.
— "Der Beitrag der Archäologie zur Geschichte Israels," *Congress Volume Oxford* 1959 (*VTSuppl.* VII), pp. 262-82.
Nowack, W. *Lehrbuch der hebräischen Archäologie*, 2 vols. Freiburg i.B., 1894.
Nyström, S. *Beduinentum und Jahwismus*, Lund, 1946.
Oehler, G. F. *Theologie des Alten Testaments*, Stuttgart, [2]1882.
Östborn, G. *Yahweh and Baal* (Studies in the Book of Hosea and related documents), Lund, 1956.
Oesterley, W. O. E. *Sacrifices in Ancient Israel*, London, 1937.
— and Robinson, T. H. *Hebrew Religion, its Origin and Development*, London, [2]1937.
Oettli, S. "Der Kultus bei Amos und Hosea," *Greifswalder Studien*, Gütersloh, 1895, pp. 1-34.
Orelli, C. "Opferkultus des Alten Testaments," *PRE* XIV, Leipzig, 1904, pp. 386-400 (E.T. (abbreviated) *The New Schaff-Herzog Encyclopedia of Religious Knowledge*, X New York (1911), pp. 163-66).
Parrot, A. "Autels et installations cultuelles a Mari," *Congress Volume Copenhagen* 1953 (*VTSuppl.* I), Leiden, 1953, pp. 112-19.
Paterson, W. P. "Sacrifice," *DB* IV, 1902, pp. 329-49.
Pedersen, J. *Israel, Her Life and Culture*, 2 vols. E.T. London, 1926 and 1940.
— "Canaanite and Israelite Cultus," *Acta Orientalia* XVIII, 1940, pp. 1-14.
Peters, J. P. "Ritual in the Psalms," *JBL* XXXV, 1916, pp. 143-54.
— *The Psalms as Liturgies*, New York, 1922.
Pettazzoni, R. *Essays on the History of Religions*, Leiden, 1954.
Pfeiffer, R. H. "The Oldest Decalogue," *JBL* XLIII, 1924, pp. 294-310.
— "Images of Yahweh," *JBL* XLV, 1926, pp. 211-22.
— "The Transmission of the Book of the Covenant," *HTR* XXIV, 1931, pp. 99-109.
— *Introduction to the Old Testament*, New York, [2]1948.
Phythian-Adams, W. J. *The Fullness of Israel* (A Study of the meaning of sacred history), London, 1938.
Pohle, J. "Sacrifice," *CathEnc* XIII, London, 1912, pp. 309-21.
Pope, M. H. *El in the Ugaritic Texts* (*VTSuppl.* II), Leiden, 1955.
Porteous, N. W. "Ritual and Righteousness," *Interpretation* III, 1949, pp. 400-14.
— "The Basis of the Ethical Teaching of the Prophets," Rowley, H. H. (ed.), *Studies in Old Testament Prophecy* (T. H. Robinson Festschrift), Edinburgh, 1950, pp. 143-56.

Porter, J. R. "2 Samuel VI and Psalm CXXXII," *JTS* N.S. V, 1954, pp. 161-73.

Press, R. "Das Ordal im alten Israel," *ZAW* LI, 1933, pp. 121-40, 227-55.

— "Der Prophet Samuel," *ZAW* LVI, 1938, pp. 177-225.

— "Die Gerichtspredigt der vorexilischen Propheten und der Versuch einer Steigerung der kultischen Leistung," *ZAW* LXX, 1958, pp. 181-84.

Evans-Pritchard, E. E. "The Meaning of Sacrifice among the Nuer," *JRAI* LXXXIV, 1954, pp. 21-33.

— *Nuer Religion*, Oxford, 1956.

Procksch, O. *Das nordhebräische Sagenbuch: Die Elohimquelle*, Leipzig, 1906.

— *Theologie des Alten Testaments*, Gütersloh, 1950.

Puukko, A. "Jeremias Stellung zum Deuteronomium," *Alttestamentliche Studien Rudolf Kittel*, Leipzig, 1913, pp. 126-53.

Quell, G. *Das kultische Problem der Psalmen*, Berlin, 1926.

Quick, O. *The Gospel of the New World*, London, 1944.

Rad, G. von. *Das Gottesvolk im Deuteronomium*, Stuttgart, 1929.

— "Das formgeschichtliche Problem des Hexateuchs," 1938 now in *GS*, München, 1958.

— "Die Anrechnung des Glaubens zur Gerechtigkeit," *ibid.*, pp. 130-35.

— "Das judäische Königsritual," *ibid.*, pp. 205-13.

— " 'Gerechtigkeit' und 'Leben' in der Kultsprache der Psalmen," *ibid.*, pp. 225-47.

— *Studies in Deuteronomy*, E.T. London, 1953.

— *Theologie des Alten Testaments*, 2 vols. München, 1957-1960.

Reeve, J. J. "Sacrifice," J. Orr (ed.), *ISBE* IV, 1947, cols. 2638-2651.

Rendtorff, R. *Studien zur Geschichte des Opfers im alten Israel*, Habilitationsschrift, Typescript, Göttingen, 1953.

— *Die Gesetze in der Priesterschrift*, Göttingen, 1954.

— "Priesterliche Kulttheologie und prophetische Kultpolemik," *ThLZ* LXXXI, 1956, cols. 339-42.

— "Der Kultus im Alten Israel," *JLH* II, 1956, pp. 1-21.

— "Opfer I: Religionsgeschichtlich II Im AT" *EKL* II, 1958, cols. 1691-1692.

Rignell, L. G. "Is lii : 13-liii : 12," *VT* III, 1953, pp. 87-92.

— "Isaiah Chapter I," *Studia Theologica* XI, 1958, pp. 140-58.

Rivière, J. "Expiation et rédemption dans l'Ancien Testament," *Bulletin de littérature ecclésiastique* XLVII, 1946, pp. 3-22.

Robertson, E. "Isaiah Chapter I," *ZAW* LII, 1934, pp. 231-36.

— *The Old Testament Problem*, Manchester, 1950.

Robinson, H. W. "Theology of the Old Testament," *Record and Revelation*, Oxford, 1938, pp. 303-48.

— "Hebrew Sacrifice and Prophetic Symbolism," *JTS* XLIII, 1942, pp. 129-39.

— *Inspiration and Revelation in the Old Testament*, Oxford, 1946.

Robinson, T. H. *A Short Comparative History of Religion*, London, [2]1951.

Rost, L. *Die Überlieferung von der Thronnachfolge Davids*, Stuttgart, 1926.

— "Weidewechsel und altisraelitischer Festkalender," *ZDPV* LXVI, 1943, pp. 205-216.

— "Sinaibund und Davidsbund," *ThLZ* LXXII, 1947, cols. 129-34.

— "Erwägungen zu Hosea 4, 13f," *Festschrift Alfred Bertholet*, Tübingen, 1950, pp. 451-60.

— "Erwägungen zum israelitischen Brandopfer," *Von Ugarit Nach Qumran* (Eissfeldt Festschrift), Berlin, 1958, pp. 177-83.
— "Die Gottesverehrung der Patriarchen im Lichte der Pentateuchquellen," *Congress Volume Oxford* 1959 (*VTSuppl.* VII), Leiden 1960, pp. 346-59.
Roubos, K. *Profetie en Cultus in Israël*, Wageningen, 1956.
Rowley, H. H. *Re-Discovery of the Old Testament*, London, 1945.
— "The Religious Value of Sacrifice," *ExpT* LVIII, 1946-1947, pp. 69-71.
— "Prophets and Sacrifice," *ibid.*, pp. 305-7.
— Review: "The Study of the Bible Today and Tomorrow," Harold R. Willoughby (ed.) *Theology Today* V, 1948, pp. 122-26.
— *The Meaning of Sacrifice in the Old Testament*, Manchester, 1950. Reprinted from the *BJRL* XXXIII, 1950, pp. 74-110.
— *From Joseph to Joshua*, London, 1950.
— "The Prophet Jeremiah and the Book of Deuteronomy," *Studies in Old Testament Prophecy* (T. H. Robinson Festschrift), Edinburgh, 1950, pp. 157-74.
— *The Unity of the Bible*, London, 1953.
— "The Book of Ezekiel in Modern Study," *BJRL* XXXVI, 1953-1954, pp. 146-90.
— *Faith of Israel*, London, 1956.
— "Ritual and the Hebrew Prophets," S. H. Hooke (ed.) *Myth, Ritual and Kingship*, 1958, pp. 236-60.
— "Sacrifice and Morality," *ExpT* LXX, 1959, pp. 341-42.
Rudolph, W. *Der "Elohist" von Exodus bis Josua*, Berlin, 1938.
Runze, G. "Ursprung und Entwicklung der Opferbräuche," I. *Neue Weltanschauung* I, (1908) pp. 401-11, II, pp. 453-57.
— "Die psychischen Motive der Opferbräuche in der Stufenfolge ihrer Entwicklung," *Zeitschrift für Religionspsychologie* II, 1908-1909, pp. 81-99.
Sanday, W. (ed.) *Priesthood and Sacrifice*, London, 1900.
Sayce, A. H. Preface to V. Z. Rule, *Old Testament Institutions*, London, 1910.
Schmid, H. "Jahwe und die Kulttradition von Jerusalem," *ZAW* LXVII, 1955, pp. 168-97.
Schmidt, W. "Ethnologische Bemerkungen zu theologischen Opfertheorien," *Jahrbuch des Missionshauses St Gabriel* I, 1922, pp. 2-67.
— *The Origin and Growth of Religion*, E.T. London, ²1935.
Schmitz, O. *Die Opferanschauung des späteren Judentums*, Tübingen, 1910.
Schötz, D. *Schuld- und Sündopfer im Alten Testament*, Breslau, 1930.
Schofield, J. N. "The Significance of the Prophets for the Dating of Deuteronomy," Payne, E. A. (ed.) *Studies in History and Religion* (Wheeler Robinson Festschrift), London, 1942, pp. 44-60.
— *Religious Background of the Bible*, London, 1944.
Schultz, H. *Old Testament Theology*, 2 vols. E.T. Edinburgh, ²1909.
Scott, M. *The Message of Hosea*, London, 1921.
— "Is. xliii : 22-25," *ExpT* XXXVII, 1925-1926, pp. 270-71.
Scott, R. B. Y. "The Service of God," Hobbs, E. C. (ed.) *A Stubborn Faith* (Irwin Festschrift), Dallas, 1956, pp. 132-43.
Sellin, E. *Gilgal*, Leipzig, 1917.
— *Mose und seine Bedeutung für die israelitisch-jüdische Religionsgeschichte*, Leipzig, 1922.
— *Introduction to the Old Testament*, E. T. London, 1923.

Sellin, E. "Wann wurde das Moselied Dtn 32 gedichtet?" *ZAW* XLIII, 1925, pp. 161-73.

Selms, A. van. *Marriage and Family Life in Ugaritic Literature,* London, 1954.

Simpson, C. A. *The Early Traditions of Israel,* Oxford, 1948.

— "The Growth of the Hexateuch," *IB* I, 1952, pp. 185-200.

— "Genesis," *ibid.*, pp. 439-57.

Smend, R. *Lehrbuch der alttestamentlichen Religionsgeschichte,* Freiburg i.B., 1893.

Smith, J. M. P. *The Moral Life of the Hebrews,* Chicago, 1923.

— *The Origin and History of Hebrew Law,* Chicago, 1931.

— *The Prophets and their Times,* Chicago, ^{2}1941.

Smith, M. "The So-Called Biography of David," *HTR* XLIV, 1951, pp. 167-69.

Smith, W. R. "Sacrifice," *EBrit* XXI, ^{9}1886, pp. 132b-138a.

— *The Old Testament in the Jewish Church,* Edinburgh, ^{2}1892.

— *Lectures on the Religion of the Semites,* London, ^{2}1894.

— *The Prophets of Israel,* London, ^{2}1895.

— "Animal Worship and Animal Tribes among the Arabs and in the Old Testament," *Lectures and Essays of William Robertson Smith,* London, 1912, pp. 455-83.

— "A Journey in the Hejâz," *ibid.*, pp. 484-597.

Snaith, N. H. "The Religion of Israel—Worship," Robinson, H. W. (ed.) *Record and Revelation,* Oxford, 1938, pp. 250-74.

— "The Priesthood and the Temple," Manson, T. W. (ed.) *A Companion to the Bible,* Edinburgh, 1939, pp. 418-43.

— "The Prophets and Sacrifice and Salvation," *ExpT* LVIII, 1946-1947, pp. 152-3.

— *The Jewish New Year Festival,* London, 1947.

— *Hymns of the Temple,* London, 1951.

— *Mercy and Sacrifice,* London, 1953.

— Review of R. K. Yerkes, *Sacrifice in Greek and Roman Religions and Early Judaism,* Theology LVII, 1954, pp. 188-89.

— "Sacrifices in the Old Testament," *VT* VII, 1957, pp. 308-17.

Snijders, L. A. "Genesis XV the Covenant with Abram," *OTS* XII, 1958, pp. 261-79.

Spencer, J. *De Legibus Hebraeorum Ritualibus et earum Rationibus,* Hagae, 1686.

Stade, B. *Geschichte des Volkes Israel,* 2 vols. Berlin, 1887-1888.

— *Biblische Theologie des Alten Testaments* I, Tübingen, 1905.

Staerk, W. *Sünde und Gnade nach der Vorstellung des älteren Judentums, besonders der Dichter der sog. Busspsalmen,* Tübingen, 1905.

Stamm, J. J. *Erlösen und Vergeben im Alten Testament,* Bern, 1940.

— *Das Leiden des Unschuldigen in Babylon und Israel,* Zürich, 1946.

— "Ein Vierteljahrhundert Psalmenforschung," *ThR* N.F. XXIII, 1955, pp. 1-68.

Steuernagel, C. "Die Weissagung über die Eliden (1 Sam 2. 27-36)," *Alttestamentliche Studien Rudolf Kittel,* Leipzig, 1913, pp. 204-21.

Stevenson, W. B. "Hebrew ʿOlah and Zebach Sacrifices," (*Festschrift Alfred Bertholet*) Tübingen, 1950, pp. 488-97.

Taylor, F. J. "Blood," Richardson, A. (ed.) *A Theological Wordbook of the Bible,* London, 1950, pp. 33-34.

Toy, C. H. "On some Conceptions of the Old Testament Psalter," *Old Testament and Semitic Studies in Memory of W. R. Harper* Vol. I, Chicago, 1908, pp. 3-34.

Trumbull, H. C. *The Threshold Covenant*, Edinburgh, 1896.

Tur-Sinai, N. H. "The Ark of God at Beit Shemesh (1 Sam. VI) and Peres ʾUzza (2 Sam. VI: 1 Chron. XIII)," *VT* I, 1951, pp. 275-86.

Tylor, E. B. *Primitive Culture*, 2 vols. reprinted as Vol. I *The Origins of Culture*, Vol. II *Religion in Primitive Culture*, New York, 1958.

Urie, D. M. L. "Sacrifice Among the West-Semites," *PEQ* LXXXI, 1949, pp. 67-82.

Vaux, de R. "Les textes de Ras Shamra et l'Ancien Testament," *RB* XLVI, 1937, pp. 526-55.

— "Les Patriarches hébreux et les découvertes modernes," *RB* LIII, 1946, pp. 321-48, LV, 1948, pp. 321-47, LVI, 1949, pp. 1-36.

— *Les institutions de l'Ancien Testament*, 2 vols. Paris, 1958-1960.

Vincent, A. "Les rites du balancement (tenoûphâh) et du prélèvement (teroûmâh) dans le sacrifice de communion de l'Ancien Testament," *Mélanges Syriens* (Dussaud Festschrift) Vol. I, Paris, 1939, pp. 267-72.

Volz, P. *Die biblischen Altertümer*, Stuttgart, 1914.

— "Die radikale Ablehnung der Kultreligion durch die alttestamentlichen Propheten," *ZSTh* XIV, 1937, pp. 63-85.

— and Rudolph, W. *Der Elohist als Erzähler: ein Irrweg der Pentateuchkritik?* Giessen, 1933.

Vorbilcher, A. *Das Opfer*, Mödling bei Wien, 1956.

Vriezen, Th. C. "The Term Hizza: Lustration and Consecration" *OTS* VII, 1950, pp. 201-35.

— *An Outline of Old Testament Theology*, E.T. Oxford, 1958.

Walker, J. C. "The Axiology of the Books of Kings," *JBR* XXVII, 1959, pp. 218-22.

Ward, W. H. "Altars and Sacrifices in the Primitive Art of Babylonia," in S. I. Curtiss, *Primitive Semitic Religion Today*, 1902, pp. 266-77.

Waterman, L. "Pre-Israelite Laws in the Book of Covenant," *AJSL* XXXVIII, 1921-1922, pp. 36-54.

Watts, J. D. W. *Vision and Prophecy in Amos*, Leiden, 1958.

Weijden, A. H. van. *Die "Gerechtigkeit" in den Psalmen*, Nimwegen, 1952.

Weiser, A. "1 Samuel 15," *ZAW* LIV, 1936, pp. 1-28.

— "Das Deboralied," *ZAW* LXXI, 1959, pp. 67-97.

Welch, A. C. *The Religion of Israel under the Kingdom*, Edinburgh, 1912.

— "Miscelle", *ZAW* XLII, 1924, pp. 163-64.

— *The Code of Deuteronomy*, London, 1924.

— "When was the worship of Israel centralised at the Temple?" *ZAW* XLIII, 1925, pp. 250-55.

— "Some Misunderstood Psalms (III)," *ExpT* XXXVII, 1925-1926, pp. 408-10.

— *The Psalter in Life, Worship and History*, Oxford, 1926.

— "On the Method of celebrating Passover," *ZAW* XLV, 1927, pp. 24-29.

— *Post-Exilic Judaism*, Edinburgh, 1935.

— *Prophet and Priest in Old Israel*, London, 1936.

— *The Work of the Chronicler*, Oxford, 1939.

— *Kings and Prophets of Israel*, London, 1952.

Wellhausen, J. "Israel," *EBrit* XIII, [9]1880, pp. 396-442.

— *Prolegomena to the History of Israel*, E.T. Edinburgh, 1885.

Wellhausen. J. *Reste Arabischen Heidentumes* (Skizzen und Vorarbeiten III), Berlin, 1887.
— *Die Composition des Hexateuchs und die Historischen Bücher des A.Ts*, Berlin, ²1889.
— "Israelitisch-jüdische Religion," Hinneberg, P. (ed.) *Die Kultur der Gegenwart* Div. I, Vol. IV, Part I, Berlin, ²1909, pp. 1-41.
Wendel, A. *Das Opfer in der altisraelitischen Religion*, Leipzig, 1927.
Westermann, C. *Das Loben Gottes in den Psalmen*, Berlin, 1953.
Westermarck, E. *The Origin and Development of the Moral Ideas*, 2 vols., London, ²1917.
Whitley, C. F. "The Sources of the Gideon Stories," *VT* VII, 1957, pp. 157-64.
Widengren, G. "King and Covenant," *JSS* II, 1957, pp. 1-32.
Wildberger, H. "Samuel und die Entstehung des israelitischen Königtums," *ThZ* XIII, 1957, pp. 442-69.
Winckler, H. *Religionsgeschichtler und geschichtlicher Orient*, Leipzig, 1906.
Wright, G. E. "The Levites in Deuteronomy," *VT* IV, 1954, pp. 325-30.
— *The Biblical Doctrine of Man in Society*, London, 1954.
— *Biblical Archaeology*, Philadelphia, 1957.
— "Old Testament Scholarship in Prospect," *JBR* XXVIII, 1960, pp. 182-203.
Wundt, W. *Völkerpsychologie*, Vols. II, 2 and II, 3, Leipzig, 1906-1909.
— *Elemente der Völkerpsychologie*, Leipzig, 1912.
Würthwein, E. "Amos 5, 21-27," *ThLZ* LXXII, 1947, cols. 143-52.
Yerkes, R. K. *Sacrifice in Greek and Roman Religions and Early Judaism*, New York, 1952.
Young, E. J. *Studies in Isaiah*, Grand Rapids, 1954.
— *The Study of Old Testament Theology To-day*, London, 1958.
Young, G. D. *Concordance of Ugaritic*, Rome, 1956.
Zimmerli, W. *Geschichte und Tradition von Beerseba im Alten Testament*, Göttingen, 1932.

AUTHOR INDEX

Albright, W. F. 24, 25, 43, 45f, 93, 120, 130, 133, 177, 191, 214
Allen, E. L. 223 f.
Allis, O. T. 188
Alt, A. 22, 34 ff., 46, 67, 80, 123, 129, 203
Anastasius the Sinaite, 166
Anderson, G. W. 179
Anderson, R. 39
Auerbach, E. 82
Auvray, R. 178

Baentsch, B. 71
Barclay, W. 10
Barton, G. A. 28, 41 f., 45, 205
Baumann, E. 214
Baumann, H. 36
Baumgartner, W. 32 f.
Baxter, W. L. 246
Bea, A. 191, 200
Beek, M. A. 167
Beer, G. 58, 60 f., 71, 99, 209
Béguerie, Ph. 175
Bennett, W. H. 11
Bentzen, A. 102
Benzinger, I. 12, 23, 125, 127
Berguer, G. 7
Berry, G. R. 74
Bertholet, A. 6 f., 13, 59, 144 f., 195, 213, 214, 216
Bewer, J. A. 87, 92 f., 197, 198, 215
Beyerlin, W. 147, 179
Binns, L. Elliott. 178, 225
Böhl, F. M. T. de L. 42 f.
Boschwitz, F. 200
Boutflower, C. 175
Bowman, R. A. 229
Brandt, W. 59
Brekelmans, C. 70
Briggs, C. A. 144 f., 156
Bright, J. 46
Brinker, R. 35
Brock-Utne, A. 50, 59
Buber, M. 42, 104
Budde, K. 103, 107, 109, 111, 116
Buren, E. D. van. 28
Burkitt, F. C. 165, 179
Burney, C. F. 38 f., 43, 91, 94 f., 128

Caird, G. B. 98, 111 f.
Caspari, W. 104, 107, 148 f.
Cazelles, H. 211, 216
Chapman, A. T. 53, 97
Chary, Th. 225
Cheyne, T. K. 8, 81, 176, 177 f.
Clarke, W. K. Lowther. 149
Closen, G. E. 51
Cook, S. A. 11, 12, 13, 24, 44, 60, 90, 235
Cooke, G. A. 31, 75, 108, 195, 198
Cowley, A. 58
Cripps, R. S. 169
Cross, F. M. 215
Cross, L. B. 62
Curtiss, S. I. 23, 28, 55

Dalman, G. 59
Davidson, A. B. 9, 10, 11, 71, 101, 174
Delitzsch, F. 51, 141, 143, 145, 172
Dewar, L. 15
Dhorme, E. 25, 27, 76
Dillmann, A. 81 f., 178, 212
Dobbie, R. 77, 162, 185, 203
Driver, G. R. 206 f., 247, 248
Driver, S. R. 11, 51, 99, 103, 109, 184, 188 f., 204
Dronkert, K. 191
Duhm, B. 143, 144 f., 147, 153, 176, 177, 185
Dumermuth, F. 164, 203
Dupont-Sommer, A. 55
Dussaud, R. 14 ff., 30 f.

Eerdmans, B. D. 24 f., 30, 60, 112, 140
Ehrenzweig, A. 50
Eichrodt, W. 108
Eissfeldt, O. 9, 13, 35, 49, 72, 75 f., 86, 92 f., 103, 127, 178, 190 f., 214, 215, 216
Elhorst, H. J. 213
Elliger, K. 194
Elmslie, W. A. L. 110

SUBJECT INDEX

SCRIPTURE INDEX